THE SUCCESSFUL AUDIT
NEW WAYS TO REDUCE RISK EXPOSURE AND INCREASE EFFICIENCY

Felix Pomeranz

BUSINESS ONE IRWIN
Homewood, Illinois 60430

To Mahvash Kalhor Albert
for untiring support and encouragement

This publication is designed to provide accurate and
authoritative information in regard to the subject matter
covered. It is sold with the understanding that neither the
author nor the publisher is engaged in rendering legal, accounting,
or other professional service. If legal advice or other expert
assistance is required, the services of a competent
professional person should be sought.

From a Declaration of Principles jointly adopted by a Committee
of the American Bar Association and a Committee of Publishers.

Sponsoring editor: Cynthia A. Zigmund
Project editor: Jess Ann Ramirez
Production manager: Ann Cassady
Designer: Larry J. Cope
Compositor: Precision Typographers
Typeface: 11/13 Century Schoolbook
Printer: The Book Press, Inc.

Library of Congress Cataloging-in-Publication Data

Pomeranz, Felix.
    The successful audit: new ways to reduce risk exposure and
increase efficiency / Felix Pomeranz.
        p.   cm.
    Includes index.
    ISBN 1-55623-391-4
    1. Auditing. I. Title.
HF5667.P594   1992
657′.45—dc20   91–29284

Printed in the United States of America
1 2 3 4 5 6 7 8 9 0 BP 8 7 6 5 4 3 2 1

FOREWORD

A pragmatic auditing philosopher, Felix Pomeranz poses thought-provoking questions to auditors and provides stimulating solutions. Why are profit margins of public accounting firms eroding at the same time that the risks of litigation and damage to professional reputation are escalating? What responsibility do public accounting firms bear for national crises such as the well-publicized failures of many savings and loan associations and the perpetration of management crimes at large defense contractors? What has caused the dramatic drop in audit productivity, and how can it be remedied without exposing auditors to an even greater risk of legal liability?

The Successful Audit: New Ways to Reduce Risk Exposure and Increase Efficiency provides a plan of action for auditors and explains the technological tools available to improve audit efficiency and effectiveness. These are not new topics, but Pomeranz provides a refreshing perspective. Much of what is written elsewhere about audit efficiency assumes that current audit practice is effective. The focus is on accomplishing the same thing faster at less cost. While pointing out that audit failures are well documented, but good audits are not accorded significant attention, Pomeranz also acknowledges the clear symptoms of lack of audit effectiveness in current practice.

Pomeranz calls on auditors to be more sensitive to the possible existence of fraud and to become better at detecting it by understanding the client's business and management. He points out that now, more than ever, "a good auditor is a good business-person" who helps the client to manage risk and who uses the client's operational information to do a better but less costly audit.

Risk assessment is the primary audit tool stressed in the so-called expectation gap *SAS*s (*Statements on Auditing Standards Nos. 53 to 61*) adopted by the AICPA's Auditing Standards Board in 1988. Pomeranz reviews the influence of these *SAS*s on the audit model and audit practice. However, his restatement of the audit model focuses first on understanding what risks the business faces and how management deals with those risks, and then on distilling that understanding as input to the auditor's risk analysis for planning and performing the audit.

This is a book about auditing, but it is not a book just for auditors. Pomeranz speaks to a diverse audience including chief financial officers, internal auditors, government accountants, audit committee members, lawyers, private investigators, law enforcement officers, and insurance adjusters or examiners, as well as practicing public accountants. To facilitate use by such a diverse mixture of readers, the book uses several devices—each chapter's essence appears in an executive highlights section, technology-related matters are shaded, examples and comments are clearly set out, checklists are provided for quick reference, and user perspectives at the beginning of each chapter identify the pertinence of topics by reader category.

Each chapter begins with a quotation that aptly captures its theme. The quotation at the beginning of Chapter 1 appropriately sets the tone of the entire book—"Action is the highest form of contemplation." Felix Pomeranz demonstrates that thinking and doing are not only compatible but essential for an auditing philosopher or auditing practitioner today.

D. R. Carmichael, Ph.D., CPA
Wollman Distinguished Professor of Accounting, Baruch College; Former Vice President, Auditing, AICPA

PREFACE

To my readers:

I became an accountant by accident. The circumstances were these: my parents were advised by a friendly neighborhood social worker that the study of accounting was a good thing for an ambitious but poor 14-year-old; the boy "could go to school at night and earn a good living during the day." Although the advice was not rooted in aptitude testing, I followed it and do not regret having done so.

I was privileged to have a front seat at some of the important events that have transformed the profession during the last 40 years. The media rarely present accountants as heroes, leaders, or even concerned citizens; yet, it is those unsung individual accountants—teachers, co-workers, partners, clients, and even competitors—who made my career worthwhile. Those accountants had an abiding concern for the public trust and gave unstintingly of themselves on both paid and pro bono bases.

Many of my beliefs and attitudes were influenced by 27 years at Coopers & Lybrand (C&L). I walked into C&L as an "expected graduate" from Columbia University; even though I lacked an appointment, I was told to start immediately. I endeavored to make the most of my opportunity and shared the American dream in its fullest sense. My work at C&L brought me into contact with some of the grand names in public accountancy, people who became role models for me; the names included Robert Montgomery, Henry Benson, and Philip Defliese.

I also served tours of duty with large industrial corporations. Here my favorite memory is of David Luke, Jr., then chairman of

Westvaco Corporation. David Luke preached *and* practiced a standard of business ethics that provided me with both inspiration and aspiration.

When I retired from C&L in 1985, I decided to begin a second career as a teacher at Miami's Florida International University. The warmth of the welcome I received from the Miami public accounting community moved me deeply and eased my teaching debut. In endeavoring to become an educator, I searched after a private vision of immortality—I hoped to pass along what I had learned in 40 years as public accountant, internal auditor, and systems analyst. In many ways, however, my hardworking and upwardly mobile students provided *me* with an unforeseen opportunity to learn and to grow. Another advantage of my new position was that it gave me access to information from many firms and people. The examples in this book are drawn from an eclectic mix of sources; it follows that they should not be attributed to a particular firm or to its audit approach. My conclusions reflect both personal belief and published material.

I decided to write this book for my students. I hope it will help ensure that the same opportunities available to me will continue to be available to them. In times of financial scandals, the search is on for scapegoats; I find it difficult to exorcise images of hectoring politicians, or even of practitioners in handcuffs, from my memory. Even more disturbingly, for awhile smaller accounting firms seemed to be abandoning the (audit) field; yet, what is needed is *more,* not less, competition. The American accountant, whose skills have been honed to a fine edge in a free market at home, stands a much better chance in the international marketplace.

The fundamentals favor the auditor. Technology, applied on the basis of incisive knowledge of the client's business, should enhance audit efficiency and effectiveness, improve profitability, and encourage competition. Technology and business knowledge together offer the only prospect of which I am aware for closing that most significant of "expectation gaps," the gap between those who legislate the rules and those whose labor is subject to the realities of an audit engagement.

Acknowledgments are due to various individuals and companies who made this book possible. DIALOG Information Services, ORBIT Search Services, and, especially, Mead Data Central provided free computer time; particular mention should be made of Mead's Dale Heider, Esq., whose encouragement was unwavering. My publisher, Business One Irwin, not only helped with a grant but provided excellent editorial support in the persons of James Childs and Cynthia Zigmund. Mark Haskins, of the Darden School of the University of Virginia, reviewed the book on the publisher's behalf and made many insightful comments. Philip Chenok, president of the AICPA, and his staff were supportive and made available numerous computer programs; software was also contributed by HavenTree Software, the publisher of Easy-Flow.

Lewis Davidson, director of the School of Accounting at Florida International University, helped me obtain a semester's leave to work on the book. Rowan Jones of the University of Birmingham asked penetrating questions and made constructive observations. My colleagues Mortimer Dittenhofer, Harvey Hendrickson, Kenneth Most, Bernadette Ruf, John Sennetti, and Richard Wiskeman reviewed portions of the book and provided valuable inputs.

Special thanks must go to a small group of individuals who imparted both knowledge and data. This group includes Antonio Argiz, past chairman of Florida's State Board of Accountancy, and the partners and employees of Morrison, Brown, Argiz & Company, especially the late Alberto Vicens; David Rosenstein and Trevor Stewart, partners of Deloitte & Touche; Stanley D. Halper of the Audit Committee Support Network; Donald W. Hunt of the Executive Development Group, Inc.; Carlos Garcia, Miguel Angel Gutierrez, and George Santana of the company I have called "Stellar Corporation."

While I am grateful to all reviewers and contributors, I wish to stress that the theoretical framework of the book, and any mistakes, are entirely my own.

Felix Pomeranz

CONTENTS

PART 1

SETTING THE STAGE

CHAPTER 1

THE NEED FOR A NEW APPROACH

Action is the highest form of contemplation.

Muhammad Iqbal*

USER PERSPECTIVE: **Items of Special Interest**

EXECUTIVE HIGHLIGHTS: All readers
INTRODUCTION: All readers

A Road Map to the Book
WHY THIS BOOK WAS WRITTEN: All readers
THE AUDIENCE FOR THIS BOOK: All readers
AN OVERVIEW OF THE BOOK: All readers
FOCAL POINTS OF THE BOOK'S PHILOSOPHY: External
auditors, internal auditors
BENEFITS TO READERS: All readers
HOW TO USE THE BOOK: All readers

The State of the Profession
THE COMPETITIVE CLIMATE: External auditors
A PROFESSION UNDER ATTACK: All readers
THOUGHTS ON THE EXPECTATION GAP: External audi-
tors, financial officers
THE STANDARDS OVERLOAD: External auditors
THE TECHNOLOGICAL REMEDY: All readers
THE UPDATED AUDIT APPROACH AND ITS IMPLICA-
TIONS: External auditors, internal auditors

---

*Pakistani philosopher and poet.

EXECUTIVE HIGHLIGHTS

Two specters loom over auditing: ineffectiveness and inadequate productivity. Improvement in audit effectiveness may mean doing more auditing, while greater audit productivity may suggest doing less.

Technology applied to the management of audit risk, to audit procedures, and to accountants' office administration is likely to offer significant relief from both problems. Particular benefits may exist for smaller firms endeavoring to maintain or reestablish themselves as providers of audit services.

Based on the author's own experiences, and on extant research, causes of unsatisfactory audit effectiveness and productivity are set out in Chapters 2 and 3 as a basis for corrective action.

This book assumes that a good auditor is a good businessperson and that business knowledge represents an auditor's most potent renewable resource. Business knowledge is also basic to understanding a client's control requirements.

The book argues that uncontrolled business risk is likely to breed audit risk. Therefore, the auditor's attention should be focused on the principal risks confronting the client and especially on those threats which the client has not controlled effectively. This latter group is likely to be synonymous with elements of the auditor's own risk.

Technology will promote continuing change in the subject matter of auditing, the composition of audit teams, auditing procedures, the timing of the audit, and the audit product. State-of-the-art auditing will prompt the involvement of senior audit personnel in the sensitive aspects of engagements.

INTRODUCTION

This chapter sets out to do two things: first, to provide a "road map" through the book, and second, to report on the current unhappy state of the accounting profession and hold out the perceived technological remedy.

A ROAD MAP TO THE BOOK

WHY THIS BOOK WAS WRITTEN

For decades, members of the accounting profession ranked near the top of all professions in terms of public esteem. Unfortunately, that esteem has eroded; certainly, accountants' reported role in the U.S. savings and loan (S&L) debacle has negatively affected their image. However, there has also been an apparent deterioration of audit productivity; at the same time, regulators, legislators, journalists, and others have questioned audit effectiveness. Improvements in audit effectiveness may mean doing more auditing, while greater audit productivity may suggest doing less. Accounting firms' profit margins have eroded as a result of efficiency and productivity problems and also because of severe price competition among those who supply audit services.

These problems must be redressed if the profession is to resume its economic growth and to continue and improve its contributions to society. The author believes technology—applied to the management of audit risk, to audit procedures, and to accountants' office administration—is likely to offer significant relief to external and internal auditors and to those who rely on their services. To the time of this writing, accountants' technology applications have tended to be uneven, halting, and tentative. Hopefully, the book will help change this situation. Other conditions that provided impetus for this book are discussed later in this chapter.

From the perspective of the practicing auditor, the challenge is "learning to do by doing."[1] This book will be guided by this approach.

THE AUDIENCE FOR THIS BOOK

Many readers will be practicing public accountants associated with firms of all sizes. These readers are likely to be bedeviled by the twin specters of deteriorating profitability and escalating au-

---

[1]The slogan was abstracted from the motto of the Finance School, U.S. Army at Fort Benjamin Harrison, Indiana.

dit failures. Hopefully, the book will reach accountants in firms of all sizes. Large accounting firms enjoy economies of scale; however, smaller firms have the advantages of close association with client principals, accompanied by hands-on knowledge of the client's business. Therefore, technology may offer particular benefits to smaller firms endeavoring to maintain or reestablish themselves in rendering audit services to public companies.

Other readers may hold posts as chief financial officers or as members of audit committees. Chief financial officers are the key people in assuring that their companies' systems conduce to the preparation of timely, accurate, and complete financial statements, and that internal controls are in place to safeguard correct financial reporting. Audit committees must have some means for ascertaining that all parties involved in the preparation of financial statements are doing their job; they should gain that comfort by monitoring the operation of key and supervisory controls built into the system.

Government accountants and auditors represent an important reader segment; in recent years they have been, and may continue to be, at the leading edge of auditing developments in the United States. This book should also be helpful to those engaged in the emerging practice of "forensic accounting": civil and criminal lawyers, private investigators, law enforcement officers, and insurance claims adjusters and examiners.

AN OVERVIEW OF THE BOOK

Part 1 Setting the Stage

Weaknesses in audit effectiveness and productivity confronting external and internal auditors and the users of their services are described. Here and throughout the book, problems are analyzed from the viewpoint of the practitioner, the audit organization, and the profession, with occasional comparative references to other professions, such as law and medicine. Attempts will be made to identify and assess causes of unsatisfactory audit effectiveness and productivity that are controllable to some degree by practitioners. To the extent that these suggestions involve technology, or closely related matters, assistance will be provided in the form of references to information resources, checklists, or examples. Also, the prevailing audit model will be analyzed and brought up to date with reference to available or emerging technology.

Chapter 1   The Need for a New Approach
The twin problems of audit ineffectiveness and lagging audit productivity are posited. The effects of endeavors to close the "expectation gap" are seen as imposing a disproportionate burden on smaller client companies, and on smaller audit organizations. Conceivably, these developments may have contributed to further concentration of audits of public companies with very large firms. Technology is suggested as a partial answer to the problems of audit organizations of all sizes, and especially as a means toward revitalizing smaller audit entities.

Chapter 2   The Ineffectiveness of Today's Auditing
If one subscribes to the theory that an expectation gap separates users of financial statements and auditors, it becomes possible to fear that the gap has widened into what an English writer has called "a chasm." The chapter assesses the reasons for both successes and failures in auditor detection of errors and irregularities. Specific types of inadequacies to which auditors are prone are set out as a basis to problem resolution, in many instances, via technology.

Chapter 3   The Erosion of Audit Productivity
Rumors abound as to the deteriorating (and differing) profit margins experienced by public accounting firms. Hard data is difficult to come by, given some public accounting firms' reluctance to issue meaningful financial statements to the public. The chapter points to likely pockets of unproductive audit work and suggests approaches to the enhancement of audit profitability. Also, attention is directed toward the development of new services, some of which could lead to the sale of "big ticket" items.

Chapter 4   The Selection of Audit Procedures
The chapter explores the state of the current professional literature concerning assessment of audit risk and the formulation of

audit objectives. An explanation is given of the interplay between client business (or inherent risk) and audit risk. Approaches are suggested for determining the inherent risk that attaches to an individual transaction or account balance and for placing the audit effort on (1) areas of uncontrolled exposure and (2) management of audit risk stemming from those areas of exposure.

Part 2   The Advent of Technology

This part describes major advances in technology in terms of their meaning to the frontline auditor and to those who rely on his services. Particular attention is given to the improved weaponry available to the "white hats" in their war on fraud. Specific facilities, programs, and techniques are considered in relation to the updated audit model.

Chapter 5   Technological Change and Its Implications for Auditing

The chapter explores technology that is either available or likely to come on-stream within the next few years; such technology is linked to ease of use by auditors. The on-line data bases are introduced.

Chapter 6   The Arsenal of the Technological Audit

This chapter constructs the foundation for a successful technological audit: physical protection of assets, circumscribed access to the computer, and independent verification of management representations. Specific guidance is given regarding effective techniques for control, and reference is made to technology-based tests and other audit procedures which have become both efficient and effective.

Chapter 7   Heightening the Auditor's Sensitivity to Fraud

The chapter argues that chances have improved for the detection of fraud of a noncollusive nature, if there is reasonable alertness and sensitivity on the part of the auditor. Diagnostic approaches to fraud detection are explored, and mention is made of trends within the emerging field of forensic accounting.

Chapter 8 Blending Technology and the Updated Audit Model

The chapter restates and refines the audit model, and provides "how to" audit guidance for using a series of tools selected by the author. Care has been taken to see that extant professional rules are complied with.

Part 3 Implementing the Updated Model

Chapter 9 Case Study

The updated model and techniques are applied to actual client situations.

Chapter 10 Working Papers

The materials in this chapter should facilitate integration of the new techniques into the readers' thought processes and professional practices. Also, hints are given for adapting or tailoring material to meet practice requirements.

Chapter 11 A Road Map to Implementing the New Technology

Step by step guidance is offered as to how to implement the updated audit procedures. Emphasis is put on the designation of a chief technology officer and on the development of a strategic plan for technological development. Suggestions are made as to the sequence in which technological advances should be introduced.

Part 4 The New Audit in Its Environment

Chapter 12 Research across Disciplines

Geometric increases are foreseen in the demand for audit research. The chapter argues for integration of academic and practice research; such integration will be essential to permit the profession to anticipate public needs, and to become more causative and less reactive.

Chapter 13 The Accountant's Organization

The familiar organization pyramid is likely to turn into a rectangle. New types of *functional* specialists will arise, responsible primarily for the maintenance of an aura of total quality. And, an upgraded type of *industry* specialist will evolve. The vision of decentralization, subject to centralized guidance, will be realized.

Chapter 14   Public Policy and Auditing
A shift is perceived in regulatory interest toward auditing, and away from accounting. A possible threat to auditors and clients involves an increase in compliance auditing, an activity unlikely to be viewed by industry as having much value. With the aid of technology, competitiveness will increase still further domestically; such competitiveness is likely to hone the capability of the American profession to strive for leadership in international accounting and auditing services.

Chapter 15   A Distillation of Experience (and a Forecast)
The rate of technological change will accelerate. Accordingly, accountancy will become a more capital-intensive profession, leading to a vigorous debate on firms' organizations and on the professional or nonprofessional status of shareholders. Some improvement may be anticipated in the legal climate; however, dramatic action could also be taken by Congress to close the expectation gap.

FOCAL POINTS OF THE BOOK'S PHILOSOPHY

Stress on Audit Fundamentals

The book espouses audit fundamentals, which at times may have become obscured by a welter of detailed rules. Advantage will be taken of available technology to a practical and cost effective degree, with appropriate consideration of negative aspects. Management of risk is discussed from client and auditor perspectives, and has been focused on areas of significant exposure.

Consideration of Possible Management and Employee Fraud

Fraud prevention and discovery should be achievable in many noncollusive instances, given a wary control approach by the client, and reasonable sensitivity to indications of fraud by the auditor. Clients should use controls to isolate a potential perpetrator from assets and other valuables, and from an opportunity for access thereto. Techniques will be mentioned for conducting a search for indications of fraud. Key and supervisory controls will be stressed as a technique for assuring corporate executives, and especially audit committee members, that controls are functioning as planned and that no undesirable conditions have arisen.

Focus on the Auditor-Businessperson

The book assumes that a good auditor is a good businessperson. That attribute will be exploited in two ways: particular attention will be given to the auditor's role in helping the client to manage business risk, and operational information will be utilized to perform a more efficient and effective financial audit.

Proactive Auditing

Historic or "score card" auditing is considered by many to have only limited benefits for users of financial information. In the future, much auditing will take place prior to performance of business transactions, or at least contemporaneously with those transactions. For example, auditors will become involved with strategic planning for systems and with systems projects undergoing development.

BENEFITS TO READERS

1. The book should be of interest to a wide readership. Hopefully, those who actually perform audits will be prime beneficiaries. However, all readers should gain a better understanding of internal and external risks to which a business is exposed, including management, employee, and third party fraud. Readers should also become aware of the impressive information resources available to financial executives and auditors to identify and manage exposures to risk, and they should become more familiar

with risk management techniques, choices, costs, and options.

2. The book argues that uncontrolled business risk is likely to breed audit risk. In other words, auditors should be deeply concerned with evaluating the client's effectiveness in managing risk.

3. External and internal auditors will be better able to avoid work that does not directly support audit objectives, unless clients specifically direct the performance of such work and are willing to pay for it.

4. Auditors, chief financial officers, and audit committee members will gain increased assurance of being in compliance with professional and regulatory requirements pertaining to preparation and auditing of financial statements, and especially with rules bearing on the profession's endeavor to close the expectation gap.

5. Auditors and financial officers will learn to apply technological tools and techniques. In many cases, the techniques will be not only effective, but also intellectually stimulating.

6. Audit committee members, as well as other readers, will have the satisfaction of having taken reasonable protective steps against audit failure, thus strengthening their own legal posture.

7. Auditors, as well as those who pay for their services, will be interested in this book's espousal of technology as a means toward increasing the rigor of an audit examination while closely monitoring its cost.

8. External and internal auditors will be in a better position to differentiate the services which *they* render from the "audit commodity" produced by others; they may be able to do this by contributing to the client's bottom line.

HOW TO USE THE BOOK

Significant issues are recapitulated in executive overviews. Technology-related techniques and instructions are highlighted by gray shading. Examples ("items") and comments have been set out separately to conserve reader time and to highlight potential pitfalls in implementation. In general, problems have been redressed by "cures" in the nature of suggestions for client and auditor risk management, controls, audit procedures, or accountants' personnel and administrative routines; there is also a summary checklist of improvement opportunities relating to audit engagements and organizations (see Figure 13–1).

At the beginning of each chapter, User Perspectives have been provided and labeled with the job titles of readers likely to find the information most pertinent.

THE STATE OF THE PROFESSION

THE COMPETITIVE CLIMATE

The remaining pages in this chapter describe the fiercely competitive markets in which accountants operate, the freely dispensed and often unjustified criticism of accountants by regulators and legislators, and the profession's defense via a "standards overload." Implementation of technology by auditors is seen as offering relief.

The merger activity that hit the accounting profession in 1988 was fueled by opportunities that may open with the removal of economic boundaries in Europe in 1992. The following U.S. revenues for fiscal year 1990 have been attributed to the "Big Six:"

Ernst & Young, $2.2 billion
Arthur Andersen, $2 billion
KPMG-Peat Marwick, $1.9 billion
Deloitte & Touche, $1.9 billion
Coopers & Lybrand, $1.2 billion
Price Waterhouse, $1.1 billion.[2]

The revenue volumes reflect the concentration of audits of major U.S. companies with large firms; similar results were ob-

---

[2]"Special Report: The Top 60 Firms," Top 60 Supplement, *Accounting Today*, September 24, 1990, p. S6.

tained in a study which compared companies listed on the New York Stock Exchange for 1956 and 1989. In 1956 the "Big Eight" audited 78.51 percent of these listed companies, while the top four firms audited 50.27 percent. In 1989 the comparable figures were 96 percent and 68.94 percent respectively.[3]

The (nonmerging) firm of Arthur Andersen is said to have been the winner among the 13 largest accounting firms in garnering new public company audit clients in 1989, with a net gain of 17, followed by nonmerging Price Waterhouse with a net gain of 6.[4] In any event, some feel that the mergers may have had an unsettling effect on the market; one commentator referred to "a zero-sum game," possible contraction in the audit function, and gains in market share achievable only at the expense of competitors.[5]

It is difficult to discern fallout from the 1988 mergers in terms of shifts of disgruntled clients away from the very large firms. Despite the reported hopes of smaller firms, especially of midsize firms (i.e., regional firms) and of "second tier" national firms, for picking up clients following the mega mergers, the large firms have continued to gain clients among listed companies. As a result, the midsize firms are said to be fighting for their survival, "doing business in a mature market enveloped in a sluggish economy," and handicapped by a "shortage of young talent, leading to escalating salaries." In 1989 the midsize group's average rate of growth was reported to be less than 7 percent, due in part to the difficulties which such firms may have in distinguishing themselves from their peers. Over the near term, these midsize firms and smaller local firms are likely to pursue specialization in terms of particular industries or services, while larger clients continue to be wooed by the Big Six.[6]

---

[3]Charles Wooten, Stanley D. Tonge, and Carel M. Wolk, "From the 'Big Eight' to the 'Big Six' Accounting Firms," *Ohio CPA Journal* 49, no. 1 (Spring 1990), pp. 19–23.

[4]"Andersen Leads in Account Gains in 1989," *Business Wire*, January 5, 1990.

[5]Albert B. Crenshaw, "Accountants Do Bitter Battle for New Clients; Coopers & Lybrand Leads the Charge in Washington," *The Washington Post*, April 23, 1990, financial sect., p. 5.

[6]Alison Leigh Cowan, "Changes in Accounting Leave Big Firms Strong," *New York Times*, Sect. D, January 8, 1990, p. 2.

A PROFESSION UNDER ATTACK

John Dingell, a noted congressional critic of the accounting profession, has repeatedly raised the cry "Where were the auditors?" The profession has responded by disclaiming blame, by trying to explain the practical and philosophical limitations of audits, and by issuing numerous new audit requirements. Some of the new rules are untried, anticipated benefits may not be supported by meaningful evidence, and startup as well as continuing costs can be significant. The pace of activity is driven by fear that "if we don't do something, the government will do it for us." It is arguable how realistic this concern is: the unique U.S. partnership of government and the accounting profession has worked effectively for more than half a century, and it is not likely to be abandoned capriciously.

In any event, the profession's zeal to anticipate governmental action has had negative effects on auditors and on their clients. Audit profitability is likely to have been affected adversely by substantial training and research efforts required to comply with complex statements such as *SAS 55*. Indeed, there are indications that small local firms are shying away from practicing auditing.

Item

In recruiting recent graduates, small firms used to highlight the numbers of "opinion audits" they performed and their prospects of picking up additional public clients. In contrast, recent applications for positions report some small firm recruiters are announcing as a virtue that their firms do no auditing, do not plan to do any, and have therefore significantly reduced their exposure to litigation.

The Views of Some Critics

The recent well-publicized failures of many U.S. savings and loan associations have furnished a rallying point for those critical of the profession. For example, a senior official of the U.S. General Accounting Office (GAO) has stated that 87 percent of savings and loan failures in Texas were caused by management fraud and that external and internal auditors had failed to detect a single case; he estimates 60 percent of S&L failures in other parts of the country also resulted from undetected management scams. In the same vein, a ranking officer of the Federal Bureau of Investigation (FBI) says that half of the nation's 100 largest defense contractors are under investigation, have confessed, or have been convicted in connection with management crimes; he adds that internal and external auditors contributed little to detection or prevention in any of these cases.

The Auditor's Role in the S&L Failures

There are varied theories as to who or what may have caused the epidemic of failures in industries such as savings and loan associations. In general, the nation's precipitate haste to deregulate—whether or not those being deregulated were capable of assuming expanded responsibilities—together with inadequate regulatory supervision and floating interest rates contributed significantly to the fiascoes.

In this regard, auditors represent one of the important components of the oversight machinery. Certainly, the auditors cannot be said to have been the causes or agents of S&L failures. Nonetheless, auditors' lack of industry knowledge, especially of novel financial instruments in the S&L industry, could have contributed to some of the alleged S&L audit failures. Moreover, some auditors may not have understood the client's business; others may not have known the client's executives, especially those who directed operations, in contrast to accounting or financial administration. Press reports suggest that public accounting firms with only a few clients in the "high-risk" S&L industry may have performed relatively less well than those specializing in the industry. (Although many large firms claim to have formal specialization programs, the nature, extent, and quality of these programs vary.) Companies in the financial services industry had created many novel and innovative financial instruments. The accounting profession has been slow to furnish auditors with guidance as to how to validate transactions involving the new instruments. This book will not endeavor to assess blame for the long lead time needed to issue professional pronouncements. There are encouraging signs of renewed activism on the part of the American Institute of Certified Public Accountants (AICPA). Moreover, the problem has been addressed, at least in part, with the creation of the Emerging Issues Task Force (EITF) by the Financial Accounting Standards Board (FASB); the move was strongly supported by the U.S. Securities and Exchange Commission (SEC). As discussed subsequently, EITF pronouncements, which represent a level of generally accepted accounting principles (GAAP), are readily retrievable "on-line" by auditors.

An additional factor, relating to the auditor's role as business advisor, should be mentioned. The American accounting profession has for a generation done relatively little to emphasize the auditor's need to understand the control implications of client *operations*. Until issuance of the expectation gap *SAS*s, especially *SAS 55*, the professional literature had guided auditors to evaluate "internal accounting controls," to de facto exclusion of "operational controls." (The last named class of controls is used by management to run the business and make decisions.)

THOUGHTS ON THE "EXPECTATION GAP"

Some leaders of the profession insist that an "expectation gap" exists between what the public expects of auditors (especially in the way of detection of fraud) and what the profession can reasonably deliver. Other leaders, including prominent auditing researchers, have stated that the alleged gap's existence has not been verified by evidence. Nonetheless, the Auditing Standards Board (ASB) has responded to this gap by pronouncing in *SAS 53* that, beginning with 1989, an auditor must design his examination so as to detect material misstatements. (Just how the auditor should execute the plan has not been made entirely clear. However, execution is likely to be affected by the uncertainties that normally surround the audit process.) It does seem that this *SAS* is a clear example of extending auditors' responsibilities; however, such extensions have confused experienced practitioners, as well as seasoned financial writers.

Whose Risk Is Being Managed?

This book will consider both the client's inherent (business) risk and the auditor's management of audit risk. Initially, an auditor must obtain an understanding of the client's industry, business, and system. Based on that understanding, the auditor assesses the business risk that attaches to a particular account or class of transactions and then makes an aggregate estimate of those risks. This process does not appear unreasonable. However, two observations seem appropriate: (1) the process has been approached entirely from the perspective of the external auditor; the practical effect is that the auditor has *not* been instructed to assess how effectively the *client* manages his own risks and (2) the professional literature provides little information as to the process to be followed in aggregating risk assessments.

In any event, there is no reason why the auditor's attention should not focus on the principal risks confronting the client, and, especially, on those threats which the client has overlooked, downplayed, or not controlled effectively. This latter group is likely to be synonymous with elements of the auditor's own audit risk. Some examples of major business risks confronting clients are noted in the two paragraphs which follow.

For the most part business risks (discussed more fully in chapter 8) are external in nature and generally include such issues as:

1. Energy shortages.
2. Material shortages.
3. Labor interruptions.
4. Inflation.
5. Capital shortages.
6. Noncompliance with laws.
7. New technology.
8. Competition—foreign and domestic.
9. New legal requirements.

The internal business risks that any business confronts may include such issues as:

1. Absence of meaningful communication up or down the line of authority.
2. Lack of a corporate charter or mission statement.
3. Excessive layers of supervision.
4. Absence of any management philosophy.

Aspects of Risk Management

Risk management is discussed in some detail in Chapter 8. Risks can be assumed, shifted to someone else, insured by an outside company, or managed by a combination of techniques, including the institution of controls. (Obviously, the extent of a company's or individual's risk averseness affects the nature of risk management.) Controls are an important risk management tool; they help to prevent loss, detect loss in timely fashion, and correct deficiencies. Of course, both internal and external auditors are experts on control and are well qualified to assist in managing business risk. The auditor's opportunities are great, especially in terms of performing preventive services; the auditor's role as a reviewer of controls built into systems while they are in the development stage illustrates the potential.

Is It an Audit Failure or a Business Failure?

There may be a communication problem between the public and some auditors as to the nature of a "failure" in relation to audit services. Leaders of the profession have urged that the public be taught to distinguish an "audit failure" from a "business failure"; they have asserted that audit failures are rare compared to business failures. Unfortunately, there are no generally accepted, or even understood, distinctions between the two sets of failures; therefore, neat slotting would seem to be impractical. Even if failures could be so classified, most businesspeople are likely to feel that their auditor should have cautioned them against engaging in imprudent decision making, making decisions based on inaccurate or incomplete information, or failing to manage business risk. Who but an auditor would be as ideally equipped to guide his client with respect to these matters?

THE STANDARDS OVERLOAD

Throughout its history the profession has created new services by responding to market demand. In recent years, however, governmental criticisms, urgings, and even threats have significantly influenced the market for accounting and auditing services. The lawsuits against auditors which began in earnest in the 70s brought to the fore the question of whether application of generally accepted accounting principles and generally accepted auditing standards resulted in a fair reflection of the nature of a client's business transactions and a faithful fulfillment of audit responsibilities, or whether such fulfillment depended on judgment exercised in a well-reasoned manner in individual cases. The accountants perceived the marketplace's hesitancy to accept such judgments as adequate defense and began to issue standards which tended to leave less and less to individual judgments. For example, during the four-year period from 1978 to 1982, the number of pages constituting *Statements of Financial Accounting Standards (SFASs)* more than tripled. The content need not concern us here, except to note that the pronouncements represent a not particularly well-ordered accumulation of concepts, objectives, detailed rules, and industry-specific guidance—all of it subject to continuing amendment, change, or reversal.

The effect of standard setting on the actions of corporate managers has not been easy to evaluate. Some have asserted that the standards favor short-term, rather than long-term, results. There is also the obvious risk that management may adjust sensible practices to influence the results that will eventually be reported. Also, there has been a gradual increase in the number and influence of Financial Accounting Foundation trustees with nonpractitioner backgrounds. Since the trustees appoint the writers of the rules, the Financial Accounting Standards Board members, there is not likely to be any decrease in the volume of detail of industry-specific rules.

The business of accounting regulation is practiced by a formidable number of agencies. Well-known names include, in addition to the FASB and ASB, the Government Accounting Standards Board, the Securities and Exchange Commission, the International Accounting Standards Committee, the International Federation of Accountants, the European Economic Community, the Organization for Economic Cooperation and Development, the United Nations, the International Organization of Supreme Audit Institutions, and regional professional or governmental groups in various geographic areas. The promulgation of accounting rules—often unsupported by cost and benefit studies, or by the establishment of threshold minimums for application—has become a cottage industry. The cost of mastering the avalanche of rules weighs heavily on accounting and auditing firms of all sizes, and disproportionately on smaller firms.

To the extent that research exists pertaining to the effect on audit quality of the standards overload, it suggests that accountants and auditors are aware of the rules, but make errors in interpretation. For example, the seminal 1983 study by St. Pierre and Anderson, which will be discussed in Chapter 4, found that 15 percent of alleged auditors' errors pertained to the interpretation of auditing standards. The interpretation of accounting principles and the implementation of auditing procedures accounted for another 33 percent of errors. The authors concluded that interpretation errors were common; the sheer number and volume of rules are likely to exacerbate these problems.

The combined effect of fear of litigation, together with the need for purchasing, reading, filing, retrieving, and interpreting pronouncements, has placed an excessive burden on smaller practitioners. This book offers succor to these practitioners.

Treadway: New Problems and Opportunities

A set of far-reaching recommendations has emerged from the work of the National Commission on Fraudulent Financial Reporting, usually referred to as the "Treadway Commission" (Treadway). Many of the important recommendations are aimed at public companies, their officers, and directors. Recommendations of particular interest to members of audit committees involve answers to the following questions:

1. Has your board of directors formally established an audit committee? Are all members independent directors?

2. Are the audit committee's duties and responsibilities set forth in a written charter?
3. Does your audit committee oversee the quarterly financial reporting process?
4. Does your audit committee review the planned scope of the independent and internal audits?[7]

Implementation of Treadway recommendations—possibly through legislation—means the responsibilities of audit committees will become formalized and significantly expanded. Greater legal exposure to directors could result. Further, Treadway is going to be costly to implement for most small public companies and especially for emerging companies. Auditors, no less than directors, will have to spend a lot of time preparing for meetings.[8]

Successful accomplishment of the audit committee's now explicit mission centers on the effectiveness of oversight: the audit committee must see to the introduction of controls to provide it with assurance that internal control and financial reporting related responsibilities are being carried out. Further, in order to gain additional protection, the committee must engage in an unrelenting search for evidence of systems breakdowns. Of course, the new responsibilities are not limited to the audit committee, which is only an arm of the board of directors—the duties are ultimately duties of all of the directors, which they have chosen to delegate.[9]

Treadway's emphasis on controls over the financial reporting process stems from an expectation that such controls can prevent and detect fraudulent financial reporting. Relevant controls are said to include the internal audit function, the audit committee itself, other components of the corporate control environment, and internal accounting controls. Therefore, an audit committee member should have some feeling for answers to the following questions: (1) which controls are really important to the preven-

---

[7]Deloitte & Touche, *DH&S Review*, July 5, 1988, p. 2.

[8]Paul Kolton, "The Treadway Commission—What Happens Next?" *Financial Executive*, May/June 1988, pp. 50–55.

[9]Hurd Baruch, "The Audit Committee: A Guide for Directors," *Harvard Business Review*, May 1980, p. 174.

tion and detection of financial fraud? (2) which of these controls have actually been put in place by my company? (3) what steps can be taken to prevent having these controls overridden by management? (4) how have the subject controls been documented by my company's systems personnel and auditors? and (5) how can an audit committee member satisfy himself that the controls are functioning as planned? This book should help to provide answers to these questions.

THE TECHNOLOGICAL REMEDY

In a recent interview the deans of three business schools mentioned "competitiveness," a term which they did not define, as the most important factor driving the environments of graduate schools of business in the 1990s. Similarly, at the 1987 Arthur Young Professors' Roundtable it was noted that competitive forces have led the auditors' clients to implement new capabilities, based on advanced information systems. Growing reliance on these systems will force auditors to respond by developing new techniques capable of dealing with the new technologies adopted by clients. Development of new auditing tools was foreseen in two basic areas: (1) tools designed to create auditable systems and (2) productivity tools to be used by an auditor in performing audits.[10]

The firm of Arthur Andersen has analyzed advances in information technology and their effect on executives. Developments likely to have a significant impact on auditors include: (1) ever-increasing computer processing speeds, due to enhancement of microchip capacities; the current rate of improvement represents fourfold increases every two years; (2) virtually unlimited data storage in the form of optical media, which can accommodate vast amounts of information in the same space and are very durable; (3) dramatic advances in telecommunications with digital trans-

---

[10]Andrew D. Bailey, Jr., Kyeong Seok Han, and Andrew B. Whinston, "Technology, Competition, and the Future of Auditing," *Auditor Productivity in the Year 2000: 1987 Proceedings of the Arthur Young Professors' Roundtable* (Reston, Va.: The Council of Arthur Young Professors, 1988), pp. 24 and 31.

mission replacing analog transmission—eventually this will lead to the transmission of voice, data, or images over the same equipment; and (4) software advances which are likely to accelerate, particularly with respect to relational data bases. Artificial intelligence is likely to awake from dormancy—hardware power and price now permit its use. In order to gain a competitive edge, corporate executives will need to closely examine and continually evaluate their use of information technology.[11]

These new tools will promote continuing change in the subject matter of auditing, the composition of audit teams, auditing procedures, the timing of the audit, and the audit product. The benefits from the changes do not represent unalloyed blessings, since new audit exposures may arise; such exposures are especially likely to affect security. This book explains how to put the new technology to work to enhance audit effectiveness and productivity, and urges a strong security ethic.

THE UPDATED AUDIT APPROACH AND ITS IMPLICATIONS

The technology described in this book will have pervasive effects on auditors and on users of audit information. For example, for many years senior personnel with auditing firms, partners and managers, have functioned as off-site and after-the-fact reviewers of information gathered by their less experienced (or even inexperienced) associates; but in the future such senior people will be involved daily with the sensitive or high-risk work required on an engagement, as well as with analysis of computer-generated data. In the future, assignments given to junior-level auditors will be less likely to involve extensive contact with client personnel in sensitive positions. As a consequence, new ways will have to be found to train, utilize, and professionally develop junior-level auditors.

Another example: currently, auditing firms are organized on

---

[11]Arthur Andersen & Company, *Trends in Information Technology: 1986* (Chicago, Ill.: Arthur Andersen & Co., 1986), 81 pp.

a functional basis into audit, tax, and consulting groups. Although "industry specialization" has become a buzzword and is practiced by different firms with varying degrees of commitment, meaningful specialization is now likely to come into its own. The new audit technology to be expounded in this book facilitates the organization of "core groups" composed of cross-disciplinary specialists, linked to each other by electronic networks rather than physical proximity. To accommodate firms of varying sizes, a group may consist of one individual, conceivably exercising this responsibility on a part-time basis, or a dedicated full-time group of specialists. The missions of the core groups will include audit research, the monitoring of audit quality while the audit is still in progress, and technical support to engagement teams.

CHAPTER 2

THE INEFFECTIVENESS OF TODAY'S AUDITING

Financial failures occur because of economic conditions, lack of management expertise, and other factors completely unrelated to fraud. . . . Many people may have lost sight of how the investment process works, and government regulators have fostered their misconceptions. . . . When are we going to start telling it like it is?

Harvey Kapnick *

USER PERSPECTIVE: **Items of Special Interest**

EXECUTIVE HIGHLIGHTS: All readers

INTRODUCTION: All readers

THE ELUSIVE NATURE OF AUDIT EFFECTIVENESS: External auditors, internal auditors, government auditors, audit committee members

THREATS TO AUDIT EFFECTIVENESS: External auditors, internal auditors

EXAMPLES OF SUCCESSFUL ERROR DETECTION: External auditors, internal auditors, government auditors, financial executives

CAUSES FOR AUDIT FAILURES: External auditors, internal auditors, audit committee members

SPECIFIC AUDIT DEFICIENCIES: All readers

SUMMARY: AREAS FOR IMPROVEMENT: All readers

---

*Harvey Kapnick was the outspoken chairman of Arthur Andersen & Co. when these remarks were published.

EXECUTIVE HIGHLIGHTS

There is an absence of literature concerning the vast majority of engagements wherein auditors took appropriate action. Consequently, it is impossible to assess the incidence of audit failures, relative to successful audits.

Audit failures can stem from client errors or irregularities (i.e., intentional misrepresentations), or both. Roughly half the legal actions against auditors have involved irregularities; management fraud comprised nearly that entire group. This suggests a need for more rigorous auditing, or for a higher degree of audit skepticism.

Agencies of the federal government have focused on audit quality from the perspective not only of errors and misrepresentations but also of compliance with professional and governmental rules. Reported inadequacies involve violations of some of the profession's basic rules, including the standards of fieldwork. It also appeared that auditors were not always aware of high-risk areas in high-risk businesses.

Failure to use operational information to confirm the accuracy of financial information may have contributed to a lack of rigor in examinations. The condition may have been compounded by the delegation of work to relatively junior personnel.

Lasting corrective actions are most likely to be brought about by appealing to the hearts and minds of those within the profession, rather than by figuratively throwing bricks from the outside. Moreover, any action to correct deficiencies must be seen from a tripartite perspective of: the auditor on the engagement, the audit organization, and the profession.

The computer's unerring accuracy, together with its data-handling capability, should lead to a more thorough and productive audit than has been performed in the past.

INTRODUCTION

This chapter is the first of two which analyze audit effectiveness and efficiency respectively; the chapter also discusses alleged audit failures. Analyses and summaries exist for fraud detected by auditors; unfortunately, the write-ups (and the police dossiers) often skirt details of the modi operandi of the culprits, or of the manner of their detection. But there is an absence of literature concerning the huge majority of engagements wherein auditors took appropriate action—that is, saw to adjusting journal entries and disclosures and expressed correct audit opinions.

It is thus impossible to determine the percentages of audits that failed, except to conclude that the incidence has been rather low relative to successful audits. It is also difficult to identify those audit procedures which were more successful than others in detecting fraud. In general, it appears that coarse analytical procedures proved more useful than other types of tests; this success could be attributed either to the substantial size of irregularities likely to be reflected in the balances, or to the fact that analytical procedures are performed early in an audit. Given the limitations of audit tests, neither tests of controls, nor tests of transactions or of account balances, appear to have been particularly productive relative to fraud detection.

Reports by the U.S. General Accounting Office (GAO) have discussed perceived failures by auditors; unfortunately, these reports may not address the specifics that caused losses or how the accounting profession might have prevented those losses.[1] Related questions include whether an effective internal audit function would have discovered the problems and whether internal auditors effectively and constantly search out, discover, and correct their organization's internal control weaknesses.[2]

There are two related issues—the discovery of fraud in the first instance, followed by its subsequent reporting. According to the *New York Times*, "the nation's accountants may soon feel [the] backlash. . . . Federal legislators are drafting a measure that would require independent auditors to alert regulators to any obvious illegal activities they discover in their audits." The article notes that

---

[1]Dan L. Goldwasser, "The Liability Ramifications of the S&L Crisis," *The CPA Journal* 60, no. 1 (January 1990), pp. 20–26.

[2]William A. Stone, "Lessons from the Thrift and Commercial Bank Industries," *Internal Auditor* 47, no. 3 (June 1990), pp. 32–40.

while accountants say they should enjoy the same protection from informing on clients that is afforded lawyers, doctors and other professionals, in the view of [the sponsor of the legislation, Congressman] Ron Wyden, accountants were not entitled to play the role of confidant to the managers of publicly held companies, because of the competing duty of auditors to serve as the public's watchdog.[3]

Author's Comment

Several critical issues are involved: it is not entirely clear to which constituency the auditor owes primary watchdog responsibility; the nature of privileged communications to auditors is mired in diverse state laws; whistle-blowing continues to be highly controversial and is likely to be the subject of an eventual accommodation between legislators, regulators, and the profession. (Similar questions are also being addressed in the United Kingdom, as discussed in Chapter 14.)

The universe of alleged failures looms large in dollar terms. A table compiled by the Federal Deposit Insurance Corporation documents the damages sought initially from major accounting firms accused of as yet unadjudicated instances of fraud, negligence, or other professional misconduct (see Table 2–1). Damages sought from Deloitte & Touche exceed $800 million; another half billion in claims has been asserted against Ernst & Young.

This chapter concentrates largely on the kind of tactical audit error that seems to point to an underlying audit deficiency. The possible causes will be listed to set the stage for exploration of audit tests and practices that might have prevented, detected, or corrected errors. The author believes that, in the majority of instances, application of new technology by the auditor could have aided discovery of a client irregularity or error, or could have mitigated its adverse effect.

This book generally discusses corrective actions from a tripartite perspective of the auditor on the engagement, the audit organization, and the profession. To the extent practical, guidance will be given to engagement personnel and to the partners and

---

[3]Alison Leigh Cowan, "S&L Backlash against Accountants," *New York Times*, July 31, 1990, sect. D, p. 5.

TABLE 2-1
Facing Damages after the Audits

Damages sought by the Federal Deposit Insurance Corporation from major
accounting firms that are accused of fraud, negligence, or other professional
misconduct. Legislation being considered in Congress would require outside
auditors to alert regulators to illegal activities discovered in audits.

Accountant	Savings and Loan	Damages Sought
Coopers & Lybrand	First Federal S&L (Shawnee, Oklahoma)	$ 7 million
Arthur Young	Imperial Savings (San Diego)	26 million
Ernst & Young	Western Savings (Dallas)	500 million
Deloitte Haskins & Sells	Sunrise Savings (Boynton Beach, Florida)	250 million
	Commonwealth Federal (Fort Lauderdale)	50 million
	Aspen Savings Bank (Aspen)	Subject to compensatory damages
	Royal Palm Federal (West Palm Beach)	None specified
Touche, Ross	Beverly Hills S&L (Beverly Hills)	300 million
	Midwest Federal (Minneapolis)	100 million
	Westwood S&L (Los Angeles)	100 million
	Peoples Federal (Bartlesville, Oklahoma)	460,000
	Lee S&L (Gidding, Texas)	38,500
Peat Marwick	Duval Federal (Jacksonville)	16.5 million

Source: Alison Leigh Cowan, "S&L Backlash against Accountants," New York Times, July 31, 1990,
sect. D, p. 1. Originally, this information was provided by the Federal Deposit Insurance Corporation.
Copyright © 1990 by the New York Times Company. Reprinted by permission.

managers responsible for directing the audit organization. Historically, the profession has endeavored to live up to public and
client expectations. Because individuals influence the profession
indirectly, lasting change is more likely to be brought about by
affecting the hearts and minds of those within the profession than
by figuratively throwing brickbats from the outside.

THE ELUSIVE NATURE OF AUDIT EFFECTIVENESS

Rulemakers have focused on investors and creditors as the primary users of financial statements. Based on this (highly arguable) premise, most assessments of audit effectiveness have involved consideration of litigation initiated by plaintiffs within those two user categories. Auditors have become increasingly defensive; many have concluded that suits charging audit failure arise in *all* instances of business failure, regardless of its cause. The auditors' perception is not correct. A comprehensive study of 472 instances of litigation against auditors between 1960 and 1985 showed that auditor litigation did not occur for the vast majority of bankrupt companies.[4]

Alleged audit failures can stem from undiscovered client errors, or irregularities, or both. The professional literature applies a test of intent to distinguish these classifications of unfortunate happenings. But, intent is extremely difficult to determine, especially when estimates and judgments are involved. The lumping of errors and irregularities is questionable for another reason; different control evaluation and test approaches may have to be considered to detect or prevent occurrences within each classification. (The risk of error should be relatively minor in a state-of-the-art environment; this is true especially when internal and external auditors have satisfied themselves that each step in new systems development or in systems modification has been properly controlled and tested.)

Management fraud can be defined as an intentional misrepresentation of a material nature, involving upper-level employees, which is being disguised by fraudulent financial reporting; management fraud is thus classified as an irregularity. The study showed that roughly half the legal actions involved irregularities; management fraud comprised nearly that entire group.[5]

Management fraud cases were resolved most frequently

---

[4]Zoe-Vonna Palmrose, "Litigation and Independent Auditors: The Role of Business Failures and Management Fraud," *Auditing: A Journal of Practice & Theory* 6, no. 2 (Spring 1987), pp. 90–103.

[5]Ibid., p. 98.

through payment of damages by auditors; cases without management fraud often resulted in dismissal of the suit against the auditors. Since professional standards have remained imprecise,
they do not appear to have offered much guidance or defense; auditors have not been shielded from litigation or from damage
awards.[6]

In recent years a new type of audit inadequacy has been publi-
cized. Agencies of the federal government have focused on audit
quality from the perspective not only of errors and misrepresentations, but of compliance with professional and governmental
rules. For example, the GAO has reported that reviewers encountered problems with a quarter of almost 10,000 governmental entity audit reports subjected to desk review. The reported instances involved "noncompliance with laws and regulations,"
including identification of internal controls studied and evaluated, lack of due professional care in preparing audit reports, and
failure to cite the auditing standards followed.[7]

Based on detailed reviews of working papers, and on consideration of the audit procedures which had been applied, almost half
the engagements reflected inadequacies. Insufficient evidence
was the most common defect. Audits were also uncovered "where
there was little or no evidence that the auditors properly planned
. . . supervised and reviewed. . . . At least two thirds of the audits
with evidence problems involved problems in the compliance
area. . . . [The examining officers] also found insufficient evidence documenting the auditors' study and evaluation of internal
control."[8]

Citations for poor work by government agencies may not result
in direct penalties. However, they can lead to significant adverse
publicity, public embarrassment, and, in noxious cases, referral to
professional and/or state regulators for disciplinary action.

---

[6]Ibid., p. 102.

[7]U.S. General Accounting Office, Accounting and Financial Management Division,
"CPA Audit Quality: Inspectors General Find Significant Problems," *GAO/AFMD-86-20*,
December 1985.

[8]Ibid., pp. 17–18.

Author's Comment

Informed commentators have voiced concern about the government's emphasis on compliance. Such an orientation has not been useful to regulators in nations where it long has been the rule. More significantly, investors and creditors are likely to balk at increased audit fees, which could be a concomitant of the compliance orientation. Hopefully, compliance reviews by auditors can be accomplished in a more efficient manner via the application of technology.

THREATS TO AUDIT EFFECTIVENESS

Research commissioned by Treadway categorized instances of fraudulent financial reporting, which are discussed in the following paragraphs. Not surprisingly, such occurrences were concentrated in receivables, inventory, accounts payable, accrued liabilities, and fixed assets.

- 44 percent of the cases . . . occurred in industries experiencing a general economic decline.
- 87 percent . . . involved manipulation of financial disclosures. . . . Frequently used techniques were improper revenue recognition methods (47 percent), deliberate overstatements of company assets (38 percent), and improper deferral of current period expenses (16 percent).
- In 45 percent of the cases against public companies, the SEC alleged that fraud occurred because of a breakdown of the company's internal controls. In many of these instances, the company had adequate internal accounting controls; these controls, however, had been overridden by management.

Author's Comment

Treadway's observation is on target. In general, regulators have pushed for a pervasive strengthening of internal control. But internal control, even if theoretically perfect, will not prevail against a predatory management, especially one skilled in the uses of corporate power.

- In 17 percent of the cases against public companies, misrepresentations were made to the company's independent public accountants.
- The SEC cited a member of upper-level corporate management as involved in 66 percent of the cases against public companies.
- In 67 percent of the cases against independent public accountants, the auditor failed to obtain sufficient competent evidential matter.
- In 36 percent of the cases against independent public accountants, the auditor failed to recognize or to pursue with sufficient skepticism certain warning signs or "red flags" that existed at the time the audit was conducted.[9]

Another study examined audit failures in terms of erroneous applications of the profession's standards of fieldwork.[10] This study pointed out:

1. The first standard of fieldwork (planning and supervision) has been somewhat ignored in the literature. Yet, time spent in conducting a preliminary audit survey and in planning the general scope and direction of an audit is likely to have a greater effect on the success of an engagement than any other phase.

2. The second standard (study and evaluation of internal control) is intended to determine how much reliance can be placed on the internal control system so that the auditor can determine the extent to which auditing procedures are to be restricted. In the light of this objective set by the profession, the author suggested that an auditor should begin by examining four major characteristics of an internal control system: separation of duties for record keeping and accounting reports from those concerned with opera-

---

[9] The points in this section are based on the report of the National Commission on Fraudulent Financial Reporting. See National Commission on Fraudulent Financial Reporting, *Report of the National Commission on Fraudulent Financial Reporting*, October 1987, pp. 112–13.

[10] Jackson A. White, "Pitfalls to Avoid in Applying the Field Work Standards to Audits," *Practical Accountant* 12, no. 4 (June 1979), pp. 35–42.

tions or asset custody; authorization and approval procedures to provide reasonable accounting control over assets; physical control over assets; and a system of internal auditing.

3. The final standard of fieldwork (gathering evidence) deals with the acquisition of sufficient competent evidential matter to afford a reasonable basis for an opinion on the financial statements. The researcher specifically emphasized that the operative key words in the standard were *sufficient* and *competent*.

Surprisingly, relatively little has been written in recent years on issues relating to the auditor's examination of evidence. Some years ago, the predecessor to the ASB, the Auditing Standards Executive Committee, ranked the competence of evidence in *SAS 31*. Assertedly, evidence from sources outside the enterprise provides greater assurance than that secured solely from within the enterprise; if internal control is satisfactory, there is more assurance as to the reliability of accounting data and financial statements than when internal control is unsatisfactory; direct personal knowledge of the auditor obtained through physical examination, observation, computation, and inspection is more persuasive than information obtained indirectly.

Author's Comment

Like many of the profession's rules, the guideline just mentioned must be applied based on judgment together with common sense; in other words, the auditor is required to be careful in applying the rules to each client situation. For example, positive confirmations from third parties depend for their effectiveness on the care with which responses are researched by the debtor; failure to reply to negative confirmations could mean either that the accounts are correct, or that the potential respondent does not take the procedure seriously!

EXAMPLES OF SUCCESSFUL ERROR DETECTION

As noted, there exists no literature on the subject of audit successes—that is, situations where the auditor took appropriate actions. Similarly, little research exists concerning auditors' management letter recommendations that were not followed by clients, but which could have prevented or detected errors and irregularities, had the client had a more constructive attitude toward the management letter.

An insightful article was coauthored by an audit principal of Arthur Andersen together with a well-known audit researcher, illustrating the types of client errors that *can* be detected.[11] The coauthors reported error size as a percentage of the account balance and as a percentage of total assets (see Table 2–2). Once again, large numbers of errors were concentrated in receivables and inventory; accounts payable and accrued liabilities together had the greatest incidence of errors; fixed assets and accumulated depreciation had the largest individual error rate.[12]

Further analysis of error incidence by account and type of er-

---

TABLE 2–2
Error Incidence and Magnitude

Account	Number of Errors	Mean Percent of Balance	Mean Aggregate Percent of Total Assets
Cash	21	1.50%	.01%
Investment securities	40	12.64	.08
Investment properties	39	4.20	.80
Receivables and related reserves	285	2.38	.52
Inventory and related reserves	218	4.36	.84
Fixed assets and accumulated depreciation	329	1.22	1.12
Accounts payable	177	10.97	.51
Accrued liabilities	306	12.09	.78
Debt	45	.91	.16

Source: Richard W. Kreutzfeldt and Wanda A. Wallace, "Error Characteristics in Audit Populations: Their Profile and Relationship to Environmental Factors," *Auditing: A Journal of Practice & Theory* 6, no. 1 (Fall 1986), p. 27. Reprinted by permission.

---

[11]Richard W. Kreutzfeldt and Wanda A. Wallace, "Error Characteristics in Audit Populations: Their Profile and Relationship to Environmental Factors," *Auditing: A Journal of Practice & Theory* 6, no. 1 (Fall 1986), pp. 20–43.
[12]Ibid., p. 28.

ror is presented in Table 2–3. Judgmental errors and insufficient knowledge of generally accepted accounting principles (GAAP) generated many of the problems; judgmental valuation errors were particularly prevalent in the bad debt reserve; incorrect applications of GAAP were most common in inventory and fixed assets. Errors of omission were common, suggesting a need for the application of more effective audit procedures.

Personnel problems and inadequate review and follow-up within the client's accounting department each accounted for nearly one third of errors. In addition, about 30 percent of the errors were due to judgment errors or biases or insufficiency of available information.[13]

TABLE 2–3
Type of Error and Magnitude:
Accounts Payable and Accrued Liabilities

Account and Type of Error	Number of Errors	Mean Percent of Balance
Accounts payable		
Omission	76	9.70%
Duplication	7	.20
Clerical	7	.42
Cutoff	37	2.44
Judgmental evaluation	24	.41
Incorrect application of GAAP	23	.59
Other	3	.50
Accrued liabilities		
Omission	128	9.22
Duplication	5	.22
Clerical	12	.67
Cutoff	34	1.01
Judgmental evaluation	93	7.81
Incorrect application of GAAP	29	.86
Other	5	.20

Source: Richard W. Kreutzfeldt and Wanda A. Wallace, "Error Characteristics in Audit Populations: Their Profile and Relationship to Environmental Factors," *Auditing: A Journal of Practice & Theory* 6, no. 1 (Fall 1986), p. 30. Reprinted by permission.

---

[13]Ibid., p. 32.

With regard to a third of the errors, there was a repetition by the client of a prior year error. This condition suggests that a client's reluctance to take action to correct the causes of past errors should alert auditors to a possible need for adjustment in the current year.[14]

CAUSES FOR AUDIT FAILURES

At this point, some conclusions may be drawn as to the causes of audit failures.

General Observations

Audit failures can stem from client errors or irregularities (i.e., intentional misrepresentations) or both. Irregularities tend to be far more dangerous to the auditors' financial health than mere errors; management fraud is involved in most irregularities.

Errors may be created by circumstances existing within the company under audit or they may be a consequence of failure to monitor outside influences or to evaluate their effect on the audited company. This suggests that a need exists for watching the environment, for spotlighting significant trends and events, and for making certain that the client introduces appropriate risk management techniques.

Irregularities (management fraud, as well as employee fraud) can be more difficult to detect than errors. The auditor gains the requisite sensitivity by understanding the client's business relative to the economy. Detection tends to be fostered by prior experience with the client, by alert interviewing, by astute observation, and by knowing what to expect from analytical reviews.

The failure of auditors to detect errors and irregularities may involve violation, misinterpretation, or disregard of general or specific rules of the profession. The GAO cited noncompliance

---

[14]Ibid.

with laws and regulations, lack of due professional care in preparing audit reports, and insufficiency of audit evidence. The Kreutzfeldt-Wallace article called attention to clients' judgmental errors, incorrect applications of GAAP, or insufficiency of available information; personnel problems and inadequate review and follow-up within the clients' accounting departments exacerbated problems. Also, it seemed likely that external auditors had not been following up on deficiencies previously reported to clients. Treadway too castigated auditors for not pursuing warning signs or red flags with sufficient skepticism.

SPECIFIC AUDIT DEFICIENCIES

The author has endeavored to identify conditions likely to lead to deficient auditing from the available research and from practice; obviously such an exercise is influenced by the author's experiences and impressions.

Professional and Personal Deficiencies

1. Auditor's confusion as to the role of independent auditors in society (i.e., their responsibility as the public's watchdogs).
2. Violations of the very basic first three standards of fieldwork relating to planning and supervision, study of internal control, and gathering of evidence, as discussed earlier in the chapter.
3. Lack of audit skepticism; willingness to accept virtually any client explanation given. The general application of blind trust may be reinforced by continuing uncertainty as to the auditor's responsibility for detecting material misstatements. Lack of skepticism may pervade the entire audit, but it is likely to represent a particular exposure in connection with the acceptance of client judgments, valuations, and estimates. For example, an SEC administrative law judge recently opined that a major

firm had "ignored or failed to perceive material facts . . . [and] failed to plan its audit procedures to test proper assertions, and relied unduly on client representations."[15]

4. Violations of specific statements on auditing standards, such as of the rules relating to newly acquired or even old clients (e.g., failure of an auditor to contact the prior auditors, or lack of communications with other auditors serving a current client).

5. Lack of a basic understanding of data processing, or of electronic record keeping generally (e.g., an auditor may not even understand that a record is merely an intangible representation of the real world—in other words, a record represents only what somebody in the client's office says it does).

Inadequate Understanding of the Client's Business

1. Inadequate understanding of the client's business (e.g., the government's lead investigator in the ESM case mentioned in a college lecture that the auditors did not fully understand the nature of a financial instrument—a repurchase agreement—used extensively by the client). There are other indications that auditors were not always aware of high-risk areas in high-risk businesses; to correct this, the Federal Deposit Insurance Corporation has now suggested that auditors focus on policy and procedures in insider transactions, director review of loan policy, accounting for loan losses, bank investment policies, and internal control of off-balance sheet activities.

2. Lack of grasp of the environment in which the client's business operates, in terms of the state of the economy and industry and the risks faced by the client.

3. Lack of knowledge of the prior backgrounds and associations of client executives (e.g., an auditor may not know

---

[15]Anonymous, "Accounting Administrative Law Judge Says Ernst Failed to Conduct Proper Audit of Medical Supply Producer," *Daily Report for Executives*, July 10, 1990, regulation, economics, and law sect., p. A7.

that the client's president pulled "scams" in a prior employment situation, using a modus operandi that she could repeat in her current position).

4. Flawed assessment of the client's control environment, especially the "tone at the top."

5. Failure to understand the client's operating environment (e.g., in a dictatorial setting, operating managers may engage in fraudulent acts either to "make" targets established by corporate management, or even to hide the fact that targets *were* made, in order to reduce future targets).

6. Failure to understand physical aspects of client products processes, and facilities.

7. Placing undue, if not total, reliance on management's representations.

8. Failure to examine the reports of other client, regulatory, or vendor service personnel who may have some type of cognizance or responsibility (e.g., the reports of systems analysts frequently reflect problems, as well as failures to solve them within the planned time frame; and the reports of government regulators can indicate emerging or imminent credit crunches, or judgmental or valuation difficulties with investment portfolios). Regulators, government auditors, and special examiners "work the same side of the street." For example, an inspector for a preferred risk mutual insurance company may recommend installation of a fire wall. Such a wall could contribute to the physical security of the data processing department; it could also result in reduced insurance premiums and quick recoupment of the cost of the wall. Hence, such matters must be pursued with diligence. (In a recent bank collapse, heated controversy was generated as to whether external auditors asked for, or failed to ask for, or saw, or didn't see, federal examiners' reports.)

9. Lack of comprehension of the mission and accomplishments of the client's internal audit department; (e.g., unthinking implementation of *SAS 9*). The new *SAS 65* provides meaningful guidance toward obtaining an understanding of the internal audit function.

Inadequate Audit Procedures

1. Failure to apply analytic review procedures properly. Several studies have shown that these procedures can detect material errors; as a result, there has been a trend toward the use of ratios. (These ratios may be calculated automatically as part of the utilization of software packages.)

Although analytic review procedures are mandated as a result of an expectation gap *SAS*, many experienced auditors have long been concerned about the value of these procedures. The coauthor of a leading text on the subject has observed in a lecture that reliance may be unwarranted, especially if risk and materiality are high; he has noted that analytic reviews usually yield value commensurate with the effort invested in the procedures. In other words, although creation of ratios at a point in time can be accomplished quickly and inexpensively, such ratios may have little or no predictive value. Further, in order to interpret the results of the procedures properly, the auditor must have informed expectations.

Item

The perils of being deceived by inappropriate ratios or unit costs are illustrated by an episode that involved three key executives of a large steamship company. This fraud involved extensive padding of stevedoring payrolls. The irregularity had started modestly enough with the creation of "ghosts" of nonexistent stevedores, and escalated into the unloading of phantom ships. The culprits reported to the corporate head office that they had handled British long tons (2,240 pounds); in reality, they had processed American short tons (2,000 pounds). Falsification of stevedoring costs per revenue ton, and use of the deceptive measure in analytical reviews, escaped both internal and external auditors who were unaware of the correct unit of measure.

Recent research has shown that analytic reviews may not provide reliable and effective bases for reducing the extent of other, more detailed, substantive tests in most cases; hence, analytic reviews should not be used for that purpose.[16] Four cleverly structured experiments did not provide any evidence that analytic re-

---

[16]James K. Loebbecke and Paul J. Steinbart, "An Investigation of the Use of Preliminary Analytical Review to Provide Substantive Audit Evidence," *Auditing: A Journal of Practice & Theory* 6, no. 2 (Spring 1987), p. 74.

view can be effectively used to reduce the extent of substantive tests. The authors noted—properly—that use of operating data or external data may improve the usefulness of the analytic procedures. They pointed to a need for the auditor to use her understanding of the client's business and to draw upon that understanding when interpreting results of those procedures.

2. Lack of capacity for behavioral interviewing. The auditor's understanding of the system is usually obtained by behaviorally oriented interviewing of (hopefully) knowledgeable people. Interviewing skills have not been emphasized in auditor training; however, as a rule, such skills are more likely to be present in partners and managers than in junior personnel. Selection of the correct interviewer and of the correct interviewing technique is the key to obtaining desired results; a selection error in this critical area will quickly short-circuit the interview into failure.[17]

3. Inability to visualize how the business "hangs together," an attribute often depicted by means of overview flowcharts. Auditors may have similar difficulties with interpreting detailed flowcharts, especially when the charts were prepared by someone else or with the assistance of a computer. Rather than turn the auditor into a graphic artist, or a computer-assisted designer, it is preferable to utilize the charts of others, and to adapt them to the auditor's purpose. In addition, before auditors immerse themselves in details, they should sketch overview charts showing how the business hangs together and how activities/documents flow from one department to another.

Some years ago, public accounting firms often confirmed the correctness of the understanding by performing a "walk through" (sometimes called a transaction review). The firms traced one or a few transactions of each type through the system to see that flowcharts or write-ups of the system were correct, that there were no breakdowns in linkages between subsystems or between parts of the same system, and that reasonable explanations and authorizations existed for the creation of new types of transactions. The issue is not how many transactions were reviewed, but whether transaction flow has received sufficient attention.

---

[17]James N. Gilbert, "Interviewing and the Protection of Assets," *Assets Protection* 7, no. 5 (Fall 1983), p. 14.

The GAO has put the walk through in perspective in discussing the objectives of a transaction flow review and analysis:

> (1) Determine and document how information flows through each selected system from initial input of transaction information through final output of reports. (2) Determine whether the outputs produced by each selected system meet users' information needs and achieve the system's control objectives. (3) Identify and document the control techniques included in each selected system. (4) Evaluate the adequacy of control techniques to implement the system's control objectives. (5) Document any material internal controls weaknesses.[18]

4. Improper or inappropriate procedures; performance of the wrong procedure at the wrong time and place, using the wrong evidence, and in the wrong manner. For example, the perpetrator in a recent scandal reported that post balance sheet date cash receipts were used to "validate" accounts receivable; it is not known whether the auditors had satisfied themselves that the remittances had been received in the mail room or that they had been sent by the debtor. In addition, the right procedure may be applied in thoughtless fashion. For example, in one case a client was reported as having shipped unordered merchandise to the Far East by surface transport; in other words, relatively expensive and lightweight data processing equipment was transported by (slow) boat. The auditors examined shipping documents to determine that title had passed, and that inventory should be relieved and sales recorded; if they had questioned the choice of an ocean carrier, they might have been less likely to accept the recorded figures. In any event, only a rather limited number of substantive test procedures are used by auditors the world over. These procedures are well known and well documented. Care must be exercised in matching the available procedures to the exigencies of a particular situation.

5. Improper performance of tests of controls (e.g., failing to react properly to exceptions because of an underlying desire to have test results demonstrate the functioning of controls, a condition called "anchoring" by statisticians). This phenomenon is explored in succeeding paragraphs.

---

[18]U.S. General Accounting Office, "Control and Risk Evaluation (CARE)–Based Methodology for Reviewing and Evaluating the Operations of Agency Accounting and Financial Management Systems," *Exposure Draft of CARE Manual*, September 28, 1984.

To be entitled to rely on controls for the purpose of restricting substantive tests, the auditor should perform tests of controls. Her sample for testing is likely to be small. This suggests that from a statistical point of view, virtually any exception should vitiate reliance on the control. Yet in most public accounting firms, the auditor will have completed an internal control questionnaire (ICQ) prior to compliance testing. Her overall budget will be based on the assumption that controls will be found in effect and functioning as planned. Thus, the auditor is conditioned to hope that controls upon which she has chosen to rely will "test out"; she is likely to accept virtually any reasonable explanation that the client may offer for a malfunction. This feeling was supported by an investigation which the author was asked to conduct by one of his employers; it was found that out of 2,000 controls "tested" by external auditors, only 1 had been identified as not being effective. The one act of rejection took courage; the auditors could no longer rely on the functioning of the control to restrict the nature, timing, and extent of substantive tests. Accordingly, they had to perform additional substantive test work, at peril to the budget.

Author's Comment

The effect of the expectation gap *SAS*s on compliance tests has not been entirely clarified. But, based on remarks by a past chairman of the ASB, compliance tests are likely to be out in many cases. If this is so, substantive tests will, in effect, become dual-purpose tests. However, the importance of controls, whether or not they impact the nature, timing, and extent of substantive tests, is beyond question. Therefore, a legitimate query can be raised as to whether dual-purpose tests will ensure that controls are functioning as planned; special audit program steps may be needed.

   6. Unimaginative or mechanical reliance on the work of the internal auditors (e.g., failure to combine available external and internal audit resources to focus on significant areas of risk).

   7. Failure to use operational information to confirm the accuracy of financial information.

Issues within the Auditing Firm

   1. Failure of partners and managers to devote sufficient time to the engagement.

2. Delegation of work to relatively junior or inadequately trained personnel.

3. Excessive personnel turnover, resulting in the constant assignment of new personnel to engagements, with a continuous training problem for partners and managers, accompanied by client resentment.

4. Pressures to make deadlines.

5. Pressures to stay within budgets.

6. Failure to exercise effective or timely supervision or quality checks during the execution of the engagement. Unfortunately, ex post facto quality control offers extremely limited protection to auditors.

7. Communications difficulties up or down the chain of audit command.

8. Lack of meaningful industry specialization.

9. Absence of participative management (i.e., of involvement of junior personnel in decision making pertaining especially to audit procedures, or to management letter contents). For example, the customer list was one of the assets changing hands when a chemical distributor was sold. The junior on the engagement reported a need for improving control over and accuracy of customer records—thereby improving prospects for client retention.

SUMMARY: AREAS FOR IMPROVEMENT

The way to help auditors out of their predicament is not based on promulgating more rules, but on following the rules which already exist, and perhaps on following them more expeditiously. Major areas for improvement include:

1. Fostering an attitude of audit skepticism and overcoming a subconscious desire to avoid trouble.

2. More faithful interpretations of and adherence to general and specific auditing standards and rules.

3. Better understanding of data processing, in terms of mastering the system and its controls and of using the computer to achieve a more effective and efficient audit.

4. A businessperson's understanding of the client's industry, business, and system, within an overall economic context.

5. Greater familiarity with the physical aspects of client products, processes, and facilities, and with related security matters.

6. A skeptical attitude toward the client's executives, especially in the absence of knowledge of their previous activities.

7. More realistic assessments of the client's control environment; more perceptive feelings for the client's tone at the top, as well as for the complementary mood among operating personnel.

8. Reading between the lines and maintaining an inquiring attitude when examining other audit reports and reacting to warnings that may be contained therein.

9. Improved ability to adequately recognize and utilize the work of internal auditors.

10. Knowledgeable application of analytic review procedures.

11. Avoidance of anchoring, especially when evaluating the results of tests of controls.

12. More perceptive programming of substantive tests in the light of the available evidence.

13. Increased emphasis on focusing the talents of experienced personnel within the public accounting firm (e.g., more timely "firing line" participation by partners and managers, meaningful industry specialization, and attention to quality while audits are ongoing).

Technology, and especially computers, bears on many of the points listed above, as will be shown in succeeding chapters. The computer's unerring accuracy and data-handling capability should lead to a far more effective and efficient audit than has been possible in the past. The opportunity seems limited only by the ability of the auditor to apply the applications' results to the problems at hand, by her knowledge of the rules of the profession, and by her sensitivity to the client and his business problems.

CHAPTER 3

THE EROSION OF AUDIT PRODUCTIVITY

Do nothing which is of no use.

Myamoto Musashi*

USER PERSPECTIVE: **Items of Special Interest**

EXECUTIVE HIGHLIGHTS: All readers

INTRODUCTION: All readers

KEEPING CURRENT: External auditors, internal auditors

THE QUESTION OF AUDIT PRODUCTIVITY: External auditors, internal auditors, audit committee members

CAUSES OF DIMINISHED AUDIT PROFITABILITY/ PRODUCTIVITY: THE FIRM: External auditors

CAUSES OF DIMINISHED AUDIT PRODUCTIVITY: THE ENGAGEMENT: External auditors, internal auditors, financial executives

SUMMARY: MATTERS FOR IMPROVEMENT: All readers

EXECUTIVE HIGHLIGHTS

Most persons engaged in other businesses would not describe the accountant's bottom line numbers as unsatisfactory. Nonetheless, many accountants feel that the twin problems of price competition and eroding audit productivity have made auditing less attractive.

---

*Renowned samurai and writer on swordsmanship.

Shrinking margins on audits have led auditors to pursue the allegedly more fully priced consulting opportunities, at times by using the audit as a loss leader. It has been estimated that more than 700 public companies change auditors yearly and that more than one third of them reduce their auditing fees in the process.

To control "lowballing," accountants could follow the lead of some lawyers. Law firms focusing on realization have been advised to seek higher realization niches, manage practice resources effectively, and apply limited resources where the highest realization can be obtained.

Productivity improvement begins with a setting of productivity objectives. The next step is the setting of quantifiable goals against which productivity can be objectively measured. Such indicators must be carefully selected to reflect productivity of individuals, engagements, and the firm as a whole.

The litigious climate has made practitioners risk averse. Their attitudes are mirrored in a tendency to overaudit, regardless of the extent of audit risk attaching to a particular account or class of transactions, or even of the flexibility built into audit standards.

Many auditors have found it difficult to rely on internal control for the purpose of restricting substantive tests. Hence, unrestricted substantive tests tend to be superimposed on internal control evaluations and on (frequently ineffectual) tests of controls. The challenge is one of determining which tasks and procedures foster achievement of engagement objectives and which represent little or no value added.

INTRODUCTION

Some public accounting firms have been reluctant to publish meaningful financial information, especially disaggregated information pertaining to product or service lines, and to geographic distribution of services. The traditional reason given for this position is "protection of partners' privacy"; some suspect that interfirm differences in audit profitability and productivity could partly explain reporting shyness on the part of those who fear that their firm's performance may be below par. Such accountants reason that actual or prospective clients might desert "shoemakers who always go barefoot."

Many public accountants have said that the profitability of audits has been eroded by a combination of unfavorable developments, including buyers' perceptions that audits are a "commodity" to be sought solely on a price basis, as well as by deteriorating productivity. The author does feel that auditors' profits have been under pressure; although this chapter discusses fee discounting, the emphasis is on audit productivity. Productivity problems tend to pertain to firms and internal audit departments of all sizes, as do the remedies. Possible causes of lagging audit productivity are explored in order to guide readers toward the corrective actions discussed in the rest of the book.

The veil covering audit profitability may have been lifted slightly: information regarding auditors' bottom lines became available recently as a result of the "mega-mergers." These numbers should be looked at with caution. The results of different firms are affected by partner, staff, and client demographics, as well as by accounting practices, and therefore may not be comparable. In addition, larger firms may have considerable clout in client fee negotiations and some capacity for absorbing general and administrative expenses. For the record, partners at Deloitte Haskins & Sells and Touche, Ross earned nearly a quarter of a million dollars a year on average before the two firms merged. In Deloitte & Touche's case, both firms had pretax margins of roughly 22 percent. The firms were more evenly matched than two competitors who also merged, Ernst & Whinney and Arthur Young. Ernst's partners were at approximately the same level of performance as Deloitte & Touche; Arthur Young lagged with pretax margins of 14.25 percent last year; Arthur Young also trailed in terms of the number of hours billed per professional.[1]

Most persons engaged in other businesses would not describe the aforementioned numbers as unsatisfactory. Moreover, there has been conjecture that some firms, not necessarily the ones mentioned, have improved productivity over the near term by ex-

---

[1]Alison Leigh Cowan, "Earnings Data Released by Deloitte & Touche," *New York Times*, January 19, 1990, p. 34.

tensive cost cutting. If cost reduction axes have indeed been wielded, one can only hope that the cuts did not affect functions concerned with improvement of audit productivity, such as industry specialization, research, and professional development.

KEEPING CURRENT

The problem of keeping current has not enhanced auditor productivity. Continuing professional education should be defined to include developments in computers (and in client use of the computers), tax and regulatory changes, and official pronouncements by the AICPA and the FASB, together with any related effects on audits. Practitioners can do little to control the effort involved, other than to determine by experiment which method of instruction is most effective in each individual's case.

Gere Dominak has reported that the number of official pronouncements has escalated:

2.2 per year from 1955 to 1964.

5.2 per year from 1965 to 1974.

12.9 per year from 1975 to 1984.

The volume of new FASB pronouncements has declined since the foregoing data were compiled, but other professional regulators, including the AICPA, may be moving to pick up any slack. However, numbers do not tell the entire story. The content of the FASB pronouncements has been changing. Some of the FASB's more recent statements deal with particular industries; moreover, many of the statements displace or amend previous pronouncements in whole or in part. These conditions do not lead to enthusiastic mastery of the materials. There also seems to be evidence that the more specific and industry-oriented a pronouncement, the more likely that revision will be required; hence, future pronouncements may be increasingly concerned with revisions of earlier statements.[2]

------

[2]Gere Dominak, "Standards Overload," *Today's CPA*, February/March 1987, pp. 25–26.

While one AICPA committee deliberated over what to do regarding the standards overload, another called for an increase in timely guidance. The two trends could conflict, inviting adversarial proceedings between the FASB and the AICPA.[3]

THE QUESTION OF AUDIT PRODUCTIVITY

Productivity has been defined as the efficient and effective use of resources entrusted to a manager. Productivity assessment requires the setting of productivity objectives. The next step, after deciding on the objectives, is to set quantifiable goals against which productivity can be objectively measured.[4]

Audit productivity has been an elusive concept. The first difficulty has been with determining what kind of service should be categorized, billed, and administered as auditing by external auditors, and should be considered auditing by clients. Some years ago, a now-superseded SEC directive required registrants to disclose consulting fees earned by external auditors; at the time there was concern that the information would not be looked upon with favor by regulators. Accordingly, auditors classified a variety of borderline services under the audit umbrella, making them nonreportable. Nonetheless, most users of audit reports would relate auditing to the expression of an opinion on financial statements; if this view is accepted, separate accounts (and meaningful timekeeping) should be maintained by auditors for audits, reviews, compilations, other accounting services, nonfinancial attestation services, and special engagements, such as operational audits, fraud investigations, and the like.

After audit services have been appropriately defined, it remains to be determined which tasks and procedures foster achievement of engagement objectives, and which represent little or no value added. In this connection, it is noteworthy that little useful

---

[3]Margaret Bartel and Harry D. Dickinson, "Legalism, Taxes, and Standards Overload," *The Virginia Accountant* 40 (1988), p. 29.

[4]Lawrence B. Sawyer, *Sawyer's Internal Auditing*, 3rd ed. (Altamonte Springs, Fla.: The Institute of Internal Auditors, 1988), p. 259.

information exists which shows how partners and managers spend their time. If a comprehensive study were to be made, it may be found that the extent of clerical activities performed by senior audit personnel resembles those of factory first-line supervisors. A study designed to discover what factory supervisors actually do determined that 80 percent of their available time was spent on accounting, including timekeeping, time analysis, and preparation of related reports. In consequence, little time remained for supervision and guidance of those in the supervisors' charge. Staff members below the partner/manager level are even more likely to be afflicted by record keeping, bookkeeping, and sundry clerical activities such as filing; the author was told that a study by one large firm determined that working paper preparation and maintenance alone represented 30 percent of staff members' time, offering a priority target for productivity enhancement.

It is not clear which measures represent the best indication of the productivity of individuals, engagements, and the firm as a whole. The following examples illustrate some possibilities:

1. Audit hours actually charged to clients, divided by total time available for audits. (This measure may be applied on a firmwide or an individual practitioner basis.)

2. Actual hours expended, multiplied by standard billing rates, divided by budgeted hours multiplied by standard billing rates. (The ratio gives an indication of the value of time budget overruns.)

3. Actual client fees earned on an engagement, divided by fees computed by multiplying time incurred by fees at standard billing rates. (The result represents "realization" on a client or an overall basis; to the extent that realization drops below a target, usually a theoretical 100 percent, a signal is provided as to the extent of "discounting" or of performance of work for which clients will not pay.)

4. Actual hours multiplied by standard billing rates of persons actually on the engagement, divided by actual hours multiplied by standard billing rates of persons contemplated in the budget. (The result indicates the effect of variances from budgeted staff mix.)

The preceding item 2 may represent the most direct opportunity for productivity measurement and enhancement, since quantifiable goals for productivity improvement can be built into budgets. Given the elfin nature of audit productivity, it is difficult to determine to what extent declines in productivity may have contributed to auditors' shrinking profit margins. And, it is not known to what extent efforts have been made to deal with productivity issues. In any event, many accountants seem to feel that the twin problems of price competition and eroding audit productivity have made audit practice less attractive. Hence, they are giving increasing attention to promoting their management consulting practices. It has become a truism among accountants that consulting carries a higher profit margin than auditing; unfortunately, the expectation does not hold true for all firms. The effects of the consulting emphasis have been quite marked. Traditionally, the Big Eight received three quarters of their revenue from audit and tax work; but by 1988 the percentage had declined to a little over half, to 56 percent.[5]

Brief comments on the competitive scene will be followed by a discussion of some causes of diminution in audit productivity.

CAUSES OF DIMINISHED AUDIT PROFITABILITY/PRODUCTIVITY: THE FIRM

Competitive Pressures

Some auditors credit the initiatives of the Federal Trade Commission (FTC) (which are designed to encourage competition), along with competitive bidding on audit engagements, for the prevalence of discounts (i.e., for unsatisfactory realization on engagements).

Mark Stevens has feelingly described the situation:

> The key to winning clients had changed from who you knew to how much you charged. . . . Clients that had retained [a particular firm] for generations were now inviting all of the giants to compete for

---

[5]Arthur Bowman, "Accounting Wars," *Georgia Trend* 3, no. 9 (May 1988), sect. 1, p. 62.

the audit, with the prize going to the lowest bidder. Overnight, the audit had become a commodity. . . . Instead of holding out against penny-pinching clients . . . the accountants fought for the crumbs and fees dropped even lower.[6]

It has been estimated that more than 700 public companies change auditors yearly and that more than one third of them reduce their auditing fees in the process.

The situation has alarmed John Dingell, chairman of the House Subcommittee on Oversight and Investigations:

> When I hear of lowball audit fees, of audits used as loss leaders to attract consulting business, that nonaudit work is the wave of the future, or that the top partners at major audit firms are management consultants, I frankly do not understand how that enhances the accounting profession's unique reputation for [applying] independent judgment as a public service.[7]

Item

(The facts in the example which follows are based on the author's own experiences in serving government agencies.) A state agency decided to seek competitive bids for the conduct of its financial audit over a three-year period. The fee of the outgoing auditor was $165,000. Careful scoping of the engagement by a competing firm showed that a minimum fee of $145,000 was required to earn a reasonable profit. The executive committee of that firm decided to submit an aggressive bid of $110,000. However, a dark horse, a third Big Six firm, submitted the winning bid of $60,000!

As mentioned, the perceived business reason—*hope* would be a better word—for lowballing may involve an eventual opportunity to bid on supposedly more highly margined consulting work. The attitude of such competitive firms is damaging and destructive to the profession, as well as to the price cutter and his clients; it is usually his longtime clients, whose fees have been repeatedly stepped up, who pay the discount. (More than a hundred years ago

---

[6]Mark Stevens, "No More White Shoes," *Business Month*, April 1988, p. 38.
[7]Ibid.

the Scottish essayist Thomas Carlyle cautioned buyers not to become a price cutter's victims.)

The zeal of the Federal Trade Commission may have been slightly dampened in its final order, which allows the AICPA to continue its ban on accepting contingency fees for preparing tax returns or tax refund claims. The AICPA can also continue to prohibit its members from accepting contingent fees or "commissions that CPAs have disclosed to their clients" for audits or other services involving attestation.

Some purchasers of audit services, notably the Intergovernmental Audit Forums (IGAFs) have suggested that proposals from auditors be rated on a variety of bases extraneous and additional to price.[8] Audit committees and other purchasers of audit services could emulate the IGAF approach, which is premised on the assumption that auditing is not a commodity, and that neither audit firms, nor audit services, are fungible. The GAO has reinforced the IGAF position by pointing out that sound procurement practices should be followed in contracting for audit services, including the monitoring of contract performance. The objectives and scope of the audit must be made clear. In addition to price, other factors to be considered include: the responsiveness of the bidder to the request for proposal; the past experience of the bidder; availability of bidder staff with professional qualifications and technical abilities; and whether the bidder organization participates in an external quality control review program.[9]

The accountants could follow the lead of some lawyers. A law firm consultant has noted that a law firm focusing on realization will: (1) seek new business in a niche that generates the highest realization on the billing rates of the firm; (2) manage practice resources effectively; and (3) apply limited resources where the highest realization can be obtained, *not* where the most hours of

---

[8]See National Intergovernmental Audit Forum, *How to Avoid a Substandard Audit: Suggestions for Procuring an Audit*, May 1988. Information may be obtained by writing to the National Intergovernmental Audit Forum, Room 6826, 441 G Street, NW, Washington, D.C. 20548.

[9]U.S. General Accounting Office, *Government Auditing Standards: Standards for Audits of Governmental Organizations, Programs, Activities, and Functions* (U.S. General Accounting Office; 1988 revision), p. I-6.

work are available. The same consultant notes the profit impact of failure to bill in timely fashion; he points out that the fee that does not flow through to the bank account represents a loss of potential revenue, to say nothing of the loss due to the time value of money.[10]

The Rise in Nonchargeable Work

The incidence and nature of nonchargeable work are not easy to assess. An example will be used to illustrate this point.

Item

> Some years ago a confidential study was conducted among large firms which compared different approaches to making qualified support personnel available to guide practitioners toward appropriate accounting and auditing treatments. The study revealed that the consultation function had been assigned as a primary responsibility to dedicated individuals in some firms, but that it was being performed on a part-time basis in others. The decentralization arrangements affected guidance personnel's training and professional development, as well as cost. (Some firms with "part-time performers," and with unmeasured results, appeared to be spending up to 10 times the amounts spent by firms with dedicated partners.)

The part-time arrangement may contribute to nonchargeable time; in addition, the more serious question can be raised as to whether programmatic goals can be achieved at all, and/or to what extent, under the "jack-of-all-trades" syndrome. For example, internal quality control programs may be assigned to numerous individuals on the theory that participation in such activities enhances competence of the reviewers. (This issue assumes greater importance at the time of this writing; the membership of the AICPA has voted to extend its peer review program; about 600 small firms appear to be affected.) Those firms which combine a training objective with compliance with a professional mandate

---

[10]William C. Cobb, "Clients Want Firms That Contain Costs," *The National Law Journal*, August 7, 1989, p. 42.

have little assurance that either objective will be achieved. In blunter terms, those who view quality control as a finishing school for the least competent or the least trained are living dangerously.

Also, many firms will comply with professional directives in grudging and unimaginative fashion; in some cases, firms will seek to comply with the letter rather than the spirit of the professional rules in order to minimize loss of time. To cure these problems, each firm should specify the desired objectives and benefits, set performance measurements, collect objective data, and assess program accomplishments; for openers, the selection of engagements for quality control review should be based on audit risk experienced by a particular client or client industry. (In all too many cases, selections have been based on a misguided desire to achieve breadth of coverage by reviewing, say, one job per partner or manager.)

Competitive pressures have led public accounting firms to create organizational units of a type usually found in commercial and industrial establishments. Marketing is but one of these innovations, and will be used as an example of the genre. It cannot be denied that there are unusual challenges to marketing professional services. Nonetheless, the turnover among major firm marketing directors has been extraordinary, a circumstance which indicates that after more than a decade of servicing accountants, the marketers may still not have "the range." The blame may rest on the shoulders of both marketers and auditors. The marketers are often alumni of consumer industries, a condition not likely to inspire confidence in some practitioners. One commentator has put all the blame on the auditors: "Accountants have become poor consumers of marketing services. . . . Accounting firms tend to be hostile environments for nonaccountants. . . . Learn the differences between marketing an accounting firm and marketing a product."[11] Relatively little has been published on the special approaches needed to market professional services; in

---

[11]Bruce W. Marcus, "Hurdles Remain for Marketing in 90s," *Accounting Today*, January 22, 1990, p. 6.

any event, orderly collection of computerized information would seem to be concomitant to marketing. More important, seasoned accounting and auditing professionals should participate actively in setting goals, missions, and tasks for the marketers.

The reported hostility of accountants to persons outside the profession may transcend marketers and include purchasing agents, personnel managers, and even systems managers and internal auditors. The obvious risk is that such laypersons may not be used properly; that is, their expertise may not be marshaled in the audit organization's interest. In other words, the functional experts may become contributors to costs, instead of to productivity.

Organization Structures May Be in Need of Updating

Most public accounting firms are organized on a functional basis into audit, tax, and consulting groups. In most cases this means that employees are accountable for satisfactory performance only to their own functional superior. This arrangement is reasonably cost effective, but lacks flexibility; it offers little or no assurance that the skills of all available persons with needed qualifications will be brought to bear on problems involving audit risk.

In other types of businesses one may find "matrix management," which calls for personnel from various disciplines to be assigned to a particular manager for assignment control purposes, and to work for him while maintaining a functional relationship to a discipline manager. This approach, rare in public accounting firms, provides flexibility, but may increase costs; it can also lead to divided loyalties.

A third or "project" approach, requires personnel to report to a project manager; this approach is well suited to major nonrecurring engagements, such as litigation support assignments. Although inflexible, it facilitates technical and cost control.

An infinite variety of possible organizational arrangements is available. For instance, some progressive industrial companies have adopted an integrated organizational format which strives to achieve the best of all possible worlds; the integrated approach emphasizes coordination, and combines matrix and project aspects.

Public accounting firms in the United States have not been in the forefront of organizational experimentation; first-rate minds of the profession have not focused on organization and personnel-related opportunities; seasoned personnel specialists have not been attracted to the profession in sufficient numbers; and adequate attention has not been focused on the design of personnel data bases. Thus, internal auditors and government auditors have paced organizational innovation. For example, in some major oil companies the internal audit effort is decentralized; a small, but elite, core group provides such essential services as quality control, research, training, and administration.

The Need for an Increased Proportion of Senior Personnel

The proportion of senior people to juniors has been rising at major public accounting firms. This phenomenon puts profits under pressure in two ways. First, it may be possible to pay a junior $15 per hour and charge $45 for her; but it may be difficult to pay a partner $100 and collect $300. Second, underutilization of juniors is likely to have a negative effect on productivity. Some firms actually try to market the services of idle juniors to engagement partners, sometimes offering inducements by marking down rates for engagement costing purposes. The problem of unassigned juniors tends to be aggravated by the external auditors' employment of paraprofessionals to perform such tasks as searching the on-line data bases. In that particular instance, and given the right conditions, the utilization of an individual skilled in library science could enhance prospects for success. As a general rule, however, the paraprofessionals need to be properly trained and closely supervised to produce useful research results or to contribute to audit quality. Junior accountants do have appropriate credentials for performing technology-related audit tasks; in any event, the juniors should be involved with such tasks as part of their professional development. The imaginative use of juniors requires the production by universities of a better-educated junior, along with a more realistic interpretation of acceptable experience by states with experience requirements.

Failure to Monitor Technological Developments

Despite intermittent efforts by professional committees, auditors have been slow to take advantage of changes in technology, and of the possibilities of utilizing technology to improve productivity. For five years, the National Center for Automated Information Retrieval (NCAIR) has funded research dedicated to the betterment of the professions of law and accountancy. Until recently, NCAIR's larger research commissions were awarded for projects advancing automation in law firms. A dramatic change appears to be in the offing; a list of NCAIR's recent research awards supports the view that mini- and microcomputers have prompted a shift in the accountants' posture toward automation. Consequently, it has now become essential for external and internal audit entities to keep up with technological developments; similarly, vendors of software and hardware should give their accounting and auditing constituency the attention it deserves. Wholesalers of data bases such as DIALOG are discovering the accountant-customer; Mead Data Central (LEXIS) and Pergamon (ORBIT) have links to the AICPA; Mead Data Central is moving aggressively to support the accountants' market.

CAUSES OF DIMINISHED AUDIT PRODUCTIVITY: THE ENGAGEMENT

The Specter of Overauditing

Practitioners have become risk averse because of the litigious climate. Not surprisingly, their attitudes are mirrored in a tendency to overaudit, regardless of the extent of audit risk attached to a particular account or class of transactions. Professor David Ricchiute of Notre Dame University lectures on examples of overauditing. It cannot be determined how representative or typical his examples are; the author believes them to be realistic based on the positive reactions of many of his own practitioner-students. The examples include:

1. Tracing bank deposit slips to accounts receivable. (This test is usually without meaning, because the deposit slips are also likely to have been the source for the accounts receivable posting. In addition, banks do not routinely compare deposit details to deposit slips. An effective substitute procedure would be to trace listings of remittances prepared in the mail room to accounts receivable.)

2. Stratifying a universe for sampling purposes, and then examining an excessively large sample drawn from an insignificant stratum.

3. Applying statistical sampling where the entire population is less than 1,000.

4. Engaging in excessively detailed verification of investment transactions.

5. Engaging in unreasonable pursuit of nonreplies to confirmation requests.

6. Engaging in excessive test counts of items included in physical inventories.

7. Performing elaborate work on the labor and overhead components of inventory when there are no significant values involved.

8. Confirming liabilities—a practice likely to detect understatements but not overstatements.

9. Performing "stand alone" work on accrued expenses; the bulk of such work can and should be linked to the related debit accounts.

10. Testing excessive details of payrolls.

Mismanagement of Audit Risk

A major firm conducted a study which cannot be cited because of its confidential character. The study showed an inverted relationship between audit risk and work effort; field auditors devoted 80 percent of their efforts to matters involving 20 percent of audit risk. This firm also identified pockets of semi-clerical effort, which were then reduced by systematic introduction of microcomputer-based tools.

Audit risk has been defined as

> the risk that the auditor may unknowingly fail to appropriately
> modify his opinion on financial statements. The standards also
> state [that] at the account-balance . . . level audit risk consists of (*a*)
> the risk [consisting of inherent risk and control risk] that the bal-
> ance contains error[s] that would be material to the financial state-
> ments . . . and (*b*) the risk . . . that the auditor's procedures will not
> detect a material error. The smaller the control risk, the greater
> the reduction that can be made in the auditor's procedures.[12]

Thus, the standards permit a reduction in the auditor's substantive tests when control risk is low, and when inherent risk is low. In
other words, an account's susceptibility to error is an appropriate
basis for adjusting substantive tests; materiality must also be considered in planning the extent of audit work.[13] Yet, many auditors
have a tendency to perform the same audit procedures without considering the different circumstances that exist with each client. Because of the need to comply with professional standards, and because clients have a right to expect audit services to be rendered in
an efficient manner, "[this] luxury of applying audit procedures in a
lockstep manner may not be available in the future."[14]

Testing Internal Control, in the Absence of Reliance

One firm views the auditor's decision as to whether or not to rely
on internal control as the key strategy decision on an engagement. The time and cost required to study, document, test, and
evaluate internal accounting control can be considerable; in some
firms, the internal control effort consumes up to 40 percent of aggregate audit time. To the extent this cost is exceeded by the cost
of substantive tests that can be reduced or eliminated, a review of
internal accounting control is an efficient procedure.

Many auditors have found it difficult to rely on internal control
for the purpose of substantive test restriction; indeed the rely/reduce

---

[12]G. William Glezen, *Opportunities for Improving Audit Efficiency* (Denton: North
Texas State University, Professional Development Institute, 1987), pp. 21–23.

[13]Ibid.

[14]Ibid., p. 25.

concept is quite alien to auditors outside the English-speaking countries. If the auditor opts for reliance on controls, he should conduct tests to establish that the controls he has selected are in effect and are functioning as planned; flawed compliance tests have been discussed in an earlier chapter. Many seasoned auditors tend to place little confidence in tests of controls, although the newer concept evaluates both design and operational effectiveness. These doubting auditors are likely to convert their negative feelings about internal control into de facto nonreliance. As a practical matter, they will simply refrain from reducing the extent of their substantive tests, or modify the tests' nature and timing. In other words, they will validate without restriction, even though they have also performed redundant tests of controls.

Author's Comment

In most cases, assuming an automated system and use of computer-assisted audit techniques, the auditor will find it cost-effective to choose unrestricted substantive tests. If he follows this approach, substantive tests will become dual purpose—that is, they will serve to validate individual transactions and account balances, and also to establish that controls are in effect and functioning as planned. Of course, the extent to which the client or a regulatory agency expects the auditor to target all or a select number of internal controls for review may require separate testing of certain controls, regardless of the auditor's reliance thereon.

From a quality perspective, a further danger exists that dual-purpose tests may not provide adequate assurance as to the functioning of important individual controls. In most cases, those controls which function as an integral part of a particular computer application will have been adequately tested; however, in some situations the auditor will also have to apply additional procedures to satisfy himself as to the functioning of key and supervisory controls, especially in sensitive areas. (The subject is discussed in Chapter 4.)

Inefficient Selection of Controls for Reliance and Testing

As mentioned, control testing has declined due to a rise in computer-based audit tests, which militate in favor of substantive tests, and because of general ineffectiveness of such tests. The controls selected for reliance, and hence for testing, by both external and internal auditors may introduce another potentially negative aspect. In instances where the auditor chooses to rely on internal control, and conducts tests of controls, professional judgment should be applied to the selection of controls for testing. Economy/efficiency considerations also bear on the selection. Usually priority should be given to:

1. Controls which process transactions to accounts with a high degree of inherent risk.
2. Controls which involve numerous transactions, or transactions with a high average value.
3. Controls which are near the end of the transaction flow, close to recording in the accounts; therefore, further opportunities for error detection are likely to be limited.
4. Controls which can be tested in association with other controls and hence yield more "bang for the buck."
5. Controls which yield more persuasive evidence of their functioning.
6. Controls which can be tested with relative ease, based on availability of evidence, or on the skill level of the audit team.
7. Controls which have been found error-prone in an earlier year.

The nature of a control—whether supervision is involved, or whether a control has managerial significance—may provide the auditor with an additional reason for its testing. If he has opted to rely on internal control, he should also consider testing those controls which management uses to run the entity. Internal reports permit management to satisfy itself that corporate policies and procedures have been followed. By their very nature these controls are important from a business perspective. Often there will be evidence of corrective action taken as a direct result of the reports; in some cases, the elimination or reduction of an unfavorable condition will provide indirect evidence of corrective action. Consequently, management reports, together with direct or indirect evidence of corrective action, may entitle the auditor to rely on the control, without having to examine the details of a selection of documents.

Flowcharting: The Efforts May Be Misdirected

Detailed flowcharting is more useful when audits are repetitive in nature, processing is relatively complicated, and the system is more or less stable. Nonetheless, many auditors prepare excessively detailed flowcharts at great cost and in unsuitable circumstances. Burdensome detail causes the auditor to lose track of the conceptual ramifications of deficiencies; conversely, flowcharts which are too skimpy may make it difficult for the auditor to detect control exposures, to say nothing of processing delays or excessive transportations of documents. The answer resides in utilization of software to prepare flowcharts, or in delegation of flowchart preparation to client personnel.

Ineffectual Supervision

It is difficult to overemphasize the importance of timely supervision. *Timely* means supervision before the audit team has gone on to other phases of the audit, or, worse, has been reassigned to other engagements; supervision during the audit can avoid unproductive rework. A former practitioner put the productivity/efficiency issue this way:

> The more direct contact each supervisor on the audit team, from the partner on down, has with the engagement, the more efficient the audit will be. . . . There are two keys to reducing inefficiency through supervision. The first is to take the time . . . to explain specific audit procedures [before work commences] . . . . There is no substitute for a precise explanation of the objectives and procedures for performing a test. . . . The second key is concurrent review. Never wait until the end of the engagement or even the completion of work in a specific section before reviewing it.[15]

Unnecessary Clerical Activities

The internal accounting systems of some firms are in a state of disarray. At such firms, time, cost, and expense information may become available long after the time for corrective action has

---

[15]Ibid., p. 79.

elapsed. The record-keeping delays and inaccuracies can force engagement personnel to maintain their own records of engagement time and costs.

A glaring example of unproductive effort involves "analysis" of the current year's actual time in light of an outdated time budget; the comparison is often accomplished without adjusting the budget for matters beyond the control of engagement personnel, such as new accounting rules, the state of the national economy or conditions within the client's industry, and changes to the client's system. More seriously, the time budget may not have been corrected for changes within the external or internal auditor's shop (e.g., personnel changes or use of computer-assisted audit techniques).

Many auditors do not use the computer for word processing. Yet, management letter findings should be recorded contemporaneously with their discovery; speedy conveyance to clients is desirable to achieve correction of control deficiencies (so as to avert additional audit work) and to permit the client to benefit from revenue enhancement or cost-cutting observations. However, in many cases findings are recorded by hand, typed, and edited (with great pain to both editor and author) by partners and managers. The management letter thus becomes a sterile document, submitted long after the opinion, with many of its benefits vitiated.

Item

A major industrial company was impressed with the cost reduction opportunities discussed in the external auditor's management letter. But the letter was usually submitted long after the opportunity had passed for achieving timely and significant savings. Accordingly, the client insisted that its audit firm submit draft letters as soon as its field staff had recorded findings.

SUMMARY: MATTERS FOR IMPROVEMENT

Major areas for improvement include:

1. Enhancing audit profitability on the one hand by reducing or controlling discounting of fees and shifting toward

higher margined services and on the other by productivity improvement.

2. Establishing an orderly plan for productivity improvement, including productivity enhancement goals, performance measures, and control and feedback of results.

3. Applying a targeted approach to keeping current, focused on the learning ability of the individual, and based on the teaching technology most appropriate to the learner.

4. Educating buyers of audit services as to the need to follow sound procurement practices that give due recognition to quality.

5. Evaluating all support activities within a firm, and eliminating dysfunctional work.

6. Making full use of all lay specialists in the firm by bringing their skills to bear on the problem solutions.

7. Analyzing the organizational structure to determine that it adequately supports the audit practice with the required industry and technical skills.

8. Bringing senior personnel experience and judgments to bear on problems as they develop.

9. Employing juniors productively, not only in performing program steps, but in professional support activities, including audit research.

10. Avoiding overauditing by seeing that each step supports audit objectives.

11. Better aligning audit risk and work effort, particularly in areas that tend to represent focal areas of exposure.

12. Timing audit supervision to be as contemporaneous with the audit work as possible.

13. Automating clerical activities, and avoiding unnecessary clerical activities.

Technology, and especially computers, bears on many of the points listed above, as will be shown in succeeding chapters. Yet, surprisingly, very little has been written on the impact of computers on audit productivity. Yet, Dr. John Willingham, partner of KPMG-Peat Marwick, avers that during the past few years computers have enabled his firm to halve the number of new staff hires. Similarly, a team of writers headed by a noted academic has asserted that the introduction of new technologies will make it possible to perform high-quality audits at considerably less cost than incurred previously.[16] However, the authors also pointed out that the capital costs of audit firms were likely to increase.

With respect to the auditor's clients, basic office functions traditionally performed by a large number of individuals with limited training may be replaced by a combination of intelligent office systems and a small professional office staff.[17] The same assumption holds true for the auditor's office.

To sum up, the impact of automation on audit productivity is likely to be beneficial; however, it is anticipated that the most important benefit will be a boost in audit effectiveness. Nessa MacErlain has pointed out that technology could even pose a threat to audit profitability. She notes that the time savings could become both a necessary good, and a necessary evil.

> Until recently, endless repetition was [mirrored in review] by three or four different supervisors, managers, or partners. . . . Firms are now using technology to reduce the incidence of . . . duplication and to focus on more interesting and appropriate audit work. . . . The development of computer technology does indeed threaten the profitability of the traditional audit. But it also liberates auditors to develop more sophisticated and higher-margin areas.[18]

---

[16]Andrew D. Bailey, Jr., Kyeong Seok Han, and Andrew B. Whinston, "Technology, Competition and the Future of Auditing," *1987 Proceedings of the Arthur Young Professors' Roundtable* (Reston, Va.: The Council of Arthur Young Professors, 1988), p. 26.

[17]Ibid., p. 28.

[18]Nessa MacErlain, "Technology's Hidden Threat," *The Independent*, March 20, 1990, p. 4.

CHAPTER 4

THE SELECTION OF AUDIT PROCEDURES

That which has made us great is the urge to tell the truth.

Robert H. Montgomery

USER PERSPECTIVE: Items of Special Interest

EXECUTIVE HIGHLIGHTS: All readers

INTRODUCTION: All readers

THE CONVERSION OF MANAGEMENT ASSERTIONS TO AUDIT PROCEDURES: All readers

THE PERILS OF APPLYING AUDIT PROCEDURES: All readers

THE MERITS OF OPERATIONAL INFORMATION: External auditors, internal auditors

THE AUDIT MODEL REVISITED AND UPDATED: All readers

SUMMARY: All readers

EXECUTIVE HIGHLIGHTS

Judicious conversion of management assertions to audit procedures enhances both audit effectiveness and productivity. There are only a few basic audit procedures; the auditor chooses the mix of procedures based on the skills of the engagement team in applying the procedures and in recognizing exceptions, on the availability of documentation suitable as audit evidence, and on the expected effectiveness of the procedures, based on the client's vulnerability to material errors and irregularities.

Audit risk may be increased by control deficiencies in three focal areas of exposure: physical protection of assets, computer access, and management representations. The last poses special hazards. Most auditors are averse to courting trouble with the client. This understandable inclination favors the auditor's acceptance of amounts which appear in the accounts and in the management representation letter.

Certain indicators of the nature of the control environment are suggested for the auditor's consideration. In any event, insofar as possible, management assertions should be verified independently by gathering external data, or by using operational information to confirm and validate financial information. Operational information can have a cachet of semi-independence. Tests of operational controls are also likely to be efficient, since evidence in the form of reports to and reactions from management is often readily obtainable.

In the author's opinion, an auditor would choose to rely on internal control only in relatively rare instances; however, internal control remains very important as an indicator of the auditee's interest in and support for corporate accountability.

The concerns raised in this and preceding chapters suggest a need for updating the conventional audit model, especially as to the risks and exposures to loss that confront the client externally and internally.

INTRODUCTION

Some accounting historians have listed "auditing by objectives" as a milestone in the evolution of the profession; others might dispute this characterization. However, there *is* agreement as to the overall objective of an examination of financial statements by an external auditor. That objective has been defined as the expression of an opinion on the fairness with which the statements present financial position, results of operations, and cash flows in conformity with generally accepted accounting principles. The challenge lies in efficient and effective achievement of this objective.

In the words of two well-known authors:

> Audit objectives are intended to provide a framework to help the
> auditor accumulate sufficient competent evidence. . . . For any
> given account balance . . . there are several *specific* audit objectives
> that must be met. . . . The framework used to develop specific audit
> objectives consists of management assertions and *general* audit ob-
> jectives. . . . Assertions are implied or expressed representations
> by management about the components of financial statements. . . .
> The general audit objectives . . . are applicable to every account
> balance, but are stated in broad terms. Specific audit objectives . . .
> are stated in terms tailored to the engagement.[1]

This chapter explores the considerations involved in setting
audit objectives based on management assertions; it also discusses the selection of audit procedures to accomplish those objectives. There are but a few types of basic audit procedures; the auditor chooses her mix of procedures based on the skills of her
engagement team in applying the procedures and in recognizing
exceptions, the availability of documentation suitable as audit
evidence, and the expected effectiveness of the procedures, based
on the client's vulnerability to material errors and irregularities.

The author believes that vulnerability to material errors and
irregularities tends to be increased by control deficiencies in
three focal areas of exposure: physical protection of assets, computer access, and management representations. The author also
holds the view that audit procedures should utilize client operational data when practical to confirm and validate financial information. For example, an expediter's list of undelivered purchased
parts may help to determine the value of work-in-process; or, an
adjustment to a sales commission may offer an indication of a
sales return. Therefore, auditors should develop their business
acumen and their ability to work with operational information to
promote achievement of financial audit objectives.

The book suggests modifications to the conventional audit
model, especially in terms of improved recognition of inherent
risk, and in selection of audit procedures suited to automation. In

---

[1]Alvin A. Arens and James K. Loebbecke, *Auditing: An Integrated Approach,* 4th ed.
(Englewood Cliffs, N.J.: Prentice-Hall, 1988), p. 141.

the author's opinion, the auditor would choose to rely on internal control only in relatively rare instances; however, internal control remains very important as an indicator of the auditee's interest in and support for corporate accountability. Robert Walker put it this way:

> At best, [internal control] is management's procedure for addressing risk. But, do those procedures help the auditor? I would say no. Auditors must bring their own independent judgment to bear regarding risks of misstatement, and design their own tests to ascertain whether management's procedures did in fact address them. . . . Good internal control simply does not reduce the need for substantive evidence.[2]

In general then, this book favors unrestricted substantive tests. The author believes that, typically, tests should not be decreased or otherwise diminished, even if internal control appears satisfactory. The opposite does not hold true; enhancements may be warranted to substantive tests, based on uncontrolled threats, particularly within the three focal areas of exposure.

THE CONVERSION OF MANAGEMENT ASSERTIONS TO AUDIT PROCEDURES

The Nature of Management Assertions

Management assertions may be categorized as follows:[3]

Existence or Occurrence
Assets, liabilities, and equities included in the balance sheet actually exist on the balance sheet date; revenues and expenses included in the income statement have actually been experienced

---

[2]Robert Walker, "Will the Real Audit Risks Please Stand Up?" *CA Magazine,* March 1990, Auditing Department, pp. 44–48.

[3]The discussion of the nature of management assertions and of general audit objectives is based on Arens and Loebbecke, *Auditing,* pp. 143–46.

during the accounting period. (The primary concern is with inclusion of amounts that should have been excluded.)

Completeness
All transactions that should be presented in the financial statements are included. (The primary concern is with the possibility of omitting items that should have been included.)

Rights and Obligations
A right exists to assets; all liabilities that are obligations of the entity have been included.

Valuation or Allocation
The component accounts of the financial statements have been included at appropriate amounts; correct allocations have been made to the right accounting periods.

Presentation and Disclosure
Components of the financial statements have been properly classified and described, and the required disclosures made.

Some Difficulties with Management Assertions

The derivation of audit objectives from management assertions (i.e., from management's expressed or implied representations) requires caution:

   1. The assertions may be incomplete; they may not meet the needs of all statement users.

Author's Comment

In early 1990 the Government Accounting Standards Board (GASB) published a research report which gave a sample presentation of service efforts and accomplishments indicators for elementary and secondary education. This report represents the first specific declaration by a body responsible for setting principles of accounting and financial reporting that financial statements of entities which disburse public funds should include indicators of efficiency and effectiveness. If such disclosures were to be widely accepted and implemented, they could be seen as written management assertions against which auditors *could* perform attestation audits.[4]

2. Management may be unaware of the nature of some or all of the assertions, of the auditor's responsibility relative to those assertions, and of the implications inherent in carrying out that responsibility. (However, professional rules require auditors to secure a management representation letter; if the letter is reasonably complete, the dangers of managerial misunderstanding may be reduced.)

3. Management may not have all the facts necessary to make accurate assertions; or management may be unaware of errors in the information that has been furnished to the auditors by its subordinates. (For example, there is a hazard that client subordinates may not know the effect on the client of all or some developments *external* to the business.)

Item

Recently, auditors for a troubled savings and loan association declined to stand for reelection. When the author asked the audit partner whether he suspected that management's integrity was not what it should be, the answer was that management was perceived as honorable. However, the partner added that numerous bad operating decisions had been caused by management being in over its head, excessively optimistic, not in possession of all facts, and a little "macho."

4. The auditors may have difficulty converting management assertions and management objectives into audit objectives, and particularly into *specific* audit objectives. For example, confusion may arise when a client has introduced a management by objectives (MBO) approach; specific audit objectives are likely to be detailed and narrowly focused, compared to broader MBO objectives.

5. The engagement team may make mistakes in selecting and assembling test procedures intended to accomplish audit ob-

---

[4]*Local Government Auditor's Newsletter* 3, no. 3 (1990), p. 6.

jectives efficiently and effectively. (There is an infinite variety of possible combinations of procedures; the choices may involve complex trade-offs.)

6. Certain desirable audit procedures may not be practical due to absence or inaccessibility of client documentation.

General Audit Objectives

Arens and Loebbecke have pointed out that all procedures performed in pursuit of audit objectives are intended to determine whether management assertions about financial statements are justified. As has been seen, general audit objectives serve as stepping stones to tailored specific audit objectives. To guide the auditor's accumulation of the necessary evidence, Arens and Loebbeke have subdivided the client management assertion relating to valuation/allocation into four separate general audit objectives. These authors have also added "overall reasonableness" as a separate general audit objective. Thus, in addition to reasonableness, the general audit objectives as redrawn by Arens and Loebbeke follow:

1. Validity—the auditor's counterpart to the management assertion of existence or occurrence.
2. Completeness—the auditor's counterpart to the management assertion of completeness.
3. Ownership—the auditor's counterpart to the management assertion of rights and obligations.
4. Valuation—the correct valuation of individual balances making up a total, including accuracy of arithmetic and recognition of declines in net realizable value.

Author's Comment

G. A. Holmes, an Australian writer, has suggested that disclosure, particularly in the United States, does not overcome the problem of unexpected failure, and that more rigorous testing of asset recoverability is necessary. Holmes believes that appropriate tests of recoverability include analysis of the company's markets for goods and services, a segment analysis of return on investment by groups of assets, a sensitivity analysis of forecast cash flows, appraisal of financial resources, and integrated ratio analysis.[5]

Author's Comment

Allowing for national differences in the approach to current value accounting and for changing U.K. rules, the observations of John F. Hogan, an Irish accountant, may also be pertinent. Hogan has suggested that auditors pay special attention to (and possibly interview) valuers of company assets included in current cost accounts. He stresses that the auditor should obtain a copy of the instruction letter that the client has issued to the valuer, the valuer's acknowledgment thereof, and an indication of the work he intends to carry out. Further, he urges consideration of the suitability and competence of the valuer. The purpose is to "ensure . . . consensus of opinion between company management, professional valuer, and auditor on the appropriateness of the valuation."[6]

5. Classification—amounts are properly classified and appropriately displayed in the financial statements.
6. Cutoff—transactions near the balance sheet date are recorded in the proper period.
7. Mechanical accuracy.
8. Disclosure—counterpart to the management assertion of presentation and disclosure.

Specific Audit Objectives

Specific audit objectives are developed for particular accounts; these objectives should be fine-tuned to reflect related inherent risk. Lynford Graham, a well known audit researcher, on the basis of a perceptive analysis of *SAS 47,* has suggested identifying the balance(s) or account(s) affected by an inherent risk condition

---

[5]G. A. Holmes, "Tests of Asset Recoverability: Audit and Accounting Implications," *The Australian Accountant,* November 1979, pp. 708–21.

[6]John F. Hogan, "SSAP 16: Auditing Professional Valuations," *Accountancy* [Ireland], October 1980, pp. 34–35.

or characteristic, the general and/or specific audit objectives pertinent to each affected balance or account, and the nature, timing, and extent of audit tests and analytical procedures sufficient to provide assurance that the financial statements are not materially misstated.[7]

The inherent risks, both external and internal, have been discussed in Chapter 1. Technological advances have made it easier to identify external risks, especially by searching the on-line data bases, as discussed in succeeding chapters; the on-line data bases may also contain information regarding client executives that could alert an auditor to potential problems. Management assertions may be flawed by (1) clerical errors, (2) errors resulting from inaccurate, incomplete, or out-of-date knowledge of business conditions, and (3) irregularities including fraud—matters which must be addressed by the design of the auditor's tests. After general and specific audit objectives have been set, suitable audit procedures can be chosen.

A New Look at Old Tests

The effectiveness of tests and other procedures depends on (1) the team which does the work, (2) available documentation, and (3) vulnerability of the documentation to errors and irregularities. (The last item should be uppermost in the auditor's mind.) Generally, the audit team should be skilled in three matters: understanding of computerized operations; capacity for using the computer to enhance audit efficiency and effectiveness; and ability to recognize problem situations. Additional considerations involve documentation: existence of *tangible* documentation suitable for gathering evidence; awareness of the possible perils of alternative evidence; and appraisal of the risk of management overrides. Arens and Loebbecke have listed seven categories of procedures and evidence, some of which have been or will be elaborated on.[8] The categories are:

---

[7]Lynford E. Graham, "Audit Risk—Part II," *The CPA Journal,* September 1985, p. 38.

[8]Arens and Loebbecke, *Auditing,* pp. 170–73.

1. *Physical examination,* the inspection or count of a tangible asset by an auditor. Auditors must be familiar with the client's facilities, security procedures, and physical and performance characteristics of the assets—or they must secure the services of someone who is.

2. *Confirmation,* the receipt of a written response from an independent third party verifying the accuracy of information. Auditors should be aware of the pitfalls in confirmation, and of the greater pitfalls which may exist in blindly following alternative procedures, such as accepting manufactured post–confirmation date cash receipts.

3. *Documentation,* the auditor's examination of the client's documents and records to substantiate information that is, or should be, included in the financial statements.

4. *Observation,* using the senses to assess certain activities.

5. *Inquiry* of the client, obtaining of written or oral information. More stress should be placed by auditors on the behavioral aspects of interviews.

6. *Mechanical accuracy,* rechecking a sample of computations and transfers of information made by the client.

7. *Analytical procedures,* using comparisons and relationships to determine whether account balances look reasonable. The obvious need is to have informed expectations.

The aforementioned procedures are applied by auditors in all nations and in a variety of circumstances. (National audit practices differ primarily in use of audit objectives, in reliance on internal control, and in the nature, extent, and timing of substantive tests.)

However, the tests comprehended by these categories also have distinctive attributes which become more important in light of the author's inclination toward substantive testing mostly at the year end. The test attributes come into play when procedures are selected to meet audit objectives. Certain test procedures *must* always be applied because of their intrinsic importance; the reading of corporate minutes represents an example. Other procedures need to be applied only when there are extraordinary exposures; for example, the author would perform a proof of cash only where there is very poor internal control over cash, or malfeasance is suspected. (A proof of cash covers a period of time and represents a reconciliation of beginning balance, receipts, disbursements, and ending balance, starting with the bank figures and closing with the book figures.) Some procedures may be variable as to the time of the year at which they are performed; for example, it may be advantageous to observe inventory counts during the year, assuming that physical controls over assets are good and that updating procedures are reliable. Finally, the extent of some procedures can be varied, depending on the auditor's assessment; variations will be influenced by the materiality of individual transactions and/or balances.

The author believes that inadequate auditing does not involve test procedures per se, as much as the manner of their application. The stage can now be set for a discussion of inadequacies in application by mentioning that errors and irregularities tend to be lumped together in the professional literature.

THE PERILS OF APPLYING AUDIT PROCEDURES

Errors and Irregularities: A Broad Category

The auditor's opinion implies that financial statements are not materially misstated due to errors and irregularities. Auditors are encouraged to design their examination to detect both types of misstatements, the *unintentional* mistake (clerical error, misapplication of accounting principles, and misinterpretation or oversight of facts) together with *intentional* distortions of financial statements (misappropriation of assets, presentation of incorrect information, or other deliberate misrepresentations).[9] Intent is used to distinguish between errors and irregularities; however, it

---

[9] John W. Cook and Gary M. Winkle, *Auditing*, 4th ed. (Boston: Houghton Mifflin, 1988), pp. 18–19.

is very difficult to determine intent, particularly in matters involving accounting estimates and judgments.[10]

The melding of different phenomena—clerical errors, errors due to inadequate information, and deliberate misstatements—could lead to misapplied audit efforts. For example, auditors may search for the results of common types of clerical errors; yet, most electronic data processing applications have built-in safeguards to avoid these errors. Review of general computer controls (discussed in Chapter 8) should provide the auditor with an indication of the extent of the risk of clerical errors, particularly when it appears that the requisite controls are in effect and functioning as planned. Moreover, computer errors, when they do occur, are likely to be noticeable and may almost cry out for correction. On the other hand, the risk of errors caused by inaccurate and incomplete knowledge on the part of management, together with possible irregularities, may call for enriched audit procedures based on consideration of threats to assets and resources and of the extent to which these threats have remained uncontrolled; fraud can represent such a threat.

Fraud: A Pervasive Problem

In the opinion of informed observers, fraud is more widespread than many people think. A recent study conducted in the United Kingdom suggests that fraud was experienced by 12 percent of respondent companies. The aggregate amounts involved in fraud can only be surmised. Georgette Bennett has estimated the annual take of persons involved in street crime at $4 billion, and that of boardroom and retail types at 10 to 50 times that amount.[11] Similarly, the U.S. Chamber of Commerce reports that 30 percent of business failures each year result from embezzlements, pilfering, and swindles by trusted employees.[12]

---

[10]Zoe-Vonna Palmrose, "Litigation and Independent Auditors," *Auditing: A Journal of Theory and Practice* 6, no. 2 (Spring 1988), pp. 92–103.

[11]Georgette Bennett, *Crimewarps: The Future of Crime in America* (Garden City, N.Y.: Doubleday, Anchor Press, 1987), p. 104.

[12]Ibid., p. 105.

Joseph Wells, considered by many to be the nation's premier fraud auditor, has taken pains to dispel what he considers myths about fraud:

1. Most people will not commit fraud. According to Wells most people will commit fraud. Wells writes that the greater the promise of reward, or the more pervasive the threat of punishment, the higher the motivation for antisocial behavior.

2. Fraud is usually not material. According to Wells, frauds are often material, because immaterial frauds have a way of turning into material ones.

3. Fraud goes undetected. According to Wells, fraud is often detected. In a continuing fraud the amounts involved get bigger and the perpetrator gets more careless about concealment.

4. Fraud is usually well concealed. According to Wells, fraud is often not well concealed. Half the instances of fraud are discovered by accident.

5. The auditor cannot do a better job at detection. According to Wells, the auditor can do a much better job at detection. However, improvement will come about only with better guidance, experience, and awareness.

6. Prosecuting some perpetrators deters others. According to Wells, prosecution may, or may not, deter others. There was no statistically significant difference in terms of losses between banks which prosecuted offenders, and those that did not.[13]

Author's Comment

While some of Joseph Wells' statements appear controversial, they are confirmed by the felon participants who lecture in Wells' training programs. These fallen luminaries include a former army colonel and a Ph.D. in computer sciences. The lesson is that individuals who normally lead blameless lives may go over the edge in certain circumstances. Hence, clients and their auditors must be vigilant

---

[13]Joseph T. Wells, "Six Common Myths about Fraud," *Journal of Accountancy*, February 1990, pp. 82–88.

to sudden behavior changes on the part of the client's employees. The author does not agree entirely with Wells' sixth point; he believes that aggressive prosecution of offenders can represent a significant deterrent—if given appropriate publicity within the victimized company.

The auditor's primary concern may lie with management rather than employee fraud; however, similar procedures may prove effective for both categories of fraud. It should be noted that relatively few management frauds involve thievery of assets or other resources. (When they do, the amounts are likely to be large.) Most management frauds feature "cooking the books" to deceive readers of financial statements. In many cases such cooking has required disregard or override of existing internal controls.

Management Overrides: A Noxious Irregularity

Management overrides have not received much attention. For example, the U.S. General Accounting Office (GAO) has repeatedly and correctly attributed savings and loan failures to weaknesses in internal control. This view is consistent with the significance of internal control as a broad indicator of the tone at the top. However, in the case of some financial institutions, particularly serious problems arose when venal managements *overrode* internal controls, or moved toward their dismantlement.

Item

In a management fraud involving an insurance company, looting of corporate assets began on the West Coast and moved east. Management's hesitation to convert the assets of a New Jersey-based affiliate was explained to the author as attributable to (1) worries over the perceived high effectiveness of New York/New Jersey state insurance examiners, and (2) the potential embarrassment created by management's need to access the programs, data, and documents involved in policy accounting. One problem was that the affiliate's computer program changes were numbered and under tight control; therefore, the first (and actually completed) move by management involved dismantling the affiliate's program change controls. Fortunately, the scandal became public knowledge before the preparations for fraud could be completed.

Most auditors track and monitor the process of preparation of the financial statements, including the creation of combining, adjusting, and consolidating journal entries. Therefore, management overrides may *precede* the creation of the unadjusted trial balance for an operating unit. Improper actions may involve creation of false documents, deliberate omission of valid documents, unsupported or fraudulent journal entries, or entry of unsupported "corrections."

Item

The division president of an industrial air conditioning manufacturer experienced difficulty in achieving profit targets imposed upon him by corporate management. Accordingly, he instructed his division controller to increase the physical inventory sufficiently to show an acceptable profit. In the course of the next weekend, the division controller created 500 "count tickets." He explained to the internal auditor that the tickets had been erroneously omitted from the inventory. The internal auditor did not accept the explanation. At inventory time he had accounted for the sequence of numbered count tickets, and had inspected the storage area to ensure that nothing had remained untagged; at that time there were no items which appeared to have been omitted from the count. Moreover, the internal auditor observed that all new tickets had been completed in the same handwriting. Needless to say, the inventory "correction" was not recorded!

Auditors should evaluate the risk of possible management overrides, both on an overall basis and with respect to individual accounts, to satisfy themselves that overrides are not likely or to introduce appropriate defensive steps. Awareness of the override hazard continues to be especially important when an auditor uses operational information to expedite the accomplishment of her audit objectives; traditionally, operational information has not been subjected to the same degree of rigorous control as financial information. For example, assume that an auditor uses customer service reports to see whether downward adjustment to accounts receivable might be necessary. If such reports are not prenumbered, or alternative controls established, and if dollar control totals are not accumulated, the auditor will have no assurance of picking up all indications of possible adjustments.

The Auditor's Achilles' Heel: Management Representations

Since management fraud is within the realm of possibility, the issue becomes one of zeroing in on areas in which such fraud might be perpetrated, of discussing control aspects, and of sensitizing auditors to the manifestations of fraud. The three most perilous areas have been mentioned. The first area involves physical protection over whatever may be worth stealing (including information), or over the hardware, software, and data needed to assure the continuity of business operations. Assuming that most companies are automated—and given dishonest managers' penchants for concealing conversion of assets or results of bad decisions by manipulating the books—access to computers, programs, and data represents the second focal point for control. These two focal points are covered elsewhere in the book, primarily in Chapter 6. The third, and most dangerous, area involves management representations, and the auditors' penchant for undue reliance on those representations in lieu of gathering objective evidence.

Most auditors are averse to courting trouble with the client; accordingly, they are comfortable with routine situations. This understandable inclination favors acceptance by the auditor of amounts which appear in the accounts and in the management representation letter; this type of bias is called *anchoring* by statisticians. Lack of auditor skepticism vis-à-vis client representations was reflected in a 1984 study in which a team of investigators examined 129 lawsuits filed against public accountants; the authors noted and cataloged 334 alleged errors by auditors.[14]

Author's Comment

A leading audit researcher in the United Kingdom has commented that the "results of the study should be interpreted with caution, both because of its restricted sample population and for its failure to consider the actual outcome of the cases analyzed. . . . Neverthe-

---

[14]Kent St. Pierre and James A. Anderson, "An Analysis of the Factors Associated with Lawsuits against Public Accountants," *The Accounting Review* 59, no. 2 (April 1984), pp. 243–63.

less, studies of this nature form a useful addition to our knowledge about situations in which an auditor might be held to have been negligent."[15]

Not surprisingly, according to the St. Pierre and Anderson study, many alleged errors stemmed from faulty interpretation of generally accepted accounting principles (GAAP) *and* generally accepted auditing standards (GAAS). Relative to GAAP, the greatest number of errors occurred when underlying issues were complex, and subject to a high degree of uncertainty in revenue recognition and asset valuation. Revenue recognition errors involved land, equipment, real estate, and construction projects. Errors involving asset valuations affected inventory, goodwill, receivables, natural resources, and real estate.[16]

Relative to GAAS, the problems concerned the testing of inventory, receivables, asset costs, current liabilities, sales, and other revenue items. Related aspects involved estimation of the proper reserve for uncollectable accounts and sending of and follow-up on customer confirmations. Allegations of inadequate inventory testing mentioned observation of physical counts, tag control, and pricing procedures. Alleged errors in testing asset costs pertained to finance, insurance, and real estate company assets included in financial statements at inflated values.[17]

The reported shortfalls seem to involve all management assertions, but especially the valuation assertion. The possible corrective measures are many and varied. They include a better understanding of the client's business, a greater feel for operations, increased audit skepticism, more pervasive and thorough testing, and greater acuity applied to audit procedures generally.

Author's Comment

In the case of certain S&Ls, appraisers seemed unable to arrive at realistic property valuations. In some states, neither the profes-

---

[15]David R. Gwilliam, *A Survey of Auditing Research* (Englewood Cliffs, N.J.: Prentice-Hall and the Institute of Chartered Accountants in England and Wales, 1987), p. 148.

[16]St. Pierre and Anderson, "An Analysis of the Factors."

[17]Ibid.

sional qualifications of appraisers, nor ground rules or standards for their work, had been prescribed; indeed, these issues had not been addressed at all by some legislatures. The federal government, in association with professional groups, strove to correct this condition in February 1990, long after the crisis appeared to have peaked. The painful experience of auditors involved in litigation related to valuation suggests that there is a need for discriminating evaluation of the credentials and procedures used by experts in whom reliance is to be placed; the rigor of this assessment should exceed present or foreseen professional requirements. In addition, the auditor's assessment of real estate valuers could be supplemented by review of the client's property trades, including inquiries into (1) the history of value "step-ups" on the properties, (2) the market values for similar properties, and (3) the arm's-length nature of the transactions.

THE MERITS OF OPERATIONAL INFORMATION

Corrective action with regard to audit shortfalls points to updating and fine-tuning of the conventional audit model based on a better understanding of the business, and the more thorough audit examination made possible by computerization. These matters are covered in some detail in the remainder of the book; a handy overview is provided later in this chapter in the section on the revisited and expanded audit model. This model also assumes the auditor will take full advantage of operational information in his financial audit.

Operational information not only represents the raw material of highly effective audit tests, but conduces to efficiency. The pertinence of operational information to auditing is traceable to the fact that managers can and should protect an enterprise from unpleasant surprises—that is, from the results of exposures—by anticipating threats and mitigating their impact. Management's actions may involve risk assumption or shifting, control through the system, or a combination of techniques to help in preventing, detecting, or correcting unfavorable developments.

In many cases, the measures designed by management to control threats will involve operational rather than financial data; or financial and operational information may be inextricably interwoven. This circumstance represents an opportunity for auditors who understand their client's business and management information system. Operational controls offer added insight into the control environment and can support the auditor's reliance on the functioning of the system. Therefore, it has been predicted that future "audits will be much more operational controls oriented than they are today. Both internal and external audit departments will have to concentrate on the operational or administrative controls, as well as on financial controls."[18]

An increased emphasis on operational controls does not conflict with the profession's interpretation of the elements of the internal control structure, which sees other policies and procedures as relevant if they pertain to data the auditor uses to apply analytical procedures.[19] In other words, the author believes that the auditor is free to consider the existence of operational controls and to identify those of audit interest. Like controls generally, operational controls function through policies, procedures, supervision, accounting, budgeting, reporting, and internal review. Controls within the last four categories are likely to be documented and replete with an audit trail. Like other audit tests, operational control tests involve observation, inquiry of client personnel, and—most importantly—inspection of evidence.

Operational information can be used in all types of audit procedures: analytical reviews, tests of controls, and substantive tests. Tests of operational controls are likely to be particularly efficient, since evidence in the form of reports to and reactions from management is often readily obtainable. Examples of the use of operational information to accomplish financial audits appear in subsequent chapters. It should be noted that, given computerized systems, operational information can be accessed quite easily and may prove particularly helpful in substantive testing. Hence, one representative example is cited in the paragraph which follows.

---

[18]Stanley D. Halper, Glenn C. Davis, P. Jarlath O'Neil-Dunne, and Pamela R. Pfau, *Handbook of EDP Auditing* (Boston: Warren, Gorham & Lamont, 1985), p. 4.

[19]Control Risk Audit Guide Task Force, *Consideration of the Internal Control Structure in a Financial Statement Audit* (New York: American Institute of CPAs, 1990), p. 2.

Author's Comment

Traditionally, auditors have examined plant, property, and equipment additions by "vouching"—that is, by examining documentation for significant acquisitions. However, the additions field of a master property record could be computer-matched to the property field of a maintenance record, assuming that the equipment requires servicing. The actions of maintenance personnel convey the cachet of semi-independent verification of the existence of assets. (Maintenance servicing without related property additions might reveal failure to close out construction in progress. Property additions without servicing might serve as a clue to omitted maintenance.)

THE AUDIT MODEL REVISITED AND UPDATED

The Conventional Model Revisited

Most U.S. auditors, at least those younger than the author, will have been trained on a systems-oriented audit model. The earliest model of the genre was developed a quarter of a century ago; changes to that model have been cosmetic rather than fundamental, even though the profession has come through a period of great change. For the record, the widely accepted phases of the model are:

1. Obtaining an understanding. In general, the understanding consists of three elements: an understanding of the position of the client in the overall economy, an understanding of the client's business and industry, and an understanding of the client's system.

2. Documenting that understanding. Many public accounting firms still enjoin staff members to document their understanding of the system by flowcharting, thereby helping to perpetuate an often inefficient technique.

3. Confirming the correctness of the understanding. Some years ago, public accounting firms often confirmed the correctness of the understanding by performing a transaction review, or walk-through. This was done by tracing

one or a few transactions of each type through the system on a cradle-to-grave basis. The practice is likely to undergo revival, assuming that portals for this capability will be built into new or modified systems.

4. Deciding on audit strategy/assessing control risk. This important decision involves a determination, usually made separately for each subsystem or "systems cycle" (e.g., sales/accounts receivable), as to whether to rely on internal control; the alternative involves the performance of unrestricted substantive tests.

5. Testing internal controls. The auditor tests those controls upon which she has chosen to rely for the purpose of restricting substantive tests.

6. Evaluating internal controls. This is often done by means of an internal control questionnaire (ICQ); Chapter 9 offers questionnaires for the focal areas of exposure. The results of the evaluation are reported to the client in a management letter and considered in developing the substantive test program.

7. Performing substantive tests; expressing an opinion.

The Disabilities of the Conventional Model

The effort involved in completing the aforementioned "magic steps" can be massive; yet, the efficiency and effectiveness of the model have been brought into question. Of course, the concerns pertaining to the model are not necessarily systemic, but lie in part in the ways in which the model is applied.

The concerns noted in this and previous chapters include: (1) In obtaining an understanding of inherent risk, the auditor may not have considered varied external and, particularly, internal business risks, and the extent to which exposures have been managed/controlled by the client. Auditors tend to be especially optimistic (read *vulnerable*) in assessing risk relating to client personnel; auditors often "see no evil, hear no evil, speak no evil." (2) Attempts to relate audit risk and audit effort have often been undisciplined; key areas of uncontrolled exposure may not have been dealt with at all or may not have been weighted appropriately in terms of audit resource commitments. (3) Flowcharting has been pursued with diligence by auditors, in spite of the fact that the exercise conveys tenuous benefits at best, and may be misleading at worst. (4) Transaction reviews appear to have become extinct, even when readily achievable. (5) Compliance tests have been performed in a manner which offers little or no assurance that the controls tested are in effect and are functioning as planned. Moreover, most auditors disregard the efficiency and effectiveness advantages of operational information for compliance testing. (6) Analytical reviews have been conducted in a superficial and unimaginative manner, confirming the adage that "you always get what you pay for." (7) Substantive tests have been conducted without reference to related operational information; few attempt to access nonfinancial information available in either public or in-house data bases.

The Updated and Expanded Audit Model

This section presents an enriched audit model and comments on tasks which should be redirected in order to help solve the twin problems of audit efficiency and effectiveness; many such tasks can be performed by using proven technology.

I. Obtain an understanding of inherent risk.

   A. Establish/update the nature of risks and exposures to loss which exist in the client's industry and business. Typically the update will involve reference to the online data bases; it will cover major types of exposures and threats to which the client is subject; in terms of information media it will include daily newspapers, periodicals, and books.

   B. Establish/update the backgrounds of the client's key executives. A search into the backgrounds, prior legal problems, and utterances of key executives may alert the auditor to the presence of people who have engaged in questionable activities in the past. (Many people previously involved in crimes demonstrate recidivist tendencies; extreme caution is required.)

C. Establish/update the nature of risks and exposures to loss which confront the client internally. The primary objective is to identify pressures on operating executives arising from commitments made by or imposed on them and to determine how unachieved commitments might be covered by cooking the books.

D. Establish/update digests of the latest legal and regulatory requirements that affect the examination. Computerized indexes can help to pinpoint authoritative sources preliminary to more complete analysis.

E. Consider analytical procedures using external information. Caution is necessary; information pertaining to different companies is often not comparable. Also, information may be late or drawn from different accounting periods.

F. Post significant business risks to a list of threats and controls, subsequently called the master tracking sheet, thereby contributing to an inventory of threats to financial statements, assets, and resources.

II. Understand the control environment.

A. Take the pulse of the control environment. Indicators of the control environment include client attitudes toward (1) internal control, (2) audit adjustments/management letters, (3) prosecution of dishonest employees, and (4) the distinction, if any, being made by executives between personal and company funds.

B. Assess the hazard of management overrides; to the extent possible, this should be done in terms of specific locations or operations. Again, the step requires a feeling for senior executives' likely responses to failure to live up to expectations.

C. Record the risk management approaches pursued by the client with respect to internal and external risks; note the extent to which risk is managed/controlled through the system; consider the desirability from a client service or audit point of view of testing related controls. In general, audit risk analysis software is under development, but has not yet become generally available. (However, other risk analysis software has been introduced which may prove helpful; for example, there is software which analyzes the reasons for network outages.)

III. Understand the system and control procedures.

A. Review flowcharts. A computerized system may be depicted by a combination of overview and detailed flowcharts. The detailed flowcharts should be prepared after the overview flowcharts; moreover, detailed flowcharting should normally not be done by external auditors. Those who prepare flowcharts will find the task of updating and maintenance greatly facilitated by state-of-the-art software.

B. Make assessment of controls in the focal areas of exposure, using the checklists which accompany Chapter 9.

C. Identify key computer applications; if practical, perform transaction reviews. Each significant type of transaction identified at the time the understanding is obtained should be considered as a candidate for a walk-through test. There is also a software technique, called *tracing*, that generates computer-printed output; the reports can be used to determine which instructions have been executed by the computer program in relation to the transaction, as well as the sequence in which they were executed.

D. Identify key controls and supervisory controls, covering both internal accounting and operating functions. Such identification is especially important with respect to the focal areas of exposure—physical control, computer access, and management representations. (The terms *key controls* and *supervisory controls* are defined in Chapter 6.)

IV. Assess control risk.

A. Perform analytical procedures to identify matters for further investigation. To the extent practical, such procedures should incorporate operational information developed outside the financial system.

    B. Consider the cost/benefit implications of the audit strategy decision, including a comparison of the cost of unrestricted substantive tests to the aggregate of restricted substantive tests and tests of controls.

Author's Comment

Unrestricted substantive tests become dual purpose—they validate individual transactions and account balances, and establish that controls are in place and functioning as planned. The auditor must be satisfied that the dual-purpose tests have confirmed that key and supervisory controls are in effect, especially in high-risk areas.

    C. Assess control risk; decide on approach. When control risk is assessed at the maximum (i.e., when there is no reliance on controls), the conclusion must be documented, but not the basis for that conclusion. When control risk is considered to be below the maximum, the precise level does not need to be documented, but the basis for the conclusion should be. (An example of documentation of an assessment at the maximum appears in Chapter 9.)

Author's Comment

In the majority of cases, given an automated system, and computer-assisted auditing techniques, it is likely that an auditor will choose not to rely on internal control.

 V. Plan audit tests.
    A. Establish program for tests of controls based on the specific need for these tests:
       1. Identify any controls not tested, or not tested adequately in dual purpose tests.
       2. Identify any tests of controls mandated by agreement with the client, or by requirements for determining compliance with laws.
       3. Consider whether to test controls in focal areas of risk; select controls for test, based on evaluating the

significance of the threats these controls have been designed to address.

4. Develop control test programs as needed. (See chapter 9.)

B. Program substantive tests.

Author's Comment

Assuming that the client has a computerized system, that controls in focal areas are in effect and functioning as planned, and that the understanding of the system has been confirmed via walk-through tests, some reliance may be placed in the clerical accuracy of computerized processing. However, particular attention must be given to verifying and evaluating management's representations; the auditor's task will be made easier if she utilizes operational controls and makes reference to the on-line data bases.

1. Develop specific audit objectives based on general audit objectives and analyses of inherent and control risk.

2. Select appropriate procedures with due regard to their nature and character:

   a. Refer to computerized banks of audit procedures.

   b. Identify available documentation.

   c. Select procedures based on audit efficiency and effectiveness, the characteristics of the procedures themselves, and the skills of the audit team. Consider information available both internally and externally; draw heavily on operational data.

VI. Convey internal control deficiencies to the client, together with other reportable events.

VII. Complete the audit.

A. Carry out the audit program, typically by using general-purpose computer audit software.

B. Conduct quality control contemporaneously with the work being done.

      C. Relay significant deficiencies to the client for corrective action as soon as practicable.

      D. Automate clerical activities relating to the consolidation and to the preparation of financial statements.

VIII. Conduct a search for errors.

      A. Identify manifestations of possible control breakdowns or exposures to loss.

      B. Evaluate available discovery/search techniques and select an appropriate approach.

      C. Implement search.

      D. Reevaluate the audit program and make any necessary changes to be applied in this and future audits.

      E. Carry out final analytical procedures.

  IX. Issue the audit report.

SUMMARY

The chapter discussed shortcomings in audit efficiency and effectiveness by highlighting the need to consider the skills of the audit team, the availability of documentation, and the risk of error and misrepresentation in applying audit procedures. Attention was called to pitfalls in the translation of management assertions to audit objectives and of audit objectives to audit procedures. The major perils were described as management fraud, management overrides, and ill-informed or misleading management assertions/representations. Three areas were singled out as focal points of risk: physical control, computer access, and management representations. Uncontrolled threats in these focal areas should give rise to reappraisal of the nature, timing, and extent of audit procedures.

    The recommended approach is substantive test oriented. Internal control was extolled as an indicator of the tone at the top but not as a means toward reducing substantive tests. The need was emphasized for an enriched understanding of the client's business, and especially of inherent risk, thoughtful application of all procedures, both computerized and manual, and use of operational information to achieve financial audit objectives.

This chapter has set the stage for describing the new technology, and the technology-driven tools that have become available to the auditor. In the remainder of the book, selected tools will be linked to the updated audit model.

PART 2

THE ADVENT OF TECHNOLOGY

CHAPTER 5

TECHNOLOGICAL CHANGE AND ITS IMPLICATIONS FOR AUDITING

The supreme goal of all theory, is to make the irreducible basic elements as simple and as few as possible without having to surrender the adequate representation of a single datum of experience.

Albert Einstein*

USER PERSPECTIVE: Items of Special Interest

EXECUTIVE HIGHLIGHTS: All readers
THE WINDS OF CHANGE: External auditors, internal auditors
TECHNOLOGICAL BREAKTHROUGHS: All readers
SOFTWARE: THE STATE OF THE ART: All readers
THE DARK SIDE OF TECHNOLOGY: Financial executives, audit committee members, external auditors, internal auditors
PUBLIC DATA BASES: External auditors, internal auditors
SUMMARY: All readers

EXECUTIVE HIGHLIGHTS

Technology has been the wellspring of change in office and factory systems. Auditors must now come to terms with technology. For over a generation, EDP auditing has tended to be a peripheral

---

*As quoted in the *Fraud Examiners Manual* (Austin: National Association of Certified Fraud Examiners, 1988), p. IV-19.

activity. With the exception of pioneers, auditors preferred to work around the computer, applying manual procedures to historic information. This approach began to change along with the clients' systems. The rate of change quickened when auditors figuratively embraced the personal computer.

Personal computers and their functioning were made possible by technological developments affecting the microchip, digitization, telecommunications, and data storage. These technological trends are expected to continue. Much of the additional processing power becoming available will be used to provide better interfaces between people and machines.

Microchips are steadily increasing in speed and capacity. Digitization represents the conversion of a signal into numerical form; it offers an opportunity to apply data processing techniques to varied applications. Networking technologies will allow most nonspecialized computers to be linked. New storage devices will enable auditors to work on client records at leisure, thereby avoiding downloading problems or the risk of contaminating mainframe files.

Software developments are likely to be particularly significant with respect to relational data bases, imaging, executive information systems, expert systems, and electronic data interchange. With imaging, forms, notes, legal documents, and photographs are scanned and stored on optical disks, indexed, and converted into standard characters. Executive information systems may be of particular value to audit committees and internal auditors.

Close attention to internal control fundamentals will be needed to overcome the negative aspects of the new technology. The list of technology-based tools is headed by the on-line data bases, which can be immensely valuable in assessing client inherent risk.

THE WINDS OF CHANGE

The first section of this book described the climate within which auditors are currently practicing. A redefined and updated audit model was presented as a partial answer to the challenges of audit effectiveness and efficiency. The model suggested increased use of the technology described in the second section of the book; the present chapter outlines technological advances in general terms.

Technology has driven change. Rudyard Kipling is said to have appreciated his five serving men "tried and true" whose names were what, when, how, why, and who. The concept of *what* is subject to audit is gradually coming to embrace all information that can be expressed in numerical terms, and is subject to control and verification; operational and financial data are blending into joint features of audit interest. *When* suggests that audits are increasingly performed either contemporaneously with or preliminary to the events subject to review. The *how* of auditing has been progressively automated; in no other area are greater opportunities available for enhancing the rigor of the audit examination. *Why* translates into greater responsiveness to information demands by the auditor's varied constituencies. *Who* refers to the people who do the auditing—increasingly task forces on which a variety of functional and industry specialists are represented—and to the recipients of audit reports, including new parties at interest, as well as the ubiquitous professional and governmental regulators.

It is time for auditors to come to terms with technology. For over a generation, EDP auditing has tended to be a largely peripheral activity. This began to change along with the clients' systems. The rate of change quickened when auditors figuratively embraced the personal computer. Three attributes of the personal computer may have speeded auditor acceptance: (1) speed of setup and processing; (2) ability to dispense with cost/ benefit analyses that formerly might have been required on mainframes (mainframe applications may be watered down or compromised for economic reasons); and (3) avoidance of the risk of an application being tampered with in a mainframe environment. The third attribute was probably especially important. When software, data, and results are under the auditor's direct control at all times, a secure environment can be provided.[1]

---

[1]Grant Brodie, "Information Technology," *CA Magazine*, April 1990, p. 33.

Personal computers and their functioning were facilitated by technological developments relating to the microchip, digitization, telecommunications, and data storage. These milestone developments will be considered next, followed by a discussion of software that may be encountered by auditors, and warnings as to the side effects that can accompany computerization. Finally, the chapter introduces the on-line data bases which typify the information age.

It is important to bear in mind that the technological trends discussed here are expected to continue. In the words of one commentator: "Things get a little better every month—no major breakthroughs, no stunning things—every month 1.2 times as much storage as the last month. . . . But, if you stand back . . . that's a big difference."[2]

The purpose of the presentation is twofold: first, to update auditors with respect to past and continuing trends in technology, in order to enable them to recognize risks of errors and irregularities; second, to invite them to adapt technology to the enhancement of audit effectiveness and efficiency.

TECHNOLOGICAL BREAKTHROUGHS

The Microchip

The distinction between sizes of computers will soon be eliminated due to dramatic improvements in chip capacity and speed; the standard chip will have either 32- or 64-bit pathways. Therefore, one word will be addressed and will travel in segments that are four to eight times larger than the eight-bit chip that IBM used in its original personal computer. Random access memories will easily exceed 1 billion words of storage.[3]

The significance to users, including auditors, of advances in chip technology may be gleaned from the following: with a 16-bit

---

[2]Jim Blinn, as quoted in a group discussion, "The Byte Summit: Anticipated Advances," *Byte*, September 1990, p. 256.

[3]Michael H. Francisco, "Riding the Dynamic Surge: Where Is Advanced Computer Technology Taking Us?" *Price Waterhouse Review* 30, no. 3 (1986), p. 30.

word, a user can handle only about 64,000 memory addresses at any one time; with 32-bit words, the number of possible addresses goes to more than 4 billion, removing constraints on programs, operating systems, and interfaces. Therefore, only minor architectural differences separate the data processing capabilities of top-of-the-line micros from mainframe computers. The most powerful of today's microprocessors perform like full-sized computers, offering a capability of 1 million instructions per second from a chip no bigger than a fingernail.[4]

The same chips will be installed in larger machines to operate as multiple processors. Thousands of chips may function simultaneously, using the sequential processing methodology of today's chips; this will result in another geometric increase in the number of processing instructions that can be handled per second. Moreover, in the future, further increases in speeds will occur, because true parallel processing will succeed sequential processing.[5]

Escalating computer speed and capacity challenge programmers to develop ever more powerful machine instructions; increasingly complex commands to the machine will be invoked with a few simple words. To benefit from information created for different purposes under different conditions, users will need convenient interfaces to the systems that provide the data. The interfaces should be flexible enough to accept information in the format in which the data source makes it available, and powerful enough to convey it to the user in an understandable fashion. Therefore, Arno Penzias believes that much of the additional processing power now becoming available will be used to provide better interfaces between people and machines.[6]

Digitization

Digitization represents the conversion of a signal into numerical form; it offers the opportunity to apply data processing techniques to varied applications. In this way, voice, sound, data, and

---

[4]Arno Penzias, *Ideas and Information* (New York: Simon & Schuster, 1989), pp. 120–21.
[5]Francisco, "Riding the Dynamic Surge," p. 27.
[6]Penzias, *Ideas and Information*, pp. 127–37.

image can be recognized, processed, and transmitted by computerized technologies. The equipment will be able to send and receive live conversations, along with video, music, and copies of memoranda from a computer file.[7] A system based on digitized images can accommodate virtually any paper document, regardless of its format; such a system offers the advantages of electronic storage by storing an exact image of the original document. The capability requires high-resolution displays and printers (to provide acceptably legible images), and high-speed data links to the storage facility.[8]

Item

The problems of controlling pictures and the information retrieved from those pictures was described some years ago in an audit report pertaining to a library of more than 1 million blueprints required to manufacture a complex consumer product. The procedures requiring timely return of issued blueprints had not been observed. More significantly, the system for authorizing, controlling, and numbering changes to the prints had collapsed. Obsolete parts were produced. The auditor's recommendations concerned control and referencing of engineering changes, disposal of obsolete blueprints, and safeguards to assure that only the latest authorized documents were issued.

Item

The transmission of virtually any kind of document can pose control problems for auditors and other users. Several years ago, the internal auditors of a European auto manufacturer sought to confirm open foreign exchange transactions. A request for confirmation was telexed to a Hungarian bank; a correct response by the Hungarians would have uncovered the existence of a large number of unauthorized transactions that had resulted in significant losses. The telex bore the name of a ranking executive. However, unknown persons successfully dispatched a follow-up telex, similarly subscribed, telling the Hungarians to disregard the earlier request.

---

[7]Francisco, "Riding the Dynamic Surge," p. 31.

[8]Penzias, *Ideas and Information*, pp. 60–61.

Telecommunications

There has been a dramatic advance in the technology underlying telecommunications. Slower speeds associated with microwave and satellite transmissions are being replaced by the ultra-high speeds of fiber optic lines using pulses of light to convey information. In addition, traditional analog transmission—suited to voice communication—is being replaced with digital transmission, the form in which information is stored in computers. When information (voice, data, or image) is in digital form it can be consolidated to reduce transmission costs. Moreover, there is an avoidance of errors that may occur during analog/digital translation.

Michael Francisco has predicted that before the end of the decade networking technologies will allow most nonspecialized computers to be linked via satellites, fiber optics, and coaxial cable. Transmission speeds will approximate 5 billion bits per second, a more than 400,000-fold increase over the speed common today. Regardless of its location, a computer will have all the capacity and speed any user might possibly require.[9]

Penzias cautions that an endeavor to connect everybody to everyone else is unnecessary and uneconomical; he favors the creation of local networks that are in turn networked together. Individual information needs would be met by participation within common interest groups linked by their own formal or informal networks. Multitasking terminals would serve an appropriately different role in each of a number of networks at the same time—with an interface to each network through a window on the terminal's display.[10] An auditor's imagination can conjure up the specter of a universal network, protected by controls which are only as strong as their weakest link.

Data Storage

Information can be etched on an optical disk and read by a laser. Optical media have major advantages over their magnetic pro-

---

[9]Francisco, "Riding the Dynamic Surge," p. 30.

[10]Penzias, *Ideas and Information*, pp. 208–9.

genitors. They can store vastly greater amounts of information in the same space and are very durable. The storage potential enables auditors to work on client records at leisure, thereby reducing the risk of contaminating data on the mainframe. Also, some disk searches may be coordinated with current information contained in the public on-line data bases. In this way, the auditor can be provided with the very latest information.

Optical disks are appropriate for storing documents and other images which cannot be encoded in numeric or alphabetic form; such documents require far greater storage space than those which can be encoded. Optical media also bestow what may be a temporary blessing on auditors: present-day optical media are mostly "write once, read many times" media. A new industry has been created which converts data to optical disks, creates the appropriate indexes to retrieve data, and enables processing against software, including audit-oriented packages.[11]

Despite limitations due to reduced retrieval speeds and higher error rates, optical technology holds great promise for the future.[12] Magnetic media, together with the attendant risk of losing information due to deterioration, are likely to be soon forgotten.

SOFTWARE: THE STATE OF THE ART

The movement to develop systems that share common data began with the advent of data base management systems; data has become the medium through which integration is achieved.[13] Yet, while hardware has been improving continuously, software development has been lagging. The software-related issues discussed in this chapter have been selected because they are be-

---

[11]The author visited one company in this field, Teletrak Advanced Technology Systems, Inc. Teletrak serves a broad customer base through a series of branches. Further information may be obtained by writing to the company at One Park Place, 621 NW 53 St., Suite 390, Boca Raton, FL 33487.

[12]Arthur Andersen & Company, *Trends in Information Technology: 1986* (Chicago: 1986), pp. 21–22.

[13]Ibid., p. 45.

lieved to be of interest to the readers of this book, and likely to be encountered by them: relational data bases, imaging, executive information systems, expert systems, and electronic data interchange.

Relational Data Bases

Relational data base management systems (DBMS) are gaining in popularity. Although relational data bases tend to use more machine resources than their predecessors, they are making inroads in higher volume transaction processing, which has been long dominated by hierarchical and network data base management systems.[14]

Mark Gillenson defines a DBMS as the "consummate middleman"; as such it represents the only means of accessing its "merchandise," that is, the data in the files. It passes data in both directions across its interface and allows data to be read from its files, and new data to be inserted or existing data to be modified.[15] No fact about the real world environment appears more than once in a DBMS. In order to provide integration of different files, it is necessary to repeat the identifying field of one file in the other; the power of data integration stems from the speed of execution of procedures which involve fields in more than one file.[16]

Relational products have proved robust for most conventional information systems applications which are likely to be involved in the maintenance of accounts and in the preparation of financial statements. However, relational products may not be as well suited for new and future needs; applications in search of a better data base are said to include computer-aided design, engineering, manufacturing, and software engineering, as well as knowledge-based systems and multimedia systems.[17] For the present, DBMS

---

[14]Ibid., pp. 31–32.

[15]Mark L. Gillenson, *Data Base: Step-by-Step*, 2nd ed. (New York: John Wiley & Sons, 1990), p. 86.

[16]Ibid., p. 87.

[17]Won Kim, "A New Database for New Times," *Datamation*, January 15, 1990, pp. 35–36.

will continue to control input to the files, changes in the files, and drawing of information from the files. The linking of various files may represent the major function of such a system.[18]

Any DBMS must be able to store data in a nonredundant way, handle multiple associations among data, integrate data, and provide direct, as well as sequential, data access. In addition to a report-generation capability, a DBMS usually includes a data description language, a data manipulation language, and a data query language. A *data description language* defines the physical characteristics of the data, such as alphabetic or numeric, and describes the relationships between data elements and between data elements and applications programs. The term *data manipulation language* refers to the mechanisms used to access and modify data. A *data query language* permits access to the data base without requiring the writing of a specific program; such a language has many uses, including inquiry by an auditor.[19] One query language, known as Structured Query Language (SQL), has been gaining in popularity; SQL is used in numerous data bases, including Ashton-Tate's popular DB IV. A data dictionary may also be of interest to auditors. This set of files is used by data processing personnel to manage their affairs. The typical dictionary lists objects or events of which track is kept, together with their names, attributes, and relationships, including security.[20]

At the time of this writing, the vendors of the popular data bases and the creators of the query languages have not entirely discovered auditors and their data extraction problems. When this situation changes—and it can be expected to change in the near future—auditors are likely to acquire another important audit tool.

Imaging Software

Recent advances in office machine technology have greatly increased the utility of digitized images. With imaging, forms, notes,

---

[18]Donald A. Watney and Peter B. B. Turney, *Auditing EDP Systems*, 2nd ed. (Englewood Cliffs, N.J., Prentice-Hall, 1990), p. 11.

[19]Ibid., p. 60.

[20]Gillenson, *Data Base*, p. 315.

legal documents, and photographs are scanned and stored on optical disks, indexed, and converted into standard characters. The indexed documents can then be retrieved by key words of fields, much like the information in a data base. By automating data that must be constantly retrieved, such as invoices, experts say that companies can increase worker productivity as much as 30 percent.[21] Such systems are especially useful in paper-intensive industries such as insurance, banking, and government.

During the next decade, America's payment systems will undergo major changes propelled by digitized image processing technology. For example, banks conventionally retrieve photocopies and microfiche to handle internal and external requests. Imaging will allow searchers equipped with sophisticated indexing techniques to stay at their workstations. Bank customers may soon be put in a position to choose between a more expensive option of receiving canceled checks and the less expensive option of receiving image copies of the checks with their statements.[22]

Author's Comment

Northern Trust Corp. handles nearly 30 million checks a year. Northern Trust has decided that it will be the first bank to implement a new generation of image-based systems for processing checks. In the next five years, Northern Trust hopes to save $50 million in operating costs.[23]

Executive Information Systems

An executive information system (EIS) has been defined as a computer-based means by which information can be created, packaged, and delivered for use on demand by high-level, nontechnical executives. EISs may incorporate features such as

---

[21]Barbara Cole, "Imaging: The End of Paper Pushing," *Accounting Today*, July 23, 1990, p. 27.

[22]"The Payment System Gets a New Image," *ABA Banking Journal*, March 1990, Computers & Operations, p. 84.

[23]Richard Layne, "Technology News: Advanced Imaging System Gets Test at Northern Trust," *American Banker*, April 24, 1990, p. 3.

trend analysis and exception and variance reporting; the system may also have a "drill down" facility that opens up automatic pathways from summary results to deeper, more detailed levels of data to reveal what could account for an anomaly.[24] With an EIS, control over the content and distribution of data may move upward in an organization. Moreover, internal auditors may truly function as the eyes and ears of management: they may participate in specifying the approach to be taken to the EIS, in seeing that data entered into the system is secure, and in reviewing results as a basis to possible audit action.

An EIS may be designed using one of two basic approaches; each approach has different internal control connotations. First, executives may be given direct access to actual records; second, data may be processed through a clearinghouse with only processed (and potentially sanitized) information available to executives. A recent article said:

> The question is whether the EIS will tap directly into the operational data bases of the enterprise, or whether it will access only its own special data base that is fed by the operational system. . . . Executives like the idea of [getting to see] raw data . . . [but] the raw data may not be organized for the most efficient retrieval . . . . Even more important, the people responsible for the data will feel exposed . . . . It follows that if an EIS is based on its own repository data base, care should be taken to protect the quality and accuracy of information and its currency, and . . . to divulge the data provider's identity.[25]

Uniform equipment and common data handling systems are prerequisites to implementation of an EIS. Further, the system and its software must be flexible enough to accommodate constant changes in user demands. The decision as to what data is needed and how it will be accessed is crucial; a rule of thumb is to include the same amount of information that executives receive through written communications and add at least one new ele-

---

[24]David Harvey, "Making Sense of the Data Deluge," *Director* 42, no. 10 (April 1989), pp. 139–40.

[25]David Armstrong, "The People Factor in EIS Success," *Datamation*, April 1, 1990, p. 75.

ment of strategic information. Further, users should actively participate in development efforts to encourage their sense of information ownership.[26]

Adaptations of EIS to meet the oversight needs of corporate directors are likely to be accelerated as a result of implementation of the Report of the National Commission on Fraudulent Financial Reporting (the Treadway Report). For example, an EIS could provide access to reports on tests of internal controls; it could also provide status information on matters such as the activities of the internal audit department, including the resolution of audit findings.

Expert Systems

So far, expert systems have been rarely encountered either in the client's office or in the auditor's tool bag, possibly due to limited or uncertain payback. The AICPA has listed some important purposes of expert systems including: education or training, assistance in quality control, improvement of personnel productivity, and handling of complex decisions. Applications can also be helpful with respect to diagnoses (interpreting symptoms to identify a situation), search problems (choosing from among many or complex alternatives), and problem solving and planning. Yet, a recent study revealed that only 2 out of 28 smaller accounting firms had even begun to develop their own systems using expert system shells.[27]

Intelligent knowledge-based systems have not yet arrived. Program development is likely to take place step by step and within the framework of a firm's audit approach. One would hope that a modest and realistic approach will not foreclose smaller firms' participation; indeed, a call for further study by firms of varying sizes seems appropriate.

---

[26]Craig Barrow, quoted in "Manager's Journal," *Computerworld*, May 28, 1990, p. 72.

[27]Anthony T. Barbera, "Personal Computer and Expert Systems Usage by Small and Medium-Sized CPA Firms," *Working Paper* (Research Opportunities in Auditing Distribution Service, Peat-Marwick Foundation, July 1988). Quoted with permission.

When this chapter was written, the time had not arrived for all but a very few audit applications of artificial intelligence.

> The focus of [the current fourth] generation of computers was primarily on increasing speed and storage capacity. . . . The fifth generation of computers is likely to provide the biggest challenge to EDP auditors of all computer generations. The fifth generation will be characterized by artificial intelligence. A system that is constantly learning and modifying itself, perhaps going through several iterations during just one auditing period, creates problems that are mind-boggling.[28]

Electronic Data Interchange (EDI)

EDI is the electronic transmission of standard business documents in machine-readable format between corporate trading partners' computers. Most EDI transactions are formatted to follow predetermined standards; the American National Standards Institute (ANSI) has prescribed how segments of documents should be structured. EDI requires standardization at the user level of data formats for input and output and standard data formats that cross industry boundaries. Standardization involves a substantial cooperative undertaking. Representatives of more than 300 companies attend periodic meetings to participate in transaction set development and maintenance.[29] There are indications that industry's needs for additional standards have escalated, putting the standard setters under severe time pressure.

"EDI has been implemented by more than 10,000 organizations to date. . . . Data transmission messages contain collections of data which traditionally were recorded in generally accepted business documents, such as purchase orders, trade and freight invoices, and bills of lading."[30] Interestingly, financial uses have lagged in EDI applications. Currently, only a relatively small

---

[28]Watney and Turney, *Auditing EDP Systems*, p. 7.

[29]Robert A. Payne, "EDI Implementation: A Case Study," *Journal of Systems Management*, March 1989, pp. 15–20.

[30]Clifford R. Buys, "EDI and Productivity in Manufacturing," *P&IM Review with APICS News*, January 1990, p. 34.

number of Fortune 500 companies is said to use EDI to transmit payments and remittances; this reluctance may have resulted from corporate treasurers' concerns with reliability and cost efficiency. Treasurers appear to require assurance that using EDI for payment transfers will not compromise security, audit trails, and established accounting procedures.[31] If the reluctance of the larger firms' treasurers is rooted in facts, a hazard may exist that smaller concerns will not be sufficiently alert to dangerous control deficiencies. Hence, auditors must be aware of the treasurers' concerns, and serve as resource personnel in this area. In other words, client managements must rely on their auditors to gain some comfort that transactions will be authorized, entered, and posted completely, correctly, and in a timely manner.

Activation of EDI requires selection of a network, choice of the appropriate software, and—most importantly—effective coordination of trading partners. EDI partners can establish direct connections among themselves, or the partners may operate through a third-party network. Each arrangement has differing internal control implications.[32] The network may have to sell trading partners on the concept, arrange for the requisite partnership agreements, make software available, provide customer service and installation assistance, and see to training and documentation; these responsibilities may also be assigned to an EDI coordinator at the hub company. Software functions include translations from an in-house system to national standard format, status reporting, and audit trails.[33]

Arrangements for EDI should clearly recognize the rights and obligations of the parties. Agreements for data exchange should cover access control and authorization, data encryption, auditing, and reporting. Each agreement should also define the types of documents involved, together with the general conditions of the agreement. The American Bar Association has created special

---

[31]Wayne Eckerson, "Financial EDI Slow to Take Root in User Community," *Network World*, November 5, 1990, p. 29.

[32]Michael A. Murphy and Xenia Ley Parker, *Handbook of EDP Auditing*, 2nd ed. (Boston: Warren, Gorham & Lamont, 1989), pp. 7-42 to 7-43.

[33]Payne, "EDI Implementation," pp. 15–20.

guidelines, published as the "Model Electronic Data Interchange Trading Partner Agreement and Commentary."[34] The legal ramifications bearing on EDI are so significant that a recent book has been devoted to the subject.[35]

The objective is to create an effectively functioning and synergistic whole out of the parties' separate systems. Auditors play a vital role. In order to make a meaningful assessment of aggregate risk and vulnerability, the auditors of the parties may have to exchange special opinions, management letter observations, and, possibly, working papers (including systems descriptions). (It is possible that professional guidance will emerge in this area.)

From a purely clerical perspective, EDI eliminates the repetitive transcriptions of data from computers to paper and the repetitive keyboard reentry of data to produce documents for interorganizational data exchange. However, EDI may also contribute to operating efficiency. For example, just-in-time manufacturing (JIT) can shift costs of storing and handling materials and product components to suppliers; EDI links the computer systems of manufacturers (which contain production schedules and requirements vital to suppliers) with the computer systems of suppliers (which contain inventory, price, and shipping data essential to manufacturers).[36]

Author's Comment

An industrial concern may transfer inventory carrying burdens to its supplier/EDI trading partner, based on application of JIT philosophy. Questions relating to reorder points (and buying and administrative lead times considered in those reorder points) and to economic ordering quantities (and the implicit optimization of inventory carrying costs and order costs) will have been shifted to the EDI partner. However, if inventory control techniques fail to work,

---

[34]"Bringing Small Business into the EDI Loop," *Corporate EFT Report* 10, no. 6 (March 21, 1990), p. 7.

[35]Lee Foote, "Management Strategies: Book Review," *Network World*, October 2, 1989, p. 27. The book is referenced as follows: Benjamin Wright, *EDI and American Law: A Practical Guide* (Alexandria, Va.: The Electronic Data Interchange Association, 1989).

[36]Buys, "EDI and Productivity," pp. 34–35.

a company may be confronted by buildups of slow-moving inventories on the one hand, and/or by possible stockouts and disruptions
of operations on the other. Consequently, the auditor will need to
consider (1) monitoring the effectiveness of the JIT arrangement at
his client, and, less typically, (2) assessing the administrati-
ve/operational controls in place within the trading partner's system, perhaps jointly with the trading partner's auditor.

Author's Comment

A related issue seems pertinent. Traditional inventory control techniques have stressed reorder points and economic ordering quantities.
JIT makes it desirable to take a new look at these techniques; up-to-
date diagnostic tools are required to control buildups of potentially
slow-moving stocks. The management objectives which may prompt
the buildups of safety stock, standby stock, or stock acquired in anticipation of customer orders also require reassessment.

The potential audit applications of EDI are just beginning to
emerge.

Author's Comment

Under current professional rules, outside evidence must be gathered to validate the existence of accounts receivable. However,
imagine a scenario where an auditee, say an auto manufacturer,
ships automobiles to dealers via a common carrier. Delivery of an
automobile to the carrier is evidenced by a bill of lading. Dealers
remit payment directly to a depository bank. If the auditor were to
access the common carrier's data base, and then to extend shipments by billing values, he would be in a position to independently
verify debits to accounts receivable. Similarly, he could utilize the
electronic records of the depository bank to verify accounts receivable credits independently!

Auditors may even seek independent audit evidence by consulting government agencies.

Item

At the Spyglass Company (the name has been changed), a suspicion
arose that payroll padding had occurred. It was thought that the

culprits would avoid attracting attention of the Social Security Administration and the Internal Revenue Service by utilizing imaginary social security numbers. The electronic search for unlikely numbers (based on the social security numbering scheme) yielded clues for the client's EDP auditors; more important, the Social Security Administration provided a list of numbers that could not be matched to employee accounts during a specified period.

Developments in the Systems Field

The Total System

The total system, an object of hype for a generation, may be coming into its own. Arthur Andersen has noted the convergence of such different systems as data processing, office automation, end-user or personal computing, and factory automation. In order to consider this phenomenon, it is helpful to consider the nature of information technologies. George Huber has classified technologies into two groups: the first group relates to basic characteristics, such as storage capacity; the second group relates to information retrieval, that is, to organizational intelligence and decision making. Huber points out that the quality of an organizational decision is largely a consequence of the quality of the organizational intelligence and the decision making process.[37] If so, amalgamation of accounting and advanced manufacturing technology information poses a special challenge. The manufacturing information differs fundamentally from traditional accounting data, which is based on transactions. In manufacturing technologies, the focus is on the quality of the product, the time to change production runs, and the ability to improve on-time delivery. Joint data collection and control methods will have to be developed, possibly based on knowledge-based systems technology.[38] Auditors would play a special role in developing strategic plans for sys-

---

[37]George P. Huber, "A Theory of the Effects of Advanced Information Technologies on Organizational Design, Intelligence, and Decision Making," *Academy of Management Review* 15, no. 1 (January 1990), pp. 47–71.

[38]David M. Dilts and Severin R. Grabski, "Manufacturing Technologies: What They Can Offer Management Accountants," *Management Accounting* 71, no. 8 (February 1990), pp. 50–53.

tems amalgamation, in monitoring the execution of plans, in seeing to the appropriate controls, and in testing the system modules and the overall system in the design phase.

Prototyping

Auditors, and particularly internal auditors, are likely to be involved with systems while they are still in the development state. Prototyping has become firmly established as a technique for software development. Prototyping permits a program or system to be built or modeled on the basis of requirements which are progressively refined to achieve greater user satisfaction and accuracy. There is no commonly accepted definition of this growing practice; however, there *is* common emphasis on user involvement in successive iterations of a program as development proceeds. The usual intention is either to put the prototype into production after minimal enhancement, or to use the prototype as a model to be replaced by a production version.

Administrative or operational problems may be encountered in prototyping—usually reflecting the fact that basic project management techniques were not applied. Prototyping can also invite poor documentation or none at all.[39] The main areas of audit concern involve project objectives, work plans, controls, procedures, and audit trail. Other areas that require audit attention include the effectiveness of user participation, the adequacy of testing, and the extent to which test results were used to modify systems, programs, and controls.

Computer-Aided Software Engineering (CASE)

CASE promises to revolutionize information systems by automating all phases of systems development and programming. But, as in the case of prototyping, data processing managers and users must understand how the tool is managed and how CASE affects the organization. Progress is measured in terms of productivity, methodology, involvement of systems personnel, user in-

---

[39]J. M. Carey and J. D. Currey, "The Prototyping Conundrum," *Datamation*, June 1, 1989, pp. 29–33.

volvement, and type of problem solution. Timely establishment of a methodology and setting and enforcement of policies, procedures, and standards enhance prospects for success.[40] The presence of the audit function should be continuous and pervasive through all stages of systems development.

THE DARK SIDE OF TECHNOLOGY

Internal Control Issues Related to Telecommunications/EDI

The audit trail has been growing more difficult to follow; matters are likely to get worse before they get better. An article in a magazine for EDP auditors notes that

> elimination of the paper trail in an electronic data interchange [EDI] arrangement might make the purchasing, accounting, and audit departments uneasy. Gone will be such things as initials okaying a payment. However, an electronic signature could be attached to EDI transaction data. . . . An audit trail is necessary to trace any item on the financial statement back to the source documents.[41]

The following questions have been raised by a team of writers as to internal control issues in an EDI environment:

1. What are the control boundaries for the sender, processor, and receiver of electronic documents? (To effectively evaluate general controls as well as application controls, each company's auditor must determine what portions of the EDI system bear on each partner's system of internal accounting controls.)

2. Where a third-party network plays an active role in processing, storing, and transmitting documents, what

---

[40]Cary T. Hughes and Jon D. Clark, "The Stages of CASE Usage," *Datamation*, February 1, 1990, pp. 41–44.

[41]Anna Carlin, "Audit Concerns in Electronic Data Interchange," *EDPACS: The EDP Audit, Control, and Security Newsletter* 17, no. 7 (January 1990), pp. 3–5.

should be its general control environment? What reports, if any, should be made available by its auditors?

3. What are the data transmission controls that assure completeness of transmitted messages and correctness at the receiving end?

4. What controls are in place to assure that authorized users, and authorized users only, may access the data?

5. Do audit objectives require modification because of sketchy audit trails?

6. Is any restructuring of internal control necessary to reduce control gaps? (Auditors can deal with problems by obtaining a thorough understanding of hardware and software control features; auditor presence during systems development is likely to be necessary.)[42]

One academic writer has taken a highly pragmatic approach. He perceives "a problem and an opportunity." He notes that there are standards, either already adopted or still in draft form, that seek to provide authenticity, integrity, and, if needed, confidentiality of EDI and electronic fund transfer (EFT) messages. He recommends the extension of "established sound internal control and accounting practices" to the total telecommunications environment. He suggests that preferred practices include:

1. All messages to be transmitted should be checked by persons authorized to initiate messages.

2. The messages *authorized* for transmission should be compared to the messages actually *transmitted*.

3. All messages provided to the communications facility should be transmitted.

4. All messages should result in cost charges; all charges should be reviewed and approved by users.

---

[42]Arjan T. Sadhwani, Ill-Woon Kim, and John Helmerci, "EDI's Effect on Internal Controls," *EDPACS: The EDP Audit, Control, and Security Newsletter* 17, no. 1 (July 1989), p. 2.

In addition, transactions should be subject to prenumbering and sequencing, limit tests, control totals, matching to supporting documents, and review by responsible parties.[43] (Most of these control techniques are discussed elsewhere in this book.)

The Auditors' Propensity to Errors

Spreadsheets

EDP processing has made traditional clerical errors less likely, but has created opportunities for other and more invidious types of errors. For example, hazards of error afflict the ever-present spreadsheet; this form of audit documentation may be passed on to a client's senior management or may be used to contaminate mainframe data. Albert Marcella has proposed 10 steps to design more efficient and better-controlled spreadsheets:

1. Make a written plan.
2. Separate data entry cells from calculation routines.
3. Never fail to use the cell protection feature built into the program.
4. Use the form layouts and formats in current use in the organization as data entry models.
5. Use separate input forms, or utilize a section of the spreadsheet for input.
6. Strive to facilitate ease and consistency of data entry.
7. Test accuracy by manual recalculations.
8. Document each application as to author, creation date, date of last modification, definition of expected input, example of output, file name, date last used, and date of last audit.
9. Establish data retention rules.
10. Test the spreadsheet.[44]

---

[43]Horton Sorkin, "EDI Tutorial: The Basics of Electronic Security," *EDI Executive,* November 1988, pp. 4–5.

[44]Albert Marcella, Jr., "Application Reviews of End-User Spreadsheet Designs," *EDPACS: The EDP Audit, Control, and Security Newsletter* 17, no. 4 (October 1989), pp. 10–14.

The Hazards of Audit Software

William Perry, well known for his writings on auditing issues, has documented some types of errors that can be caused by an auditor's simple carelessness. He cautions auditors to recognize that whatever is entered into the software will determine output; therefore, the nature of possible errors should be anticipated. He points to the importance of controls already built into the software; these controls depend on the ingenuity of the vendor and include audits of the validity of data entered, limit checks, prompt warning messages, and menus designed to lead the auditor through processing. His four-step prescription to minimize errors follows:

1. Identify audit software risks.
2. Identify vendor-provided controls.
3. Add any additional controls that may be necessary.
4. Test the software.[45]

Viruses

A computer virus has been defined as a software code specifically designed to invade the systems of unsuspecting computer users and to perform some self-propagating act there. Hackers have gained unauthorized access to computers engaged in work related to national security and aroused widespread fears as to the safety of data and programs.

Viruses may be implanted within an organization by a dishonest or disloyal employee; they may also be contracted from outside. The illicit code may instantly reproduce itself or lodge copies of itself deep within the computer's operating system; it may then give commands to make room for a copy of itself on every data diskette or every program stored on the hard disk of the infected computer. The act may involve damage, such as data deletion, alteration, or even destruction of hardware.

A Dutch article drew parallels to control over epidemics. It suggested that "epidemiologist system managers" discourage the using or sharing of programs from unknown sources, be alert

---

[45]William E. Perry, "The Problem with Audit Software," *EDPACS: The EDP Audit, Control, and Security Newsletter* 17, no. 4 (October 1989), pp. 14–17.

to any evidence of the presence of a virus, and have a plan for isolating the infection. Several products designed to protect microcomputers from viruses have appeared; relatively little has been reported concerning experience with these products.

Companies might set out environmental rules such as:

1. Establish policies requiring great care in using electronic bulletin boards and public domain software; restrict the downloading of files and software from electronic bulletin boards.
2. Require software to be certified virus free by persons who have a degree of independence. (This could represent an emerging product line for independent public accountants.) Alternatively, software could be tested hard upon its entry on the premises.
3. Maintain tight control of master copies of programs, and periodically compare production programs to master programs.
4. Restrict direct access to disk content from terminals; turn off terminals that are not in use.
5. Where storage must be accessed from the outside, set up segments of storage space with controlled connections between the segments.
6. Consider using workstations that lack a floppy disk drive. Such stations could help to prevent infections and would be easier to control.

Auditors should be aware of viral hazards, and of the precautionary measures that can be taken: selection and isolation of certain computers for testing and evaluating new software, use of "vaccine" software programs, checking of programs on hard disks, use of virus auditing software, and keeping virus defenses current.[46] Auditors should also be able to assess the effects of a suspected virus and help localize the damage. They should also be in a position to advise relative to the reconstruction of affected records.

---

[46]Gregory L. Ameres and Victor Goldberg, "Computer Viruses," *Management Issues for Colleges and Universities* (KPMG-Peat Marwick), September 1990, p. 6.

Industrial Espionage

Technology has modernized some very old crimes. Successful defense against penetration via bugs and similar devices requires pooling the ideas of the best available security officers with the ideas of the most informed auditors. Periodic security checkups, perhaps including sweeps of offices, represent sensible precautions. Management and employee computer crimes are covered in Chapter 7.

PUBLIC DATA BASES

The On-Line Data Bases

The technology-based tools available to auditors are discussed in the next chapter. To prepare readers for this discussion, on-line data bases will be introduced at this point; these data bases can be immensely valuable in assessing inherent risk. Moreover, their usefulness seems to be a rather well-kept secret, which the author hopes to make public.

Owen Davis and Mike Edelhart have defined data bases as resources which contain "facts that people will want to use." They also noted that "[such a] collection is not static." They indicated that "a base is something you build upon, [and that] data bases by and large, are information resources designed to get started."[47] Alfred Glossbrenner, a guru of on-line data base developments, has noted that the creation of data bases starts with a vendor's desire to make a buck. "Once printed information has been digitized into a pattern of bits and stored on a platter, what could be more profitable than selling that same pattern in the form of electronic impulses over and over again? No ink. No paper. No postage."[48] The

---

[47]Owen Davis and Mike Edelhart, *Omni On-Line Data Base Directory 1985* (New York: MacMillan, 1984), p. 2.

[48]Alfred Glossbrenner, *How to Look It Up Online* (New York: St. Martin's Press, 1987), p. 24.

TABLE 5-1
Eight Major Data Base Wholesalers

BRS/SEARCH and BRS/After Dark
  BRS Information Technologies
  1200 Route 7
  Latham, NY 12110
  (800) 227-5277
  (518) 783-7251 (Collect)
  TWX: 710-44-4965
	LEXIS/NEXIS from Mead Data
	Central (MDC)
	  Mead Data Central
	  9393 Springboro Pike
	  P.O. Box 933
	  Dayton, OH 45401
	  (800) 227-4908

CompuServe
  CompuServe Information
    Service, Inc.
  5000 Arlington Center Boulevard
  Columbus, OH 43220
  (617) 457-8600
	NewsNet, Inc.
	  NewsNet, Inc.
	  945 Haverford Road
	  Bryn Mawr, PA 19010
	  (800) 345-1301
	  (215) 527-8030

DIALOG and the Knowledge Index
  DIALOG Information Services,
    Inc.
  3460 Hillview Avenue
  Palo Alto, CA 94304
  (800) 334-2564
  (415) 858-3792
  Telex: 334499 (DIALOG)
  TWX: 10-339-9221
	ORBIT Search Service
	  ORBIT Search Service
	  Pergamon ORBIT InfoLine, Inc.
	  8000 Westpark Drive
	  McLean, VA 22102
	  (800) 421-7248
	  (703) 442-0900

Dow Jones News/Retrieval Service
(DJN/R)
  Dow Jones News/Retrieval
  P.O. Box 300
  Princeton, NJ 08543-0300
  (609) 452-1511
  (800) 522-3567
	VU/TEXT
	  VU/TEXT Information Services,
	    Inc.
	  325 Chestnut Street, Suite 1300
	  Philadelphia, PA 19106
	  (800) 323-2940
	  (215) 574-4400

Source: Alfred Glossbrenner, *Personal Computer Communications,* 3rd ed. (New York: St. Martin's Press, 1990). Copyright © 1983 by Alfred Glossbrenner. Reprinted with special permission of St. Martin's Press, Inc., New York, NY. This book contains a wealth of information, including objective descriptions and evaluations, not readily available elsewhere.

addresses and phone numbers of eight large data base wholesalers are shown in Table 5–1.

On-line data bases are likely to prove of immense help to an auditor in obtaining an understanding of the client's industry, business, and people. Two academics have noted that:

the audit professional can quickly and efficiently obtain information about the current conditions of a certain industry or company when seeking to develop a potential client or to make an informed audit decision. Some data bases of a more specialized nature can identify audit reports which have been issued in unique situations or predecessor audit reports and financial statements for a company which may become a new client.[49]

Moreover, the on-line data bases will prove useful in substantiation of account balances; the full range of company-wide and account-oriented applications is covered in Chapters 8 and 9.

Most of the material in the on-line data bases is in English; this may not impose serious constraints, because of the importance of English as the language of business. The economic consolidation of the European Community in 1992 will give impetus to data base development in Europe. European Economic Community telecommunications ministers have agreed to liberalize certain types of services; value-added services such as electronic mail and banking were scheduled for liberalization as early as 1990, while private companies will be free to offer data communication services, after a transitional period, at the beginning of 1993.[50]

A Special Case: EDGAR

The Electronic Data Gathering Analysis and Retrieval System, popularly known as EDGAR, represents an outgrowth of electronic filing of annual and other reports with the Securities and Exchange Commission (SEC); the public will be able to retrieve data upon payment of a fee. Mead Data Central (MDC) will operate the EDGAR dissemination system for the SEC. The SEC will regulate the wholesale market for EDGAR, selling the service to companies such as MDC; the secondary market for EDGAR will be unregulated. MDC expects EDGAR to be available on either its NEXIS or LEXIS libraries; filings will be available no later than 8 A.M. the day after they are made. Disclosure, Inc., which has been disseminating SEC filings since 1968, already offers on-line access

---

[49]Gail B. Wright and Raymond L. Slaughter, "Are Electronic Data Bases a Viable Audit Research Tool?" *Florida CPA Today,* February 1988, p. 12.

[50]*Eurecom* 2, no. 1 (January 1990), p. 3.

to SEC documents; it will use EDGAR when the service becomes available. (The future second phase of EDGAR has been modified in terms of the sophistication of its analytical or review capabilities; it is not clear whether and on what terms second phase information will be made available to the public.)

EDGAR will make it easier for registrants to meet filing deadlines. The opposite side of that benefit is lack of time within which to correct erroneous information; there may also be some security exposure. (The latter probably could be remedied by encrypting data before it is transmitted to the SEC.) However, the greatest future benefit of EDGAR may lie in a user's ability to draw off individual account data, and to format his own financial statements. This capability is significant because the Financial Accounting Standards Board perceives that the important users of financial statements are investors and creditors; EDGAR will permit *all* users of financial statements to produce their own customized statements. For example, a potential or actual creditor who wishes to omit goodwill from a debtor's assets could readily do so; a potential investor could evaluate the benefit of historic cash flows received from particular assets; a union leader could identify and compare benefit funding practices for all companies in a particular industry.

In addition, EDGAR will facilitate intercompany comparisons of companies and implementation of analytical procedures. EDGAR will permit a focus on accuracy, completeness, and conformance with generally accepted accounting principles (GAAP) of the individual account, rather than of the financial statements as a whole. It is entirely possible that the emphasis of an engagement will shift gradually to the individual account. Moreover, future auditors may be required to attest to a system or a client data base, together with the related controls, as well as to the data processed. (A precursor of this product line can be seen in some public accountants' reports on computer software.)

SUMMARY

There appears to be a three- to five-year time lag between client adoption of hardware and software improvements, and the development of related audit tools. In the client universe, synthesis may be expected in the next few years between office automation, information systems, and the automated factory. This new and more solid technical infrastructure, accompanied by continuing advances in basic technology, will make it necessary for auditors to speed up their acceptance of change; it is also likely that new or extended professional and regulatory requirements will lend impetus to imaginative audit uses of technology.

Combinations of hardware and software, the latter embedded in client programs, are likely to be used by auditors on a proactive basis and/or as the events subject to audit are taking place. Accordingly, auditors will have to monitor emerging technological developments to be certain that they understand the new systems on an up-front basis, and that they will be in a position to achieve their audit objectives effectively and efficiently.

This chapter has identified present and continuing trends in both hardware and software; the emergence of EDI appears to hold great promise (as well as threats) for both clients and their auditors. Problems of accuracy and completeness of data transmission and of authorization to access programs and data may still not be receiving adequate attention from vendors, users, auditors, legislators, and regulators. The market for relational data bases is likely to continue its gains; auditors will use inquiry languages to develop audit evidence. Executive information systems will be improved; these systems should enable corporate managers, directors, and auditors to carry out new responsibilities—provided such systems are appropriately controlled.

On-line data bases (both public and private) have proliferated in terms of quantity and quality; these data bases have great potential as audit procedures. The public data bases are likely to achieve an apogee in popularity with full activation and user acceptance of the SEC's EDGAR data base.

CHAPTER 6

THE ARSENAL OF THE TECHNOLOGICAL AUDIT

Be not the first by whom the new are tried,
nor yet the last to lay the old aside.

Alexander Pope

USER PERSPECTIVE: Items of Special Interest

EXECUTIVE HIGHLIGHTS: All readers
INTRODUCTION: All readers
PHYSICAL PROTECTION OF ASSETS: All readers
COMPUTER ACCESS: All readers
MANAGEMENT REPRESENTATIONS: All readers
ON–LINE DATA BASES (PUBLIC AND PRIVATE): All readers
OBTAINING AN UNDERSTANDING OF THE SYSTEM:
BEHAVIORAL INTERVIEWING: External auditors, internal
auditors
DOCUMENTING THE UNDERSTANDING: Audit committee
members, external auditors, internal auditors
EVALUATING INTERNAL CONTROL: All readers
SUBSTANTIVE TESTING: All readers
SUMMARY: All readers

EXECUTIVE HIGHLIGHTS

Information technology and personal computers could enable
large organizations to match the flexibility of smaller companies,
while letting small organizations emulate the information-

130

gathering power of large organizations. Audit organizations are no exception. Indeed, significant benefits may accrue to smaller firms that combine their knowledge of clients' operations with imaginative computer auditing.

Technology should foster the effectiveness and efficiency of controls, as well as of the audit process itself. Nonetheless, the true deterrent value of controls lies not so much in their physical attributes as in an organization's control philosophy and in the extent to which awareness of controls has been inculcated in managers and subordinates. (See Figure 6–13 for an audit committee's tools for oversight.)

The issue of access to assets (and to information) can be viewed from the perspective of granting access to certain people and denying it to all others. Each asset, including information resources, should receive protection appropriate to its nature, value, and proneness to theft, wastage, or diffusion. Computer access controls are intended to prevent (rather than detect) unauthorized use of the computer.

Use of the on-line data bases holds vast promise for (1) tasks involving the financial statements as a whole and (2) procedures affecting one or more individual accounts. Hints are provided to help readers become successful users of the on-line data bases. Meaningful involvement of audit personnel at all levels, but especially of partners and managers, represents part of the price of admission.

Other electronic tools facilitate research of the professional literature, drawing of flowcharts, and design of audit programs. Audit software offers great advantages in substantive testing, because computers can process large volumes of data. Test results are more conclusive when all data contained in a file are examined, rather than just a sample.

INTRODUCTION

In the preceding chapter, assessments were made of trends in technology generally, followed by discussion of software or approaches to programming likely to be encountered on the client's premises. This chapter initially describes some of the techniques available to strengthen client internal controls, especially in the focal areas of exposure. Next, on-line data bases are considered, primarily from the perspective of the auditor's assessment of inherent risk, and secondarily as a tool for verifying management's representations. The final part of this chapter describes examples of current audit techniques in terms of the updated audit model discussed in Chapter 4.

In essence, this chapter presents technology-based devices, data bases, and software thought suitable to strengthen internal control in critical areas and to accomplish various audit objectives. The purpose is to get readers to "test the water." After they have done so, they will develop approaches tailored to their own needs. It was not the author's purpose to survey the software market, to evaluate packages, and to make recommendations; in other words, no seal of approval is bestowed on the products mentioned. There is an approbation of a limited sort: the author has used most of the products himself, or has seen them applied; the techniques work, and they are relatively easy to use. (Proprietary products created by public accounting firms may be available to outsiders only under special conditions, if at all. Hence, much of the discussion emphasizes products distributed through the AICPA.)

Information technology and personal computers have been described as enabling large organizations to match the flexibility of smaller companies, while letting small organizations emulate the information-gathering power of large organizations. Accounting firms are no exception. The author believes that technology offers tremendous opportunities to virtually every accountant and auditor who wishes to assume leadership in a period of accelerating change. She will be in a position to determine what needs doing and, in most cases, will be able to proceed.

The opportunities for professional firms have been described by Kate McKeown, who heads a small consulting firm. "We can use data bases such as DIALOG to monitor society at large, and statistical packages . . . to analyze change. We can [get] the Congressional Record on a disk . . . and we track current and potential customers on [a] Trinet . . . data base." She concludes: "A leader can only create an environment in which people are inclined to motivate themselves. . . . The best climate for motivation in the 1990s is one of purpose-driven freedom."[1]

---

[1]Kate McKeown, "Everyone Can Be a Leader; Using Computer Technology to Enhance Communication, Commitment," *PC Computing* 3, no. 1 (January 1990), p. 110.

The paragraphs which follow present relatively new control techniques in relation to the focal areas of exposure.

PHYSICAL PROTECTION OF ASSETS

Asset Protection Awareness

The deterrent value of controls lies not so much in their physical attributes, as in an organization's control philosophy and in the extent to which awareness of controls has been inculcated in managers and subordinates. Each asset should receive protection appropriate to its nature, value, and proneness to theft, wastage, or diffusion. The term *asset* includes all things owned, including such intangibles as the auditee organization's books, records, and information resources.

High-Tech Progress

Physical devices may incorporate computerized applications, thereby offering possibilities for capturing entry and exit information and for tracing an individual's movements within a facility.[2] In the recent past, progress has been made in the following areas: (1) biometric identification, (2) cryptography, and (3) electronic surveillance.

Biometric identification allows computer users to be identified by voice, fingerprint, hand geometry, palm print, retinal pattern, and signature.

Cryptography provides an additional lock to safeguard data and other EDP resources; a user's ability to get the system to translate encrypted data into usable information tends to authenticate her identity. Accordingly, encryption/decryption must be under effective control in order to provide the necessary protection. The basic security issues are similar to those encountered in the case of passwords; carelessness (such as employees taping

---

[2]Michael A. Murphy and Xenia Ley Parker, *Handbook of EDP Auditing*, 2nd ed. (Boston: Warren, Gorham, and Lamont, 1989), p. 30-13.

their passwords to their computers) is at the root of security problems. Fortunately, additional safeguards are available in distributing and managing crypto keys; for example, encryption may be employed to transmit crypto keys.[3]

Electronic surveillance may be applied to both people and objects. The challenge is to select a product that gets the job done efficiently and effectively. For example, a unit of On-site Research uses time-lapse cameras to monitor in-store traffic patterns and shopper behaviors. The system can: (1) catalog interaction between consumer and product; (2) chart the product selection process; (3) evaluate point-of-purchase displays; (4) examine traffic patterns; (5) evaluate employee training; and (6) serve as part of an employee training program.

In a different vein, it has become possible to create integrated building management systems that monitor and control life safety, intrusion, and environmental systems over a single cable, thereby simplifying wiring requirements. This capability has resulted from multiplexing, the sequential or simultaneous transmission of various pieces of information at very high speed over a common communications link.

The newer techniques supplement, rather than supplant, the older. Simple devices such as safes, vaults, door locks, guards, badges, and bullet resistant barriers continue to be important. An equally significant role continues to be played by passwords, access codes, and access cards. Kinsley F. Nyce has summarized certain basic considerations involved in physical security. His example pertains to a shipping and receiving dock. He has noted that "traffic patterns can be controlled . . . to avoid peak delivery periods." His prescription for defending the dock includes: (1) a fire plan, easily accessible extinguishers, and training; (2) compacting trash and locking monitored disposal units; (3) rotating personnel assignments; and (4) tracking contractors and transient workers.[4]

---

[3]Ibid.

[4]Kinsley F. Nyce, "Defending the Dock," *Security Management* 34, no. 7 (July 1990), pp. 47–49.

Asset Protection: Reemphasis

The issue of access to assets (and to information) can be viewed from the perspective of granting access to certain people and denying it to all others. Therefore, a security system performs three functions: (1) it processes a claim to be a certain person; (2) it assesses proof of the claimed identity; and (3) it determines the allowable actions for that individual.[5] The system checks each attempted access to the protected assets, programs, or data. Inappropriate or unauthorized attempts are prevented and reported in a computer-generated log.

Item

At Spyglass Corporation, accounts payable clerks were authorized to process payments to vendors. However, the clerks did not have the authority to assign or modify vendor codes; such codes were intrinsic to processing payments. The system stopped 17 attempts by an unknown, unauthorized person to access the vendor code file; the attempts were reported in a computer-prepared log. However, no attention was paid to these log entries for two days; finally, a college intern glanced at the log and informed corporate management. An investigation was initiated; its objective was to determine whether any penetration of the code file and consequent improper disbursement(s) had taken place. (None had.)

The Auditor as Verifier of Assets

Thievery and substitution of assets may not be detected by auditors. Also, auditors may encounter difficulties in taking, observing, or attending a physical inventory; some assets present challenges of identification, determination of ownership, confirmation of genuineness, and measurement of quantities.

---

[5]Horton Lee Sorkin, Barron Harvey, and Margaret Hicks, "Four Vital Control Areas in Complex EDP Environments," *Internal Auditing*, Fall 1988, pp. 26–28.

Item

The difficulty of measuring and valuing large coal piles, a portion of which may have sunk into the ground, has been cited as a classic example of a challenge in taking inventory. In one case, an auditor turned the problem into an opportunity via a valuable management letter recommendation. He urged that a study be made to determine whether the existing anthracite bedding coal could be replaced by a cheaper blend of coal mixed with crushed stone. The client, a large public utility, eventually adopted this method for all coal yards.

In some cases, auditors may have failed to demonstrate professional judgment while attending inventories. For example, it has been reported that auditors attempting to verify the existence of a fictitious historic restoration project were impressed by the presence at the site of individuals wearing T-shirts emblazoned with the client's name. In a case involving another firm, auditors agreed to the inclusion in the inventory of a fraudulent count card which the client reported as just having been found; if the auditors had had the slightest perception of the size of the product, and of the warehouse space necessary to store the alleged find, they would not have accepted the representation.

With respect to validation of asset existence, hand-held counting and recording equipment can enhance accuracy and productivity. In some cases, the recorded information can be uploaded to personal computers, possibly for automated computation of inventory adjustments. (The popular laptops have this capability, too.)

Forward Planning

Forward planning is especially important with respect to areas in which exposures may exist or which tend to be nontraditional in terms of audit effort. (1) The auditor must anticipate any potential identification, measurement, counting, and valuation problems, relative to significant assets. For example, inventories may require specialized measurement, sampling, evaluation, and analysis; patents may require searches of patent data bases and expert evaluations; valuation of properties may require appraisal. (2) The auditor may have to help locate, evaluate, and recruit any needed experts, and see that they are properly instructed. (3) The auditor may wish to add procedures using operational information to his audit program. He will have to select the operational data, controls, or reports he wishes to utilize, consider their value as evidence, assess whether they are appropriately controlled, consider the risk of management overrides, and draft an efficient and effective audit program.

Risk Management for Auditors

More and more auditors will be using risk management software to plan engagements; some tools along these lines are available within the larger firms. Increased use of risk management packages by auditors is foreshadowed by explosive growth in specialized types of risk analysis programs. For example, 15 packages are said to be available just to evaluate the probability and potential consequences of network failures; these products help users assess the effectiveness of their network and information system security by posing questions concerning equipment and procedures. Barton Crockett notes that currently available products offer a wide range of options. "Some, such as Rank-It (a $95 PC package sold by Jerry FitzGerald & Associates, 506 Barkentine Lane, Redwood City, CA, (415) 591-5676), provide a standard procedure to prioritize the importance of different information systems and networks and to assess how vulnerable they are to an outage."[6]

COMPUTER ACCESS

Emphasis on Prevention

Computer access controls are intended to prevent (rather than detect) unauthorized use of the computer. The preventive controls include such time-honored techniques as separation of duties, job

---

[6]Barton Crockett, "Users Contemplate Risk Analysis Tools," *Network World,* April 10, 1989, Management Strategies, p. 27.

rotation, personnel briefings, and documentation standards, along with the access controls.

One writer points out that there are three ways of restricting access to assets, computers, or data bases; these ways may be based on something you know, something you have, or something you are. Restricting access by something you know requires the use of a secret identification code or password. Second, access can be restricted by something you have, such as a key; the key may be an electronic key containing secret encrypted numbers. Third, access may be restricted by something you are, such as by one or more of your physical characteristics.[7]

Protection of Data Integrity

After computer access has been authenticated, data integrity must be protected by insuring completeness and accuracy of data input. Completeness of input is controlled by several "old standbys," including computer sequence checks of serially numbered documents, computer matching with data held on master or suspense files, agreement of manually established batch controls, and one-on-one test checking of individual documents to listings developed on the computer.

Computers have a marked ability to supplement access controls and to promote accuracy by means of programmed edit checks. Edit checks include parity checks and check digit verification. The parity bit is assigned a value of 0 or 1 to create an odd or even parity in combination with the data bits in each byte. (A bit is a binary digit; a byte is a unit of bits, known as a character.) The control system counts the number of bits in each individual byte and then checks for an odd or even value, or parity. Both horizontal and vertical parity checks can and should be used; a vertical parity check applies to a character, and a horizontal parity check to a string of characters.

A check digit represents a computed numeric value which

---

[7] Jerry FitzGerald, *Business Data Communications,* 3rd ed. (New York: John Wiley & Sons, 1990), p. 506.

bears a preestablished mathematical relationship to preceding digits, and therefore conveys some assurance that the original value has not been entered incorrectly or altered. According to Murphy and Parker, other edit checks include:

1. *Reasonableness:* test whether the contents of the data entered fall within a predetermined limit.

2. *Dependency:* test whether the contents of two or more data elements or fields on a transaction bear the correct logical relationship.

3. *Existence:* test that the data codes entered agree with valid codes held on the file or in the program.

4. *Format:* check the existence of expected numerical or alphabetic characters of a transaction.

5. *Mathematical accuracy:* check calculations.

6. *Range checks:* check to see whether a number falls within a predefined set of numbers, or range.

7. *Prior data matching:* the new data to be processed is entered together with old data which is subject to updating; validity is assured because the old data is compared to the file.

8. *Document reconciliation:* check the mathematical accuracy of the entry of numerical data; this technique represents a hash total (a total of numbers that has no significance of its own) as applied to a single transaction.[8]

MANAGEMENT REPRESENTATIONS

As pointed out in Chapter 4, when an auditor develops her program for the audit of individual accounts, she does so to substantiate management's assertions. Historically, auditors have tested management's valuation assertions and other judgments by scrutinizing (primarily client-furnished) documentary evidence. However, a better understanding of the business, particularly of operational controls, and availability of the on-line data bases, as

---

[8]Murphy and Parker, *Handbook of EDP Auditing*, pp. 14-20 to 14-25.

discussed in succeeding paragraphs, should equip the auditor to utilize independent information to make her own assessment of the representations.

ON-LINE DATA BASES (PUBLIC AND PRIVATE)

Nature, Advantages, and Utilization

Data bases represent systematic collections of information in electronic form, organized for rapid retrieval. The accountant is concerned with public or private data bases that may contain information related to actual or potential clients. Public data bases are maintained by publishing companies, academic institutions, professional associations, and government departments; they are usually made available to customers through wholesalers. Data base publishers sell two things: access to the data base for searching, plus individual items of information identified as a result of that access.

The advantages of on-line services have been persuasively cataloged as: (1) finding in minutes what would otherwise take hours or weeks; (2) finding in minutes what could be practically impossible to find in printed sources; (3) consulting up-to-the-minute sources; (4) extending the research reach worldwide; and (5) paying for what is needed, when it is needed.[9]

Computer-assisted *tax* research has developed into an important tool mostly in the larger public accounting firms. Mead Data Central's LEXIS shows heavy usage overall and in the Big Six–type firm. But, the story is different with respect to *audit* uses of the data bases. In 1988 the author reported the results of a research study intended to determine the extent of accountants' usage of on-line data bases, the reasons for nonusage, and the potential for increased use in audit applications. The study was directed specifically at south Florida practice locations of public accounting firms, internal

---

[9]Jean M. Scanlan, Ulla de Stricker, and Anne Conway Fernald, *Business Online: The Professional's Guide to Electronic Information Sources* (New York: John Wiley & Sons, 1990), pp. 29–32.

audit departments, and government agencies. In general, usage of the on-line data bases tended to be both scant, and (with one exception involving internal auditing) unimaginative. Among Big Eight public accounting firms, significant usage existed primarily at two firms; ironically, these two firms have now merged.

When the nature of the applications was examined, the results became even more disappointing. Audit applications can be slotted into one of two nondiscrete categories: (1) tasks involving the financial statements as a whole—utilization was rare; or (2) procedures affecting one or more individual accounts—utilization did not exist. The first category relates to the obtaining of an understanding of the client's industry and business to identify inherent risk. In the case of a potential new client, these procedures should help the auditor decide whether to accept the client. In the case of a recurring client, the auditor could expect to become sensitized to potential problems as a basis for further investigation. The second category should be helpful in substantive tests of account balances.

Getting Started

The use of the on-line services involves effort and cost. Meaningful involvement of audit personnel at all levels—especially of partners and managers—represents an important part of the price of admission. Furthermore, the resources of the on-line data bases cannot be viewed in a vacuum; they are closely linked to other human, published, and electronic resources available to an accounting firm or internal audit department. One highly useful resource must be mentioned at this point: the Library Services Division of the AICPA. The performance of the Division is second to none in terms of efficiency and effectiveness. An ACCOUNT-ANTS data base fact sheet, prepared by the AICPA Library Services, appears in Figure 6–1.

A recent book describes what a professional user needs to interact with an on-line service:[10]

---

[10]In writing this section, reference has been made to Scanlan et al., *Business Online,* p. 52.

FIGURE 6–1
ACCOUNTANTS Data Base Fact Sheet

On-line service	ORBIT Search Service 8000 Westpark Drive McLean, VA 22102 Tel.: (800) 456-7248 or (703) 442-0900
Producer	American Institute of Certified Public Accountants, Library Services Division; contact: Linda Pierce (212) 575-6326
Printed equivalent	*Accountants' Index*
Scope	Worldwide English-language literature of accounting, auditing, data processing, financial management, investments and securities, management, and taxation. Special businesses and industries are also included.
Years of coverage	1974 on
Frequency of update	Quarterly
File size	245,021 as of 6/91; 4,000 records each update (approximately)
Source documents	80% journal articles (338 current journal titles); 20% books, pamphlets, etc.
Unit record	Citation and assigned terms
Structure of assigned index terms	Hierarchical (controlled vocabulary)
Document availability	Members of the AICPA and special libraries may borrow items listed in the Accountants' Data Base from the AICPA Library.
ORBIT rate	$88/hour, connect time; $.47/on-line print; $.52/on-line full or tailored; $.56/off-line print; $.61/off-line full or tailored
User aids	*ORBIT User Manual for Accountants,* available from ORBIT Search Service. *Accountants' Index Master List of Subject Headings* and *AICPA Library Classification Schedule,* available from AICPA Order Department. *Journals List,* by title and subject, available from AICPA Library Services Division.

Source: Library of the American Institute of Certified Public Accountants, Inc.

1. A personal computer, or terminal.
2. A modem. (This device modulates and demodulates. *Modulation* is the conversion of digital pulses into an analog

signal; the analog mode is compatible with the various transmission media. *Demodulation* is the translation of data from analog form back to digital form.)

3. Communications software. The auditor has a choice of utilizing software provided by the data base wholesaler, or generalized communications software which requires customizing. The author has had favorable experiences with Mead Data Central's LEXIS/NEXIS Communications Software and CROSSTALK XVI. The latter is a command-driven communications program; it has the ability to build and store automatic log-on scripts, is fast, and supports three error checking protocols.[11] Of course, from time to time software houses issue new versions of popular programs; buyers should make certain that they have the version that is either the most recent or the most productive for them.

4. Access to a communications network. The user needs to know which telephone number must be dialed to reach a communications network.

5. A service subscription. Subscriptions tend to be of two types, each with a different cost effect: (1) pay as you go; and (2) use time against a deposit paid in advance. The choice is the user's and depends on the nature, number, and frequency of applications.

6. A working knowledge of the differences in conventions and annotations existing for the different data base providers. To speed learning, abbreviated usage guides have been included in this book. See Guidelines for Using DIALOG (Figure 6–2), Guidelines for Using NEXIS (Figure 6–3), Guidelines for Using ORBIT (Figure 6–4), DIALOG List of Data Bases of Interest (Figure 6–5), LEXIS/NEXIS List of Data Bases of Interest (Figure 6–6),[12]

---

[11]FitzGerald, *Business Data Communications,* p. 369.

[12]The LEXIS service consists of general and specialized legal libraries. The general libraries include GENFED, the general federal library; specialized libraries include FEDSEC, the federal securities library. Both libraries feature combined files which afford thorough coverage to accounting and auditing practitioners.

FIGURE 6–2
Guidelines for Using DIALOG

Terminal: CONNECT

Accountant: Return (twice)

Terminal: TERMINAL =

Accountant: ct12

Terminal: @

Accountant: 41548

Terminal: 415 48 CONNECTED (Note: User identification and password not shown)

Note: It is assumed that the terminal is operating in recording mode, that is with "capture on." On CROSSTALK this may be accomplished by accessing the communications program, and giving the command CA ON. Similarly, after the terminal is off-line, the CA OFF command should be followed by saving of the file, and by exit from the communications program.

BASIC COMMANDS (In most cases, the contents show the command, its abbreviations, and an explanation.)

BEGIN   B   Connect to database

SELECT STEPS   SS   Create set(s) of records containing the search term(s) specified by the auditor; this command assigns individual set numbers to each search term, each proximity operator, and to final results. The numbered sets are easier to work with, especially when users are relatively inexperienced.

PROXIMITY OPERATORS

(W)   The WITH operator (W) specifies that two terms must occur next to each other and in the order specified. A number placed in front of the W allows up to the specified number of words to occur between the search terms.

(nW)   Terms within *n* words of each other in the order specified.

(N)   The NEAR operator (N) specifies that the two terms must occur next to each other, but in any order. A number placed in front of the N allows up to the specified number of words to occur between the search terms.

(nN)   Terms within *n* words of each other in any order.

OR   The OR operator is used for alternative expressions.

AND   The AND operator requires words to exist somewhere in the same document. Typically, it is used to join ideas.

ORDER IN WHICH INSTRUCTIONS ARE EXECUTED

The sequence is: Not, and, or; terms within parentheses are always executed first.

(continued)

FIGURE 6–2 *(concluded)*

TRUNCATION

? Denotes an undefined number of characters following the stem.

? Any embedded character where the question mark has been entered.

SEARCH TIPS

Suffix codes are used to restrict retrieval to specified basic index fields of a record. For example, the search statement "SS Audit? and efficien?/TI" means that the search terms must appear in the title.

Prefix codes are used to search additional indexes available within a data base. For example, the search statement "SS Audit? and efficien? and PY = 1986" means that the search is to cover only publications in 1986.

KWIC	K	Display only those portions of selected records which include the search term. K permits a judgment to be made of the relevance of search results. K may be used as part of a command which includes a print format, such as in "T S3/5,K/all," or it may be used as in "T S3/K/all."
TYPE	T	Type search results at the terminal. The command format is usually expressed as "T S3/5/S3," wherein the number following the first slash indicates the format, and the number following the second slash identifies the documents to be typed.
SORT		Rearrange the records in your final search results by specific fields. Search results are sorted alphabetically or numerically depending on the nature of the field. Sorts are usually in ascending order, unless a descending order is required; in such cases the letter D (,d) follows the sort statement.
SAVE TEMP		Store strategy for seven days. A retrieval number will be assigned to the search strategy, to be used in subsequent execution.
EXECUTE STEPS		Run search/save that has been stored on-line.
LOGOFF		End search session and disconnect terminal from DIALOG.

Description of NEXIS Files (Figure 6–7), ORBIT and BRS List of Data Bases of Interest (Figure 6–8), and Important Data Bases and Where They Can Be Found (Figure 6–9).

Four different wholesalers of data bases will be mentioned. The data bases distributed by them are likely to be of interest to accountants.[13]

- *Mead Data Central, Inc. (MDC)* is a leading electronic publisher of legal developments, general, accounting, business, and financial news, and other information, mostly in full text format. The primary services and libraries of interest to accountants include LEXIS, NEXIS, and NAARS. LEXIS provides instant access to U.S. federal and state court decisions, state statutes, and administrative agency decisions and rulings, as well as other authoritative legal material. NEXIS provides the full text of articles from more than 350 news sources, including newspapers, newsletters, magazines, and wire services, plus certain abstracts.

  NAARS is made available by agreement with the AICPA and provides annual reports and proxy statements for many U.S. public corporations, government documents, and authoritative and semi-authoritative accounting literature. Accountants and auditors may wish to refer to both current and superseded accounting literature from the Financial Accounting Standards Board (FASB), the Government Accounting Standards Board (GASB), the Securities and Exchange Commission (SEC), the AICPA, the International Accounting Standards Committee, the International Federation of Accountants, and the Cost Accounting Standards Board, among others.

  Certain other NEXIS data bases complement information in NAARS; examples of such data bases are the Code of Federal Regulations (CFR) and the Federal Register (FEDREG). The latter includes rules and regulations from federal agencies and departments keyed to the Code of Federal Regulations, amendments, interim or temporary rules, and final

---

[13]In writing this section, general reference has been made to Scanlan et al., *Business Online*, pp. 139, 141, 269, 356, 357, and 359.

FIGURE 6–3
Guidelines for Using NEXIS

Note: It is assumed that LEXIS/NEXIS Communications Software has been acquired. This software is inexpensive and easy to use. The software establishes communication, as illustrated in the paragraphs which follow.

BASIC COMMANDS (In most cases, the command will be shown, together with its abbreviation, and an explanation.)

Selection of library; directed by interactive software command. (A "service" is a collection of related libraries. A "library" is a collection of related files. A "file" is a collection of related documents.)

The selection of a file is also directed by interactive software command.

PROXIMITY OPERATORS

W/n   The WITH operator W/ specifies that two terms must occur close to each other and in any order. A number, n, placed after the W/ allows up to the specified number of words to occur between search terms.

OR   The OR operator is used for alternative expressions.

AND   The AND operator requires words to exist somewhere in the same document. It is typically used to join ideas.

ORDER IN WHICH INSTRUCTIONS ARE EXECUTED

The sequence is: Or, w/n, and. A parenthesis is not required to have "or" operate first. But, the connectors used inside parentheses have priority over connectors used outside parentheses.

TRUNCATION

!   Denotes an unspecified number of characters following the stem.

*   Denotes any character embedded where the asterisk has been entered, except the first character.

SEARCH TIPS

Searches may be restricted to specified segments of a record. For example, the search statement "Title (Audit! and efficien!)" means that the search terms must appear in the title.

SEARCHING

It is preferable to enter commands via the keyboard, using *dot* commands. (The alternative approach, which uses the numeric personal computer keypad, can be more vulnerable to transmission difficulties.)

NEXT DOCUMENT	.nd	Display next document.
PREVIOUS DOCUMENT	.pd	Display previous document.
NEXT PAGE	.np	Display previous page of a document.
PREVIOUS PAGE	.pp	Display previous page of a document.
MODIFY	.m	Modify the search. The modification must begin with a connector.

(continued)

FIGURE 6–3 *(concluded)*

CHANGE FILE	.cf	Change file.
CHANGE LIBRARY	.cl	Change library.
NEW SEARCH	.ns	Conduct new search.
SEGMENTS	.se	Obtain list of segments available for searching.
DATE		Limit requests to specific date by typing DATE followed by IS, AFT, or BEF, and by the date searched for. (Example: "Market w/2 share and Big w/1 Six and date aft December 31, 1989.")

DISPLAY FORMATS

KWIC	.kw	Display documents with search terms in the context in which they appear.

Note: The use of the KWIC format can be especially helpful when full text data bases are being searched; KWIC establishes the relevance of a particular document before displaying its full text. Conversely, KWIC tends to be only marginally useful when displaying records from abstract data bases.

FULL	.fu	Display the full text of a document.
CITE	.ci	Display a list of bibliographic references.
SIGNOFF	.so	

---

rules; it also features notices to the public of proposed rules and regulations. CFR represents a codification of general and permanent rules published in FEDREG.

- *DIALOG Information Retrieval Service.* DIALOG, a widely used on-line retrieval service, offers access to over 320 data bases that collectively cover more than 100,000 publications. DIALOG carries the full text of articles from over 500 magazines, newspapers, trade journals, and newsletters, plus data bases of abstracts and bibliographic indexes. Its "One Search" technique permits a user to search as many as 20 data bases at the same time. DIALOG also offers strong training programs.

- *ORBIT.* This wholesaler carries the Accountants' Index, which provides extensive coverage of English-language literature in accounting and related business and finan-

FIGURE 6-4
Guidelines for Using ORBIT

Terminal: CONNECT

Accountant: Return (twice)

Terminal: TELENET 305 110A

Terminal: =

Accountant: D3

Terminal: @

Accountant: C ORBIT

Terminal: ORBIT CONNECTED (Note: user identification and password not shown.)

Note: It is assumed that the terminal is operating in recording mode, that is with "capture on." On CROSSTALK this may be accomplished by accessing the communications program, and giving the command CA ON. Similarly, after the terminal is off-line, the CA OFF command should be followed by saving of the file, and by exiting the communications program.

BASIC COMMANDS (In most cases, the contents show the command, its abbreviations, and an explanation.)

FILE		To enter a data base, use the FILE command followed by the name of the data base.
SEARCH STATEMENT	SS	To select sets of records containing the search term(s) specified by the auditor. A set number is assigned to the final result.

PROXIMITY OPERATORS

(W)　　The WITH operator (W) specifies that two terms must occur next to each other and in the order specified. A number placed in front of the W allows up to the specified number of words to occur between the search terms.

(nW)　　Terms within *n* words of each other in the order specified.

(S)　　The SENTENCE (S) operator specifies that the two terms must occur in the same sentence, in any order.

OR　　The OR operator is used to combine terms or sets either of which may appear in a retrieved record.

AND　　The AND operator is used to combine terms or sets both of which appear in a retrieved record. Typically, it is used to join ideas.

ORDER IN WHICH INSTRUCTIONS ARE EXECUTED

The sequence is: and, not, or; terms within parentheses are always executed first.

TRUNCATION

:　　Denotes an undefined number of characters following the stem.

#　　Any embedded character where the symbol has been entered.

(continued)

FIGURE 6-4 *(concluded)*

SEARCH TIPS

Prefix or suffix codes are used to search one or more specified fields in a document record. For example, the search statement "Audit: and efficien:/TI" means that the search terms must appear in the title.

The Basic Index includes single words from the subject fields of the record, usually, TI, AB, or IT (Index Term). The index terms include single and multi-word terms.

A range of years from which a document selection is to be made, such as the years from 1983 to 1986, may be indicated by adding the following words to a search statement "and 83-86."

TERM LINESIZE N or TERM LS N	Change the character line length from 80.
PRINT PRT	Print five bibliographic records.
PRINT, field	Print the fields you want to search for each record in the specified order. Example: To print accession number, author and title, use "PRT AN AU TI."
PRINT SET	Print the entire set, including certain fields designated by the data base provider.
PRINT FULL SET	Print the entire set; all fields.
SAVE	Retain all search statements entered in session.
RECALL	Execute a saved search.
STOP	To exit program.

---

cial areas, including cost and managerial accounting, auditing, data processing, financial reporting, financial management, investments and securities, management, and taxation. The data base includes more than 220,000 records. Eighty percent of the file represents journal articles; the remainder, books and pamphlets. Over 300 journals are covered. Searching is simplified by the AICPA's controlled vocabulary. Because of the great importance of the Accountants' Index and its on-line version, ACCOUNTANTS, a list of journals covered has been included as Figure 6-10.

- *COMPUSERVE.* This popular service carries a number of data bases of interest to business professionals, especially

---

FIGURE 6–5
DIALOG List of Data Bases of Interest

ABI/INFORM	Investext
Business Dateline	M&A Filings
Business Software Database	Magazine ASAP
Computer ASAP	Magazine Index
Computer Data Base	Management Contents
Congressional Record Abstracts	Microcomputer Software Guide
Criminal Justice Periodical Index	Moody's Corporate News
D&B-Dun's Financial Records Plus	Newspaper Abstracts
D&B-Dun's Market Identifiers	Newswire ASAP
D&B-Million Dollar Directory	NTIS
Dialog Quotes and Trading (Quotes)	PAIS International
	PTS Prompt
Disclosure Database	SEC Online
Disclosure Spectrum Ownership	Social SciSearch
Federal Index	The Software Directory
Federal Register	Standard & Poor's Corporate Descriptions
Federal Register Abstracts	
Financial Times Company Abstracts	Standard & Poor's News
	Tax Notes Today
Financial Times Full Text	Trade & Industry ASAP
FINIS: Financial Industry Information Service	Trade & Industry Index
	Trinet Establishment Database
Infomat International Business	

---

those in the financial services industry. The offerings range from brokerage house reports to stock quotations and company financial data. The IQuest service provides a gateway to over 800 data bases available on about 15 other on-line services.

Usage Hints

The challenge in searching through data bases involves picking the right data bases and finding the needed information in the shortest period of time. As in so many other accounting and auditing endeavors, planning is of the essence; in this case, plan-

---

FIGURE 6–6
LEXIS/NEXIS List of Data Bases of Interest

The NEXIS Service

  NEXIS Library—Group files
    CURRNT—Stories dated 1987 or later from full text files
    CURABS—Abstracts dated 1987 or later from abstract files
    OMNI—All stories from all files

The NEXIS Financial Information Service
  COMPNY—Combined brokerage house reports, SEC filings, SEC abstracts
  ALLABS—Combined business abstract files
  CONEWS—Combined wire service reports

The National Automated Accounting Research System (NAARS) Service

  Accounting Information Library
    GR—Combined 1988/9, 1987/8, 1986/7, and 1985/6 files for governmental
      unit annual reports
    AR—Combined 1990/1, 1989/90, 1988/9, 1987/8,1986/7, 1985/6, and
      1984/5 files for corporate annual reports
    LIT—Authoritative and semiauthoritative accounting literature
    JNLACC—*Journal of Accountancy*

The LEXIS Service

  General Federal Library
    CFR—*Code of Federal Regulations*
    FEDREG—*Federal Register*

  Federal Securities Library
    OMNI—Combined court and SEC release files

---

ning involves identifying the specific information needed, deciding on search strategy, setting out key search terms, and formulating the search statement—before the computer is accessed. Russ Lockwood notes that "with on-line meters running at up to $250 an hour, the time you save by searching efficiently translates into significantly reduced costs. Some on-line services charge by the number of citations [pulled] from the data base as well as by the hour, so downloading the wrong information can hit the budget twice as hard." In searching, overlapping or replicating coverage can be put to use. For example, DIALOG has a feature called DIALINDEX that sorts 320 data bases by subject. The user picks the subject and enters the search terms; DIAL-

FIGURE 6-7
Description of NEXIS Files

NEXIS contains full-text sources of business information focused on international, national, regional, and local topics:
- Newspapers (PAPERS)
- Magazines (MAGS)
- Newsletters (NWLTRS)
- Wires (WIRES)

Descriptions of Individual Files

Business Dateline (BUSDTL) focuses on more than 180 regional business publications and 14 daily newspapers. In addition to local issues and stories on major firms located in the regions, the data base includes valuable information on start-ups and private companies, as well as facts about their management personnel.

Businesswire (BWIRE) contains the unedited text of news releases from over 10,000 diverse news sources. Approximately 90 percent of all releases are business/financial, covering every category of business and industry. News releases include all information on earnings, dividend announcements, mergers and acquisitions, major contract awards, new products, new security offerings, takeovers, restructurings, and more. All releases carry the name and telephone number of a contact person within the company.

PR Newswire (PRNEWS) covers over 80,000 press releases a year, most of which are issued by publicly-owned companies, including 85 percent of the *Fortune* 1,000 and most companies trading on the stock exchanges. The major focus is on business and financial news, including information on mergers and acquisitions, tender offers, earnings, dividends, contracts, and management changes. The file also includes releases from public relations firms, trade associations, labor unions, political parties, governmental agencies, and cultural and educational institutions.

NEXIS also contains a collection of abstracted information from business, general news, marketing, and financial sources. (ALLABS)

Descriptions of Individual Files

Financial Industry Information Service (FINIS) provides marketing information on organizations that comprise the financial services industry and on products and services offered to corporate and retail customers. The content coverage includes items relating to the activities of: banks, brokers, credit unions, insurance companies, investment houses, real estate firms, thrift institutions, and related government agencies.

COMPNY is the financial information library.

Summary Descriptions of Individual Files

FILING contains the full text of 10-Qs, 10-Ks, annual reports, and proxy statements for select numbers of public parent companies.

SECABS contains the abstracts of registration statements, Forms 13D, 13G, 14D-1, 14D-9, 13E-3, 13E-4, 8K, and 4S.

(continued)

FIGURE 6–7 *(concluded)*

Descriptions of Individual Files

Company/Industry Reports (COIND) provides the complete text of financial research reports from over 125 of the leading investment banking firms in the United States, Europe, Canada, and Japan. These primary research reports contain independent sales and earning forecasts, market share projections, research and development expenditures, and related data. The reports cover more than 14,000 companies in 53 industries and contain competitive analysis, market research, and financial forecasting data.

Disclosure (DISCLO) provides in-depth financial information on over 12,000 companies that have at least 500 shareholders and at least $5 million in assets. The data is derived from reports filed with the SEC by public companies, including: 10-Ks, 10-Qs, annual reports, registration statements, M/A filings, and more. The contents include full financials, including footnotes, the management discussion and president's letter to the stockholders, significant corporate events, a list of all SEC filings for the past 18 months, and ratios comparing a company with its competitors within the industry.

Trinet Company Data Base (TRICO) provides current address, sales, and market share information on U.S. single and multi-establishment companies. Covers both public and private manufacturing and non-manufacturing companies in all product areas and sections of industry. The company must employ 10 or more employees to be included in the data base.

Trinet Establishment Data Base (TRIEST), a companion to the Trinet Company Data Base, focuses on branch locations.

Standard and Poor's Register of Corporations (SPCORP) contains information on over 10,000 publicly held and 45,000 private U.S. companies, including parent companies, subsidiaries, divisions, and affiliates. A company must have either annual revenues of one million dollars or more, or retain a minimum of 50 employees. Records include current company address, financial and marketing information, and a listing of officers and directors.

Standard and Poor's Register of Directors and Executives—Biographical (SPBIO) contains biographical information on nearly 70,000 active business executives and directors of major U.S. and non U.S. corporations, both publicly and privately owned. Provided for each individual is information such as principal business affiliation with official title, principal business address, residence address, and, where obtainable, year and place of birth, college and year of graduation, and fraternal membership.

Company News (CONEWS) is a collection of wire stories which focus on timely company and financial news stories. Includes Businesswire (BWIRE) and PR Newswire (PRNEWS) from NEXIS. The coverage also includes Canadian and international news events.

Source: Most of the material in this section was taken from unpublished material presented at the Software Tools Conference—1989 held November 13–15, 1989, in Orlando, Florida. This material was prepared and presented by Susan Klopper, information specialist with the firm of Arthur Andersen in Atlanta, Georgia, and is presented with her permission.

FIGURE 6–8
ORBIT and BRS Data Bases of Interest

ORBIT
  Accountants
BRS
  ABI/Inform
  Business Dateline
  Business Software Database
  Computer Database
  Disclosure Database
  Disclosure Spectrum Ownership
  Federal Register Abstracts
  FINIS: Financial Industry Information Service
  Magazine Index
  Magazine Contents
  Micro Software Directory
  NTIS
  PAIS International
  PTS/Prompt
  PTS/F&S and PTS/Prompt merged file
  Social SciSearch
  Trade and Industry ASAP III

INDEX lists the number of "hits" in each data base included in the subject category.[14]

Consideration of People Risks

On a first-year audit it is usually helpful to gain perspective as to the backgrounds of client executives, to consider their uttered or published comments, and to search for any prior legal difficulties they, or the auditee organization, may have experienced. Legal data bases, such as MDC's LEXIS, include judgments in state and federal courts, and administrative decisions and regulatory information from federal agencies. Also, of course, data bases which cover newspapers and magazines may provide information or clues in relation to executive personnel. Sometimes the *absence* of information can be revealing.

---

[14]Russ Lockwood, "The Searchers: On-Line Heroes of the Business World," *Personal Computing* 12, no. 12 (December 1988), p. 128.

FIGURE 6–9
Important Data Bases and Where They Can Be Found

ABI/INFORM abstracts literature from business and management journals to provide information on corporate strategy, company case histories, and personnel. Trends in areas such as banking, real estate, telecommunications, and health-care industries are included. Available through BRS, DIALOG, ORBIT, and VU/TEXT; charges on DIALOG are $96 per connect hour plus 68 cents per full record, typed or displayed.*

Business Dateline contains the full text of over 100 regional business publications throughout the U.S. Available through DIALOG, Dow Jones, and VU/TEXT; charges on DIALOG are $96 per connect hour plus $4 per full record, typed or displayed.*

COMPUTER Database summarizes technical and business articles in the electronics, computers, and communications fields. Available through BRS and DIALOG; charges on DIALOG are $96 per connect hour plus 50 cents per full record, typed or displayed.*

DISCLOSURE contains detailed financials from SEC filings for over 12,000 publicly-held companies. Available through BRS, DIALOG, Dow Jones News/Retrieval, Mead Data Central-NEXIS, and VU/TEXT; charges on DIALOG are $45 per connect hour plus $7 per full record, typed or displayed.* DIALOG and Mead allow researchers to search and sort over 200 indexed fields, some of which are arithmetically searchable. These two services allow sorting by sales and other financial statement line items so that comparisons can be made on a number of companies. Using custom print formats, it is possible to extract only the necessary portions of the records.†

D&B Dun's Market Identifiers provides company facts for over 2 million U.S. and Canadian private and public companies with 10 or more employees or $1 million in sales. Available through DIALOG and direct through Dun's Marketing Services; charges on DIALOG are $100 per connect hour plus $2.50 per full record, typed or displayed.*

Investext contains the full text of investment banking, brokerage, and research reports for companies and major product areas within 52 major industries. Available direct through Business Research Corporation, BRS, DIALOG, Dow Jones News/Retrieval and NewsNet; charges on DIALOG are $96 per connect hour plus $4.50 per full record, typed or displayed.*

The financial portions and footnotes of selected annual reports to shareholders can be located in NAARS on LEXIS/NEXIS. The footnotes, of particular interest to accountants, can be searched free text or with descriptors assigned by the AICPA.†

Predicast's Marketing and Advertising Reference Service (MARS) abstracts information on the marketing and advertising of consumer goods and services. Advertising by account, agency, campaign, media, and slogan is provided in addition to target and markets. Available through BRS and DIALOG; charges on DIALOG are $150 per connect hour plus 58 cents per full record, typed or displayed.*

FIGURE 6–9 *(concluded)*

Predicast's PROMPT contains information from international, national, and regional trade and business sources that shows market share, new product announcements, company activities, and production and trends for many industries. Available through BRS, DIALOG, and VU/TEXT; charges on DIALOG are $126 per connect hour plus 63 cents per full record, typed or displayed.*

SECABS offers abstracts of M&A (merger and acquisition) filings, registration statements, significant corporate events, and insider holding amendments. The abstracts, provided by States News Service exclusively to Mead, are derived from SEC filings and other information sources. SECABS is an excellent source to pinpoint the exact date or nature of a corporate event in a particular 8-K filing.†

SECNEW is a digest of events provided by the SEC to Mead Data Central. It contains daily summaries of SEC filings and registration statements.†

SEC ONLINE provides full-text 10-K's, 10-Q's, annual reports to shareholders, and proxies for public companies. 10-K reports contain the exhibit index and selected exhibits, including the list of subsidiaries. Available on Mead Data Central—NEXIS, DIALOG and INVESTEXT/PLUS; Mead's features allow the extract of pages containing relevant information.†

Standard & Poor's Corporate Descriptions provides in-depth financial and corporate information for over 7,800 publicly held U.S. companies. Available through DIALOG; charges on DIALOG are $85 per connect hour plus $3.50 per full record, typed or displayed.*

TRINET Establishment Database identifies public and private companies with 20 or more employees with primary emphasis on the branch/establishment level. Available through DIALOG, Mead Data Central—NEXIS, and direct through Control Data's Business Information Services; charges on DIALOG are $90 per connect hour plus 50 cents per full record, typed or displayed.*

*Judith Sovner-Ribbler, "Which Database Solves Which Marketing Problem?" *Sales and Marketing Management* 140, no. 9 (July 1988), p. 52. Reprinted with permission.
†Margaret W. Nicol and Christina M. Darnowsky, "On-Line Access to SEC Filings," *Database* 12, no. 4 (August 1989), p. 28. Reprinted with permission.

Item

A real estate developer was accused of using "bait and switch" tactics in selling lots, "stepping up" valuations, and reneging on promises made to purchasers. Developer executives thought that a state-of-the-art accounting system would help its defense and offer safeguards against a repetition of the alleged occurrences. A systems manager with an allegedly vaunted reputation was hired to preside over the revitalization of the company's system. The auditor searched the on-line data bases and determined that there was no mention of the systems man in practitioner and academic journals, as either newsmaker or contributor. This type of signal should have given pause for concern.

FIGURE 6–10
Journals List for Accountants' Index/ACCOUNTANTS Data Base*

ABA Banking Journal
ABA Journal
†*Abacus* (Australia)
Accountancy (England)
Accountancy Ireland
Accountancy SA (South Africa)
Accountant (England)
Accountant (Kenya) (1983)
†*Accountants Digest* (England)
Accountants' Journal (New Zealand)

Accountants Journal (Republic of the Philippines)
Accountant's Liability Newsletter (AICPA) (1982)
Accountant's Magazine (Scotland)
Accounting and Business Research (England)
Accounting and Finance (Australia) (1979)
Accounting, Auditing and Accountability (England) (1988)
Accounting, Business and Financial History (England) (1990)
Accounting Education News (1981)
Accounting Educators' Journal (1988)
†*Accounting Historians Journal* (1977)

Accounting History (AAANZ) (1989)
Accounting Horizons (1987)
Accounting Issues (Bear Stearns)
Accounting, Organizations and Society (England) (1976)
†*Accounting Review*
Accounting Systems Journal (1989)
Across the Board
Administrative Science Quarterly
Akron Business and Economic Review
American Business Law Journal

American Economic Review
Annals of the School of Business Administration, Kobe University (Japan)
API Account (1978)
Appraisal Journal
Armed Forces Comptroller
Asset (Missouri Society of CPAs)
Association Management
Attorney-CPA
†*Auditing* (1981)
Auditor's Report (1979)

Australian Accountant
Australian Tax Forum (1984)
Bank Accounting & Finance (1987)
Bank Management (formerly *Magazine of Bank Administration*)
Bankers Magazine
Bankers Monthly
Baylor Business Review (1980)

FIGURE 6–10 *(continued)*

†*Behavioral Research in Accounting* (1989)
Benefits Law Journal (1988)
Best's Review (Life/Health)

Best's Review (Property/Casualty)
Black Enterprise (1987)
Bowman's Accounting Report (1987)
British Accounting Review (1987)
British Tax Review
Bulletin for International Fiscal Documentation (Netherlands)
Business
Business and Society Review
Business and Tax Planning Quarterly (formerly *Business Planning Quarterly*)
    (1985)
Business Credit (formerly *Credit & Financial Management*)

Business History Review
Business Horizons
Business Lawyer
Business Marketing
Business Month (formerly *Dun's Business Month*)
Business Week
CA Magazine (Canada)
California Management Review
Canadian Business Review
Canadian Tax Journal

Certified Accountant (England)
CFO (1986)
CGA Magazine (Canada)
Charter (Australia)
Chartered Accountant (India)
Chartered Accountant (Sri Lanka) (formerly *Journal of the Institute of Chartered
    Accountants of Sri Lanka*) (1978)
Club Management
CMA (Canada) [formerly *Cost and Management* (Canada)]
Columbia Journal of World Business
Columbia Law Review

Commercial Lending Review (1986)
Company Accountant (England) [formerly *Accountants Record* (England)] (1977)
Compensation & Benefits Management (1984)
Computer Security, Auditing and Controls (1979)
Computer Security Journal (1981)
Computers in Accounting (1984)
Concepts in Action (Deloitte & Touche) (1989)
Connecticut CPA Quarterly
Consultation: An International Journal (1989)

Contemporary Accounting Research (Canada) (1984)
Continental Bank Journal of Applied Corporate Finance (1988)
Controllers Quarterly (1985)

(continued)

FIGURE 6–10 *(continued)*

Cooperative Accountant
Coopers & Lybrand Executive Briefing [formerly *Coopers & Lybrand Newsletter (Executive Alert)*] (1978)
Cornell Hotel and Restaurant Administration Quarterly
Cornell Law Review
Corporate Accounting International (Ireland) (1989)
Corporate Controller (1988)

Corporate Finance (1986)
Corporate Practice Commentator (1986)
Corporate Taxation (1988)
Cost and Management (Bangladesh) (1984)
†*CPA Journal*
CPA Personnel Report (1986)
Critical Perspectives on Accounting (England) (1990)
Datamation
De Ratione (South Africa) (1987)
Decision Sciences

Dental Economics (1987)
Directors & Boards (1976)
EDP Auditor Journal
Edpacs
Engineering Economist
Entrepreneurship Theory and Practice (formerly *American Journal of Small Business*) (1983)
†*Estate Planning*
European Accountant (Ireland) (1990)
Executive Accountant (England) (1986)
Expert Systems: Planning/Implementation/Integration (1989)

Faulkner & Gray's Bankruptcy Law Review (1989)
Federation of Schools of Accountancy Newsletter (1980)
Finance & Development
Financial Accountability and Management (England) (1985)
Financial Analysts Journal
Financial & Accounting Systems (formerly *Journal of Accounting and EDP*) (1985)
Financial Executive
Financial Independence (KPMG-Peat Marwick) (1990)
Financial Management
Financial Planning (1987)

Florida CPA Today (1986)
Forbes (1975)
Fordham Business Review [formerly *Balance Sheet* (Fordham Business Review)]
Fortune
GAO Journal (1988)
†*Georgia Journal of Accounting* (1980)
Government Accountants Journal
Government Finance Review (1985)

FIGURE 6–10 *(continued)*

Harvard Business Review
Harvard Law Review

Healthcare Financial Management
Highlights of Financial Reporting Issues (FASB) (1981)
Hong Kong Accountant (1988)
Hospital & Health Services Administration
Hospitals
Hotel & Motel Management
IASC News (England) (1990)
In Our Opinion (AICPA) (1983)
INC. (1983)
Indiana Law Journal

Industrial Accountant (Pakistan) (1975)
Institutional Investor
†*Internal Auditing* (1985)
Internal Auditor
International Accountant (England)
International Accounting Bulletin (Ireland) (1983)
†*International Journal of Accounting Education and Research*
International Journal of Government Auditing
†*International Tax Journal*
Interpreter (1976)

Iowa Law Review
Issues in Accounting Education (1986)
†*Journal of Accountancy*
†*Journal of Accounting and Economics* (Netherlands) (1979)
Journal of Accounting and Public Policy (1982)
†*Journal of Accounting, Auditing and Finance* (1977)
†*Journal of Accounting Education* (1983)
†*Journal of Accounting Literature* (1982)
†*Journal of Accounting Research*
Journal of Agricultural Taxation & Law (1987)

Journal of American Insurance
Journal of Applied Business Research (1988)
Journal of Bank Accounting and Auditing (1988)
†*Journal of Bank Cost & Management Accounting* (1985)
Journal of Business
Journal of Business Ethics (1986)
Journal of Business Finance & Accounting (England)
Journal of Business Forecasting Methods and Systems (1982)
Journal of Career Planning & Employment
Journal of Commercial Bank Lending

Journal of Compensation and Benefits (1985)
Journal of Corporate Accounting & Finance (1989)
†*Journal of Corporate Taxation*
Journal of Corporation Law (1975)
Journal of Cost Analysis (1984)
Journal of Cost Management for the Manufacturing Industry (1987)

(continued)

FIGURE 6–10 *(continued)*

†*Journal of Equipment Lease Financing* (1988)
Journal of European Business (1989)
Journal of France
Journal of Financial and Quantitative Analysis

Journal of Financial Planning (formerly *Journal of the Institute of Certified Financial Planners*) (1979)
Journal of Financial Planning Today (formerly *Financial Planning Today*) (1979)
Journal of Futures Markets (1983)
Journal of Information Systems (1986)
Journal of Information Systems Management (1984)
Journal of International Financial Management and Accounting (1989)
Journal of International Taxation (1990)
†*Journal of Management Accounting Research* (1989)
Journal of Management Consulting (1982)
Journal of Marketing

Journal of Marketing Research
Journal of Partnership Taxation (1984)
†*Journal of Pension Planning and Compliance* (formerly *Pension and Profit-Sharing Tax Journal*)
Journal of Property Management
†*Journal of Real Estate Taxation*
Journal of Retailing
Journal of S Corporation Taxation (1989)
†*Journal of State Taxation* (1986)
Journal of Systems Management
†*Journal of Taxation*

Journal of Taxation of Estates & Trusts (formerly *Journal of Taxation of Trusts & Estates*) (1988)
Journal of Taxation of Exempt Organizations (1989)
†*Journal of Taxation of Investments* (1985)
Journal of Taxation of S Corporations (1989)
Journal of the Academy of Marketing Science
Journal of the American Society of CLU & ChFC
†*Journal of the American Taxation Association* (1979)
Kent/Bentley Journal of Accounting and Computers (formerly *Kent/Bentley Review*) (1985)
Kobe Economic & Business Review (Japan) (1979)
Laventhol & Horwath Perspective

Law and Contemporary Problems
Law Office Economics and Management
Law Practice Management (formerly *Legal Economics*) (1987)
Lodging Hospitality
Malaysian Accountant (1981)
Management Accountant (India)
Management Accounting (England)
†*Management Accounting* (NAA)
Management Consultant International (Ireland) (1989)

FIGURE 6–10 *(continued)*

Management Science
Managerial Auditing Journal (England) (1988)
Massachusetts CPA Review
Medical Economics
Mergers & Acquisitions
Michigan CPA
Michigan Law Review
Mid-Atlantic Journal of Business (formerly *Journal of Business*)
Modern Healthcare
Money
Monthly Labor Review (1975)

Mortgage Banking
Motor Freight Controller
Municipal Finance Journal (1986)
National Public Accountant
National Tax Journal
New Accountant (1985)
New York University Law Review
Newspaper Financial Executive Journal (formerly *Newspaper Controller*)
Nigerian Accountant (1979)
Nursing Homes and Senior Citizen Care

Ohio CPA Journal
Oil & Gas Finance and Accounting (England) [formerly *Journal of Oil and Gas Accountancy* (England)] (1987)
Oil & Gas Tax Quarterly (1990)
Oklahoma Law Review
Optometric Management (1987)
Outlook (California Society of CPAs)
Pacific Accounting Review (New Zealand) (1988)
Panorama (Pannell Kerr Forster) (1975)
Pennsylvania CPA Journal
Pension World

Personal Financial Planning (1989)
Personnel
Petroleum Accounting and Financial Management Journal (formerly *Journal of Petroleum Accounting*) (1982)
Physician's Management (1987)
Planner (AICPA) (1986)
Planning Review (1980)
†*Practical Accountant* (1986)
Practical Lawyer
Practical Tax Lawyer (1986)
Practice Development—Insights for Growth (1986)

†*Practicing CPA* (AICPA) (1978)
Price Waterhouse Review
Probate and Property (1988)

(continued)

FIGURE 6–10 *(continued)*

Production and Inventory Management Journal (formerly *Production and Inventory Management*)
Production & Inventory Management Review with APICS News (1986)
Public Accounting Report (1981)
Public Finance and Accountancy (England)
Public Opinion Quarterly

Public Personnel Management
Public Relations Quarterly
Public Utilities Fortnightly
Quarterly Review of Economics and Business
Rand Journal of Economics (formerly *Bell Journal of Economics*)
Real Estate Accounting & Taxation (1986)
Real Estate Review
Real Property, Probate and Trust Journal
Research Bulletin of the Institute of Cost and Works Accountants of India (1986)
Restaurant Hospitality
Retail Control

Review of Business and Economic Research (1981)
†*Review of Taxation of Individuals* (1977)
Risk Management
†*S Corporations: The Journal of Tax, Legal and Business Strategies* (1988)
Sales & Marketing Management
SAM Advanced Management Journal (formerly *Advanced Management Journal*)
Savings Institutions
School Business Affairs (1990)
SEC Accounting Report (1975)
Securities Regulation Law Journal

Selections (1986)
SGV Group Journal (Republic of the Philippines)
Singapore Accountant
†*Small Business Taxation* (1988)
Southern Collegiate Accountant (1989)
Spectrum (NABA) (1986)
St. John's Law Review
Stanford Law Review
Stanger's Investment Advisor (formerly *Stanger Register*) (1987)
Status Report (FASB) (1986)

Systems Integration (formerly *Mini-Micro Systems*) (1976)
†*Tax Adviser*
†*Tax Executive*
†*Tax Law Review*
†*Tax Lawyer*
Tax Management Compensation Planning Journal (1989)

FIGURE 6-10 *(concluded)*

†*Tax Management Estates, Gifts and Trusts Journal* (formerly *Estates, Gifts and Trusts Journal*) (1976)
Tax Management Financial Planning Journal (1985)
Tax Management International Journal
Tax Management Real Estate Journal (1984)

Tax Planning International Review (England) (1988)
Taxation in Australia (1989)
†*Taxation for Accountants*
†*Taxation for Lawyers*
†*Taxes—The Tax Magazine*
Today's CPA (Texas Society of CPAs) (1983)
Trusts & Estates
University of Miami Law Review
Valuation
Vanderbilt Law Review

Veterinary Economics
Video Store (1986)
Virginia Law Review
†*Virginia Tax Review* (1989)
Washington and Lee Law Review
Washington Law Review (1979)
Wisconsin CPA
†*Woman CPA*
World (KPMG-Peat Marwick)
World Accounting Report (England) (1981)

Yale Law Journal

*Coverage in ACCOUNTANTS data base is from 1974, unless otherwise indicated.
†Denotes indexing in entirety. All other titles indexed selectively.

Source: Library of the American Institute of Certified Public Accountants, Inc.

Analytical Review (with or without the On-Line Data Bases)

Benefits from the application of analytical review procedures tend to be proportionate to the user's knowledge of the subject company, and to the realism of the relationships she expects to find. Nonetheless, analytical procedures, discussed in Chapters 8 and 9 of this book, can reveal out-of-line conditions; in this way the procedures provide a starting point for further inquiry.

Professional Rule Retrieval

The AICPA's Electronic Index to Technical Pronouncements (EITP) is available in disk format. EITP can be used by an auditor to locate specific references to AICPA, FASB, GASB, SEC, and certain other professional and regulatory bodies' pronouncements. The details of each specific reference can then be looked up in the hard copy of the pronouncement. Alternatively, the reference can be used to retrieve the relevant text on NAARS.

The auditor may also need to be aware of accounting-related rules being considered in other countries in which her clients have operations. She should know what new reporting requirements are emerging, when they are likely to be implemented, what information might be needed to comply, and how much effort will be necessary. The on-line data bases may carry news of regulatory developments abroad. Moreover, judicious planning may help to produce the new information with minimal effort.

Item

The government of Trinidad and Tobago considered whether to require reporting of special payroll information in order to track the relative job progress of its own nationals, given the presence of foreign supervisors. When it became apparent that the information *was* going to be required, moderate systems modifications would have facilitated easy retrieval. However, those who waited to collect the information until after promulgation of the directive were confronted by an extensive task of payroll coding and information reconstruction.

The Emerging Issues Task Force (EITF): Of Special Interest

EITF has generally been successful in providing timely guidance with respect to newly conceived financial instruments and transactions. This guidance has usually taken the form of a consensus of the views of Task Force members. EITF issue summaries, as well as minutes of meetings, are readily retrievable from NAARS' LIT (literature) file. (See Figure 6–11.) EITF minutes represent a component of authoritative literature, although at a lower level of authority. (See Figure 6–12.)

FIGURE 6–11
NAARS Literature File Contents

Content summary: The literature files contain both current and superseded authoritative accounting literature from the Financial Accounting Standards Board (FASB), Government Accounting Standards Board (GASB), the Securities and Exchange Commission (SEC), the AICPA, the International Federation of Accountants and the Cost Accounting Standards Board.

Standard segments: Types of literature: the types of documents listed below are not separately searchable files. However, if a user wishes to limit a search to a particular type of document, this can be easily accomplished through a document segment search. Type doc, followed by an acronym from the list below, enclosed in parenthesis, e.g., doc (feitfis). This will retrieve FASB Emerging Issues Task Force Issue Summary Packages. Types of documents in the accounting literature files include:

Type of Literature	Acronym
Accounting and Auditing Enforcement Releases	AAER
Accounting Research Bulletins	
Accounting Series Releases	ASR
Accounting Standard Executive Committee Pronouncements	ASEC
APB Opinions, Statements, and Interpretations	AC
Cost Accounting Standards Board Pronouncements	CASB
Ethics—Concepts, Rules of Conduct, Interpretations of Rules of Conduct and Ethics Rulings	ET
FASB Concepts	FASBC
FASB Emerging Issues Task Force Dates of Discussion and Disposition	FEITFDDD
FASB Emerging Issues Task Force Issue Summary Packages	FEITFIS
FASB Emerging Issues Task Force Meeting Minutes	FEITFM
FASB Interpretations	FASBI
FASB Statements	FASBS
FASB Technical Bulletins	FASBT
Financial Reporting Releases	FRR
GASB Interpretations	GASBI
GASB Statements	GASBS
GASB Technical Bulletins	GASBT
Industry Accounting Guides	ACTG
Industry Audit Guides	AUDG
International Accounting Standards Committee Pronouncements	IAS
International Federation of Accountants Committee Pronouncements (Auditing)	IAUG
Issue Papers	ISUPAP
Regulations S-K	SK
Regulations S-X	SX

(continued)

FIGURE 6–11 *(concluded)*

Type of Literature	Acronym
Staff Accounting Bulletins	SAB
Statements on Auditing Standards (SAS)	AU
Statements on Management Advisory Service	SMAS
Statements on Quality Control	QCS
Statements on Quality Control Interpretation	QCSI
Statements on Standards for Accounting and Review Services	SSARS
Statements on Standards for Accounting and Review Interpretation	SSARSI
Statements on Standards for Attestation Engagements	SSAE
Technical Information Service Technical Practice Aids	TIS

Retrieval of Information: In-House Data Bases

An in-house data base would seem to be essential to a public accounting firm or an internal audit department. (Deloitte & Touche's comprehensive DaTa represents a good example of this type of knowledge base; it includes the firm's international audit approach, accounting and auditing bulletins, examples of financial statement presentations, and a large body of FASB, AICPA, and SEC materials.) Other in-house data bases can serve many needs ranging from tracking marketing opportunities to planning employee career paths.

However, many auditing organizations do *not* have a technical data base which bridges the details of (1) professional rules, (2) published annual reports, which reflect decisions of other accountants, and (3) the firm's own internal decisions and advisories. Lack of such a data base makes it difficult to conform accounting treatments on a firmwide basis; precedents become hard to find and apply. The author believes that such a data base should represent full text rather than abstracts, and that careful thought must be given to indexing procedures, especially to identification of key words. (The AICPA maintains a master list of subject headings, prepared in connection with the Accountants' Index; the list is obtainable through the AICPA Library Services Division.)

FIGURE 6–12
Authoritative Literature

Highest Level of Accounting Authority

1. Nonsuperseded sections of the *Accounting Research Bulletins* issued by the Committee on Accounting Procedure.
2. Nonsuperseded sections of the *APB Opinions* issued by the Accounting Principles Board.
3. *Statements of Financial Accounting Standards* issued by the FASB.
4. *Interpretations* issued by the FASB.
5. *Statements* and *Interpretations* of the Governmental Accounting Standards Board (for governmental units).

Next Level of Accounting Authority

1. AICPA *Industry Accounting* and *Auditing Guides.*
2. AICPA *Statements of Position.*
3. FASB and GASB *Technical Bulletins.*
4. Industry accounting practices.
5. AICPA *Accounting Interpretations.*

Lower Level of Accounting Authority

1. Guidelines published by SEC and other regulatory agencies.
2. FASB and GASB *Concept Statements.*
3. APB *Statements.*
4. AICPA *Issues Papers.*
5. *Minutes* of the FASB Emerging Issues Task Force.
6. Other professional association statements.
7. Accounting textbooks, reference books, and articles written by recognized authorities in the field.

Source: Jeffrey R. Miller, L. Murphy Smith, and Robert H. Strawser, "Sources of Accounting Literature," *The CPA Journal,* April 1990, Accounting, p. 54. Reprinted with permission from *The CPA Journal,* April 1990, copyright 1990. It should be noted that the levels of accounting authority were under review at the time of writing.

Compact Disk–Read Only Memory (CD-ROM): Supplementing the On-Line Services

A CD-ROM disk physically resembles an audio compact disk. Data once written to CD-ROM by a data base provider cannot be erased or overwritten but can be read many times. Large capacity—the five-inch version can hold the equivalent of 250,000 pages—makes disks suitable for storing an entire data base, or selected excerpts from one or more. Data is recorded by laser beam. The disks and the data are immune from wear; therefore, the disks represent an economical investment for frequent and repeat users. These disks supplement the on-line services without matching their currency; the disks may be used to best advantage in combination with the data bases. Some data base vendors have developed software that will automatically update CD searches for material added to the data base since the CD was cut.[15]

There are two types of disks on which data *can* be written by users. One type is referred to as WORM—write once, read many; the WORM device enables users to write data while on-line to the computer. A second possibility for erasure and rewriting is represented by a relatively new erasable optical storage medium.[16] The latter development raises a number of issues, including the internal control exposure, the risks of accidental erasure, and the introduction of protective measures over accessibility of data.

CD-ROM makes it possible to custom-assemble data bases of special interest to the user. A library of accounting or tax reference sources can be placed on 10 or fewer disks; it is likely that software will be developed to facilitate movement across data bases. Mead Data Central, together with the AICPA, reportedly has been developing a CD-ROM version of its NAARS data base. DIALOG and its data base providers are also marketing a wide range of CD offerings.[17]

In the last section of the present chapter, computer-related approaches will be considered in terms of the audit model.

OBTAINING AN UNDERSTANDING OF THE SYSTEM: BEHAVIORAL INTERVIEWING

The High-Tech Challenge

Interviewing is, of course, a time-honored technique of obtaining or updating an understanding of the system. However, when that

---

[15]Scanlan et al., *Business Online,* p. 134.

[16]Charles E. Price, "Compact Disks—A New Technology for Finding Answers to Clients' Questions," *The CPA Journal,* March 1990, The Practitioner and the Computer, pp. 62–64.

[17]Ibid., p. 64.

system has high-tech aspects, special challenges exist for the interviewer. For example, words used during an interview must be understandable to both interviewer and interviewee. In addition, an understanding of the psychological forces at work during an interview should make it easier to minimize negative aspects. Stated differently, the interviewer should try to see the world through the eyes of the interviewee. Types of questions described by Murphy and Parker include:

1. *Open-ended questions.* These questions cannot be answered "yes" or "no." The interviewee is forced to think about the answer.

2. *Direct questions.* These questions ask for explanations or expansions on a particular point.

3. *Closed questions.* These are direct questions that have a narrow range of possible responses. Preferably, such questions should be asked only by interviewers who have a good grasp of the subject. However, a question which an interviewee perceives as threatening may not be answered directly and can create barriers to further communication.

4. *Yes/no questions.* Unfortunately, this type of question tends to be used by an inexperienced interviewer. While it is useful for the purpose of filling out forms and obtaining specific facts, it limits the amount of information obtained. Dangers may arise when internal control questions are answered on a basis of an interview (rather than the auditor's knowledge), especially when the interviewer does not understand the meaning and significance of the questions. Long lists of questions should also be avoided. Otherwise, the interview may turn into an interrogation, and negative interviewee reactions may be induced.[18] In the author's view, turning an internal control questionnaire (ICQ) over to a client for unsupervised completion does not yield acceptable results.

The author believes that auditors should be trained in behavioral approaches to interviewing. It may be concluded that a successful interview should be conducted by individuals tending to

---

[18]Murphy and Parker, *Handbook of EDP Auditing,* pp. 18-3 to 18-10.

be more knowledgeable in the subject matter of the interview and in interview techniques (i.e., partners and managers, rather than relatively junior personnel).

DOCUMENTING THE UNDERSTANDING

Flowcharts: To Draw or Not to Draw

There are many ways of documenting the logic of computer systems or programs, including narratives. A recent book lists 17 types of diagrams, including types of flowcharts familiar to auditors.[19] The author favors *utilization* of flowcharts by accountants and auditors—and under certain circumstances by members of audit committees—primarily because this form of documentation has enjoyed substantial user acceptance.

Flowcharts are of two types: (1) overview charts, which reflect interdepartmental relationships and (2) detailed charts of transaction processing. Whether an auditor should *prepare* detailed charts depends on the complexity of the application, on whether the application tends to be static, on the materiality of the accounts involved, on risk, and on whether the audit is recurring. Typically, charting is more likely to be done by internal, rather than external, auditors.

Charts should contain enough detail to track operations, documents, approvals, controls, files, and reports. This detail should permit the auditor to (1) identify controls, including those which are considered key, and (2) distinguish supervisory controls. In this context, *key* controls are those which bear on the accuracy and completeness of the financial statements; *supervisory* controls are intended to ensure that other controls are functioning. These controls and other matters of interest to audit committee members are covered in Figure 6–13, Audit Committee Tools for Oversight.

---

[19]James E. Patterson, "Diagramming Techniques for Analysts and Programmers," *Government Computer News* 7, no. 22 (October 24, 1988), p. 49. The article reviews the book *Diagramming Techniques for Analysts and Programmers,* by James Martin and Carma McClure.

FIGURE 6–13
Audit Committee Tools for Oversight

Assessing the Control Environment

1. Does management demonstrate concern for the adequacy of internal control?

   Examples of information

   - Written requests are made by management urging external and internal auditors to comment on internal control within as short a time as possible—conceivably verbally, subject to written confirmation—so that needed improvements will not be delayed.
   - Internal auditors are customarily assigned to see that controls are built into systems under development, and that such controls are appropriately tested; the auditors' assignment sheets and resulting reports are available for review.
   - Findings and recommendations made by both internal and external auditors are tracked into resolution.

2. Is management reasonably receptive to audit adjustments?

   Examples of information

   - Management accepts *reasonably* complete documentation of adjustments.
   - Management does not insist on netting debatable items with a view toward waiving aggregated adjustments. The nature of adjustments can be established by reviewing supporting documentation.

3. Is management aware that corporate assets are not its personal piggy bank?

   Examples of information

   - Company policy, instructions, and practices require employees to pay for personal expenses; for example, employees reimburse the company for non-business lunches and dinners, or for travel of dependents.
   - Cost consciousness pervades the organization, especially with respect to travel expenses, and is mirrored in such matters as expense report approval routines, and, particularly, requests for downward revisions to expense reports.
   - If relatives are employed, they are subject to the same compensation, perquisites, and expectations as nonrelatives. Their expense reports are available for review.
   - Studies have been performed indicating the elements and amounts of prevailing compensation.

4. Are offenders prosecuted?

   Examples of information

   - Informed, documented, and approved decisions are made whether to prosecute offenders; the decisions are based on the nature of the crime and on the record of the offender.
   - Except in unusual circumstances, publicity is given to prosecutions.
   - Controls are reassessed by the internal auditors to determine whether ''retrofitting'' is necessary; audit programs are revised accordingly.

(continued)

FIGURE 6–13 *(continued)*

Oversight of the Internal Audit Function

5. Has a charter been authorized by top management, and by the audit committee, that gives internal auditors broad scope, freedom of access to all facilities, and protection from interference by those under audit?

Examples of information

- The internal auditors' charter spells out matters mentioned in the question. Audit reports reflect that broad mandate.
- Reports published by internal auditors do not pull any punches.
- Reports are issued in timely fashion, pursuant to the audit schedule and the dates of completion of field work, without excision of subject matter or undue delay.

6. Does the chief auditor have the right of access to the audit committee?

Examples of information

- Memoranda, explanations, and briefing materials are provided to committee members on a regular basis by the chief auditor.
- To the extent that action by committee members was required, the nature of that action was documented.

7. Are the best available talents brought to bear on problems?

Examples of information

- Joint internal/external auditor assignments are made insofar as possible on the basis of the (educational and experience) qualifications of individuals perceived to be helpful in dealing with audit risk.

8. Are findings and recommendations in internal audit reports monitored into resolution?

Examples of information

- Operating managers are recorded as agreeing with the accuracy of the facts in the reports.
- Documentation exists that operating managers are concerned with taking corrective actions, based on evaluations of alternatives, and that orderly plans are established for completing such actions, including target dates and manpower assignments.
- Reports are submitted as to the status of pending corrective actions.
- Complete and accurate inventories are maintained of pending matters, and delays in resolution of reported deficiencies are questioned and/or investigated.

Internal Control

9. Has an orderly approach been taken to risk management?

Examples of information

- Business risk is evaluated, and an optimum approach taken to its management. Documentation is on file to support the evaluations and the selected actions.

FIGURE 6-13 *(continued)*

- Assuming that insurance represents part of the risk management approach, documentation is available in the form of claims status reports and in reports showing claims filed in relation to claims accepted.

10. Have standards of internal control been published?

   Examples of information

   - The standards document.
   - Staff evaluations and surveys are made concerning separation of duties, especially between those who have access to assets and those responsible for the related record keeping, and between those who engage in systems design and programming and those who operate computers.
   - Auditors evaluate how effectively separations of duties have been achieved.
   - Policies exist relating to matters such as required vacations, overtime, and job rotation.

11. Is there management awareness of the controls which are in place, and of the controls which might be missing?

   Examples of information

   - Flowcharts have been marked with key controls and supervisory controls.
   - Internal and external audit reports are followed up relative to uncontrolled threats.

12. Is it possible to assess the broad accuracy of the financial statements by applying an algorithm or model to transaction flows of the auditee, and, if so, is such a computation made?

   Examples of information

   - If a company renders personal services, the hours for which payment was made to employees, and the hours billed to clients should be reconcilable.

13. Has security been evaluated, and has a formal security program resulted?

   Examples of information

   - There is a formal study, conducted by a person with reasonable independence, that incorporates facts, conclusions, and recommendations.
   - The study was reviewed by persons with appropriate authority and a formal program adopted.
   - The security program is subject to periodic tests; the test results are analyzed and any needed upgrading is undertaken.
   - The program is reexamined, evaluated, and updated periodically by individuals with an appropriate degree of independence.

14. Are assets, including information resources, and related records, including supplies of blank forms of sensitive documents, under physical control?

   Examples of information

   - Results are reported for physical inventories.
   - Reports are made of violations of physical access, together with exploration of the reasons and initiation of needed corrective actions.

(continued)

FIGURE 6–13 *(continued)*

- Reports are made of inspections by guards.

15. Is access to computers and terminals tracked in terms of the identity and authority of persons seeking access, the place of attempted access, the nature of the item to which access is sought, and the nature of the transaction?

    Examples of information

    - Computer logs reflect unauthorized access, together with the actions taken.

16. Are physical, logical, and computer-based controls in place to monitor data entry in terms of completeness and accuracy?

    Examples of information

    - Reports exist of rejections, possibly aged in terms of the date on which the error was detected.
    - Reports detail the techniques used to resolve rejections, especially to ensure protection of sensitive information.
    - Suitably supported journal entries and adjustments are processed to correct errors.

17. Are program change controls in effect to make sure that programs cannot be changed except on appropriate authority?

    Examples of information

    - Program change authorizations are required, together with accompanying documentation.
    - Actual production programs are compared to authorized programs by individuals with appropriate independence, such as internal auditors.

Financial Statement Preparation

18. Have instructions been issued relative to the assembly of information required for preparation of financial statements, especially interim financial statements?

    Examples of information

    - A policy is implemented, together with procedures and operating instructions.
    - Letters of admonition or similar memoranda concern compliance with procedures relative to the nature, quality, and timing of information received.

19. Is the audit committee involved in regular and recurring reviews of (annual and interim) financial statements?

20. If so, is the committee given:

    Enough time?
    Enough lead time to accommodate deadlines?
    Supporting documentation?
    Required clerical support?

    Examples of information

    - Minutes of committee actions.
    - Records are maintained of corrections to the interim statements.

FIGURE 6–13 *(continued)*

21. Has a person been designated to monitor business, regulatory, and technical developments in the economy and in the auditee's industry and business?

    Examples of information

    • Periodic status reports exist, and recommendations as to any actions that might be necessary.

22. Are the directors apprised of lawsuits that have been asserted, or that are about to be asserted, or of governmental or regulatory actions that could significantly impair assets or profitability?

23. Is there evidence that reports of current business problems and opportunities are considered in the preparation of either interim or annual financial statements?

    Examples of information

    • Adjustments to the statements reflect additional or improved disclosures.

24. Do the external (or internal) auditors review the interim financial statements?

    Examples of information

    • Engagement letter.
    • Adjusting journal entries or other records of corrections exist to the statements and accounts.
    • Critical comments of the interim statements by the external (or internal) auditors are aimed at seeing that required minimum disclosures were made.

25. Are management's assertions supported by evidence to assure their reasonableness in the light of outside information bearing especially on:

    Existence?
    Valuation?
    Reporting and disclosure?

    Examples of information

    • Printouts from the on-line data bases.
    • Appraisers' reports.
    • Credit reports or investigators' reports.

Codes of Conduct

26. Have the internal auditors been assigned to monitor:

    Compliance with laws?
    Conflicts of interest?
    Giving or accepting gifts or gratuities?
    Competitive bidding?
    Political contributions?
    Waivers of compliance with policies?
    Actions in case of discovered fraud?
    Protection of the human rights of whistleblowers?

    Examples of information

    • Internal audit reports.

(continued)

FIGURE 6–13 *(concluded)*

27. Are employee acknowledgments and periodic reporting requirements under the ethics code maintained on a current basis?

Examples of information

- Reminder letters to employees.
- Summarizations of responses.
- Internal audit reports.

Search for Out-of-Line Conditions

28. Is a relentless search, using modern techniques, such as especially written software and discovery sampling, conducted for violations of policies, procedures, and practices, especially by fraud, illegal acts, thefts, etc.?

Examples of information

- Reports by internal auditors or by counsel.

Flowcharts should permit the auditor to trace the flow of documents from their creation to their burial in the accounts. Sudden flow termination, or other untoward events, such as the creation of a new transaction type without a meaningful, documented, and approved reason, may indicate impropriety.

The selection of a flowcharting package depends on ease of use, cost, the extent to which it permits identification of controls, and whether it presents a level of detail appropriate to auditing.

Several different approaches can be followed with respect to flowcharting, including automation of the drawing process. For example, HavenTree Software Limited's interactive EasyFlow allows the user to create and modify flowcharts and merge them with text notes.[20] Douglas Van Kirk has noted that EasyFlow copes with the effort inherent in flowcharting, and with the difficulty of editing the charts: "EasyFlow . . . [lets you] create flowcharts, organizational charts, and dataflow diagrams on your PC. With EasyFlow you don't have to worry about text formatting, redrawing lines or moving symbols. Everything is auto-

---

[20]John W. Yu, "Creating Forms and Flowcharts," *CGA Magazine,* September 1988, p. 8. HavenTree can be reached at P.O. Box 1093-G, Thousand Island Park, NY 13692; the phone numbers are (613) 544-6035 or (800) 267-0668.

matic."[21] Other software houses have also striven to ease flow-charting burdens; a recent article lists five packages, including EasyFlow.[22] Still another article writes up ABC Flowcharter by Roykore, a Windows-based package which links multiple charts; it makes it possible to structure a flowchart hierarchically to show the big picture at the top level; additional components of the chart can then be created for subordinate levels.[23]

Some software houses have created computer programs that will automatically generate flowcharts by analyzing source code from a copy of a program in a high-level computer language. If the auditor can ensure that the source code thus analyzed has served in actual processing, she may assume that the computer-prepared flowchart represents the operation of the program.

Computer-aided software engineering may provide job control language (JCL) flowchart programs which may be helpful in understanding and confirming systems flows. (JCL programs provide an interface between an application program and the computer's operating system.)

Confirming the Accuracy of the Flowcharts

It is desirable (although not a professional requirement) to ensure the currency and accuracy of flowcharts by tracing at least one transaction of each significant type through the system on a cradle-to-grave basis. This may be accomplished manually or with the computer. The computer technique is called *snapshot.* A series of images is taken of a transaction, and of the information available to it, as it progresses through the system. Audit trails must be printed for each snapshot point. Audit routines may also continously monitor all transactions and report those that pass or fail established criteria; the embedding of data collection portals

---

[21]Douglas Van Kirk, "Go with the Flow: Software Review: HavenTree Software Easy-Flow Flowcharting Program Toolkit," *PC Computing* 3, no. 2 (February 1990), p. 149.

[22]Steve Rosenthal, "Products; Flowcharting Graphics Software," *PC Week* 6, no. 9 (March 6, 1989), p. 95.

[23]John Walkenbach, "Roykore's ABC Flowcharter Offers Power, Ease of Use," *InfoWorld,* April 30, 1990, p. 72.

into production systems is usually accomplished while systems are still in the development phase.

EVALUATING INTERNAL CONTROL

The Return of Separation of Duties

Traditionally, auditors have examined internal control as a basis of determining the extent to which substantive tests could be restricted, modified, or shifted in time. While this hitherto basic objective of the internal control review may be changing, two attributes of internal control have been gaining in importance. The first of these is attention to separation of duties; the second is the use of internal control as a barometer of a particular client's sensitivity to corporate accountability.

Custody of assets should be divorced from the related record keeping, and computer operations from programming and systems design. The success of separation of duties hinges on the extent to which supervisors observe and enforce rules and standards. Again, technology may be helpful. Deloitte & Touche has developed a program, named "Control Plan," for identifying conflicting duties of accounting personnel. Control Plan represents an endeavor to highlight situations wherein an employee has access to assets, and also a degree of access to records of accountability over those assets. Control Plan may be used to create "what if" scenarios that help to determine the effect of organizational changes on the system of internal control.

The developers of Control Plan have focused on two matters: structures that could be used to represent the evaluation rules of the model, and the program itself (which interprets and executes the evaluation rules). In the language of knowledge-based systems, the set of rules is the *knowledge base,* and the program the *inference engine.* Deloitte has also created a Control Plan derivative oriented toward banks.[24]

---

[24]Trevor Stewart and Randy Finch, "Developing a Microcomputer Program for Evaluating Internal Control," *Internal Auditing,* Summer 1986, pp. 31–39.

SUBSTANTIVE TESTING

Substantive Testing and Audit Software

Audit software offers great advantages in substantive testing, because computers can process large volumes of data. Test results are more conclusive when all data contained in a file are examined, rather than a sample. In addition, it is often more efficient to carry out extended substantive tests than to evaluate and test the system of internal control. The available software includes the utilities that usually accompany an operating system (e.g., MS-DOS' COMP, COPY, FIND, and SORT), public domain (free) programs of various types, packages designed to audit particular applications or applications for certain industries, custom-written programs, and generalized audit software.

The role of a general purpose computer audit program is not changed in a PC environment. Micro-based generalized audit software packages add, identify exceptions, select and analyze data (such as age accounts receivable or inventories), select samples, combine files by matching common data items, and prepare and follow up on confirmations. If generalized audit software is to be used, data must be downloaded from the client's system into the auditor's computer. Given mixed formats and file types, the first task that the software performs is to convert client files into files the audit software can read and manipulate. In general, a trade-off may exist between ease of use of the packages and their flexibility and/or ability to access complex structures of files.

An interesting approach has been developed by the Canadian Institute of Chartered Accountants (CICA); the program, known as Interactive Data Extraction and Analysis (IDEA), is distributed in the United States by the AICPA. CICA suggests that IDEA be thought of "as an integrator, allowing [the auditor] the capability to analyze and manipulate data in a variety of ways."[25]

---

[25]*Interactive Data Extraction Analysis: Version 3.1,* (Toronto: Canadian Institute of Chartered Accountants, 1987), p. xii.

IDEA:

- Extracts data based on various criteria.
- Finds out how many transactions meet specified criteria.
- Browses through transactions.
- Refines and analyzes selections.
- Manipulates files in a variety of ways; for example, compares files, links files, adds fields to a file, and enters data into records.
- Performs statistical (and non-statistical) sampling.
- Ages by date.
- Checks for gaps and duplicates.
- Performs arithmetical calculations.

IDEA cannot be custom-tailored through programming or report generation. (The author used IDEA version 3.1.) Nonetheless, IDEA is both powerful and easy to use. In the words of one reviewer, "This may be an ideal package for the auditor who wants to use generalized audit software but is concerned about his or her lack of the technical skills necessary to use such software."[26] One example will help to make this point: in most cases, the import of data from files prepared by use of popular programs will be almost automatic. However, there may be conditions which require the auditor to define files to be imported to IDEA. IDEA has made definitions virtually painless for the auditor; IDEA has the capability of comparing the source file layout to the auditor's definition to signal errors.

Audit Program Generator

AICPA has created an electronic practice aid that should allow accountants to concentrate on making professional judgments while the software handles the mechanical aspects of creating audit programs and checklists. The AICPA's program, Audit Program Generator (APG), facilitates the creation of full-text pro-

---

[26]Scott D. Jacobson and Christopher Wolfe, "Auditing with Your Microcomputer," *Journal of Accountancy,* February 1990, p. 76.

grams in outline format, modification of items in existing programs, and the development of libraries of programs; programs can be tailored to new clients or new situations. The program print layout includes space for initials and dates of performance and working paper references.

Consolidation-Related Programs

The AICPA has created a family of tools. Accountant's Trial Balance (ATB) helps accountants prepare and work with trial balances. ATB creates trial balances, makes different types of journal entries, defines lead schedules, computes up to 34 preprogrammed analytical ratios and compares them with prior period, budget, and industry averages, and prepares variance analyses of various types. ATB has been supplemented by a Consolidations Module (CM) which helps accountants prepare and work with consolidated trial balances. The consolidated trial balances are linked to the individual ATB trial balances; changes to individual trial balances are brought forward automatically. A Financial Statements Module (F/S) facilitates financial statement preparation.

In addition, systems are being developed that are responsive to the needs of the multinationals. One system now being built can compute exchange gains or losses on dealings between foreign subsidiaries on a transactional basis. The most important feature of the emerging programs is a rate of speed that has enabled some companies to reduce to hours consolidations that used to take days.[27]

Macro Program Statements

Auditors may be in a position to retrieve data from client data bases by issuing the proper commands. A query language is the set of commands that orders the computer to examine or change the data stored in the data base. Structured query language (SQL) is the standard vocabulary for most data bases. Various software houses

---

[27]Steven M. Cowherd, "PCs Lead Progress for Consolidations," *Accounting Today,* February 5, 1990, p. 30.

are refining their SQL versions; use of the languages by auditors is likely to become more widespread within the next year or two. In the meantime, some end users have begun building their own PC applications using macro languages. For example, Peter Chen, a senior manager with Arthur Andersen and Co., used the macro language in Microsoft Corp.'s Excel spreadsheet software to create an internal control evaluation program. Users who customize their own PC applications tend to work with familiar programs; the extent of customization, the value of these efforts, and their significance to the audit mission cannot be readily assessed.[28]

Custom Programs

Few auditors are likely to write special programs, due to the difficulty and expense involved. Therefore, custom audit software is likely to be developed only because packaged software is not available for a particular computer, the output required is very specialized, or the computations and data handling are particularly intricate.[29] The state of New York has provided some interesting examples of the use of specialized computer-assisted audit techniques (CAATs). In performing their audits, the auditors first analyzed the system's computer programs to determine what controls (edits) were in place. In most cases, the EDP auditors then wrote review programs in high-level languages, such as COBOL; vendor-supplied software packages were also used. The results were highly significant from an operational point of view; for example, CAATs identified 2 million questionable transportation claims, totaling $56 million, for which no corresponding medical services had been billed. Another example: one hospital billed the system at its general inpatient rate, rather than at the correct specialty rate (half the general rate), leading to overbilling of more than $6 million.[30]

---

[28]John McMullen, "End Users Create PC Applications: Macro Language Usage," *Datamation* 35, no. 23 (December 1, 1989), p. 41.

[29]*Advanced Computer Audit Techniques,* (New York: EDP Auditors Foundation Monograph Series, 1987), p. 18.

[30]David DeStefano, "Using Computer-Assisted Audit Techniques in Public Sector Audits," *Association of Government Accountants Journal,* Fall Quarter 1989, pp. 43–50.

Statistical Methods

J. B. Mandel has described discovery sampling, along with a number of other graphic or analytical techniques, as useful in detecting errors and irregularities. Other techniques he mentions include rank analysis (listing of attributes in order of magnitude), control charts (which track a particular measure within bounds of acceptability), record matching, graphic analysis (plotting of variables on a scale with simple x and y axes), and analytical review. However, Mandel believes that the value of these methods may be limited because usage tends to occur at intervals of a year or longer; quantitative methods based on relatively short periods of continuous data collection and analysis can discover problems earlier. The auditor should consider utilizing discovery sampling. If she observes at least one unfavorable development of a defined nature, given a specified rate of occurrence in the population, that development would provide a basis for inquiry into why the problem had not been detected previously, given the audit procedures employed.[31]

The meaning of discovery sampling results is clear: if there are no occurrences of the critical attribute in the sample, the auditor has gained the assurance specified in her test design; if one or more occurrences are found, the auditor must consider their effect on the audit in the case. (Appendix A presents a brief tutorial on discovery sampling.)

SUMMARY

This chapter has presented specific devices that promise to strengthen control in the focal areas of risk: physical protection of assets, access to the computer, and verification of management representations. The on-line data bases have been introduced, and their potential role in the audit explored. In addition, men-

---

[31]J. B. Mandel, "How Statistical Methods Can Detect Possible Fraud or Abuse," *The White Paper* 4, no. 3, (May–June 1990), pp. 6, 11.

tion has been made of a number of software programs, which have been related to the audit model. In Chapters 8 and 9 guidance and examples will be given relating to certain software.

The impact of technology can be put into perspective by considering that the new tools can put the auditor in a position to accomplish a more efficient and effective audit, subject to better control over audit risk. However, there is a prerequisite. The auditor must bring an enriched perspective to the audit—that of the broadly educated auditor/businessperson.

Before technological tools can be considered in the light of the details of the updated audit model, consideration is necessary in Chapter 7 of the auditor's current responsibilities relating to fraud.

CHAPTER 7

HEIGHTENING THE AUDITOR'S SENSITIVITY TO FRAUD

He who has been burned blows on the yogurt.

Greek proverb

USER PERSPECTIVE: **Items of Special Interest**

EXECUTIVE HIGHLIGHTS: All readers
INTRODUCTION: All readers
THE FRAUD EQUATION: All readers
THE PROTECTIVE RINGS: All readers
SOME NEGATIVE ASPECTS OF TECHNOLOGY: External auditors, internal auditors
PROFESSIONAL SKEPTICISM AND SENSITIVITY TO FRAUD: External auditors, internal auditors, government auditors
THE FUTURE: ALERTNESS: External auditors, internal auditors
SUMMARY: All readers

EXECUTIVE HIGHLIGHTS

Fraud exists in unexpected places and has become a worldwide scourge.

Managers, even of enterprises previously victimized by fraud, tend to delude themselves with the thought that "it can't happen here." Ironically, technology has equipped the "white hats" with better tools for detecting fraud. But, increased sensitivity to fraud, sometimes called *audit skepticism*, is an attitudinal prerequisite.

For fraud to take place there must be (1) an item worth stealing, (2) a potential perpetrator willing to steal, and (3) an opportunity for the crime to take place.

Many people will steal, as long as they can rationalize their behavior to their own satisfaction. The opportunity for illegal access to assets usually arises from knowledge acquired by the perpetrator, and/or from lack of security awareness on the part of other employees.

Isolating the perpetrator from the asset, and from the opportunity and knowledge for access, involves the creation of a series of rings around each part of the fraud equation. An eclectic mix of physical, logical, and computer-based devices should protect assets and safeguard computer access.

Periodic diagnostic checkups should be conducted by qualified consultants to ensure continuing viability of risk management programs, to foster separation of duties, to confirm that loss prevention controls continue to function as planned, and to ensure the company is in a position to take advantage of technological developments as they break.

The recidivist tendencies of felons, and especially of financial "operators," bear noting. Therefore, the prior associations and activities of client executives may need to be checked through the on-line data bases.

INTRODUCTION

Chapter 6 described techniques and devices that contribute to internal control, information resources thought to be useful to auditors, and audit software. The subject matter of this chapter is similar, except that the focus is on fraud prevention or detection and on sensitizing the auditor to indications of fraud. Fraud exists in unexpected places and has become a worldwide phenomenon.

Item

A city on the Texas border operates an international bridge. It had long been thought that mechanical devices embedded in the pavement would discourage thefts by toll collectors. However, the fact that U.S. government vehicles were exempt from tolls made it difficult to reconcile counts reported by the devices to bank deposits. In

1989 new electronic surveillance devices were installed which permitted a count of vehicles, accompanied by visual identification. It was quickly determined that a significant shortfall existed in collections turned in. Experienced fraud examiners were called; the collectors' eventual confessions revealed a long-standing practice of passing through collectors' friends and relatives!

The story is interesting for its use of technology—as well as for the ingenuous attitudes of the collectors and their extended families. Seemingly, fraud is more common than may have been thought. Another example: 12 percent of respondents to a U.K. survey said that their company had suffered a significant fraud in the last three years. Perhaps not very logically, almost half the respondents thought that their controls against fraud were good, although in need of some improvement.[1] A different survey showed that managers of U.S. banks, irrespective of whether they were located in rural or urban areas, held similar views. The majority of these managers was of the opinion that the likelihood of a breach of security was low, while they admitted that such a breach could be costly. However, the managers also agreed that checking account files and savings account files represented high-risk areas, since these files were accessed by the widest variety and number of employees.[2]

Given what seems to be a persistent laissez-faire attitude toward fraud, opportunities for thievery will continue to tempt those whose actions are not subject to checks and balances via separation of duties. Of course, security involves far more than merely

> guarding premises and carrying the weekly wages from the bank to the factory. . . . Perhaps most significant among assets [now requiring protection] is information [which] exists in a number of forms. . . . Many businesses have still not absorbed the security ramifications and vulnerability of the telephone. . . . Managers have not yet perceived the disbenefits of computers. . . . Most computer crimes

---

[1]"U.K. Auditors' Responsibility on Fraud," *The Financial Times, World Loss Report,* March 9, 1990, Finance/Business.

[2]R. Leon Price, John S. Cotner, and Warren L. Dickson, "Computer Fraud in Commercial Banks: Management's Perception of Risk," *Journal of Systems Management* 40, no. 10 (October 1989), p. 28.

are committed not by "hackers" on the outside of organizations, but by "gropers" within the company itself.[3]

The situation is not hopeless; technology has equipped the "white hats" with better tools for detecting fraud. However, increased sensitivity to fraud on the part of internal and external auditors—better expressed as eternal vigilance—is a prerequisite. (Professional bodies, particularly the Institute of Internal Auditors (IIA), have long stressed the need for such vigilance.) The Treadway Commission's report includes the following highly pertinent recommendation: "The assumption of management integrity is one of the key areas where [professional] guidance should be changed. . . . To aid auditors in designing audit tests, the guidance should recognize the difficulties in assessing risks, designing tests, and evaluating audit evidence and it should require substantial involvement by seasoned audit professionals."[4]

The profession has endeavored to follow through on Treadway. *Statement on Auditing Standards (SAS) 53* states that auditors should design the audit to provide reasonable assurance of detecting errors and irregularities material to the financial statements. Auditors are also enjoined to exercise due care in planning, performing, and evaluating results of an audit, and to exercise the proper degree of professional skepticism. *Montgomery's Auditing* puts it this way:

> The way the auditor meets the obligation to not assume unquestioningly that management is honest is by maintaining an attitude of professional skepticism through the audit, especially when gathering and evaluating evidence, including management's answers to audit inquiries. . . . When "red flags" appear, the auditor should reconsider the audit testing plan in order to obtain sufficient competent evidence that the financial statements are free of material misstatements.[5]

---

[3]Paul Abrahams, "Corporate Security: Guarding the Standard," *Financial Times*, October 17, 1989, Survey, p. 17.

[4]*The Report of the National Commission on Fraudulent Financial Reporting* (National Commission on Fraudulent Financial Reporting, 1987), p. 51. Further information may be obtained through the American Institute of Certified Public Accountants, 1211 Avenue of the Americas, New York, NY 10036.

[5]Philip L. Defliese, Henry R. Jaenicke, Vincent M. O'Reilly, and Murray B. Hirsch, *Montgomery's Auditing*, 11th ed. (New York: John Wiley & Sons, 1990), p. 108.

As to internal auditors, *Statement on Internal Auditing Standards No. 3* recommends that they have sufficient knowledge of fraud to be able to identify indicators that fraud might have been committed. If significant control weaknesses are detected, additional tests conducted by internal auditors should include tests directed toward identification of other indicators of fraud.[6]

Keeping the need for vigilance in mind, discussion will begin with a summary of conceptual matters which bear on controls designed to prevent or detect fraud.

THE FRAUD EQUATION

In order for fraud to take place there must be (1) an item worth stealing, (2) a potential perpetrator willing to steal, and (3) an opportunity for the crime to take place.

The Asset

The potential target may not even have been identified or assigned a value by the auditee entity; also, the item may not be protected by records and/or physical devices. Thus, management's initial, mundane task in achieving better security may involve identification of what is to be protected. Once an inventory has been taken and recorded, decisions must be made relative to managing against the threats of fraud and theft; a plan must be developed, implemented, and its execution evaluated. Chapter 8 sets out the basic steps in risk management procedure. Of course, auditors are well equipped by training, experience, and orientation to participate in planning and conducting the inventory, evaluating the costs and benefits of risk management alternatives, testing controls, and reporting deficiencies.

Item

A company in the development stage owned a single asset, a proprietary computer program created to prepare drawings for automo-

---

[6]Lawrence B. Sawyer, *Sawyer's Internal Auditing*, 3rd ed. (Altamonte Springs, Fla.: The Institute of Internal Auditors, 1988), p. 1006.

tive dies. The program was loaded to an early (and insecure) mini-computer. The external auditor prepared a management letter in which he suggested that the client safeguard the program by instituting physical and computer access controls. The client's chairman demurred; he did not think that any potential perpetrator (in his words, "that kind of person") was working at his company. Shortly thereafter, the program was copied without authorization and sold to a competitor. When legal action was taken against the apparent thief, he entered a counterclaim; he asserted that *he* was the program's author and that the program had been taken from him without adequate compensation!

The Perpetrator

The identification of potential perpetrators (as part of the hiring process and, subsequently, when previously trusted employees cross the line into thievery) affords opportunities for prevention. Traditionally, it has been assumed that most people turn to crime only when serious personal financial pressures push them over the edge. Similarly, perpetrators have been thought to fit a certain age and gender profile. Unfortunately, it is no longer valid to pigeonhole potential culprits.

Most people will steal, as long as they can rationalize their behavior to their own satisfaction. Theft may be prompted by a macho attitude: a criminal may think that he is smarter than the boss, but unappreciated; therefore he sets out to show who is better. Consequently, employers must do more than endeavor to minimize smoldering employee resentments; they should monitor and investigate patterns of—or changes in—employee appearance and behavior.

Item

An internal auditor for a bank was assigned to a branch examination. He noticed a slovenly, poorly dressed youngster who drove a late-model BMW and frequently made large cash deposits. The auditor, in remarks to a teller, wondered whether "the kid was into drugs." The teller replied that the auditor was wrong and offered this reassurance: "That's the mail boy from the head office." Subsequent investigation revealed that the boy was a "bag carrier" for a gang that had developed an elaborate scheme to defraud the federal government on insured mortgages. The bank's internal affairs division's documentation of the fraud was cited by federal officials as an example of how things should be done.

The Opportunity for Illegal Access

Opportunity for illegal access to assets usually arises from knowledge acquired by the perpetrator, and/or from lack of security awareness on the part of other employees. Successful protection involves isolation of the asset, monitoring of the behavior of the perpetrator, and safeguarding of access knowledge, all implemented in a security-conscious atmosphere.

A 1987 U.K. survey of computer fraud and abuse concluded that "there is a disturbing lack of [those] basic, well-defined control mechanisms which the text books have been extolling for years. The most obvious control which was absent or deficient in nearly all reported cases was that of separating the functions of a particular process so that one individual [did] not have absolute control." Almost 10 percent of the participants in the U.K. survey reported incidents. Input to the computer was involved in the largest proportion of these frauds, and in the largest proportion of financial losses. Only 40 percent of the incidents were discovered by day-to-day control procedures, whereas 44 percent of incidents were detected by accident. The survey wound up on a pessimistic note by foreseeing ever-increasing problems affecting both the public and private sectors in the United Kingdom.[7]

THE PROTECTIVE RINGS

Isolation of the perpetrator from the asset, and from the opportunity and knowledge for access, involves the creation of a series of rings around each part of the equation. Personnel and administrative countermeasures should be instituted along with controls.

Personnel Countermeasures

Human factors affecting data security should be reflected in the design of the system and in the way it is managed. For example, the security design of a data processing operation should mini-

---

[7]The Audit Commission, *Survey of Computer Fraud and Abuse* (London: Her Majesty's Stationery Office, 1987).

mize the number of people to be placed in a position of trust, as well as the extent of trust placed in them.

Personnel countermeasures are well known and include reference checks, background inquiries, tests for honesty or for inclination toward fraud, and bonding company investigations. The effectiveness of these techniques lies in the skill with which they are applied. Auditors are familiar with the implications of control weaknesses in the personnel function, because they traditionally test the documentation underlying payroll changes; this experience should help them to evaluate the completeness and suitability of the client's procedures. For example, an auditor could recommend that the client make reference checks, not with the persons listed as references by an applicant, but with others more likely to make a realistic assessment of his performance. The benefits of intelligent reference checks are illustrated by the following tale:

Item

A man named Wilbur sought a position as an internal auditor. In so doing, Wilbur assumed the total identity of a foreign-born audit executive. Wilbur's impersonation was detected by a bonding company investigator who discussed Wilbur's (nonmatching) *physical* characteristics with persons listed as references by the foreign-born auditor. The most recent communication pertaining to Wilbur was an inquiry from the warden of Fort Leavenworth; the warden wanted to place his newly arrived charge in suitable rehabilitative employment. Ironically, the warden viewed internal auditing within the penitentiary as one possibility of such employment.

In addition to reference checks, employers may also introduce integrity tests and interviews. Polygraph testing pertaining to public safety and local police is permitted, as is federal government testing in areas of national security intelligence.[8] Emerging technology supports reference checking in another way. Some business groups have established data bases of persons who have previously been convicted of, or have confessed to, a crime. When

---

[8]June P. Schafer, Brian C. Jayne, William G. Harris, Ryan A. Kuhn, Kelley V. Rea, and Charles R. Carroll, "The Ways and Means of Screening," *Security Management*, July 1990, Supplement, pp. 20A–25A.

persons apply for a position, a search of the data bases is conducted. The technique works: in the case of a retail industry data base in a large northeastern city, in some months up to two thirds of 1 percent of applicants have been listed as felons or as self-confessed perpetrators.

Administrative Countermeasures

Risk Management

Companies' protective actions are predicated on the theory that, to some extent at least, unfavorable possibilities can be anticipated and their effects shifted or otherwise mitigated. Some examples of shifting risk to an insurance company follow. One commentator, writing in a banking industry publication, advised executives to focus on a variety of insurance products involving legal liability, disaster recovery, and computer security. Liability coverage for computer theft can protect vendors from intentional, unlawful employee acts that produce financial loss to customers; banks that provide data processing services were advised that they should consider purchasing insurance for data processing errors and omissions as a backup to the service contract.

Proactive Approaches

The entire area of risk management represents a good example of a proactive approach; it incorporates the idea that management should improve control over operations before, rather than after, money has been lost. Security controls are familiar to most accountants and auditors; security should be built into a management information system when it is first designed. Further, the functioning of controls could be tested by use of test data as part of the auditor's involvement in the system development process.

Awareness

Management must create companywide awareness of the need for security. If that awareness permeates all levels of the organization, employees will observe commonsense precautions likely to frustrate potential perpetrators. For example, modems will be switched off when not in use, thus helping to prevent unauthorized access; passwords will be secured from prying eyes; employment contracts will specify rights to intellectual property; copying machines will be monitored on a surprise basis, and so forth.

The internal or external auditor should be able to ascertain that security consciousness raising programs are under way; one aspect of such a program could involve communication to employees of the implications of active prosecutions, and of the related punishments. Prudent risk management requires judicious inquiry into the mores and backgrounds of potential clients and even suppliers, before the auditee organization enters into an association with them. Ford Motors' Jerry Guibord has commented: "[The hallmarks of a good security program are] the commitment from the top, the policy statement, . . . involvement [by] operations, a sanity check [testing policy implementation in practice] . . . and, a program quality assurance review."[9]

Item

While Treadway has focused, properly so, on the tone at the top, insufficient attention may have been paid to the tone at intermediate tops, or to general employee awareness of the problem of fraud. Accordingly, the events described in this paragraph may not be atypical. A Spanish-speaking individual appeared at a local branch of a large bank. He explained that he was a fugitive from Sandinista Nicaragua, who had just been admitted to medical practice in the United States. Over the next few months he visited the branch repeatedly; he engaged in small talk and made deposits and withdrawals. One day he appeared in a bloodstained surgical gown, and allowed that he had just left the operating room. He asked to cash a $5,000 check; the teller sought the branch manager's approval. At this point, the surgeon's beeper went off; he was being paged to return immediately to the operating room to minister to his failing patient. The manager thereupon cashed the check and thrust the bundle of bills upon the doctor as he rushed from the bank. (The "doctor" was caught at the third reenactment of his little playlet; by that time his fame had spread to all the neighborhood banks.)

Internal Controls and Internal Control Standards
As mentioned in Chapter 6, separation of duties is alive and well. There is a need for foreclosing opportunities for fraud by separat-

---

[9]Patricia M. Fernberg, "Securing Your Best Corporate Interests," *Modern Office Technology* 35, no. 4 (April 1990), p. 65.

ing custody of assets—or other items subject to conversion—from record keeping, authorization of transactions from execution, planning from operations, and systems analysis and programming from computer operations. Ironically, professional firms, especially law firms, do not appear to be attentive to internal control generally, and to separation of duties in particular. This may be due to lawyers' penchants for (1) practicing law, rather than office administration and (2) taking employees at their word. In law firms, problems are considered likely to arise in memorandum accounts (involving such items as unbilled time) and trust fund accounts, circumstances which could make such firms particularly vulnerable to thievery.[10]

In addition to separation of duties, the amorphous term *audit trail* is frequently mentioned, but rarely defined. The audit trail and its comprehensive nature, as applied to retailing, were described as follows in an English journal: (1) a terminal identifier; (2) a salesperson identifier; (3) a transaction record number; (4) a transaction date and interday sequence; (5) a transaction type; (6) transaction details; and (7) a file change image."[11]

Periodic Checkups

Periodic diagnostic checkups should be conducted by qualified consultants to ensure continuing viability of risk management programs, to foster separation of duties, to confirm that loss prevention controls continue to function as planned, and to make certain that the company is in a position to take advantage of technological developments as they break. Preferably, the consultants' reviews should extend to contingency plans and to rehearsals for the handling of emergencies, prevention and detection of damage from fire, air conditioning failure, and other environmental threats, protection against hostile acts, and backup practices. When choosing consultants, it should be remembered that technology has softened the turf demarcations used previously to distinguish between auditors, EDP auditors, and EDP consultants. However, what *is*

---

[10]Steven L. Siemborski, "Controlling Internal Theft and Fraud," *Law Office Management*, March 20, 1989, p. 22.

[11]Belden Menkus, "How an Audit Trail Aids in Maintaining Information Integrity," *Computers & Security* 9, no. 2 (April 1990), pp. 111–16.

new and noteworthy is the blending of audit and security responsibilities to provide broader and more responsive services to the organization and to protect shareholder value.[12]

Codes of Conduct

The Treadway Commission urged publicly held companies to install corporate codes of conduct. No research has been performed
to demonstrate that such codes have value; in any event, the
value, if any, would be realized from *implementation*, rather than
promulgation, of the codes. In the absence of related tests of controls, or dual-purpose substantive tests, an auditor would be ill-
advised to trust in the efficacy of codes of conduct. Moreover, it is
unusual to find a code that is (1) well written, (2) relatively complete (especially with respect to the protection, if any, that is afforded whistle-blowers), and (3) enforced. One of the few examples
of a good code comes from a large guard service company. Although the company considers the document confidential, an extract seems appropriate. "It is imperative that we adhere to the
highest standards of conduct. We know that if we deal honorably
with ourselves, our clients and our company, we will achieve a
level of both business and personal integrity of which each of us
will be justly proud."

Controls[13]

Controls may be purely physical, they may involve some computer logic, or they may be entirely computer-based. Discussion
in this section will begin with physical controls.

Electronic Surveillance of Objects and People

The new surveillance technology differs from traditional social
control in that: (1) the technology is not impeded by distance,
darkness, or physical barriers; (2) records are provided for easy

---

[12]Bank Administration Institute Audit and Security Commissions, and Information
Systems Audit & Security Committee, "Assets at Risk," *The Magazine of Bank Management*, January 1990, Banking in the 1990s, p. 44.

[13]Certain material in the controls section is based on an article by the author; that article includes a complete bibliography. The reference is Felix Pomeranz, "Technological Security," *Annals of the Academy of Political and Social Sciences* 498 (July 1988), pp. 70–81.

storage, retrieval, and analysis; (3) the concern is with reducing risk and uncertainty; and (4) those under surveillance often become active partners in their own monitoring. Quality of the devices' output has been significantly improved; this facilitates careful and in-depth study by auditors and by internal affairs personnel.

Safes and Vaults
Safes, vaults, and bullet resistant barriers represent physical countermeasures. Sandia National Laboratories has had a major physical security program in effect for over ten years. The program includes identification of items subject to loss, assessment of risk, and selection of protective techniques of optimum effectiveness.

Access Codes and Access Cards
Small cards may use various technologies, including magnetic strip, magnetic dot, embedded wire, or passive proximity. (The choice of technology depends on assessment of individual needs.) The effectiveness of the cards depends on the protection they are given by holders and on how difficult the cards are to forge or alter. Specialized technology with countermeasure capability includes three-dimensional holograms, ultraviolet ink, fine-line printing, two-sided embossing, carbonless sales slips, and so-called smart cards. The latter may embody an integrated circuit chip to increase security and reduce fraud. Management's challenge is to select from the technological tools those that will be the most efficient and the most effective.

Logical Countermeasures
Controls using logic may strengthen physical protection and safeguard computer access. Biometric security techniques allow computer users to be identified by voice, fingerprint, hand geometry, or retinal patterns. Biometric techniques depend on who a person is, rather than on what he knows. For example, the Ridge Reader from Fingermatrix works by scanning a person's fingerprint and using proprietary algorithms to compare the configurations of specific points along the print's ridges with those stored in the system for that person. Other logical controls may be concerned with determining who is seeking access, the place from which ac-

cess is sought, and what the accessing individual is authorized to do with the information.

Machine Shutdowns

These techniques include machine shutdowns after a number of unsuccessful access attempts and machine searches of a table of authorized transactions or of authorized users and of the extent of their authority. Authorization from a person with specific clearance may be required before a machine that has shut down is restarted or resumes processing.

Encryption

Encryption, touched on in Chapter 6, represents another tactic for enhancing computer security and may be an idea whose time has come, in light of the advent of distributed data processing and sophisticated telecommunications. One expert views computer security as a layered approach:

> One layer is a log-on identification that identifies the user to the computer. A second layer is a password associated with that ID to prevent unauthorized users from using the ID. A third layer is a data access control package that determines who can get to what data and what they can do with it . . . . A fourth level of security is encryption, [used especially] where the data will reside outside [the] normal control environment.

An encryption algorithm, DES, developed by IBM more than a decade ago, has been authorized for commercial use by the National Bureau of Standards and the National Security Agency. To date, encryption has been widely applied in automated teller machine networks, and has been mandated for Federal Reserve regional fund transfers. The spread of encryption seems assured.[14]

Source Data Automation

Source data automation can also help to reduce both errors and irregularities. Firms are abandoning mechanical time clocks in favor of electronic systems that are comparable in price, but elimi-

---

[14]G. Berton Latamore, "Do You Know Where Your Data's Been? Data Encryption Is Re-emerging as a Security Solution for Sensitive Electronic Transactions," *Computerworld*, June 1, 1987, p. 75.

nate labor costs and manual errors. Computerized units provide management with an effective means of integrating labor reporting into the payroll system and of monitoring employee activity. Electronic clocks eliminate labor-intensive tasks, prevent employees from punching in too early or too late, eliminate underpayments or overpayments, and forward data to a payroll processor.

Security Packages
The mainframe security market is dominated by three packages: IBM's RACF and Computer Associates International, Inc.'s Top Secret and ACF2. (By contrast, the personal computer security market is wide open with an anticipated annual growth rate of about 10 percent per year. A myriad of add-on and add-in products is offered, ranging from risk analysis packages to software locks and password systems to data encryption and diskless workstations.)[15] Two IBM data communications monitors, Information Management System (IMS) and Customer Information Control System (CICS), represent approaches designed to strengthen access security.

The National Institute of Standards and Technology and the National Computer Security Center have set up a risk management research lab to test risk analysis software and develop management guidelines; the lab helps government agencies develop comprehensive risk management programs. Wisely, potential clients have been advised to determine what they want to accomplish before shopping for automated tools.[16] (That advice is equally pertinent in the private sector.)

SOME NEGATIVE ASPECTS OF TECHNOLOGY

Herbert Edelhertz, a former chief of the U.S. Justice Department Criminal Division's fraud section, sees a clear relationship between an increase in computer-assisted crime, the numbers and

---

[15]Patricia Keefe, "It Can't Happen Here: Blasé Attitudes Spell Trouble," *Computerworld*, April 6, 1988, Corporate Vigilance, p. 13.

[16]Kevin Power, "NIST Lab Studying Security Risks and Analysis Tools," *Government Computer News* 9, no. 18 (September 3, 1990), p. 110.

sizes of transactions, the use of data communications, and the level of international trading that involves wire transfers. He adds that "if a piece of paper looks like what it is supposed to look like and comes from where it is supposed to come from, then it is going to be accepted as being what it purports to be." He notes that internal controls and protective devices may deter attempts at computer fraud—even though "the reported crimes [might not have] been discovered by detection approaches."[17]

The career of Mark Hoffman provides an instructive illustration of undetected forgery. Hoffman, a history buff and rare documents dealer, converted his basement into a chemical, photographic, and computer laboratory; he created a series of unique documents relating primarily to the early Mormon church. Initially, he established credibility by deceiving selected antiquarians along with numerous functionaries of the church; as Hoffman became increasingly worried about being exposed by teams of experts, he turned to murder—which led to Salt Lake City's "case of the century."[18]

The remainder of this chapter emphasizes the need for being alert to indicators of fraud throughout an audit engagement.

PROFESSIONAL SKEPTICISM AND SENSITIVITY TO FRAUD

The Ten Commandments

"The Ten Commands for Fraud Auditors"[19] provide an appropriate introduction to the subject of audit skepticism. These auditors' tablets include the following:

---

[17]Lois Paul, "Internal Auditing: White-Collar DP Crime Climbing in 80s," *Computerworld*, January 25, 1982, p. 12.

[18]Steven Naifeh and Gregory White Smith, *The Mormon Murders*, (New York: Weidenfeld & Nicholson, 1988).

[19]The origin of "The Ten Commandments" is not clear. The author first saw the list in a publication of the Pacific Northwest Intergovernmental Audit Forum; the reference is *Auditing for Fraud—A Resource Guide*, (Seattle: Pacific Northwest Intergovernmental Audit Forum, 1982), pp. 21–22.

I. Assume anyone can commit fraud.

II. Think dirty.

III. Remember that good documentation does not mean something happened—only that somebody *says* something happened. (This advice seems particularly pertinent in relation to computerized systems.)

IV. Pay attention to the details of documents (numbers, dates, amounts, corrections, and other alterations, typefaces, addresses, endorsements, bank notations, quantities, items, erasures, differences in pens used, thickness of marks on paper, and reasonableness of totals against individual amounts). Review for raising amounts, forgery, counterfeiting, fake billings, destruction of data, breaks in serial sequence, and substitution of copies for original documents.

V. Pay attention to the reasonableness of accounting entries, especially corrections and adjustments.

VI. Pay attention to rumors of wrongdoing, and follow up on them.

VII. Check out hunches. As an old Indian chief reportedly said, "walk a mile in the other man's (i.e., the potential malefactor's) moccasins." It is appropriate to begin an audit by brainstorming what irregularities might exist, how they might be disguised, and how they might be uncovered.

VIII. Be nosy—especially when something does not seem clear.

IX. Use statistical sampling to select items that would not be examined otherwise.

X. Look for both patterns and unusual transactions.

Inherent Risks: The Economy and the People

Poor business and economic conditions increase the risk of management fraud. Some public accounting firms have developed assessment tools to identify audit engagements that require special tasks, timing, or staffing, due to above-average risk of management fraud. According to Lawrence Sawyer, consultants specializing in investigations have identified a set of symptoms which he regards as reliable indicators of an improper condition. The symptoms include: consistently late reports; managers who regularly assume subordinates' duties; noncompliance with corporate directives and procedures; managers dealing in matters outside their profit center's scope; payments to trade creditors supported by copies instead of originals; negative debit memos; commissions not in line with increased sales.[20]

The recidivist tendencies of felons, and especially of financial operators, bear noting. Therefore, the prior associations and activities of client executives could, and in many cases should, be checked through the on-line data bases.

Item

One creative Floridian invented a concept of unsecured mortgages, known euphemistically as "equal dignity mortgages." Worthless securities valued at $40 million were vended to unwary investors, many of them senior citizens. Although the organizer of the scheme was ultimately put out of business and jailed by the state of Florida, he had been accused of scams in two other states. The details of his legal entanglements were reported in the on-line data bases; however, as far as is known, none of the investors' accountants, lawyers, or financial advisers thought to research the promoter's background on-line.

Information resources related to fraud have been documented by the Office of Special Investigations of the U.S. General Accounting Office (GAO). This organization has published a booklet entitled *Investigators' Guide to Sources of Information.* The sources listed are divided into four general categories: business, finance, people, and property. Details are given as to the information maintained by each source. (However, some of the information may be obtainable only through the legal process.) In addition, the Guide includes a data base section which features investigative and law enforcement data bases, as well as commercial data bases, and research and reference services. See Appendix B.[21]

---

[20]Sawyer, *Sawyer's Internal Auditing*, p. 1036.

[21]U.S. General Accounting Office, Office of Special Investigations, *Investigators' Guide to Sources of Information*, GAO/OSI-88-1, March 1988.

The Control Environment: Red Flags

As noted in Chapter 4, a quick assessment of the moral tone of an organization may be made by looking at a few pulses, including the auditee's attitude toward internal control. Contempt for internal control can have serious consequences.

Item

One interesting case involved a company which provided subscribers with financial information. Deficiencies in control existed over salesmen engaged in renegotiating sales contracts with clients. A senior executive announced, "We don't have dishonest salesmen here," and expressed a lack of interest in imposing "unrealistic" control requirements. Ultimately, customers stated that they were being defrauded by being pressured into unnecessary or excessive contracts; the damage suits involved millions of dollars.

Red flags may wave for both the audited entity and individual employees. An imperious management style portends trouble; the danger signals include autocratic management, low trust of employees, short-range planning, management by crisis, negative feedback, poor promotion opportunities, hostile working relationships, high turnover and/or absenteeism, low company loyalty, and a reactive management philosophy. (Many frauds occur where an autocratic management arbitrarily sets budgets for lower level managers. When these budgets prove unattainable, the managers have a choice to either cheat or fail.)

There are three categories of employee-specific red flags: (1) personal financial factors, (2) personal habits, and (3) personal feelings. In addition to these factors, personal red flags include abruptly changed behavior, a wheeler-dealer attitude, consistent rationalization of contradictory behavior, and a strong desire to beat the system.[22] Perceived inequities in the workplace can lead to low employee loyalty and to attempts to correct such injustices as:

---

[22]Joseph T. Wells, W. Steve Albrecht, Jack Bologna, Gilbert Geis, and Jack Robertson, *Fraud Examiners Manual* (Austin: National Association of Certified Fraud Examiners, 1988); some of the discussion in this section, especially that pertaining to criminology, draws upon the contents of this Manual.

1. Being passed over for a raise.
2. Being assigned to undesirable jobs.
3. Being subjected to disciplinary action.
4. Favoritism shown to other employees.
5. Feeling that pay is inadequate.
6. Resentment of superiors.
7. Frustration with the job.
8. Boredom.

Environmental and personal red flags are related; problems may feed on each other. Conversely, a supportive counseling and financial assistance program could head off fraud by an employee who is considering problem solving via thievery.

Obtaining an Understanding of the System

When the auditor reviews detailed flowcharts (and/or conducts transaction reviews) he should be alert to the reasons for the creation of new types of transactions.

Item

Mr. X, a whiz kid of the record industry, requested and was granted a separate bank account. Checks written on the new account were to be signed manually by X and his executive assistant. The ostensible purpose of the account was to expedite promotional payments to disk jockeys and others. However, the account was used largely to pay X's expenses, some of which were subsequently alleged to be of a personal nature. The alleged peculations were uncovered by internal auditors in the course of vouching disbursements; the allegations led to X's dismissal.

A skilled interviewer may detect clues to wrongdoing in what a subject talks about, which matters he embellishes and which he skirts, and his body language. Auditors could benefit from improved interviewing skills, and from a better understanding of the behavioral aspects of interviewing. The *Fraud Examiners Manual* describes the fluid line between an interview and an interrogation, and gives useful guidelines to the conduct of both

procedures.[23] An experimental approach called cognitive interviewing may have some favorable implications for fraud auditors
of the future. The cognitive interview is a memory-enhancing
technique aimed at getting crime victims and witnesses to remember more than they would under standard questioning.
Some training by a qualified psychologist seems desirable to apply this technique effectively. However, it appears that the techniques can be learned relatively easily.

Analytical Review and Substantive Testing

A wealth of pertinent information has become accessible to auditors through the inquiry capabilities available on certain data bases, or by special programs written to retrieve particular information. For example, Georgette Bennett reports that insurance
companies may access in-house data bases in endeavoring to find
answers to questions such as these:

Has the same person made several claims?

Has the same article been subject to multiple claims?

Does the claimant hold similar policies with several companies?

Has the policy been written recently?

Are all claimants in an accident being treated by the same
doctor?

Is the article claimed relatively expensive compared to the
face amount of the policy?

Did the reported burglary take place while the claimant was
on vacation?

Is it likely for a person to lose a sable coat on a plane bound for
Hawaii?

Can a person be suffering from an injured back, if he was seen
recently playing tennis for two hours?

---

[23]Wells et al., *Fraud Examiners Manual,* pp. 1-14 to 1-31.

Was business bad for the two years prior to the fire that destroyed claimant's restaurant?[24]

The same point can be illustrated with an example from a payroll audit; let us assume that the auditee renders guard and cleaning services, that its work force is composed of persons with relatively limited education, and that turnover is heavy. Let us further assume that activities are administered in decentralized fashion and that there are deficiencies in controlling changes to standing (i.e., repetitively used) data in the payroll files.

The auditor's arsenal includes general-purpose computer audit programs, specialized industry programs, data base programs, public domain security utilities, and disk operating system (DOS) utilities.[25] In the subject case, a simple program was written to develop:

1. The identification of the same social security number submitted with different names. (This may be an indication of payroll padding.)
2. The identification of the same social security number, utilizing the same name, in different departments. (This may be an indication of double-dipping or of payroll padding.)
3. The identification of individuals bearing different names, but residing at the same address. (Further investigation may uncover payroll padding involving no-shows.)
4. The identification of individuals consistently working overtime beyond limits established by company policies. (Further investigation may reflect favoritism.)
5. The identification of individuals having had an unreasonable number of promotions, or unreasonably large pay raises. (This, too, could point to favoritism.)

---

[24]Georgette Bennett, *Crimewarps: The Future of Crime in America* (Garden City: Doubleday, Anchor Press, 1987), p. 104.

[25]Jerry FitzGerald, *Online Auditing Using Microcomputers* (Redwood City, Calif.: Jerry FitzGerald & Associates, 1987). This book is accompanied by an extremely useful series of selected public domain programs.

6. The identification of individuals lacking certain payroll deductions, including withholding taxes and hospitalization. (This could point to ghosts on the payroll.)

7. The identification by the Social Security Administration of social security numbers that were claimed by employees, but that do not exist. In other words, social security taxes were paid but could not be credited to a legitimate account. (The condition could point to ghosts on the payroll.)

8. Travel and expense reimbursements which may be inflated or duplicated; a particular risk of duplicate payments exists when reimbursements may be made at the employee's option, either via payrolls and/or by separate disbursements.

9. Particular client complaints referenced to units or individuals. (This may reveal a variety of irregularities, including assignment of personnel with qualifications or ratings below those stipulated in the contract with the client, "soldiering on the job," and payroll padding.)

When implementation of special computer programs reveals problems, immediate steps should be taken to (1) correct the condition, (2) if practicable, take steps toward recovery, (3) repair the controls to prevent the situation from recurring, and (4) amend the audit program as necessary.

Use of operational information can accomplish a more efficient and effective financial audit. Moreover, the auditor may gain a fringe benefit in terms of detecting possible fraud. Operational information tends to move through channels apart from the financial information network. Thus, operational information that may have originated in a quasi-independent manner can be used by an auditor to verify the accuracy and completeness of financial information.

Item

Paternalistic Paper Corporation heated its employees' homes with power generated at a company-owned utility, at very low cost to the employees. The chief engineer of the utility reported an inexplicable decline in revenues and advised his auditors to be especially alert; he also established that steam output in terms of British thermal units (BTUs) was being measured correctly. The auditors reviewed the tonnage of coal input, applied the expected BTU generation factor, and simulated the utility's financial statements. The simulated financial statements differed substantially from the actual financial statements. Since the variances could not be explained, Geiger counters were used to trace the steam pipelines. An illicit tap was discovered.

Conducting a Search for Errors

Depending upon the terms of the engagement, or the auditor's assessment of the control environment, a search may be initiated for symptoms of possible fraud or for surrogate evidence of fraud. (Such a search may involve discovery sampling, which was mentioned in Chapter 6.) In a sense, a search represents a way of testing controls. The test seeks indirect confirmation of the results of the application of controls; it does not involve direct testing of the functioning of controls.

Item

Although the following example relates to a special engagement, it illustrates the mind-set desired in a search for fraud. An independent accounting firm was engaged to determine whether the chief executive of C Corporation, a large nonclient movie theater chain, had enriched himself at shareholders' expense. C Corporation not only operated cinemas but also owned numerous parcels of land and buildings. Published annual reports represented the only documentation available to the examiners. Review of footnotes concerning the executive bonus plan provided the proverbial smoking gun. The executive bonus plan had been designed to spur better operating performance by theater managers. However, C's president had decided to supplement his own bonus in slow years by including capital gains from theater dispositions in the bonus computation; his interpretation of the bonus base varied from year to year, depending on the extent of the bonus he wished to earn. The auditor's review set the stage for a shareholder suit.

Expert systems may help in fraud prevention. Security Pacific recently installed an expert system which monitors certain kinds of financial transactions in order to detect and deter fraudulent activities. The fraud investigator's expertise is modeled in the expert system shell as a set of backward chaining rules. The basic rule says that if a symptom of fraud is detected in a data base of electronic transactions, then the likelihood of fraud can be anticipated with a particular certainty factor. The expert system might decide to block the account, to call for further investigation, or to refer to accounts where no fraud has been detected. In the author's words, "financial applications are one of the most promising directions . . . of expert systems. . . . [In fraud detection] the knowledge and experience of the senior fraud investigator can be made available on-line to everybody.[26]

THE FUTURE: ALERTNESS

External and internal auditors will have to continue to stay alert to fraud, partly because security breaches may be facilitated by the current trend toward connectivity. Because greater access leads to greater vulnerability, decentralization necessitates the placing of significant responsibility for security increasingly in the hands of end users.

Technology does not offer radically new answers to managements attempting to protect companies from fraud, industrial espionage, or sundry types of sabotage. The solution lies in awareness at all levels, unwavering management support for security— including appropriate budgets—and realistic and enforced policies and procedures. Basic internal control—including separation of duties—and adequate audit trails continue to represent the bedrock of protection against fraud. Attempts to prevent fraud are likely to become increasingly proactive. Security functions represent a tried and proven proactive audit application; auditors should assess and test the controls incorporated in systems as development proceeds, and indeed, throughout the life cycle of the systems.

The special fraud audit, part of the growing field of forensic accounting, is likely to show significant growth. With the forma-

---

[26]Koenraad Lecot, "Using Expert Systems in Banking: The Case of Fraud Detection," *Expert Systems Review* 1, no. 2 (1988), p. 17–20.

tion of the National Association of Certified Fraud Examiners (NACFE), its licensing programs, continuing professional education requirement, and code of professional ethics, generally accepted forensic auditing standards may not be far behind. And, NACFE's active research program can be expected to make significant contributions to the state of the art.

SUMMARY

A series of rings should be drawn around the factors in the fraud equation (the asset, the perpetrator, and the opportunity). The rings involve redesign and/or fine-tuning of administrative and personnel procedures, risk analysis, and above all, controls. An eclectic mix of physical, logical, and computer-based devices will protect assets and safeguard computer access.

The most fundamental change required of auditors relates to attitude and sensitivity. No longer will auditors "speak no evil, hear no evil, and see no evil"; having become newly suspicious, their work will be assisted by electronic tools. For example, new data bases will be created which will eventually include criminals' modi operandi and the manner of detection. Intelligence relating to executives and their prior activities and utterances will be gathered by monitoring the on-line data bases. Analytical procedures will be performed largely by using quasi-independently developed operational data and by making incisive associations of financial and operational information. In addition, substantive tests will become more efficient, due to the emerging capability of querying data bases, entrapment of information for subsequent audit review, knowledge-based decision aids, more powerful computer audit programs, and use of the on-line data bases to develop corroborative information.

CHAPTER 8

BLENDING TECHNOLOGY AND THE UPDATED AUDIT MODEL

"You must be able to dance if you are to heal people," [the old Indian healer] said . . . . "I can teach you my steps, but you will have to hear your own music."

*Carl A. Hammerschlag**

USER PERSPECTIVE: Items of Special Interest

EXECUTIVE HIGHLIGHTS: All readers

INTRODUCTION: All readers

THE MASTER TRACKING SHEET: All readers

UNDERSTAND INHERENT RISK: External auditors, internal auditors, audit committee members

UNDERSTAND THE CLIENT: ON–SITE: External auditors

UNDERSTAND THE CONTROL ENVIRONMENT: External auditors, internal auditors

UNDERSTAND THE SYSTEM AND CONTROL PROCEDURES: External auditors, internal auditors, audit committee members

ASSESS CONTROL RISK: All readers

CONDUCT SUBSTANTIVE TESTS: External auditors, internal auditors

SUMMARY: All readers

---

*Carl A. Hammerschlag, M.D., is the author of the recent book *The Dancing Healers* (New York: Harper & Row, 1988).

EXECUTIVE HIGHLIGHTS

A relationship exists between the ambience created by management, the "tone at the top," and the risk of misstatements, particularly in accounting estimates; controls may prevent or detect misstatements or, at least, make them more difficult.

The client should have a systematic approach to risk management. Potential or actual threats should not be viewed as "acts of God." Risk management techniques may be employed to control many exposures or at least to mitigate their negative impacts.

To run the business, management must have reasonable assurance that controls are functioning as planned. That assurance can be gained by installing supervisory controls designed to detect nonperformance in a timely manner.

The auditor should maintain a running list of potential threats, called a master tracking sheet. Controls can then be matched to the threats to permit audit procedures to focus on areas of likely audit risk, and to facilitate the formulation of recommendations for control enhancement.

Internal risks include management and employee fraud, poor communication, disorderly or excessively authoritarian actions, and employee morale and turnover problems. Deficiencies can reflect themselves in inability to make timely deliveries of goods and services at appropriate cost or to meet product and service quality standards.

The plant and/or office tours should give the auditor an impression of the extent to which assets are protected from theft or deterioration, of the complexity and size of materials, and of security awareness—or lack thereof—on the part of employees.

Audit risk is likely to be reduced by extensive substantive examinations, compared to less extensive substantive examinations; and, examinations at year end are favored over examinations at interim.

INTRODUCTION

This chapter blends what has been covered in Chapters 4 and 6 relative to the expanded audit model; the discussion focuses on technological tools available to accomplish the phases in the audit approach including general and specific audit objectives. Chapter 4 capped the first section of this book, Setting the Stage, while Chapter 6 was the penultimate chapter in the second section, The Advent of Technology. (However, Chapter 7 was no outlier; it was intended to sensitize auditors to indications of fraud.) This chapter should enable auditors to comply with the expectation gap *SAS*s. By way of introduction, reference is made to *SAS No. 55*, "Consideration of the Internal Control Structure in a Financial Statement Audit"; this *Statement* became effective for periods beginning on or after January 1, 1990. *SAS 55* requires the auditor to document his understanding of the internal control structure (i.e., of the control environment, accounting system, and control procedures) for the following purposes:

- To identify types of potential misstatements.
- To consider factors that affect the risk of material misstatements.
- To design substantive tests.

During 1989, an AICPA task force developed an audit guide to assist auditors in implementing *SAS 55*. Figure 8–1 presents the two basic strategies in the guide, which depend on the degree of control risk assessed by the auditor.

A significant relationship exists between the ambience created by management, the tone at the top, and the risk of misstatements, particularly in accounting estimates; controls may prevent or detect misstatements, or, at least, make them more difficult. Moreover, a thorough understanding of the system, focused on control-related matters, is basic to the design of meaningful audit procedures.[1]

---

[1]Raymond N. Johnson, "Practical Application of *SAS 55*," *The CPA Journal*, May 1990, pp. 14–21.

FIGURE 8-1 Guide to *SAS 55* Basic Strategies

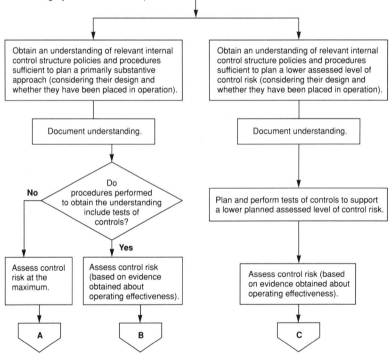

Flowchart of the Auditor's Consideration of the Internal Control Structure and Its Relation to Substantive Tests for Significant Assertions Related to Each Significant Account Balance and Class of Transaction

Consider a preliminary audit strategy (for significant assertions related to each significant account balance and class of transaction) to obtain an understanding sufficient to plan the audit based on a planned assessed level of control risk or planned level of substantive tests.

Audit strategy: Obtain an understanding relevant to an assertion sufficient to plan a primarily substantive approach. (Evidence about operating effectiveness acquired while obtaining this understanding will normally result in a control risk assessment at or slightly below the maximum.)

Audit strategy: Obtain an understanding relevant to an assertion and perform tests of controls to support a lower planned assessed level of control risk.

Obtain an understanding of relevant internal control structure policies and procedures sufficient to plan a primarily substantive approach (considering their design and whether they have been placed in operation).

Obtain an understanding of relevant internal control structure policies and procedures sufficient to plan a lower assessed level of control risk (considering their design and whether they have been placed in operation).

Document understanding.

Document understanding.

Do procedures performed to obtain the understanding include tests of controls?

No

Yes

Plan and perform tests of controls to support a lower planned assessed level of control risk.

Assess control risk at the maximum.

Assess control risk (based on evidence obtained about operating effectiveness).

Assess control risk (based on evidence obtained about operating effectiveness).

A

B

C

Note: This flowchart presents only one conceptual way to view the auditor's consideration of the internal control structure, and it does not imply a specific sequencing of steps in the performance of an audit. In addition, there may be other strategies that the auditor may follow.

FIGURE 8–1 *(concluded)*

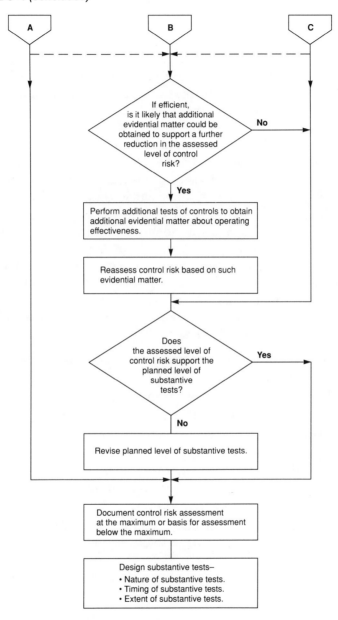

Source: Adapted from *Audit Guide, Consideration of the Internal Control Structure in a Financial Statement Audit* (New York: American Institute of Certified Public Accountants, 1990), pp. 10–11. Reprinted with permission.

THE MASTER TRACKING SHEET

The auditor should maintain a running list of potential threats. The list will be referred to as the master tracking sheet. The sheet represents an adaptation of an approach developed by Jerry FitzGerald for computerized systems. FitzGerald calls for identification of the component parts that make up the system and of the threats these components face. Threats are listed across the top of the sheet, components down its side.[2] A threat is defined as a potentially adverse occurrence or an unwanted event that could be injurious to the organization. Controls prevent or detect threats that may cause damage to the components, the system, or the organization. When the master tracking sheet is prepared as a spreadsheet, or with word processing software, its flexibility is enhanced; for example, lines can be made available under each threat to explain either existing or recommended controls. Components, threats, and controls are client dependent. The FitzGeralds have defined the components listed below; additional components, such as assets and resources, can be added as needed:

1. Reports: reports and manual files, documents, logs, and so forth.
2. Microcomputers or terminals: these units may be connected to a host mainframe or to other networks.
3. Mainframe or minicomputers: central site computers, disk and tape drives, and related hardware.
4. Terminal operators: terminal operators, temporary employees, and other employees or outsiders who have access to the organization's terminals.
5. Communication circuits: communication circuits connecting the organization to either local or wide area networks.

---

[2]Jerry FitzGerald, "How to Conduct a Security Review," *ISP News*, September/October 1990, pp. 5–7.

6. Data and data base files: the organization's data files on disk drives, in file cabinets, or in long-term storage.

7. Programs: application programs and other software for mainframes or microcomputers.[3]

Threats were described as follows:

1. Breach of privacy: unauthorized access to confidential data.

2. Errors and omissions: errors that occur during document preparation, processing, or output.

3. Illegal system access: unauthorized access to data bases, networks, computer programs, sensitive documents, etc.

4. Fraud or theft: theft of an organization's data or other assets by manual or computerized means.

5. Lost or corrupted messages: misdirected, lost, unprocessed, or delayed messages, whether occurring manually, during computer processing, or on networks.

6. Disasters and disruptions: physical disasters, including fires, floods, electrical failures, storms, and earthquakes.[4]

Author's Comment

Jerry and Ardra FitzGerald recommend application of the Delphi technique to accomplish comparative risk ranking of threats. The technique involves selection of a few experts who have in-depth knowledge of the system being reviewed; after discussing the threats, the experts combine their opinions to form a consensus as to which threat might cause the most damage or delay. The author expects that it will not be necessary on most engagements to formally implement the Delphi technique. He believes that senior external and internal audit personnel have excellent qualifications for arriving at an informal view of the risk that attaches to uncontrolled threats and of the affected accounts.

---

[3]Jerry FitzGerald and Ardra F. FitzGerald, *Designing Controls into Computerized Systems*, 2nd ed. (Redwood City, Calif.: Jerry FitzGerald & Associates, 1990), p. 32.
[4]Ibid.

UNDERSTAND INHERENT RISK

Consider the Auditee's Position Relative to Its Industry

The auditor may wish to see how the client has fared compared to others. That comparison is often based on the U.S. government's Standard Industrial Classification (SIC) code. (Dun & Bradstreet has developed a more detailed form of segmentation, called the *2+2 SIC Code System.*) Auditors are cautioned that the selection of an SIC code can be difficult, given the conglomerate nature of many U.S. companies. Moreover, companies change SIC codes to reflect new corporate directions; in less commendable fashion, some companies may window-dress comparisons by reporting codes likely to show better comparisons.

> **Item**
>
> Reference will be made from time to time to an actual company about which the author has written previously. The entity was originally chosen at random; its name will be disguised. It will be referred to as Discover Corp. (Discover). The on-line records for Discover sport three SIC numbers, none of which bears more than a casual relationship to the company's business. In general, external and internal auditors should verify the correctness of SIC codes, since the client may find the choice difficult.

SAS 56 requires the auditor to use analytical procedures at different audit stages, including planning. Comparing a client's financial results with those of other companies in its industry may help to focus audit efforts.[5] After the auditor has satisfied herself as to the reasonableness of the SIC code, she can access either D&B-Dun's Financial Records Plus, available on DIALOG, or Disclosure, Inc.'s data base, available on both DIALOG and Mead Data Central. In the case of Dun's, the record includes 14 measures; half of these can be searched arithmetically. The client can be compared to the median of a preselected sample of companies.

---

[5]Deloitte & Touche has opted for what it calls a *peer group analysis*, drawn from the Compustat data base. The peer group is defined by matches on major industry category, size, standard industrial code, and geographical region.

(See Figure 8–2.) In the case of Disclosure, 32 financial ratios are displayed for a three-year period. (See Figure 8–3.)

FIGURE 8–2
D&B-Dun's Financial Ratios

D&B-Dun's Financial Records Plus, available on DIALOG, feature the following ratios, together with a comparison of the client to industry norms, expressed in upper, lower, and median quartiles:

Solvency:
Quick ratio
Current ratio
Current liabilities/net worth
Current liabilities/inventory
Total liabilities/net worth
Fixed assets/net worth

Efficiency:
Collection period (days)
Sales/inventory
Assets/sales
Sales/net working capital
Accounts payable/sales

Profitability:
Return on sales
Return on assets
Return on net worth

FIGURE 8–3
Disclosure, Inc. Financial Ratios

Disclosure Database, available on both NEXIS and DIALOG, features the following ratios, shown for the last three years:

Quick ratio
Current ratio
Net sales/cash
Sales, general, and administrative expenses/sales
Receivables turnover

Receivables day sales
Inventories turnover
Inventories day sales
Net sales/working capital
Net sales/net plant and equipment

(continued)

FIGURE 8–3 *(concluded)*

Net sales/current assets
Net sales/total assets
Net sales/employees
Total liabilities/total assets
Total liabilities/invested capital

Total liabilities/common equity
Times interest earned
Current debt/equity
Long term debt/equity
Total debt/equity

Total assets/equity
Pretax income/net sales
Pretax income/total assets
Pretax income/invested capital
Pretax income/common equity

Net income/net sales
Net income/total assets
Net income/invested capital
Net income/common equity
R&D expenditures/net sales

R&D expenditures/net income
R&D expenditures/employees

Item

Readers may be interested in Discover's quick ratio (cash plus marketable securities plus net current receivables, all divided by current liabilities) over a three-year period compared to similar entities:

	1989	1988	1987
Discover	1.13	2.19	2.47
Competitor A	5.77	7.23	10.66
Competitor B	1.76	18.71	14.24
Competitor C	.35	.24	1.79
Industry leader	6.87	2.06	.28

Identify Client's Approach to Risk Management

External risks may affect revenues or costs. Major threats to revenues include declining customer demand, gluts in the market-

place, and consequent price erosion. In addition, the general state of the economy may affect a company's ability to turn receivables and other assets into cash. Major threats on the expenditure side involve inflationary increases in the cost of purchased materials, labor, and capital. Production disruptions may arise from scarcity of materials, inadequate energy supplies, nonavailability of labor, or shortages of capital. Technical advances in the United States or abroad may diminish the value of the company's products, services, and inventories on hand. Legal actions, at times frivolous, may be brought against a company on a broad band of issues, including patent infringements and social law violations relating to employees, environment, and communities.

In any case, potential or actual threats should not be viewed as acts of God. Risk management techniques may be employed to control many of them, or at least to mitigate their negative impacts. Risk management goes beyond the purchase of insurance, although insurance can be integral to risk management. The decision that must be made is whether to assume a particular risk—often appropriate in the case of a relatively small risk, or a risk which cannot be insured—shift the risk to others (including vendors, employees, customers, and insurance companies), or manage the risk through the system and the controls built into that system.

Risk management decisions may be complex; they may involve ethical and moral considerations in addition to cost/benefit trade-offs. Even when management succeeds in shifting the risk, it still has an important stake in keeping losses down; where there is insurance coverage, loss claims may result in higher rates. Where risks are assumed by contractors, there is the possibility that a contractor will not be able to make good.

Jerry FitzGerald has presented the major steps in business risk management:

- List the potential causes of loss.
- Estimate the value of the asset, or of the related revenues to be protected, or the potential for cost increases or revenue losses.
- Identify the expected threats likely to cause loss.
- For each threat, estimate the probability of its occurrence.

- Quantify the estimated loss.
- Determine the approach to be taken to control.
- Introduce the requisite safeguards.[6]

If the client practices risk management, the auditor can begin where the client left off, except that the auditor's perspective is one of *audit* risk. Audit risk tends to involve uncontrolled threats. The auditor performs two steps: (1) she identifies threats, noted during the current audit, plus uncontrolled threats carried forward from a previous audit (giving particular attention to the focal areas of exposure), and posts these threats to her master tracking sheet; and, (2) as the audit progresses, she records any controls introduced to manage risk through the system.

Some examples of client risk management approaches are given in succeeding paragraphs:

1. *Energy shortages.* The typical approach shifts risk to the energy provider via long-term supply contracts. It may be possible to secure favorable rates from utilities by granting them the right to interrupt service. For example, assume a continuous production process with interruption of power (heat) not operationally feasible. In such a case consideration might be given to possible construction of standby liquid propane gas facilities; these facilities would permit the manufacturer to seek advantageous electric rates.

2. *Material shortages.* The usual approach is to shift the risk to vendors via long term contracts. Merely having more than one vendor to choose from may afford a degree of protection. Beyond this, it may be possible to share key materials, such as spare parts for crippled machines, with others in the same industry. This practice is followed in capital-intensive industries. Of course, inventory controls, which strike a balance between acquisition costs and carrying charges and aim to protect the continuity of production, can also reduce the impact of shortages.

---

[6]Jerry FitzGerald, "EDP Risk Analysis for Contingency Planning," *The EDP Audit Control and Security Newsletter*, September 1978, pp. 1–8.

3. *Labor interruptions.* Management must be constantly alert to conditions that could give rise to legitimate grievances. While these conditions are being evaluated, hopefully with a view toward problem resolution, contingency planning can be under way to resequence critical operations, and/or to stockpile supplies to cushion the effects of a possible strike.

4. *Inflation.* It may be possible to shift the risk of inflation to vendors, by limiting or capping escalation clauses in long term contracts.

5. *Capital shortages.* Active cash management should help to control cash inflow, outflow, and turnover, and should have a positive influence on earnings over the short and long term. Cyclical peaks and valleys in cash balances must be evaluated; gaps may be closed by introducing suitable financing.

6. *Violations of laws.* One way of coping with the legal and regulatory maze is to have attorneys compile lists of laws, regulations, rulings, and court decisions that could affect the auditee. The list should include rules and regulations that are still under consideration, but are likely to be implemented. The compilation can be used as a basis for monitoring compliance.

Author's Comment

The task of listing laws is formidable. For example, a railroad that sought to modernize or add about 150 miles of rail, found itself subject to 1,700 different ordinances and codes. However, the act of compiling the list of laws proved highly beneficial, since it permitted many of the rules to be satisfied on the basis of a single search through the records.

Item

Some years ago, a law was being considered which required the installation of devices to detect the buildup of potentially explosive fumes on oil tankers. One major oil company ordered the devices built into tankers under construction, an action which avoided subsequent, more costly modification of ships after they had entered service.

7. *Technological changes.* Care must be taken to track technological developments in progress, to weigh their effect on costs and revenues, and to take protective action necessary to mitigate unfavorable effects.

> The auditor may obtain some feeling for the inherent risk that confronts an entity by reading the 10-K—the annual report to the Securities and Exchange Commission (SEC). (Considerable information concerning risk may also be gleaned from reading the documents filed in connection with an initial securities offering.) The detailed 10-K is available from SEC Online, Inc. via NEXIS, and also through DIALOG; the complete 10-K may contain more information than the Disclosure, Inc. (DISCLO) version; the latter is also available on both DIALOG and NEXIS.

In the case of Discover, management's discussion and analysis of financial condition and results of operations included in the 10-K revealed that a quarter of the company's revenues stemmed from a gain from the sale of oil and gas properties. The footnote dealing with the accounting for the transaction made it clear that the purchaser was an affiliated entity. This gain is discussed more fully later in this chapter.

The author randomly selected a second company to further illustrate the information content of the 10-Ks; this concern will be called Adult Toy Ltd. (Adult). In the case of Adult, accounts receivable declined by half from the previous year, although sales rose. Management's discussion and analysis of financial condition and results of operations disclosed that the company entered into an agreement with its largest customer for the sale of products at reduced margins. In return for this concession, the company received immediate payment on a large sale to the customer.

An indication of risk may also be obtained by reading newspaper articles. The results of a successful search of regional papers on NEXIS (included in the CURRNT group file) proved humorous in addition to sending a message. An article described a visit with Discover's former chairman, who is still a director and a very large shareholder: "It's a quiet Monday in the summer, but the scent of a deal is in the air . . . . 'Are you single?' [the former chairman asks the reporter] . . . 'I've got the perfect girl for you.' " The reporter summarizes the subject's characteristics as follows: "A little bit of sincerity, a little bit of bluster, a lot of hard sell."

In the case of Adult, the CURRNT file was equally helpful. An article was found in a regional paper, which described the company as appealing to "the child that lives in the adult." The reporter added that this embryonic creature had to have plenty of disposable income. More disturbingly, the company's principals were described as saying that they don't bother with consumer tests or other surveys in deciding whether to market a new product. In other words, the principals are hunch players. Given the histories and performances of similar companies with similar philosophies, and the possibility of a protracted downturn in the economy, the article should alert the auditor to problems that could involve almost every account.

Search of another NEXIS file (*Daily SEC Abstract*) disclosed that, presumably influenced by cash flow problems, Adult had filed an open (shelf) registration with the SEC for the issuance of new securities valued between $5 and $6 per share. However, fiscal relief may not be in sight; Adult's stock presently trades for less than half of the stipulated range of values.

The auditor's knowledge of external risk, acquired before she actually begins her audit and integrated into her thinking as potential audit risk, equips her to ask the hard questions when she arrives on the client's premises.

Communicate with Former Auditors

If the client is new, the auditor should follow professional rules (*SAS 7*) and contact the prior auditors to obtain their insights and, conceivably, information for the permanent files; for example, the former auditors could assist in historic analyses of goodwill, long-term liabilities, capital, and similar accounts. The new auditor should be satisfied that the auditor change notification requirements of the SEC have been observed. These requirements, which must be accomplished within a narrow time frame (which could get progressively more narrow), involve the client's reporting of the auditor change, concurred in by the former auditor. The pertinent form, 8-K, deals with major corporate events and is readily retrievable from the on-line data bases.

Adult's 1988 8-K shows three audit firms—last year's auditors, the incoming auditors, and a third firm, not otherwise identified. The situation would seem to make it incumbent upon an incoming auditor to seek out the letters submitted by the outgoing auditor and by the third auditor to see whether the letters offer clues to disagreements with the client.

Another example: a more dramatic brace of 8-Ks was filed in October 1990 by Financial News Network (FNN) and an affiliate (see Figure 8–4). FNN announced the appointment of interim chief executive officers; the registrant also said that it had learned that the SEC had issued a formal order of investigation with respect to possible securities law violations. A few days earlier a related company, Infotechnology, Inc., and its independent accountants, Deloitte & Touche, "mutually agreed" to terminate Deloitte's audit engagement. Deloitte indicated that certain financial statements could not be relied upon due to the audit firm's inability to satisfy itself about investments in FNN.

Update Knowledge of Professional and Regulatory Requirements

The AICPA's Electronic Index to Technical Pronouncements (EITP) was mentioned in Chapter 6, along with the literature file (LIT) of NAARS, the National Automated Accounting Research System. The recovery from the LIT file of an issue addressed by the Emerging Issues Task Force (EITF) appears in Figure 8–5. Of course, an auditor should be aware of both existing and emerging rules. She should know what new reporting requirements are emerging and when, what information might be needed to comply, and how much effort may be required. The auditor may wish to advise the client on implementation of the new rules to minimize negative impact.

Debrief Staff

The external or internal auditor should debrief all staff members with significant previous exposure to the auditee. The information sources include auditors previously assigned to the engage-

FIGURE 8–4
8-K Examples

LEVEL 1 - 1 OF 11 REPORTS
Copyright © 1990 Mead Data Central, Inc.; prepared by States News Service
SEC Abstracted Filings

Form 8-K

FILING-DATE: October 30, 1990

REGISTRANT-NAME Financial News Network Inc.

DATE-OF-REPORT: October 23, 1990

COMMISSION FILE NO.: 1- 8374

INCORPORATION: California

ITEM-5:
On Oct. 24, 1990 the registrant announced that Alan J. Herschfield and Allan R. Tessler will serve as interim co-CEOs. On Oct. 25, 1990 the registrant learned that the SEC had issued a formal order of investigation with respect to possible federal securities laws violations by the registrant.

ITEM-7/ EXHIBIT-INDEX:
Exhibit 1 -- Press release dated Oct. 24, 1990.

2 -- Press release dated Oct. 23, 1990.

LEVEL 1 - 3 OF 8 REPORTS
Copyright © 1990 Mead Data Central, Inc.; prepared by States News Service
SEC Abstracted Filings

Form 8-K

FILING-DATE: October 12, 1990

REGISTRANT-NAME: Financial News Network Inc.

DATE-OF-REPORT: October 4, 1990

COMMISSION FILE NO.: 1- 8374

INCORPORATION: California

ITEM-4:
On Oct. 11, 1990 the registrant engaged Coopers & Lybrand to replace Deloitte & Touche, who was dismissed Oct. 4, 1990 as its independent accountant. In Sept. 1990 the registrant engaged Henry R. Jaenicke to consult with the registrant on certain accounting issues with respect to the fiscal year ended June 30, 1990.

ITEM-7/ EXHIBIT-INDEX:
Exhibit 1 -- Letter of Deloitte & Touche.

Source: Represents output of search of Mead Data Central, NEXIS Service, SEC Abstracts of Filings, 8-K, prepared by States News Service. NEXIS® and Related Services Guide. Reprinted with the permission of Mead Data Central, Inc., provider of the LEXIS®/NEXIS® Services. Copyright 1990, Mead Data Central, Inc. No copyright is claimed as to any part of the original work prepared by a government officer or employee as part of that person's official duties.

FIGURE 8–5
EITF Issue Memorandum Example

LEVEL 1 - 9 OF 287 ITEMS
FASB; FINANCIAL ACCOUNTING STANDARDS BOARD; EITF; EMERGING
ISSUES TASK FORCE

MARCH 8, 1990

ISSUE SUMMARY NO. 90-5; FEITFIS 90-5
EXCHANGES OF OWNERSHIP INTERESTS BETWEEN ENTITIES UNDER COMMON
CONTROL

TEXT:
ISSUE:EXCHANGES OF OWNERSHIP INTERESTS BETWEEN ENTITIES
UNDER COMMON CONTROL

Prepared by: Arthur Andersen & Co.

Date Prepared: January 31, 1990

Raised by: Arthur Andersen & Co.

Summary Description of Transaction/Event

A parent company exchanges its ownership in subsidiary Sub B (either wholly or partially owned) for additional shares of its partially owned subsidiary Sub A.

ISSUE SUMMARY NO. 90-5; FEITFIS 90-5 MARCH 8, 1990

A. Sub A may or may not issue shares for the minority interests of Sub B.

Accounting Issues and Status AICPA Accounting Interpretation 39, "Transfers and Exchanges between Companies under Common Control" of APB Opinion No. 16, Business Combinations, indicates that the transfer of net assets or an exchange of shares between entities under common control are excluded from Opinion 16 and should be accounted for at historical cost in a manner similar to a pooling of interests. An accounting issue arises when the parent company's basis in the subsidiary transferred is different than its underlying equity of that subsidiary.

1. Should the consolidated financial statements of Sub A reflect the assets and liabilities of Sub B at their bases on the books of Sub B or at their bases in the consolidated financial statements of the parent?

2. If Sub A acquires the minority interests of Sub B, does the basis used by Sub A to record the minority interest of Sub B depend on whether Sub A issues cash or stock?

Authoritative Accounting Literature

FASB Technical Bulletin No. 85-5, Issues Relating to Accounting for Business Combinations, . . . , Question No. 2, "Stock Transactions between Companies under Common Control."

APB Opinion No. 16, Business Combinations, paragraphs 5 and 43.

AICPA Accounting Interpretation 26, Acquisition of Minority Interest, of APB Opinion No. 16, Business Combinations.

AICPA Accounting Interpretation 39, Transfers and Exchanges between Companies under Common Control, of APB Opinion No. 16, Business Combinations.

---

ment, consultants, systems analysts, and tax advisors. It is especially important to draw on the recollections of persons at lower staff levels who may have knowledge of problems and who could contribute ideas to enhance audit efficiency and effectiveness. If the engagement is large, a formal preengagement planning session may be helpful.

Evaluate People Risks

The assessment of people risks can cover client executives, investors, investees, vendors, and customers, among others. The point is probably best made by example.

Item

Congress investigated Robert J. Thompson, a one-time aide to the President of the United States, who reportedly assisted James M. Fail in acquiring 15 insolvent savings and loan associations, with a pledge of $1.85 billion in federal aid, together with $70 million in borrowed money and a personal investment of only $1,000. Purchaser Fail was cleared for the acquisition with a simplified procedure; high officials testified that they did not know of any prior difficulties Fail might have had with regulatory authorities.

The author ran Mr. Fail's name through LEXIS' federal and state files and discovered the following: "the collateral, originally and allegedly still owned by Atlas Financial Corp., a company allegedly controlled by James M. Fail, through Atlas United Financial Corp., has now in effect been transferred in a series of questionable transactions to another company also owned by Mr. Fail, United Security . . . . The various transactions described in this paragraph are presently the subject of a pending action in Alabama to recover for alleged common law fraud and fraud under the Securities Exchange Act of 1934 . . . . [T]hese transfers raise a sufficient inference or 'badge' of fraud at this time to warrant the appointment of a receiver to preserve the status quo."[7]

The moral of this story is that federal agencies, including Resolution Trust Corporation, would do well to expand their use of LEXIS

---

[7]John G. Bookout as receiver of *Modern Home Life Ins. Co.* v. *Atlas Financial Corp.*, 395 F. Supp. 1338 (N.D. Ga. 1974).

or of a similar data base. (One of LEXIS' competitors is the U.S. Department of Justice's JURIS data base.)

Personnel Implications

In the remainder of this chapter, attention will be called to steps which require active participation by the most senior auditors available, typically by the engagement partner and manager, or their counterparts in internal auditing. For example, the steps in the present section (Understand Inherent Risk) warrant substantial involvement by the partner.

UNDERSTAND THE CLIENT: ON–SITE

Perform Internal Analytics

SAS 56 requires the auditor to carry out analytical procedures. A *reasonableness test*, a type of analytical procedure, has been described as requiring the auditor to consider the financial *and* operating factors (independent variables) relevant to the amount being estimated (dependent variable). It has been noted that such a test may confer benefits "since it can capture the relationship between operating and financial data and thereby explain a greater portion of the behavior of the account than could be obtained, from, say, a simple trend analysis."[8]

While analytical procedures should be applied with caution, they *can* detect errors when the auditor has realistic expectations. The apparent effectiveness of analytical procedures in detecting errors becomes more significant because the cost of these procedures tends to be relatively low. Caution is in order; some researchers have stressed the need to consider the nature of evidence on *each* engagement: "Analytical review may be the strongest form of evidence in detecting material errors for a stable long-term client, while it may [constitute] the weakest avail-

---

[8]Edward Blocher and John J. Willingham, *Analytical Review: A Guide to Evaluating Financial Statements* (New York: McGraw-Hill, 1985), p. 119.

able evidence for a high-risk client with only moderately effective internal controls."[9]

The extent to which analytical review may be used by an auditor to reduce other work has been described as involving the following considerations:

1. *Risk.* The auditor evaluates the potential for material error to occur in the account and to remain undetected by existing controls.

2. *Materiality.* The auditor assesses the impact on the financial statements as a whole if the account balance is substantially misstated.

3. *Precision.* The auditor evaluates the precision associated with the use of the analytical review method for the account, including the auditor's confidence in the projections and results of the method.

4. If the results of the analytical review indicate no unusual or unexpected relationships for the account, the auditor *may* be able to reduce the scope of subsequent substantive testing, if she is satisfied as to risk, materiality, and precision for the account.[10] (However, as pointed out in chapter 2, caution is advised.)

It has become easy to produce certain types of analytical information. Microcomputer audit software, including the AICPA's Accountant's Trial Balance (ATB), automates many labor-intensive tasks associated with an audit. Programs of this genre may, among other things: (1) aid in preparing financial statements, (2) prepare analyses of fluctuations between periods on a percentage or amount basis, (3) calculate standard and nonstandard ratios, (4) calculate a common size for a series of accounts, financial lines, or subheadings, and (5) produce account, financial line, ratio base, or ratio result data for export to popular spreadsheet programs.[11]

---

[9]Arnold Wright and Theodore J. Mock, "Toward a Contingency View of Audit Evidence," *Auditing: A Journal of Practice and Theory* 5, no. 1 (September 1985), p. 97.

[10]Ibid., p. 118.

[11]Michael A. Murphy and Xenia Ley Parker, *Handbook of EDP Auditing*, 2nd ed. (Boston: Warren, Gorham, and Lamont, 1989), p. 12-31.

Personnel Involvement

While detailed work can be done by a relatively junior person, the interpretation of the results, especially of financial ratios, calls for partner or manager attention.

Assess Prior Communications, Including Internal Audit Reports

The auditor should review the prior year's working papers, audit report, and letter to the client. However, she is cautioned to avoid the hazard of anchoring. *Anchoring* occurs "when a decision maker focuses on an initial value and then adjusts judgments from that value [the anchor]. Typically, the adjustment is in the correct direction, but is of insufficient magnitude . . . . In audit planning, staff may rely too heavily on prior working papers [the anchor] and fail to adapt audit procedures to client or industry changes."[12]

Internal audit reports represent another source of information. Report contents must be viewed through the prism of the mission and competence of the internal audit department. What is, or should be, the main concern of internal auditors has been aptly described: "In some companies, the internal auditors are considered the control specialists. Their main responsibilities are to study, evaluate, and test the system of internal control . . . . [They] represent a higher level of control that determines whether the system is functioning."[13] One well-known internal auditor wrote:

> The internal control structure, which includes the internal audit function, has emerged as a critical element in strategic and policy-making decisions at successful organizations . . . . While emphasis on proactive leadership is important, [the trend] also reflects an even more important shift in the scope of the audit function. Where once the auditor's tasks were limited to periodic transaction tests,

---

[12]Wright and Mock, "Toward a Contingency View," p. 96.

[13]Ernst & Young, *The Audit Committee: Functioning in a Changing Environment: A Brief Guide* (Cleveland: Ernst & Whinney, 1988), p. 26.

today's strategies focus on audit methodologies that look at entire control systems.[14]

Internal auditors must enjoy de facto independence from operating management, especially with respect to the reporting of findings. If internal auditors prepare a follow-up list of findings and recommendations, and track deficiencies into resolution, the external auditor can review open findings and assess their significance, along with the adequacy of resolutions. The inventory of unresolved audit exceptions represents a key indicator of managerial attitude. Management's reluctance to implement audit recommendations and/or adjustments may indicate a lack of desire for improvement; merely acknowledging deficiencies is not enough; findings must be corrected or otherwise resolved. (Unresolved findings should also be carried to the master tracking sheet.)

The auditor should obtain any draft or final reports submitted during the review period by state or federal auditors or by other examiners that perform functions similar to auditing. Unfortunately, questions have arisen in several recent cases as to whether the external auditors asked for, read, or reacted to regulators' reports.

There are good reasons for reviewing prior audit reports, prior regulatory actions, and prior records of litigation. Persons guilty of malfeasance tend to repeat similar acts of omission or commission at different times and places. Moreover, entities that have been found guilty of violating health, safety, employment, or environmental regulations may also be inclined to violate other laws which may have a more direct financial impact. In this regard, the auditor may find it helpful to search case-law data bases and administrative rule and regulation data bases to see whether there are references to the audit entity, its executives, and their associates.

The auditor may also benefit by reviewing reports of violations prepared by various categories of inspectors.

---

[14]John B. Ptak, "Internal Audit Emerges," *The Magazine of Bank Administration*, December 1988, Management and Finance, p. 40.

The auditor should also review plans and programs of the organization's systems and procedures function. These documents often reflect not only what is, but what should be. Consequently, when systems projects are not completed on schedule, the plans can represent a mother lode of matters of audit concern. Moreover, examination of a systems group's project plans and staffing arrangements may offer comfort that internal auditors have an appropriate involvement with systems development.

Personnel Involvement
Analytical review and review of reports on file can be conducted by audit staff. However, supervision by the manager is important.

Identify Internal Risks

Internal risks include management and employee fraud, poor communication, disorderly or excessively authoritarian acts, and employee morale and turnover problems. Deficiencies can reflect themselves in inability to make timely deliveries of goods and services, to understand and manage change, or to meet product and service quality standards. The risk management concepts, discussed previously in this chapter, are identical for internal and external risks.

Take Plant and Office Tours

Auditors take plant or office tours to accomplish three objectives: (1) to sensitize themselves to the possible existence of accounting or operational problems; (2) to assess physical security and the extent of employee awareness of security; and (3) to see whether there are asset identification or valuation issues which may affect engagement planning for staff personnel and/or outside consultants. The auditors' tour should have been cleared with top management and should have its demonstrated support; the cooperation of lower levels of management should have been mandated by a directive from the top. The tour conductor must be an individual knowledgeable in operations and, hopefully, in financial matters; if an individual with both attributes is not available, operations knowledge should be given priority.

If the auditee entity operates a manufacturing plant, the tour should follow the progress of materials through the facility. In other words, the tour should move from the receiving department, through manufacturing, to shipping. The auditor should observe potential exceptions, and make notes or recordings during or immediately after the tour. (Apparent threats should be carried to the master tracking sheet.)

The plant or office tour may have professional development benefits; at the conclusion of the tour it may be helpful to debrief junior personnel. This process should heighten staff acuity by alerting members to conditions that they may not have noticed (but should have), and which could be symptoms of deficiencies.

As a result of the plant and/or office tours, auditors may become aware of any general lassitude in control that may affect access to assets, computers, programs, and data. Figures 8–6 and 8–7 list matters that may be observed in the course of a plant or office tour, the techniques for documenting such matters, and the possible implications of deficiencies.

Personnel Involvement

All personnel assigned to the engagement should participate in the assessment of internal risk. In the plant/office tour, it is especially important that the partner and manager participate.

UNDERSTAND THE CONTROL ENVIRONMENT

There appears to be a significant relationship between management's philosophy and operating style and the risk of misstatements. As noted in Chapter 4, strong signals are conveyed when management holds internal control (and management letters) in contempt, views the corporate treasury as its personal piggy bank, and avoids publicity by not prosecuting wrongdoers.

FIGURE 8–6
Plant Tour

Plant Tour Symptom	Documentation	Possible Causes
	Receiving Department	
Long lines of trucks	Demurrage payment schedule	Improper staging of incoming shipping
	Overtime payments in receiving department	Insufficient number of bays
	Gate attendant's log	
Idle outside truckers	"Work" or "no work" observations	Failure to enforce agreements with shippers
	Review of contract with shippers	Poorly drawn agreements
Idle client employees	Compare shipping volumes to staffing tables at selected times or dates	Staffing based on peak periods
		Inadequate or "thin" supervision
Poor unloading techniques Typical examples: Bags versus pallets Magnets versus dump trucks Hand trucks versus forklifts Brooms versus vacuums Old-type railcars versus garage-door type	Review with client's personnel; client to provide estimates of "damages"	Materials-handling function not assigned Absence of coordination between traffic and receiving groups
Backlog of undelivered goods	Aged schedule of articles, including indications of their dollar importance and of their importance to plant operations	Insufficient or unsupervised labor Inadequate facilities or equipment Improper staging Lack of delivery plan
Many partial deliveries	Comparison of receipt dates and quantities with purchase orders or release requests	Vendors unable to deliver needed quantities because insufficient lead time
Many deliveries by air freight, airmail, etc.	Analysis of premium freight paid by client	Inability to plan procurement activity Inadequate reorder points or economic lots Customer accommodations

FIGURE 8–6 *(continued)*

Plant Tour Symptom	Documentation	Possible Causes

Paperwork problems
  Typical examples:
    Stale files of open
      receiving reports
    Repetitive preparation
      of receiving reports
	Aging of open paperwork	Failure to clear files
		Systems function not
		  assigned or ineffective

Incoming Inspection

Plant Tour Symptom	Documentation	Possible Causes

No such activity	Review analysis of causes
	  of rejections; ask client
	  to determine whether
	  early inspection would
	  have minimized
	  damages
		Function not assigned

Backlog of uninspected
  articles
	Aged schedule of articles
	Record of rework
	Record of rework billed to
	  vendors
		Insufficient inspectors
		Insufficient testing
		  equipment
		Absence of instructions as
		  to what is to be inspected
		  (e.g., checklists)

Paperwork problems
  Example:
    Heavy rejection pattern
	Review vendor evaluation
	  files
	Compare client's
	  specifications with
	  published specifications
		Failure to inform
		  purchasing department
		  of rejections
		Purchasing department
		  fails to police vendors
		Specifications too tight

Absence of log sheets,
  summaries of activity,
  etc.
	Review staffing tables (for
	  all shifts); discussion with
	  chief inspector
		Function not adequately
		  planned or controlled

Materials Handling

Plant Tour Symptom	Documentation	Possible Causes

Forklift trucks: Many
  different types
	Fixed asset records
	Summary of repair orders
	Spare parts inventory
	  movement
		Disorderly procurement
		Vendors have ready access
		  to operating people

Cranes:
  Not heavy enough
	Report of nonstandard
	  routings where
	  necessary to "work
	  around" heavy jobs
	Summary of maintenance
	  work orders reflecting
	  special "move
	  materials" charges
	Property appropriation
	  request files
		Lack of communication
		Cost justification
		  requirements not
		  properly drawn

(continued)

FIGURE 8–6 (continued)

Plant Tour Symptom	Documentation	Possible Causes
Other equipment problems: Insufficient elevators Bins too small No cushioning pads, etc.	Spot-check incidence and length of waiting time Discussion with client's industrial engineers	Insufficient funds for modernization Needs not properly communicated
Safety questions: Lack of head guards on forklifts Lack of safety railings Lack of "all clear" buttons Extinguishers not inspected Improper extinguishers Lack of sprinklers, firewalls, etc.	Review of workers' compensation claims Review of accident and lost time reports Review of insurance inspectors' reports	Failure to recognize hidden costs of inadequate safety precautions
Careless handling: "Chewmarks" on goods Leaning towers Rust Exposure to elements Absence of proper moisture and humidity controls (especially for instruments) Poor housekeeping	Write-offs of damaged goods Buildups of unmarketable "base stocks," per inventory records Repeated charges for instrument calibration services Housekeeping-committee minutes	Poor training Poor supervision Lack of instructions Unsuitable storage space
Storage: More than one location Lack of bin labels Lack of locator files Storage plan not evident Aisle blockage Cartoned versus uncartoned, from space utilization standpoint	Review of floor plan Number of "stock chasers" Discussion with warehouse superintendent Warehouse activity reports and ratios Damaged merchandise reports	Floor space not considered in planning Lack of communication

Production Activities

Layout: Flow of materials not discernible Feeder lines not distinguishable from main assembly line Backtracking of materials in process Long distances from receiving to storage to production Control points not discernible	Plant map Flow diagram Layout charts Materials-handling costs relative to total direct labor; other similar ratios Maintenance work orders—"Rube Goldberg" approaches to layout modification	Facilities questions not considered in planning Lack of communication

FIGURE 8–6 *(concluded)*

Plant Tour Symptom	Documentation	Possible Causes
Paperwork: None—no route sheets, no travelers Loading-board backups	Interviews with foremen to determine how much time is spent on nonsupervisory activities Tests of delivery performance Tests of cost performance Overtime patterns Rejection rates Scrap reports	Lack of uniform scheduling, routing, dispatching techniques—laissez-faire approaches Orders accepted beyond plant's delivery capabilities
Work force: Idle—soldiering on the job Clocking-out early Obvious personnel shortage	"Work" or "no work" observations Review of idle time report Review of performance report Analysis of control over timekeeping Test of time clock lineup On-the-job headcount Report of "split" assignments Premium labor charges Review of efficiency patterns	Supervision failure Absence of work force preplanning Lack of standards or other performance measurements
Machines: Idle machines Machine bottlenecks Goods piled to an excessive degree	Interview with chief engineer Downtime report Machine-loading records Shortage or backlog reports; aging of merchandise on floor Delivery performance or late-shipment records	Inability to debug Deficient maintenance Inadequate scheduling; shop imbalances Failure to secure needed machinery—poor planning Obsolescence
Shop practices: Conveyors not used—workers stoop Small pieces inefficiently placed on hangers	Confirm with industrial engineers	Lack of industrial engineering function Morale problems Communication problems

Mark Haskins and Robert Henarie have developed an extensive rank ordered listing of what 146 auditor-respondents believed to be attributes relating to the control environment. The authors emphasize that "auditors should be hesitant to set aside the control environment cues that [lead] to an initial concern and [advise that] . . .

FIGURE 8–7
Office Tour

Office Tour Symptom	Documentation	Possible Causes
Idle employees Checking out early Obvious shortage of help	Compare document processing volumes to staffing tables for selected times or dates "Work" or "No Work" observations Review of idle time report Review of span of control Review of performance reports Analysis of control over time-keeping On-the-job headcount Report on "split" assignments Premium labor charges Test of time clock line-up	Staffing based on peak loads Inadequate or thin supervision
Deliveries by air freight or airmail	Analysis of premium freight paid	Poor coordination
Paperwork problems: Delays in processing Excessive corrections Excessive handling and transportation Large volume of on-line corrections Unprocessed backlogs Numerous complaints from correspondents Failure to date or time stamp	Flowchart analysis Aged listing of pending corrections Batch reconciliations Analysis of nature of errors Analysis of delays Analysis in terms of the nature of the complaint (e.g., accuracy or timeliness) Observation	Crisis management Poor supervision Lack of exception reports or no action thereon Excessive reliance on computer edits Lack of instruction
Storage: More than one location Lack of bin labels Lack of locator files Storage plan not evident Aisle blockage	Review of floor plan Discussion with storage supervisor	Inadequate space planning
Office equipment: Idle machines Machine bottlenecks Unprocessed paperwork Equipment from a variety of different vendors	Downtime report Machine logs Property, plant, and equipment records	Deficient maintenance Unused or uncontrolled warranties Lack of proper procurement policies Absence of control over systems development and related activities

---

FIGURE 8–7 *(concluded)*

Office Tour Symptom	Documentation	Possible Causes
Office supplies: Rag rather than chemical papers Engraved letterheads Heavy bond paper for airmail	Analysis of purchase orders	No standardization on preferred items No catalogue Personal preferences
Safety: Fire extinguishers not charged Lack of drills Wrong type of extinguishers	Charge records	Absence of safety program
Temperature/humidity lighting/amenity problem	Employee complaints	Disorderly approach to resolution

Source: Felix Pomeranz, "Planning the Independent Government Audit," in *Applying Government Auditing Standards,* ed. Mortimer A. Dittenhofer (New York: Matthew Bender & Company, 1990), pp. 5-10, 5-11. Copyright © 1990 by Matthew Bender & Co. Inc. and reprinted with permission.

skepticism arising from these preliminary cues should be carried over to extended year-end substantive tests." The flavor of the list may be sampled by considering the first four items: (1) existence of an appropriate policy for the authorization of transactions; (2) proper segregation of duties among client employees whose work is related to the financial reporting process (e.g., financial management, EDP, accounting, and internal audit personnel); (3) effectiveness of general EDP controls; and, (4) effectiveness of physical safeguards over records and assets.[15] The entire list is reproduced in Figure 8–8.

Personnel Involvement
Direction and participation by the partner and manager are essential.

[15]Mark E. Haskins and Robert L. Henarie, "Attributes and Audit Impact of Client's Control Environment," *The CPA Journal,* July 1985, pp. 18–26.

FIGURE 8–8
Ranked List of Control Environment Concerns

1. Existence of an appropriate policy for the authorization of transactions

2. Proper segregation of duties among client employees whose work is related to the financial reporting process (e.g., financial management, EDP, accounting, and internal audit personnel)

3. Effectiveness of general EDP controls

4. Effectiveness of physical safeguards over records and assets

5. Appropriateness of the internal audit staff's assigned duties, responsibilities, and lines of reporting

6. Existence of factors that might motivate managers to circumvent or override existing controls (e.g., tight credit, low working capital, bonus plans, need to meet forecasts, decaying industry)

7. Compulsion on the part of the client's top executive management for reporting the most favorable financial picture

8. Effectiveness of the internal audit staff in reporting detected deficiencies

9. Extent of knowledge on the part of the client's controller concerning FASB and SEC (where appropriate) guidelines

10. Promptness with which errors in internal financial reports are detected and corrected

11. Potential for errors in internal financial reports

12. Reputation of the client's top executive management for taking unusual business risks

13. Effectiveness of internal financial reports in adequately highlighting, identifying, or isolating problems

14. Extent of turnover in the client's top executive management positions and the reasons for it

15. Effectiveness of coordination among related functions for financial reporting purposes (e.g., sales, accounting, and production)

16. Inferences that can be drawn concerning the relationship between prior audit adjustments and the competence of the relevant personnel

17. Appropriateness of separate accounting systems for each of the client's diversified business endeavors (e.g., a client might have a mining division and a banking division)

18. Effectiveness of the client's policies and procedures manuals in regard to the financial reporting process

19. Manner in which recommendations of internal and external auditors have been dealt with in the past

20. Conscientiousness of the audit committee in the execution of its duties and responsibilities

21. Adequacy of a client's analysis of budget variances

22. Timeliness with which financial managers receive the information they need

23. Extent to which the client's top executive management is dominated by one or a few individuals

24. Adequacy of the client's budgetary process in covering all units or functions

25. Appropriateness of the client's actions in response to the Foreign Corrupt Practices Act of 1977

26. Extent to which native personnel managing the client's foreign operations are allowed to exercise their discretion to financial reporting decisions

27. Appropriateness of the client's chart of accounts

28. Accessibility of supervisors to employees, both of whose work is related to the financial reporting process (e.g., financial management, EDP, accounting, and internal audit personnel)

29. Appropriateness of client policies and practices of required vacations and rotation of duties for employees whose work is related to the financial reporting process (e.g., financial management, EDP, accounting, and internal audit personnel)

30. Extent to which the client's line personnel (i.e., operations) review internal financial reports

31. Congruency of responsibility with authority for the client's employees whose work is related to the financial reporting process (e.g., financial management, EDP, accounting, and internal audit personnel)

32. Manageability of the workloads of client personnel whose work is related to the financial reporting process (e.g., financial management, EDP, accounting, and internal audit personnel)

33. Adequacy of the process by which operating budgets are revised

34. Incompatibility (if any) of centralized client management over decentralized operations

35. Extent to which the client investigates the backgrounds and references of new employees whose work is related to the financial reporting process (e.g., financial management, EDP, accounting, and internal audit personnel)

36. Qualifications of the members of the board of directors

37. Qualifications of the members of the audit committee

38. Extent of client bonding of all employees who handle cash, securities, etc.

39. Effectiveness of a client's communication of formal codes of conduct

40. Appropriateness of client training programs for new or promoted employees whose work is related to the financial reporting process (e.g., financial management, EDP, accounting, and internal audit personnel)

41. Relevance of an internal financial report to the person receiving it

42. Adequacy of client planning for staff needs in regard to employees whose work is related to the financial reporting process (e.g., financial management, EDP, accounting, and internal audit personnel)

43. Existence of client programs for ongoing evaluation of employees whose work is related to the financial reporting process (e.g., financial management, EDP, accounting, and internal audit personnel)

44. Compatibility of the client's *formal* organizational structure with their organizational goals

45. Extent of a client's monitoring of their competition

46. Compatibility of the client's *informal* organizational structure with their organizational goals

47. Appropriateness of the information bases used in determining raises and promotions for the client's employees (management and staff) whose work is related to the financial reporting process (e.g., financial management, EDP, accounting, and internal audit personnel)

48. Appropriateness of the information bases used in determining raises and promotions for the client's employees (management and staff) whose work is not directly related to the financial reporting process

Source: Mark E. Haskins and Robert L. Henarie, "Attributes and Audit Impact of Client's Control Environment," *The CPA Journal*, July 1985, pp. 18–26. Reprinted with permission from *The CPA Journal*, copyright © 1985.

UNDERSTAND THE SYSTEM AND CONTROL PROCEDURES

Conduct Interviews

Some of the behavioral aspects of interviewing, notably the types of possible questions, have been discussed in Chapter 6. The common-sense guidelines in this section should expedite the interview process. Interviews should be planned carefully, but executed with an appearance of spontaneity. The sequence in which interviews are conducted should follow the flow of paperwork; in most cases, relatively low-ranking personnel should be interviewed first. This approach will permit an auditor to compare subordinates' answers with those of their bosses. Interviews should be conducted by the most experienced person available, who should endeavor to discover subsurface exposures. Ron Weber has presented 10 rules of conduct:[16]

1. Minimize digressions from the main purpose of the interview.

Author's Comment

The topic of the interview should pertain to a defined component, function, or area, and should include questions such as: "where do you get the papers?" or "how do you know you have all of them?" and ending with "to whom do you give your output?" or "how do you know that what you have given is accurate?"

2. For the most part be a listener.

Author's Comment

Interviewers should focus not only on what is being said, but on what is *not* being said, and on the respondent's body language.

3. Allow the respondent some thinking time.
4. Avoid condescension and criticism; be polite.

---

[16]Ron Weber, *EDP Auditing: Conceptual Foundations and Practice*, 2nd ed. (New York: McGraw-Hill, 1988), pp. 730–31.

5. Avoid sarcasm and be careful with humor.
6. Avoid jargon and buzzwords; clearly state the question.
7. Be attentive and interested.
8. Avoid disagreements and confrontations.
9. Answer the respondent's questions courteously.
10. Maintain relaxed formality; avoid familiarity.

The results of interviews should be recorded as quickly as practical. Pocket recorders can be used to make notes *after* an interview has been completed. The use of recorders, or even the appearance of a pencil and writing tablet in the auditor's hands, may cause a respondent to clam up.

Personnel Involvement
Partners and managers should be deeply involved in interviews of employees engaged in sensitive activities.

Item

The purchasing director of a large midwestern city was questioned by a partner on why large purchases of snow removal chemicals had been made on an emergency basis (i.e., with competitive bidding waived). The emergency purchase prices were 5 to 10 percent higher than the prices that could have been secured by competitive bidding. The purchasing director replied that only God could predict whether it would snow. The comment was relayed to the city's mayor, who took immediate action to see that future purchases were made in accordance with good business practice (and the city charter).

Document the Understanding

The advantages of flowcharts and the effort involved in their preparation have been discussed. Overview flowcharts, which show the relationships of activities conducted by various departments of the business, offer a pictorial image of the business. Auditors tend to evaluate specific controls on a basis of subsystems, sometimes called *systems cycles*, which they define for audit purposes. Any cycle with significant control problems involving physical security, computer access, and management judgments should be given priority attention.

Detailed cycle flowcharts can be costly to prepare, and embody the risk of not seeing the forest for the trees. From an audit perspective, the value of detailed flowcharts increases if (1) key controls and (2) supervisory controls are marked directly on the flowcharts; this should be done by drawing a single circle around key controls, and a double circle around supervisory controls.

Key controls have been described in Chapter 6 as bearing on the accuracy and completeness of financial statements. The FitzGeralds mention important concerns:

Are the Controls Effective and Reliable?

Consider the effectiveness and reliability of other key controls in place within the system.

Consider the effectiveness and reliability of (nonkey) controls in place within the system.

Are the Preventive Controls Adequate?

Preventive controls may affect or soften actions or stop an individual from acting or an event from occurring; for example, a password may prevent illegal entry into a system.

Deterrent controls discourage or restrain a person from acting or proceeding. They also restrain or hinder an event from taking place; for example, a guard or a security lock on a door may deter an attempt to gain illegal entry.

Are the Detective Controls Adequate?

Detective controls reveal or discover unwanted events and offer evidence of trespass. For example, special software can search out illegal journal entries, out of balance accounts, or overdrafts.

Reporting controls document an event, a situation, or a trespass; for example, the same software that detects an illegal act or problem should report it, so that a person, or an automated process, can take remedial action.[17]

---

[17]J. FitzGerald and A. FitzGerald, *Designing Controls*, pp. 44–45.

To run the business, management must have comfort that controls are functioning as planned. That comfort can be gained by installing supervisory controls designed to detect nonperformance in a timely manner. Supervisory control procedures frequently involve operational information. The procedures may consist of specific, observable administrative routines which are often documented. Examples of documentation include checklists, exception reports, initials evidencing review of batch controls, bank reconciliations, vouchers, logbooks for review routines, and, most importantly, written reports.

In computerized systems, such reports often represent a product of processing; in most cases, an executive should have been made responsible for seeing to corrective actions with respect to out-of-line conditions reflected in the reports; often her corrective actions will also be documented. (Conversely, when corrective action has not taken place, auditors should inquire into the reasons with a view toward identifying emerging business problems, or even management overrides.)

The importance of supervisory controls is hard to exaggerate, since these controls ensure that other controls are working. In addition, audit committee members, influenced by the Treadway Commission's recommendations, are likely to pay particular attention to overseeing the functioning of key and supervisory controls. (The oversight activities of audit committees have been described in Figure 6–13.)

Personnel Involvement
While work in this area can be performed by staff at various levels, close supervision by partners and managers is necessary, in light of audit committee members' concerns.

Make Sure the Understanding Is Correct

Auditors should be able to trace one transaction of each significant type, or resulting information, through manual and programmed procedures. (Auditors who evaluate controls while a system is being designed should see that the completed system will allow transaction reviews to be conducted.) Methods used to confirm the adequacy of programmed procedures may involve reperforming the procedures, reviewing program documentation, and even reading some source code. Thus, special skills and experience may be necessary to carry out transaction reviews in a complex EDP system.[18]

Personnel Involvement
The engagement manager should review transaction test documentation.

Test Controls as Necessary

Auditors are likely to be partial to supervisory control tests, especially when the controls are in the format of reports to and reactions from management. In addition, and irrespective of reliance on internal control, the auditor may find it desirable to perform tests of key/supervisory controls in which the client has placed special confidence, or which are in the focal areas of exposure. The client may *ask* the auditor to conduct tests of controls. The auditor must also assess which key and supervisory controls are being tested adequately by substantive tests, and which controls may warrant separate testing; such controls often involve lists of open items, or of items in suspense, such as a report of undelivered purchases.

Compliance tests may also be required in a government audit. GAO policy calls for a vulnerability assessment to be made to determine the extent of compliance testing. (The vulnerability assessment determines the probability that a law/regulation related to engagement objectives will not be complied with, or that the area being reviewed is susceptible to noncompliance or abuse.) The higher the vulnerability, the more extensive the compliance testing.[19]

Traditionally, in most cases compliance tests have involved reperformance by the auditor of the functioning of a particular control. However, it is also possible to evaluate the functioning of a control by searching for evidence of its malfunctioning. (For ex-

---

[18]Murphy and Parker, *Handbook of EDP Auditing*, p. 18-18.

[19]U.S. General Accounting Office, Office of Policy, "Assessing Compliance with Applicable Laws and Regulations," *GAO/OP-4.1.2*, December 1989.

ample, if the purpose of the control is to see that approval has been given to a sale, based on an authorized credit limit, the functioning of the control could be assessed by searching for credit limits that may have been exceeded without approval having been obtained.)

Personnel Involvement
Managers must pay particular attention to the way in which exceptions discovered in the course of tests of controls are evaluated, cleared, and tracked into resolution.

ASSESS CONTROL RISK

The auditor may have been working with the master tracking sheet, which shows threats across the top of the page and affected components down the left-hand column. On the flowcharts, or in a write-up, key controls and supervisory controls will have been identified for each systems cycle. The auditor now considers each component and the threats thereto, posts existing key and supervisory controls, and assesses the nature of uncontrolled threats.

Internal control issues can be tracked on the master tracking sheet, especially when a spreadsheet or word processing program is used. As previously noted, space can be expanded to allow for as many rows of controls as necessary. The columns of the matrix continue to represent causes of loss. The auditor can perform four types of evaluation: a columnar evaluation, a row evaluation, an evaluation by component, and an evaluation by systems cycle. Weber notes that little definitive guidance exists as to how the evaluation is to be made. He observes that some professional bodies have published minimum control standards that must be achieved before an auditor can consider controls over a cause of loss as satisfactory.[20] For example, the Office of the Comptroller of the state of New York has promulgated a list of internal control standards (Appendix C). The merits of standards are also dis-

---

[20]Weber, *EDP Auditing*, pp. 49–50.

cussed in a recent article in *Internal Auditing*; the article mentions that "once control standards have been documented, the auditor is better able to evaluate the effectiveness of the control systems."[21]

Cerullo has referred to *Pareto's law* in considering EDP controls; Pareto wrote that a relatively small number of items in a group can constitute those of greatest significance. It seems to follow that significant security controls may be implemented for a relatively insignificant dollar investment. Cerullo concludes that management should initially concentrate its security and control budget on installing general controls, which provide high protection for relatively small cost. Management should then proceed to install more costly and/or complex controls.[22] The general controls are listed in Figure 8–9.

Focus on Security

Computer security has become a managerial problem, because of its potentially dramatic impact on the success or failure of an organization.[23] Many auditors will have no difficulty in mastering some emerging security issues. For example, they can influence their clients to introduce business contingency/recovery plans. Such plans include phases such as (1) getting management support, (2) determining the applicability and scope of the plan, (3) inventorying resources, (4) creating and documenting the plan, (5) testing the plan, and (6) updating the plan.[24] Of course, technological change also involves continuing efforts by auditors and their clients to stay current. For example, for some years fires have been the number one cause of computer outages. However, according to international agreements, fire suppression systems

---

[21]Kim Schotzel-Isles, "Using Financial Control Standards to Improve the Control Framework," *Internal Auditing*, Spring 1988, pp. 11–22.

[22]Michael J. Cerullo, "EDP Security and Controls Justification," *Internal Auditing*, Fall 1989, pp. 13–26.

[23]Hossein Bigdoli and Reza Azarmsa, "Computer Security: New Managerial Concern for the 1980s and Beyond," *Journal of Systems Management*, October 1989, pp. 21–27.

[24]Randall M. Coleman, "Six Steps to Contingency Planning," *ISP News*, March/April 1990, pp. 8–9.

FIGURE 8-9
Internal Control Questionnaire—EDP General Controls

Organization and Operation Controls

1. Are the following duties segregated within the EDP department:
   - Systems design?
   - Computer programming?
   - Computer operations?
   - Data entry?
   - Custody of systems documentation, programs, and files?
   - Data control?
2. Are the following duties performed only outside the EDP Department:
   - Initiation and authorization of transactions?
   - Authorization of changes in systems, programs, and master files?
   - Preparation of source documents?
   - Correction of errors in source documents?
   - Custody of assets?

Systems Development and Documentation Controls

1. Is there adequate participation by users and internal auditors in new systems development?
2. Is proper authorization, testing, and documentation required for systems and program changes?

Hardware and Systems Software Controls

1. Are built-in hardware and systems software controls adequate to detect equipment malfunctions?
2. Are systems software changes properly authorized, tested, and documented?

Access Controls

1. Is access to computer facilities restricted to authorized personnel?
2. Is access to data files and programs restricted to authorized personnel by a librarian?

Data and Procedural Controls

1. Is there a data control function that controls data input, processing, and output?
2. Is there a disaster contingency plan to ensure continuity of operations?
3. Is there off-premises storage of backup files and programs?

Source: The material in this questionnaire was reproduced with permission. It was taken from the following volume: Walter G. Kell, William C. Boynton, and Richard E. Ziegler, *Modern Auditing*, 4th ed. (New York: John Wiley & Sons, 1989), p. 233. Copyright © 1989 by John Wiley & Sons, Inc. and reprinted with permission.

that utilize Halon™ are to be outlawed by the year 2000. As a result, radically new alternatives may be emerging, such as detection systems that rely on warm air movement.[25] Given developments of this nature, it may be wise for auditors who do not feel comfortable with technological change to arrange access to qualified security consultants.

Personnel Involvement
Since the partner and manager are the most experienced personnel on an engagement, they must be sensitive to security matters.

CONDUCT SUBSTANTIVE TESTS

Strive for Efficiency and Effectiveness

The performance of efficient and effective substantive tests reflects an auditor's knowledge of technology, as well as her personal working style. For example, the auditor may use a word processor with windowing capabilities. One window may feature a supporting schedule, the other a management letter. When the auditor wishes to note a finding, she jumps to the letter window and writes the comment, while the evidence remains on the screen in the first window. Another example involves replacement of the traditional, multicolored audit tickmarks with footnote references entered on the word processor.[26]

Relatively few types of substantive tests are available to gather sufficient and competent evidence. The basic type of test procedures have been listed in Chapter 4. The timing and extent of test performance will be commented on at this time. Some procedures may be variable in terms of the effort to be applied (VE), or in terms of timing (VT). In general, variability in the extent of tests

---

[25]George Vorsheim, "Computer Fires Cause Most Downtime," *ISP News*, March/April 1990, p. 47.

[26]Wayne J. Socha, "Practical Tips for Automating the Auditor," *Internal Auditor*, February 1989, pp. 54–59.

(VE) would be influenced primarily by reliance on internal control and, conceivably, by materiality. Variability as to the timing of tests (VT) similarly depends on internal control reliance, and, possibly, on absence of key and supervisory controls; in other words, a lack of such controls makes it inappropriate to shift tests from the year end. The marking of test procedures with the aforementioned letter codes may help the auditor to focus her efforts.

The author believes that audit risk is likely to be reduced by extensive substantive examinations, compared to less extensive substantive examinations; the author also feels more comfortable with examinations at year end, compared to examinations at interim. Of course, in considering program steps, the auditor will be mindful of the uncontrolled threats appearing in the master tracking sheet. This philosophy is illustrated in Chapter 9 in the assembly of programs via the AICPA's Audit Program Generator (APG).

Seek Independent Verification of Management Representations

SAS 19 requires the auditor to obtain a representation letter from management. The letter affirms management's responsibility for preparing the financial statements and its belief in the accuracy and completeness of the information contained therein and furnished to the auditor during her examination. The *SAS* contains specific recommendations as to matters to be included; the letters typically refer to cash and bank accounts, receivables, inventories, and liabilities. As pointed out by Arens and Loebbecke, a client representation is a written statement from a nonindependent source and therefore cannot be regarded as reliable evidence: "The letter provides minimal evidence that management has been asked certain questions; but, its primary purpose is psychological; [it is designed] to protect the auditor from potential claims by management that it was unaware of its responsibilities."[27] Representation letters can induce auditors to audit toward the representa-

---

[27]Alvin A. Arens and James K. Loebbecke, *Auditing: An Integrated Approach*, 4th ed. (Englewood Cliffs, N.J.: Prentice-Hall, 1988), p. 748.

tions, thereby risking anchoring. One antidote to this problem lies in the auditor's independent verification of the management representations by using the information contained in the on-line data bases.

Utilize the On-Line Data Bases in Substantive Testing

In Chapter 4 we discussed setting general and specific audit objectives based on management's assertions. This chapter will show how the on-line data bases can be used to accomplish these objectives. Again, the two companies introduced before, Discover and Adult, will be used as illustrations. The on-line data bases can assist in documentation related matters:

1. *Examination/reading*: reasonably detailed study of a document or record to determine specific facts about it.
2. *Comparison*: comparing information in two different locations.
3. *Scanning*: less detailed study of a document or record, usually to determine whether closer examination is warranted.
4. *Analytical procedures*: reasonableness reviews of financial information made by studying and comparing relationships among data and trends in the data; examples include fluctuation analyses, ratio analyses, comparisons of accounting data with operating data, and comparisons of recorded amounts to the auditor's expectations.

The data bases contain information on companies, products, markets, trends, and management techniques; hence, an imaginative auditor will find unlimited opportunities to expedite achievement of audit objectives. The on-line data bases should help to collect independent information relating to virtually all financial statement assertions, but especially to existence or occurrence, valuation or allocation, presentation, and disclosure.

The remainder of the chapter gives examples of on-line data base applications for substantive and other testing. Hints for becoming a new user of the on-line data bases have been given in Chapter 6. Darvin Melton has emphasized the need for the auditor to set a reasonably precise research objective. For example, he suggested that a search to obtain a company's financial history might be narrowed by including the stock exchange symbol, the information desired, the number of years' history required, balance sheets, income statements, and selected ratios. Melton also pointed to the variety of available data bases; there are over 500 on-line information services, which market 1,700 on-line data bases.[28]

With exceptions, data base distributors do not hold *exclusive* rights to data bases. In choosing the distributors mentioned in this book, the author proceeded on the basis of his own experiences. (Although some books survey the choices, this has not been the author's purpose.) In many cases the data bases cited will be available from LEXIS/NEXIS; others are vended through DIALOG or through both LEXIS/NEXIS and DIALOG.

Use the Data Bases for Tests that Bear on the Financial Statements as a Whole

Such information may assist the auditor in meeting the standards related to the going concern concept established by *SAS 59*.

1. Assess the overall financial health of the client's industry. (Danger signals may be found in sluggish sales, declining prices, changes in technology, new products, foreign competition, excess capacity, idle capacity, cash flow problems, restructuring, or new regulatory or professional rules.) The information can be found in full text, as well as in abstract data bases.

Item

Search of NEXIS' SECABS file showed that in mid-1990 Adult sold a $150,000 note, convertible into units made up of one common share and one warrant at a price equal to one half of that to be charged at a planned public offering of the units. (Two Adult officers secured the loan with personal stock, then valued at about $400,000.) The auditor will have to see that the arrangement is reflected correctly in Adult's 1990 financial statements.

---

[28]Darvin C. Melton, "Information at Your Fingertips," *Journal of Accountancy*, December 1990, pp. 42–48.

2. Compare disclosures made by the auditee entity relative to accounting policies and related matters to those of companies with similar SIC codes.

Item

The fluid SIC codes of Discover came to mind in reviewing the annual report to the SEC in NEXIS' 10-K file. (The 10-K file is useful for this purpose, since it tends to represent an image of the actual filing.) The SIC code shown in the 10-K relates, apparently correctly, to oil/gas field services. However, the president's letter observes that the company has "redeployed certain assets . . . into financial services and investment banking services." He claims that the company will be the managing partner for an intended series of partnerships to drill natural gas wells. He also refers to a sale of a property interest for $700,000, resulting in a profit of $420,000. The property was sold to a limited partnership with seven limited partners, of whom two are directors of Discover and an additional two are family members of the company's directors. The reported gain virtually equals Discover's entire income before special charges and extraordinary items.

Questions can be raised as to whether (1) the transaction represented window dressing or (2) the price was appropriate (allegedly, the affiliated partnership was the highest bidder in an event described as a "competitive, arms-length, bidding procedure").

Item

Discover's 10-K balance sheet contains an account described as "accounts payable and accrued expenses" which exceeds $2,000,000. No similar items existed in the prior year. The company described itself as an escrow agent for a partnership "affiliated with an affiliate"; assertedly, the escrow agreement required the company to remit the net operating profits of the partnership to a bank creditor. However, it was stated, Discover's affiliate had now requested that the remittances cease, resulting in the subject payable. In effect, nonpayment has enabled the company to make investments in marketable securities as discussed subsequently.

Questions can be raised (1) as to Discover's responsibility as escrow agent, (2) the conditions under which the principal becomes payable to the bank creditor, and (3) the possibility that interest may become due on the loan.

3. Compare auditee to others in the industry, especially to companies with similar SIC codes.

4. Check for open federal regulatory actions, fines, and assessments. NEXIS' SECNEW file, a daily news digest, carries summaries of SEC actions with regard to civil or criminal cases and summaries of SEC releases.

5. Search for new professional and regulatory actions. For instance, the Federal Register file, FEDREG, carried by NEXIS, posts emerging federal rules.

6. Review Securities and Exchange Commission filings for abstracts of outstanding corporate events reported on Form 8-K, insider trading reports on Forms 3 and 4, and tender offers and 5 percent ownership reports on various schedules. This information is available in NEXIS' SECABS file.

Use the Data Bases to Test Individual Accounts

Investments

1. Determine that market value for current and non-current portfolios has been properly computed. Trace quoted market prices to competent published sources when possible.

Item

Discover made a significant investment in a company we shall call Cold Fusion, Inc. (Fusion). Fusion was underwritten by a Discover affiliate. Fusion has four types of publicly traded securities—common stock, A stock, warrants, and units. At the end of calendar year 1989, Discover's short-term investment in Fusion totaled $1,340,000 and had a market value of $1,795,000. Discover is a significant shareholder and holds between 5 and 10 percent of the outstanding securities. The substantial increases in the market values of Fusion's securities give rise to the following questions: (1) are the market values realistic? (2) who are the market makers, and to what extent is the market affected or created by Discover affiliates? (3) is the market sufficiently liquid to handle the sale of a large block of stock, such as that owned by Discover? and (4) is valuation at market appropriate in the circumstances?

All Discover investments were traced to the Market Guide (MG) and, except for the investment in Fusion, to the Quote (QF) data base on NEXIS. (Fusion prices were traced to the pink sheets, which list prices in the nonautomated over-the-counter market; the auditor should note the spread between bid and asked prices, and should consider the degree to which a valid market appears to exist.) Investments in marketable securities other than Fusion were not material. Fusion's market value has been increasing, although MG reported escalating losses at Fusion due to increases in research and development expenses. Twelve-month earnings per share were a negative $2.07, while book value was a mere $2.88; these figures do not augur well for Fusion and lend urgency to the questions raised previously.

2. Make certain that there are competent independent sources for substantiating declaration and remittance of investment income.
3. For investments in nonpublic entities and investments carried on the equity method, compare carrying values to information in the most recent audited financial statements.
4. With respect to joint ventures, check the treatment to the books of the partner.
5. Develop information for appropriate valuation of restricted securities, nonmarketable securities, or other investments which may have suffered impaired values.

Accounts Receivable

1. Substantiate the existence of significant accounts receivable by reference to the TRINET Company data base and the TRINET Establishment data base available on both LEXIS and DIALOG.
2. Develop information pertinent to major accounts by examining financial information, credit information, and news reports. Financial information pertaining to large public companies may be found in the Disclosure, Inc. data base available on both NEXIS and DIALOG and in filings with the SEC available on NEXIS and DIALOG, such as the 10-K annual reports. D&B-Dun's Financial Records Plus, available on DIALOG, contain financial in-

formation, industry comparisons, and company history and operations information on approximately 650,000 U.S. business establishments; an additional 1.2 million privately held companies are included with history and operations information only.

Inventories

1. Review the nature of items and quantities on hand in light of market forecasts and economic conditions.
2. Consider price trends in the auditee's industry, market share, techniques likely to be used by the auditee to boost or sustain its market position, and the auditee's strength as a leader in pricing.
3. Compare the client's sales forecast to industry forecasts or to forecasts by individual competitors to the degree possible, considering major product lines and marketing areas.
4. Establish whether losses exist on open purchase commitments.

Property, Plant, and Equipment

1. See whether the auditee has experienced idle capacity, abandoned property, or property held for sale; if so, consider the effect on valuation of property, plant, and equipment.

Item

Discover's 10-K states that "capitalized costs of producing properties are periodically reviewed for impairment and, if necessary, written down to estimated recoverable amounts. Capitalized costs for unproved properties are periodically reviewed for impairment, and, if necessary, a valuation allowance is provided." With respect to oil and gas leases, a similar valuation allowance is provided.

Author's Comment

According to Walter Schuetze, formerly of the FASB, the accounting treatment of impaired long-lived nonmonetary assets has become an urgent problem. He has pointed out that no uniform practice exists for recognizing and measuring impairment. He has suggested that "for fair values that are difficult or costly to obtain, a standardized measure of cash flow should be disclosed when it is negative.''[29]

An article by Don Eggington provides a list of indicators that suggest that a write-down be considered, such as "currently underused assets, currently idle assets, recent decline in demand, expected decline in demand."[30] 10-K's, including that of Discover, usually do not explain the procedures used to determine impairment; auditors should inquire into and evaluate the procedures used by the auditee to discern and report impairment.

> 2. Identify dispositions of major parts of the business to search out a need for possible write-downs in the value of goodwill.

Personnel Involvement

The manager on the engagement should be involved in choosing the data bases, in determining the search approach, in formulating search statements, and in evaluating results.

SUMMARY

This chapter has set out various actions to enhance audit efficiency and effectiveness that have become possible with the assistance of modern technology. Many of these actions are illustrated in the case study in Chapter 9. Significant matters include:

1. Identification of major external risks faced by the client and of his approaches to risk management; the auditor is invited to think through the financial statement implications of the threats, the extent to which threats were controlled, and the effect on audit risk of the uncontrolled threats. The on-line data bases play a significant role in identifying problem buildups.

---

[29]Walter Schuetze, "Disclosure and the Impairment Question," *Journal of Accountancy*, December 1987, pp. 26–32.

[30]Don Eggington, "When Is a Fixed Asset Overvalued?" *Accountancy*, September 1986, pp. 101–102.

2. Professional and regulatory updates, determination of applicable rules—via electronic searches.
3. Evaluation of people risks. Legal and regulatory data bases can be used, along with newspaper and magazine data bases.
4. Identification of major internal risks, of risk management approaches, and of the implications for audit risk. Use of operational information is encouraged to identify out-of-line conditions for individual accounts.
5. Risk-sensitive and behaviorally aware interviewing in relation to obtaining an understanding of control policies and procedures; identifying key controls and supervisory controls.
6. Confirming the accuracy of the understanding; transaction reviews.
7. Conduct of substantive tests in the light of exposures; use of the on-line data base to verify management's assertions independently.

PART 3

IMPLEMENTING THE UPDATED MODEL

CHAPTER 9

CASE STUDY

However forcefully a man develops and seems to leap from one contradiction to the next, close observation will reveal the dovetailing, where the new building grows out of the old . . . . Nature never jumps.

Friedrich Nietzsche

USER PERSPECTIVE: **Items of Special Interest**

EXECUTIVE HIGHLIGHTS: All readers

INTRODUCTION: All readers

UNDERSTAND INHERENT RISK: All readers

UNDERSTAND THE CLIENT: ON SITE: External auditors, internal auditors

UNDERSTAND THE CONTROL ENVIRONMENT: External auditors, internal auditors

UNDERSTAND THE SYSTEM AND CONTROL PROCE-DURES: All readers

ASSESS CONTROL RISK: Financial executives, internal auditors, external auditors

ALLOCATE AUDIT EFFORT: External auditors, internal auditors

CONDUCT SUBSTANTIVE TESTS: External auditors, internal auditors

SUMMARY: All readers

EXECUTIVE HIGHLIGHTS

Much of the case study refers to Stellar Corporation, a partly fictional entity. The partners in Stellar's audit firm are recognized for the value of the general business advice they provide bundled with audits.

The auditors updated their understanding of Stellar's place in its industry by using public on-line data bases. Stellar's financial ratios were compared to three publicly held companies. Not unexpectedly, the comparison showed that Stellar had a tight cash situation and weak current and quick ratios.

The auditors also referred to data bases which showed that the business of the client's industry was split among a few large and hundreds of small companies. For all, except the apparent industry leader, sales were sluggish or had suffered slowdowns. Extensive capital investment, needed to respond to technological change, represented a potential challenge for Stellar.

The auditor's interest in operational controls serves two purposes: first, absence or malfunctioning of the controls, and the related impact on profitability, can provide a real opportunity for service by furnishing grist for the management letter; second, operational controls can be used to achieve a more efficient and effective audit.

Tests of controls in the focal areas of exposure can add special value. These tests would focus on supervisory controls.

Uncontrolled deficiencies as posted to the master tracking sheet suggested an audit time budget at Stellar which allocated roughly 50 percent of available time to substantive tests of accounts receivable, inventories, and costs.

INTRODUCTION

This chapter further illustrates some of the techniques mentioned in Chapter 8. The figures in the present chapter feature considerable detail and may be used as reminders on actual engagements. Underlying concepts and the results of applications are summarized in the main body of the chapter. On occasion, the discussion refers to an actual company, herein called *Stellar*. Stellar typifies the difficulties and opportunities found at small growth enterprises; to the extent practical, selected audit procedures will be demonstrated by reference to Stellar.

Summary Description of Stellar and Its Audit Firm

The information relating to Stellar is based on an actual company which has been successful in an industry long described as a buyer's market. Certain of Stellar's internal controls are deficient, while others are reasonably good; Stellar's principals compensate for control deficiencies by actively supervising operations. However, well-controlled companies do not necessarily yield instructive examples; further, a company that is *not* well controlled may present particular challenges and opportunities to an auditor. Accordingly, the author exercised poetic license at Stellar and created a partly fictional entity.

Stellar Corporation was started in Florida about 20 years ago. The organizers were first-generation Cuban immigrants imbued with a work ethic and a drive to succeed. They chose to enter the business of electric motor repair. Competition in this fragmented industry was and is fierce and involves quality, service, performance, and price—Stellar opted to compete in all aspects, and has done so successfully.

Stellar does not manufacture complete electric motors, although it does sell coil assemblies. Stellar's operations are located in a new building in an attractive industrial park; the property acquisition was financed via tax-exempt industrial revenue bonds. Sales are running at an annual rate of $15 million. Stellar employs 150 persons. Mirroring the owners' paternalism, employee turnover tends to be low. The coming of age of a new generation of owners has not diminished the company's traditional concern with quality, but has given new impetus to plans for eventually going public and becoming an important factor in its industry.

Since Stellar is still a private company, certain SEC-related aspects will be illustrated by reference to another company in the same industry. See Figure 9–1 for excerpts from an annual report on Form 10-K which include a description of the electric motor business and the registrant's properties.

Stellar does not have an audit committee. If and when the con-

---

FIGURE 9–1
10-K Example

1989 COPYRIGHT SEC ONLINE, INC., 1, *1

BALDOR ELECTRIC COMPANY
5711 SOUTH 7TH STREET
FORT SMITH, ARKANSAS 72902
(501) 646-4711

FOR FISCAL YEAR ENDED: 12/30/89
COMMISSION FILE NUMBER: 1- 7284
STATE OF INCORPORATION: MO
IRS EMPLOYER I.D.:   43-0168840

SECURITIES REGISTERED PURSUANT TO SECTION 12(b) OF THE ACT:

TITLE OF EACH CLASS	NAME OF EACH EXCHANGE ON WHICH REGISTERED
COMMON STOCK, $ .10 PAR VALUE	NEW YORK STOCK EXCHANGE
COMMON STOCK PURCHASE RIGHTS	NEW YORK STOCK EXCHANGE

SECURITIES REGISTERED PURSUANT TO SECTION 12(g) OF THE ACT:

TITLE OF EACH CLASS	NAME OF EACH EXCHANGE ON WHICH REGISTERED
NONE	NONE

INDICATE BY CHECK MARK WHETHER THE REGISTRANT (1) HAS FILED
ALL REPORTS REQUIRED TO BE FILED BY SECTION 13 OR 15(D) OF THE
SECURITIES EXCHANGE ACT OF 1934 DURING THE PRECEDING 12
MONTHS (OR FOR SUCH SHORTER PERIOD THAT THE REGISTRANT WAS
REQUIRED TO FILE SUCH REPORTS), AND (2) HAS BEEN SUBJECT TO
SUCH FILING REQUIREMENTS FOR THE PAST 90 DAYS.
YES   x   NO

THE AGGREGATE MARKET VALUE OF VOTING STOCK HELD BY
NON-AFFILIATES OF THE REGISTRANT BASED ON THE CLOSING PRICE
ON FEBRUARY 28, 1990 WAS $144,377,000.

AT FEBRUARY 28, 1990 THERE WERE 9,650,006 SHARES OF THE
REGISTRANT'S COMMON STOCK OUTSTANDING.

[*2]   [HARDCOPY PAGE 2]

FIGURE 9-1 *(continued)*

PART I

ITEM 1. BUSINESS

Baldor Electric Company ("the Company") was incorporated in Missouri in 1920 as a manufacturer of industrial electric motors. Baldor has subsequently expanded principally through internal growth. Baldor's single line of business is the design, manufacture and marketing of electric motors and related electronic products.

Industrial electric motors, ranging in size from 1/2 through 300 horsepower A.C. and 1/50 through 700 horsepower D.C., is the principal product line representing over 90% of the Company's sales. These products are built primarily for industrial use as distinguished from home appliance use. The Company's electric motors are designed and manufactured to individual customer specifications ("custom products") and for general purpose uses ("stock products").

The Company also designs, manufactures and markets industrial grinders, buffers and dental polishing lathes. In addition, as a result of an acquisition in 1986, the Company's product line was expanded to include solid-state electric motor starters.

The Company also designs, manufactures and markets advanced-technology industrial control systems. These include a broad range of transistor servodrivers and servomotors. During 1986, the Company announced the formation of a Motion Products Group that consolidated several related operations to market these products in North America.

Sales and Marketing

The products of the Company are marketed in all 50 states of the United States and in approximately 40 foreign countries. The Company's field sales organization consists of almost 50 independent manufacturers' representative groups including 24 in the United States, and the remainder in Canada, Europe, Latin America, Australia and the Far East.

Custom products and stock products are sold to original equipment manufacturers ("OEMs"). Stock products are sold to independent distributors for resale, often as replacement components in industrial machinery which is being modernized or upgraded for improved performance.

The Company conducts business with a large number of customers, and it does not believe that the loss of any single customer would have a material adverse effect on its total business.

(continued)

FIGURE 9–1 *(continued)*

1989 COPYRIGHT SEC ONLINE, INC., 1, *3

Competition

The Company faces substantial competition in the sales of its products in all markets served. Some of the Company's competitors are larger in size or are divisions of large diversified companies and have substantially greater financial resources. The Company competes on the basis of quality, service, availability, performance and price.

[*3]   [HARDCOPY PAGE 3]

The Company is not aware of any industry-wide statistics from which it can precisely determine its relative portion of the industrial electric motor industry. In the United States, certain industry statistics are available from the U.S. Department of Commerce and the National Electrical Manufacturers Association. However, these sources do not include all competitors or all sizes of motors. The Company believes, however, that it is a significant factor in certain markets served.

Manufacturing

The Company manufactures many of the components used in its products including laminations, motor hardware, capacitors and aluminum die castings. Manufacturing many of its own components permits the Company to achieve a high degree of cost and quality control. In addition to the manufacture of components, the Company's motor manufacturing operations include machining, stamping, welding, assembling and finishing operations.

The raw materials necessary for the Company's manufacturing operations are available from several sources. These materials include steel, copper wire, gray iron castings, aluminum and insulating materials, most of which are purchased from more than one supplier. Although some materials are purchased from single suppliers, the Company believes that alternate sources are available for such materials.

Patents, Trademarks, Licenses and Franchises

The Company owns numerous patents but believes the knowledge and expertise it has, as evidenced in the development of products, product applications and production methods, is of greater importance to the company than the development of patents.

Research and Development

The Company's design and development of electric motors and related products includes both the development of products which extend the

FIGURE 9-1 *(continued)*

1989 COPYRIGHT SEC ONLINE, INC., 1, *4

Company's product lines and the modification of existing Company products to meet new application requirements. Additional development work is done to improve production methods. Costs associated with research, new product development and product and cost improvements are treated as expenses when incurred and amounted to approximately $8,500,000 in 1989, $7,200,000 in 1988, and $6,000,000 in 1987.

Environment

Compliance with laws relating to the discharge of materials into the environment or otherwise relating to the protection of the environment has not had a material effect on capital expenditures, earnings or the competitive position of the Company and is not expected to have such effect.

Employees

At December 30, 1989, the Company had 2,900 employees.

Executive Officers of the Registrant

Information regarding executive officers is contained in Part III, Item 10, and incorporated herein by reference.

[*4]   [HARDCOPY PAGE 4]

Foreign Operations

The Company's products are distributed in approximately 40 foreign countries, principally in Canada, Europe, Australia, the Far East, and Latin America.

The Company's foreign operations include the Baldor ASR group of companies ("ASR"), acquired in 1983. ASR has sales offices located in Switzerland, West Germany, and the United Kingdom, with research and manufacturing operations in West Germany. The Company has a majority interest in Baldor Electric (Far East) Pte. Ltd., located in Singapore, and Australian Baldor Pty. Limited, with two locations in Australia. Finally, the Company has a minority interest in Baldor de Mexico, S.A. de C.V., located in Mexico City. The Singapore, Australian, and Mexican affiliates are sales operations.

The Company believes that there are additional risks attendant to foreign operations including currency fluctuations and possible restrictions on the movement of funds. However, these risks have not had a material adverse effect on the Company's business.

(continued)

FIGURE 9-1 *(continued)*

1989 COPYRIGHT SEC ONLINE, INC., 1, *4

For each of the three years in the period presented, export and foreign sales have increased, representing approximately 10.9% of consolidated sales in 1989, 10.6% in 1988, and 10.5% in 1987.

Material Changes

Except as discussed in preceding sections, there have been no material changes since the beginning of the fiscal year in the business done and intended to be done by the Company and its subsidiaries.

ITEM 2. PROPERTIES

The Company believes that all of its facilities, including equipment and machinery, are in good condition and adequately maintained and insured. The following table sets forth certain information with respect to the Company's properties.

LOCATION	PRIMARY USE	AREA (SQ. FT.)
Fort Smith, AR.	AC motor production and aluminum die casting	328,900
	Distribution and service center	112,300
	Administration and engineering offices	60,100
St. Louis County, MO.	Metal stamping and engineering toolroom	114,500
	DC and repulsion—induction motor production	55,600
Columbus, MS.	AC motor production	140,300
Westville, OK.	AC and DC motor production	155,000
Charlotte, NC	DC motor and tachometer production	76,000
Clarksville, AR	Subfractional motor production	63,000
Thirteen properties with less than 50,000 sq. ft. each	Servodrivers, electronic servomotors, metal stamping and electrolytic capacitor production	199,100
		1,304,800

[*5]   [HARDCOPY PAGE 5]

FIGURE 9-1 *(continued)*

1989 COPYRIGHT SEC ONLINE, INC., 1, *5

Certain properties listed above (509,500 sq. ft. in the aggregate) are leased, principally pursuant to Industrial Revenue Bond agreements, and where material are accounted for as capitalized lease obligations. Certain lease agreements contain purchase options at varying prices and/or renewal options at reduced rentals for extended additional periods.

ITEM 3. LEGAL PROCEEDINGS

The Company is party to a number of legal proceedings incidental to its business, none of which is deemed to be material to its operations or business.

ITEM 4. SUBMISSION OF MATTERS TO A VOTE OF SECURITY HOLDERS

Not applicable.

PART II

ITEM 5. MARKET FOR THE REGISTRANT'S COMMON EQUITY AND RELATED STOCKHOLDER MATTERS

Information under the captions "Dividends Paid," "Common Stock: Price Range," and "Stockholders" on the inside back cover of the Annual Report to Stockholders for 1989 is incorporated herein by reference.

ITEM 6. SELECTED FINANCIAL DATA
Information under the "Eleven Year Summary of Financial Data" for years 1985 through 1989 for net sales, net earnings, net earnings per share, dividends per share, long-term obligations and total assets on page 23 of the Annual Report to Stockholders for 1989 is incorporated herein by reference.

ITEM 7. MANAGEMENT'S DISCUSSION AND ANALYSIS OF FINANCIAL CONDITION AND RESULTS OF OPERATIONS

Management's Review and Analysis of Financial Condition and Results of Operations on pages 10 and 11 of the Annual Report to Stockholders for 1989 is incorporated herein by reference.

ITEM 8. FINANCIAL STATEMENTS AND SUPPLEMENTARY DATA

The consolidated financial statements of the Company on pages 14 through 21, the report thereon of Ernst & Young on page 22, and the "Summary of Quarterly Results of Operations (Unaudited)" on page 23 of the Annual Report to Stockholders for 1989 are incorporated herein by reference.

(continued)

FIGURE 9–1 *(concluded)*

1989 COPYRIGHT SEC ONLINE, INC., 1, *5

DATE: SEPTEMBER 10, 1990
CLIENT: STELLAR
LIBRARY: FEDSEC
FILE: FILING

Your search request is:
BALDOR ELECTRIC

Number of FILINGS found with your search request through:
LEVEL 1 . . .   32

To display the next screen of text of the FILING you were viewing, press the
NEXT PAGE key.

To redisplay the screen of text of the FILING you were viewing, press the
TRANSMIT key.

For further explanation, press the H key (for HELP) and then the TRANSMIT key.

Source: Represents output of search of Mead Data Central, NEXIS® Service, 10-K, SEC On-line, Inc.
Reprinted with the permission of Mead Data Central, Inc., provider of the LEXIS®/NEXIS® services.
Copyright 1990, Mead Data Central, Inc. No copyright is claimed as to any part of the original work
prepared by a government officer or employee as part of that person's official duties.

cern goes public, such a committee will be created pursuant to the requirements of the National Market System (NMS) of the National Association of Security Dealers (NASD). In addition Stellar does not maintain a separate internal audit department; however, Stellar is planning to initiate certain functions akin to those performed by internal auditors.

Stellar is an audit client of a prestigious Miami accounting firm. This firm conducts a thriving audit practice and prides itself on having a number of public company clients. The auditors provide a broad range of accounting, auditing, consulting, and tax services. In addition to the firm's considerable size within its market, it enjoys substantial prestige in the community and among professional accountants. The firm's partners are recognized for the value of the general business advice they provide bundled with audits. The firm has been notably successful in recruiting, retaining, and seeing to the professional development of outstanding partners and employees.

Stellar has been a client since 1987. The relationship between Stellar and its auditors has been satisfactory and mutually beneficial. Stellar's sales have doubled over the last few years. Stellar's executives acknowledge that their auditors have had a part in Stellar's success. Stellar has been responsive to (infrequent) suggestions for audit adjustments, and/or to comments and recommendations. The latter are first communicated to management verbally and recorded in the engagement working papers subsequently. Its cooperativeness with its auditors notwithstanding, Stellar asks that audit adjustments and comments and recommendations be supported by adequate evidence.

UNDERSTAND INHERENT RISK

Consider Stellar's Position Relative to Its Industry

The auditors updated their understanding of Stellar's place in its industry by using public on-line data bases. Information on private companies, including Stellar, can be found in D&B-DUN'S MARKET IDENTIFIERS (DIALOG File 516) and D&B-DUN'S FINANCIAL RECORDS PLUS (DIALOG File 519). D&B-DUN'S FINANCIAL RECORDS PLUS provides up to three years of comprehensive financial statements for more than 650,000 U.S. business establishments. The information includes balance sheets, income statements, widely used business ratios, and history and operations discussions. The file also contains an abbreviated history and operations background for an additional 1.2 million companies. The audit senior looked up Stellar to determine whether any changes had occurred which might have audit implications; none had. However, the client's financial statements in File 519 were out of date, a matter which was brought to the attention of Stellar's controller.

In the case of *public* companies, extensive and detailed financial information is available through either Disclosure On-line Data Base (DISCLO file) or SEC On-line, Inc. (10-K file), carried by both Mead Data Central (MDC) and DIALOG.

Author's Comment

Although tradeoffs exist whenever different wholesalers provide the same data bases, it is difficult to determine the effect of varying prices on the user's bottom line. Subscription plans differ. The ongoing cost of using an on-line service may depend on the amount of time spent on-line and on the volume of information displayed and/ or printed; these usage factors are difficult to predict until experience has been gained with a particular vendor.[1]

Stellar's financial ratios were compared to three publicly held companies in its industry; two of these companies are among the industry's figurative blue chips. DISCLO features 32 financial ratios; the results of the comparison are shown in Figure 9–2. Not unexpectedly for an emerging company, the comparison showed that Stellar had a tight cash situation and weak current and quick ratios. Moreover, Stellar was highly leveraged in terms of borrowings. On the other hand, inventory turnover and receivable collections were somewhat better than at the larger companies, presumably reflecting managerial attention.

Identify Stellar's Approach to Risk Management

The auditor decided to supplement the financial information already obtained by referring to other data bases likely to yield further information on current inherent risk. Four data bases were selected initially: ABI/INFORM (available on DIALOG and ORBIT), MANAGEMENT CONTENTS (DIALOG), PAIS INTERNATIONAL (DIALOG), and PTS PROMPT (DIALOG). ABI/INFORM has been described in Figure 6–9. MANAGEMENT CONTENTS provides current information helpful to business decision making and forecasting; articles from over 120 U.S. and international journals, as well as proceedings, newsletters, and other research materials, are indexed and abstracted. PAIS INTERNATIONAL relates primarily to social

---

[1]Jean M. Scanlan, Ulla de Stricker, and Anne Conway Fernald, *Business Online: The Professional's Guide to Electronic Information Sources* (New York: John Wiley & Sons, 1990), pp. 46–47.

FIGURE 9–2
Comparative Ratios

	Stellar 04/30/90	A 06/30/89	B 12/30/89	C 07/31/88
Quick ratio	.46	1.63	1.54	.47
Current ratio	.82	3.75	3.06	1.19
Net sales/cash	111.76	318.05	41.46	341.41
SG&A expenses/sales	.21	.18	.19	.14
Receivables turnover	6.30	5.65	6.20	4.27
Receivables day sales	57.14	63.67	58.05	84.28
Inventories turnover	8.02	4.47	5.88	2.63
Inventories day sales	44.89	80.62	61.24	136.77
Net sales/working capital	NA	3.30	4.03	9.98
Net sales/net plant & equipment	2.39	7.10	4.2	6.72
Net sales/current assets	3.37	2.42	2.71	1.60
Net sales/total assets	1.39	1.73	1.52	1.27
Net sales/employees	100000	86220	97056	42718
Total liabilities/total assets	.88	.52	.38	.94
Total liabilities/invested capital	1.76	.66	.52	2.82
Total liabilities/common equity	7.09	1.09	.62	15.27
Times interest earned	1.71	4.54	16.09	1.29
Current debt/equity	4.07	.07	.01	.33
Long-term debt/equity	3.02	.65	.2	4.42
Total debt/equity	7.09	.72	.21	4.75
Total assets/equity	8.09	2.09	1.62	16.27
Pretax income/net sales	.03	.06	.08	.01
Pretax income/total assets	.05	.10	.12	.01
Pretax income/invested capital	.09	.13	.16	.09
Pretax income/common equity	.38	.22	.19	1.18
Net income/net sales	NA	.04	.05	.04
Net income/total assets	NA	.07	.07	.02
Net income/invested capital	NA	.09	.10	.07
Net income/common equity	NA	.16	.11	1.00
R&D expenditures/net sales	NA	.07	NA	NA
R&D expenditures/net income	NA	1.51	NA	NA
R&D expenditures/employees	NA	5620	NA	NA

Note: "NA" means not applicable or available.

science, economics, and business issues. This data base represents a bibliographic index, enriched by very brief abstracts; it covers more than 1,200 journals and 8,000 books; many of its sources have an international orientation. PTS PROMPT provides broad international coverage of companies, products, markets, and applied technologies.

A single search was made on DIALOG of all four data bases. The articles retrieved showed that:

the electric motor manufacturing business is a $4 billion business, split among a few large, and hundreds of small, companies. Baldor Electric represented the exception to an industrywide slump. Baldor's sales rose 25 percent in 1988 over 1987; exports were up over 50 percent. The manufacturers of fractional horsepower motors were hard hit by Japanese and Mexican imports. Sales were also hurt by sluggish residential construction and reduced capital spending by users of integral motors.

Further, the industry suffered from a lack of technological developments, high prices for copper and for bearings, and 20 to 30 percent greater costs required to build a high efficiency motor, compared to a standard one.[2] Two additional articles were found and given to Stellar's president; the first story outlined the quality strategy pursued by a large German electric motor manufacturer; the second dealt with improvements to the energy efficiency of electric motors.

The DIALOG search also led to an article which asserted that the technology available in 1990 can provide the means to save 75 percent of all electrical energy being consumed in the United States. Lighting and electric motors use up the greatest portion of electrical energy. This writer asserted that the energy used to power industrial electric motors can be reduced by using electronic speed controls and new, high efficiency motors.[3] If his statement is correct, a need would exist for research at Stellar, and for closely monitoring inventories in all stages of production. In order to assist Stellar's management, the audit manager authorized an expansion of the search to include two technical engineering data bases, which resulted in 41 primarily technical references, mostly relating to the manufacture of higher efficiency motors. A typical article said "fuel consumption can be reduced substantially in all major sectors through more efficient electric motors."[4]

---

[2]Thomas F. Dillon, "Variety and Competition in Motors," *Purchasing World* 32, no. 11 (November 1988), pp. 67M1–68M2.

[3]Amory B. Lovins, "The Megawatt Revolution," *Across the Board* 27 (September 1990), p. 18.

[4]Cheryl Jones, Paul Grad, and Ian Hammond, "Standby & Alternative Power: Australia Has a Huge Untapped Resource—Energy Wasted Through Inefficiency," *Journal of the Institute of Engineers (Australia)* 61, no. 10 (June 2, 1989), p. 24.

According to information found in PTS PROMPT, sales in Stellar's business continued to be sluggish, or suffered from slow-downs. Baldor Electric continued to do comparatively well during 1990 "as a result of conversion to more efficient plant processes in recent years."[5] In 1990 alone, eight articles were found concerning the electric motor repair business; three of these articles involved sales or acquisitions of facilities, one a plant closure, and another a new plant. The remaining three articles discussed innovative services being rendered by General Electric—that is, predictive maintenance analysis services and motor efficiency enhancement during rewinding.

Finally, as a service to Stellar, a look was taken at a data base of the *Journal of Commerce* (on DIALOG) which includes leads and bidding invitations supplied by the U.S. Department of Commerce and others. Based on some 24 announcements, there appeared to be export opportunities. The technical and marketing references were turned over to the client for follow-up.

In essence, the search of the data bases revealed an increasingly competitive situation in Stellar's industry, flat sales, and a trend toward costly plant modernization. These developments affect sales, accounts receivable, inventory movement, and cash flow. Stellar should monitor developments and take appropriate action, possibly with its auditors' help. The auditors must be similarly watchful, given a potential threat to the client's status as a going concern.

Identify Internal Risks

Inherent risk is composed of external and internal elements. The principal risks confronting a business are external; however, internal risks, such as those involving inability to make deliveries, cope with technological change, or meet quality standards, must also be considered. Internal risks may involve deep-seated mala-

---

[5]M. Plummer of Stephens, Inc., "Baldor Electric—Company Report," *Investext*, November 1, 1990, p. 1-1.

dies such as failure to communicate effectively, lack of an overall
managerial philosophy, excessive layers of supervision, and even
fear. The internal risks may be considered by the auditor prior to
or after his arrival on site.

Item

A transportation company hired a new chief executive in the person
of a (hitherto unknown) scion of an aristocratic family. The new executive made extravagant commitments as to the profit targets he
would achieve. When it became apparent to him that he would be
unable to meet his goal, he deferred payments of vendor invoices.
Eventually, many file drawers were filled with unpaid invoices.

Inherent Risk: A Summing Up

The auditors must understand inherent risks confronted by their
client, the control techniques used to mitigate those risks, and any
remaining exposures from uncontrolled risk.[6] The master tracking
sheet endeavors to deal with these concerns; instructions for completing the master tracking sheet appear in Figure 9–3. The purpose of the sheet is to assemble in one place all components of the
system and all assets that could be subject to threats, identify the
threats, determine which are uncontrolled, note the accounts affected, and estimate the seriousness of uncontrolled threats.

A master tracking sheet, partly completed for Stellar, is
shown as Figure 9–4. For purposes of illustration, only *uncontrolled* threats are shown (i.e., the sheet does not reflect any key or
supervisory controls bearing on these threats). Significant uncontrolled threats (i.e., audit risk) existed with respect to accounts receivable, inventories, and costs—considerations which militate in
favor of unrestricted substantive testing at the end of the year. In
addition, adverse business conditions, which are likely to continue, call for imaginative management responses to protect the
entity's ability to continue as a going concern.

---

[6]Melvin M. Kann, "How to Initiate Control Management and Conduct Investigative Auditing," *The Journal of Bank Accounting & Auditing* 2, no. 4 (Summer 1989), p. 30.

FIGURE 9-3
The Master Tracking Sheet

Instructions

---

1. Identify the component parts of the system, together with assets, intangibles, or other company resources that could be at risk and subject to threats. Give special attention to the focal areas of exposure.
2. Identify the threats faced by components and weigh their relative seriousness in terms of the organization:
   a. SR   = Security related:
       BP   = Breach of privacy.
       EO   = Errors and omissions.
       IA   = Illegal system access.
       FT   = Fraud or theft.
       LCM = Lost or corrupted messages.
       DD   = Disasters and disruptions.
   b. Other:
       MS   = Material shortages.
       LI   = Labor interruptions.
       I   = Inflation.
       CS   = Capital shortages.
       VL   = Violation of laws.
       TL   = Technological change.
       SD   = Sales decrease.
       CI   = Cost increase.
3. Identified threats are usually based on:
   a. Matters reported previously and not corrected.
   b. Exposures to risk recognized during the current audit.
   c. Threats noted during the plant or office tours or at any other time while on the client's premises, or while communicating with the client's employees.
   d. Threats detected in the focal areas of risk.
   e. Threats detected in the course of reviews of flowcharts, narratives, and internal control questionnaires or checklists.
   f. Control weaknesses, errors, misrepresentations, etc. noted during testing.
4. Refer to existing key controls and supervisory controls identified from flowcharts, narratives, interviews, or reviews of checklists. Enter such controls following the related threats.
5. With respect to threats which have not been fully addressed by controls, consider the recommendations to be made to the organization being audited.
6. Enter the accounts potentially affected by uncontrolled threats.
7. Rank uncontrolled threats as high, medium, or low. (These rankings will be used to allocate audit effort.) (See Figure 9-18.)

FIGURE 9–4
Stellar Corporation Master Tracking Sheet*

Components	Threat	Accounts Affected	Seriousness of Threats
Focal areas of risk:			
Physical security of assets			Medium
Cycle count results may not be controlled	FT	Inv.	
Inaccurate counts due to articles consigned	EO	Inv.	
Inaccurate counts; lack of instructions	EO	Inv.	
Computer access	SR	All	High
Management representations	FT	All	Low
External inherent risk:			
Competitive markets; price cutting	SD	Inv.	High
High commodity prices, especially copper	CI	Cost	Medium
Rising costs of building high-tech items	CI	Inv.	Medium
Deteriorating backlog	SD	Inv.	Medium
Internal risk:			
Bored work force; proneness to error	EO	Cost	High
Uncertain structure of quality control program	EO	Cost	Medium
No emphasis on plant safety	CI	Cost	Medium
Insufficient emphasis on security	FT	All	Medium
Tight cash situation	CS	A/R	High
Weak financial ratios	CS	All	Medium
High debt leverage	CS	All	High
Other weaknesses or exceptions:			
Sales/accounts receivable cycle			
Little information on bidding effectiveness	SD	Sales	Medium
Questionable profitability of coil business	SD	Sales	Low
Rising sales compensation relative to sales	SD	Inv.	Medium
Purchasing/accounts payable cycle			
Commodity buying volumes unavailable	CI	Cost	Medium
Incomplete data to expedite custom buys	EO	Cost	Low
Absence of control over vendor code issuance	FT	A/P	Medium
Rising purchased parts inventories	CI	Inv.	High
Production/inventory cycle			
Inadequate temporary reservation system	CI	Cost	Low
Lack of formal paperwork	EO	Cost	Medium
Unexplained rework	CI	Cost	Medium
Round-the-clock work	CI	Cost	Medium
Time clocks not under supervision	FT	Cost	Low
Data processing			
Lack of plan for systems development	EO	All	High
Lack of systems documentation	FT	All	High

FIGURE 9–4 *(concluded)*

Components	Threat	Accounts Affected	Seriousness of Threats
Incompatible order entry/receivables systems	EO	A/R	Medium
Contract programmer handles all work	FT	All	High

Summary of evaluations for effort allocation:
Focal areas
  Computer access issues

Accounts receivable	High
Inventories	High

Inherent risk

Accounts receivable	High
Inventories	High
Costs	High

Codes of threats
SR = Security related:
BP = Breach of privacy.
EO = Errors and omissions.
IA   = Illegal system access.
FT = Fraud or theft.
LCM = Lost or corrupted messages.
DD = Disasters and disruptions.

Other:
MS = Material shortages.
LI   = Labor interruptions.
I   = Inflation.
CS = Capital shortages.
VL = Violation of laws.
TL = Technological change.
SD = Sales decrease.
CI = Cost increase.

*The sheet has been completed for selected matters only. Neither existing nor recommended controls have been shown.

Update Knowledge of Professional and Regulatory Requirements

An auditor consults on-line data bases to consider the effect on his client of changes in governmental and professional rules. Mention has been made previously of the AICPA's Electronic Index to Technical Pronouncements (EITP), along with the literature file (LIT) of the National Automated Accounting Research System (NAARS). NAARS, a product of the AICPA, is available exclusively through MDC. NAARS' LIT file covers accounting- and auditing-related rules issued by key government agencies, as well as pronouncements of the profession. Although NAARS is not difficult to learn, there is an additional convenient way in which smaller audit organizations, or audit organizations that think of themselves as one-time users of data bases, may avoid a start-up effort: They can engage the AICPA (1-800-223-4158) to conduct a search on their behalf. Accountants and auditors may also wish to search additional files available on MDC, such as SECREL (Interpretive and other SEC releases), FEDREG (Federal Register), and CFR (Code of Federal Regulations).

Stellar's auditors determined that their client's one open accounting problem involved a question as to whether the warranty cost accruals should include both labor and materials. In its 1990 annual report, Stellar's policy had been described as follows: "Estimated warranty costs are accrued at the time revenues from repairs are recognized, based on past operating history. Expenses related to unusual warranty repair problems are recorded in the period the problem is identified." The computation of Stellar's warranty reserve was based on a three-year average of chargebacks to gross income.

In connection with warranty costs, EITP was used to identify pertinent pronouncements, primarily *Statement on Financial Accounting Standards (SFAS) 14*, paragraphs 3, 8, and 24. The rules leave the methodology of computation to each company. Accordingly, a search was made of footnotes of companies with pertinent SIC codes. The DISCLO file, which can be accessed on either MDC or DIALOG, was used to retrieve footnotes. (NAARS' Annual Report file (AR) or SEC On-line's 10-K file represent alternative sources of footnotes.)

The search revealed several approaches to warranty cost computation. One company stated: "Product warranty costs, principally labor charges [parts and components are substantially covered by the manufacturer's warranty] are provided." Another said that "management does not believe, based on historical experience, that the Company will incur significant warranty costs on its products." Two others gave no details beyond statements that they provided currently for the estimated cost to repair or replace products under warranty provisions in effect at the time of the sale. Equipped with this information, Stellar's auditors plan to discuss the current year's computation with the client.

Evaluate People Risks

Employee turnover has not been a problem at Stellar. If turnover had been a problem, and senior employees had been hired, the on-line data bases would offer opportunities for gaining insights into their prior associations. MDC's NEXIS/LEXIS services make it easy to look up individuals and their written or oral utterances, activities, and possibly litigious pasts.

UNDERSTAND THE CLIENT: ON–SITE

Perform Internal Analytics

Subsequent to their arrival on the client's premises, auditors should continue to gain or update their understanding of the client. Internal analytical procedures are applied to identify out-of-line conditions for investigation. There are two related categories of analytical procedures: (1) analytical procedures based solely on data appearing in financial records, and (2) analytical procedures involving operating data. One advantage of using operational information stems from the circumstance that financial personnel are not likely to have been deeply involved in generating the information; the information therefore has a cachet of semi-independence.

However, there are negative aspects to audit use of operational information; the information may not have been subject to appropriate internal control, and could also have been targeted for management overrides. A list of operational controls for various subsystems (systems cycles) appears in Figure 9–5. The auditor's interest in these controls serves two purposes: first, absence or malfunctioning of the controls, and the related impact on profitability, can provide auditors with a real opportunity for service by furnishing grist for the management letter; second, operational controls can be used to achieve a more efficient and effec-

---

FIGURE 9–5
Examples of Operational Controls*

Whether the auditor utilizes operational controls for substantive test purposes
depends not only on considerations of audit efficiency and effectiveness, but
also on the hazard of management overrides. Overrides involve a conscious
or directed disregard of company policies. (These policies should stress
compliance with ethical standards, adherence to acceptable control
procedures, oversight by an audit committee, and reviews by internal and
external auditors. Less commonly, policies may prohibit overrides of controls
designed to prevent or detect transactions that are illegal, improper, or
unethical, while other types of overrides may require specific executive
approval.)

Operational controls may function as integral parts of the data processing
system. To make an informed decision as to the extent of reliance on
operational controls, the auditor must be knowledgeable as to the entity's
philosophy toward control generally, the involvement of persons with
appropriate independence in the process, and the nature of review and
approval routines applied by them.

Operational control tests involve observation, inquiry of client personnel, and,
most importantly, inspection of evidence. The tests are usually efficient, since
evidence in the form of reports to and reactions from management should be
readily obtainable.

The operational controls, problems involved in their functioning, and the
significance of breakdowns in operational controls are outside the scope of
this book. The list of operational controls presented in succeeding paragraphs
is *not* comprehensive, although it includes many controls likely to affect audit
risk. The operational controls are presented on a subsystems or systems
cycle basis; such cycles are usually defined to the requirements of a
particular audit.

Sales/Accounts Receivable Cycle

Sales budgets (including quotas, forecasts, and goals)
Order backlog
Bidding effectiveness reports
Sales statistics
Sales price variance reports
Shipping records
Traffic statistics
Traffic standard cost variance reports
Salespeople's compensation analysis
Salespeople's performance evaluations
Quality assurance analysis
Report of missed delivery dates
Analysis of order cancellations
Customer service reports
Analysis of accounts receivable claims, credits, and allowances

(continued)

FIGURE 9–5 *(concluded)*

Purchasing/Accounts Payable Cycle

Purchase volume statistics by commodity and vendor
Purchase budget variance report by commodity and vendor
Analysis of expediting activities
Vendor performance reports in terms of quality, time, and service
Analysis of order cancellations
Purchase price variance reports
Analysis of the results of incoming inspections
Receiving statistics
Traffic statistics
Incoming traffic standard cost variance reports

Production/Inventory Cycle

Inventory position and turnover reports by product, area, warehouse, customer, salesperson, etc.
Production performance reports
Rework reports
Production cost variance reports
Machine loading reports, including backlogs
Overtime planning versus actual performance reports
Premium payment reports
Scrap reports
Stockout reports
Quality control reports
Warranty service reports
Claim adjudication reports
Analysis of inventory shrinkages

---

*The Institute of Internal Auditors stocks a number of quality publications relating to operational auditing. The Institute's address is 249 Maitland Avenue, Altamonte Springs, FL 32701-4201. The phone number is (407) 830-7600.

---

tive audit. The use of operational controls to accomplish substantive testing is discussed in subsequent paragraphs.

A guide to analytical review using operational information is represented by Figure 9–6. At Stellar, comparison of analytical relationships showed that the ratio of order backlog to receivables had declined, although sales had increased significantly; this could indicate future erosion of sales prices or quantities, and could eventually threaten the company's cash flow. The ratio of sales compensation to sales also increased, reflecting ongoing hard sell efforts, and possibly, presaging slower inventory turnover in the future. The purchased parts component of inventories rose relative to other inventories, indicating a need for better inventory control, especially in light of market conditions. Results of the ratio analysis were carried to the master tracking sheet and will receive further consideration in audit planning; it is apparent that audit attention must be given to inventory movement, especially of purchased parts, and that management must monitor selling costs. Furthermore, existing borrowing arrangements (which hinge on maintenance of a specified dollar level of current, not past due, accounts receivable) must be watched to ensure compliance and to support a case for eventual loan renegotiation.

Assess Prior Communications, Including Internal Audit Reports

As noted, Stellar's external auditors convey findings, comments, and recommendations verbally; the reasons are to minimize the client's financial exposure, to minimize expansion of the audit to overcome deficiencies, and to stanch any ongoing erosion of client profitability.

Internal audit at Stellar is in a pre-startup phase. Stellar's external auditors will monitor such activities, together with the accompanying professionalism, technical competence, and independence of the individuals involved, to determine the reliance, if any, that should be placed on their activities in the future.

As noted in the preceding chapter, formal or informal reports rendered by examiners or inspectors provide important pieces toward completing the mosaic of the client's control environment. The auditor should endeavor to obtain formal or informal reports rendered by tax examiners, systems analysts, fire inspectors, safety, health, and environmental reviewers, insurance examiners, and wages and hours auditors, and review them in the light of his audit objectives. The auditor should determine: (1) which agency conducted a review; (2) the nature of report(s) submitted and to whom; (3) the current status of any findings or recommendations; (4) the impact upon client profitability of resolving, or not resolving, findings and recommendations; (5) the financial significance and materiality of any fines; and (6) the effect of findings, recommendations, unresolved issues, and fines upon the accounts and mandated disclosures. During the period no reports were ren-

FIGURE 9–6
Analytical Review

The objectives of analytical review have been described by Blocher and
Willingham as follows:*

Accounts receivable: assess collectibility.

Inventory: assist in inventory pricing; detect misclassifications in overhead
allocations; examine for obsolete inventory, improper handling of
shrinkages, and improper cutoff.

Property, plant, and equipment: test accuracy of allowance for depreciation
and related current expenses; examine utilization of assets to evaluate the
need for writedowns.

Accounts payable, unrecorded liabilities, and other liabilities: evaluate
completeness of disclosure; evaluate reasonableness of contingent
liabilities.

Revenue: test validity of reported sales; test for unrecorded sales.

Expenses: evaluate whether accounts are completely and properly stated.

The following operationally oriented procedures may be of interest relative to
analytical tests of balances of accounts receivable, accounts payable, and
inventories. The list is not intended to be complete or comprehensive, nor
does it include examples of all representative types of analytical procedures.

Accounts Receivable

Ratio of order backlog (in dollars) to receivables
Order cancellations to order backlog
Dollar volume of successful bids to total bids
Receivables turnover (i.e., the ratio of credit sales to receivables)
Sales discounts to credit sales
Sales returns and allowances to sales
Sales divided by physical measure of shipments or traffic
Sales compensation to sales
Sales incentives to sales
Order cancellations to sales
Analysis of quality assurance reports
Analysis of customer service calls
Analysis of warranty service reports

Accounts Payable

Accounts payable to production budget
Purchase discounts to purchases
Purchase returns and allowances to purchases
Purchases divided by physical measure of volume of incoming traffic
Purchase order cancellations to purchases

(continued)

FIGURE 9–6 *(concluded)*

Inventories

Comparison of the ending balance of (finished goods) inventories to sales
 budgets
Comparison of the ending balance of raw materials to budgeted production
Trends in the composition of inventories by cost component
Rework to finished goods inventories
Analysis of unusually large purchases toward the year end.

---

*Readers seeking additional information can consult their book: Edward Blocher and John J.
Willingham, *Analytical Review: A Guide to Evaluating Financial Statements* (New York: McGraw-Hill,
1985).

---

dered to Stellar by examiners or inspectors. (It should be pointed
out that MDC's LEXIS and NEXIS services include specialized
data bases dealing with environmental, health, insurance, energy, and other matters. These files would not be searched by auditors in all cases; they are mentioned because of their value as
potential information resources.)

Take Plant and Office Tours

The engagement team toured Stellar's facilities and recorded its observations. The tour was guided by Stellar's vice president for engineering. The audit manager prepared an internal memo pertaining
to the plant tour (see Figure 9–7). The memo was written so as to fit
easily into a management letter. Major deficiencies included lack of
physical security over inventory, absence of information for procurement purposes, lack of a comprehensive production control system,
and badly documented data processing. To help plan for attendance
at the annual physical inventory, the senior prepared a separate
memorandum giving his impression as to the extent to which assets
were protected physically (see Figure 9–8).

UNDERSTAND THE CONTROL ENVIRONMENT

Knowledge of the control environment enables an auditor to determine (1) whether it conduces to an effective accounting system
and integral control procedures, and (2) whether it minimizes the

FIGURE 9–7
Stellar Corporation Plant Tour Notes

General

1. There is no evidence of management instructions intended to improve product quality; it is not certain how the quality control program is structured.
2. Some new motors were observed in storage. These units were on consignment from vendors. Care should be taken to make certain that these motors are excluded from the physical inventory.
3. Stellar has introduced a cycle counting program for unassembled parts. This ought to be reviewed by audit staff for cutoff procedures, instructions, etc.
4. Stellar may shift the date of the physical inventory from the year end. Possibly, the company will take the inventory twice a year. The costs of inventory taking are likely to be reduced by the cycle counting program. (However, until the production control system has been improved, percentage of completion applied to assemblies in progress will continue to represent a "guesstimate.")
5. The electric motor repair business involves intense competition based on quality, service, performance, and price. Actions to strengthen the Company's hand in these areas should receive priority attention.
6. Two men were observed in the sales counter area, where business was nonexisting. Excess crewing should be watched carefully, as should security in the area.
7. There seems to be no plant safety emphasis. This could be a significant exposure.

Sales

8. The Company provides finished coils to a major manufacturer of electrical equipment. In light of the fact that this customer is known as an astute bargainer, Stellar should evaluate the profitability of this business, together with the accompanying advantages and disadvantages.
9. Stellar has little information on its bidding effectiveness. In other words, the Company does not know why it is successful on certain bids, and not on others.
10. Stellar is not engaged in significant government business. Yet, it seems that in a time of broad cutbacks in industry, marketing to government agencies might be attempted to make up some of the lost private sector business.
11. Most of Stellar's customers are in South Florida. The area is defined by geographic, rather than marketing, factors. Therefore, Stellar may wish to study its self-imposed marketing area; perhaps opportunities exist in bordering counties or in the rest of the state.
12. When a quotation is submitted, production facilities have to be reserved in the hope that the quotation will turn into a firm order. This capability of entering temporary calls on machine and manpower loading should be built into the Company's production control system.

(continued)

FIGURE 9–7 *(continued)*

Accounts Receivable

13. It appears that the accounts receivable system does not work with the existing general ledger package; a new general ledger package is being run in parallel. This condition reflects lack of a long-term plan for systems development and software acquisitions.
14. Similarly, the new receivables package has to be linked to the old order entry and invoicing system. The Company should be alert to the danger of additional clerical work, or errors, that could result from the need to interface differing applications.

Purchasing

15. Stellar should consider accumulating information regarding dollar purchase volumes for significant commodities. The Company might wish to consider negotiating buying contracts, subject to periodic releases.
16. Stellar also needs to protect itself from supply disruptions—possibly by long-term (longer than a year) buying contracts or blanket purchase orders.
17. Stellar should look into reordering routines, that is into how reorder points and economic ordering quantities are set. If these control techniques do not work properly, there could be stockouts on the one hand, and unassembled jobs and slow-moving parts on the other. Premium freight could be another symptom.
18. There are no part numbers which distinguish special order items, a condition which makes it more difficult to see to expediting and to promote timely deliveries.

Accounts Payable

19. The assignment of new vendor codes seems to be in the hands of the accounts payable department. This could represent an exposure; in other words, new and fictitious supplier accounts could be established preliminary to fraudulent payments of such accounts. (However, the exposure is lessened because the officer who signs checks has full supporting details available to him. The supporting papers are canceled after they are signed.) Three suggestions are: there should be software controls to prevent duplicate payments, a search should be made for duplicate payments that may have been made, and vendor code assignments should be made only by persons with special file access privileges.

Production

20. Only very limited paperwork exists in connection with the scheduling, routing, and dispatching of production orders. There is no bill of materials system. Jobs are not always accompanied by paperwork. There may be dangers of inventory imbalances, idle (or backlogged) machines, and feast-or-famine staffing patterns.

FIGURE 9–7 *(concluded)*

21. The tour did point up a number of idle machines, which may reflect informal scheduling.
22. Missed deliveries could be another symptom of ad hoc production scheduling, and would be easily documentable. Premium (rush) freight could also pose problems.
23. Production workers maintain both a time log and a parts log. Neither log has been automated. Apparently, the records are error prone. Special review routines, perhaps on a sampling basis, could be considered to improve accuracy.
24. We were informed that workers get bored. While the auditors walked through the plant there was some rework going on. The reasons for rework should be carefully documented in order to deal with the causes.

Payrolls

25. Apparently, three shifts are being worked. The need for work beyond the first shift should be documented, and informed managerial choices made between overtime, shift premiums, etc.
26. Time clocks were not under anyone's supervision, a condition which may invite employees' clocking in or clocking out as a favor to co-workers.

---

incentives and opportunities for management to deliberately distort the financial statements.[7] A quick environmental assessment, the taking of the pulse of an organization's moral tone, was mentioned in Chapter 4. In addition, a rank-ordered listing of attributes relating to the control environment was included in Chapter 8.

Based on the auditors' close working relationships with Stellar's directors and officers—and especially with the chief financial officer—their good experiences with the client's records, and the client's constructive attitude toward audit adjustments and internal control in general, the control environment was felt to be sound.

---

[7]Philip L. Defliese et al., *Montgomery's Auditing*, 11th ed., college version (New York: John Wiley & Sons, 1990), p. 226.

FIGURE 9–8
Stellar Corporation Comments on Physical Security

On the basis of the plant tour, taken on October 2, 1990, the following observations are made:

In general, security in the parts warehouse, as well as on the production floor, appeared weak. No special precautions had been taken to protect either copper (a material likely to "move," particularly in the form in which it was stored in the plant) or valuable small parts. Moreover, no outsider-oriented safety or security precautions (such as visitors' logs, visitors' badges, or hard hats) were observed.

If the client shifts the timing of its inventory from year end, and even if two inventories are taken, the second of the two inventories should be at or proximate to the year end. This inventory should be guided by comprehensive instructions. In addition, the inventory should be attended by checkers, representing nonproduction personnel, and auditors. Discrepancies should be investigated with great care and the records adjusted. Improved security appears warranted for the more valuable items, especially copper.

UNDERSTAND THE SYSTEM AND CONTROL PROCEDURES

Stellar's auditors have maintained summary descriptions of hardware, software, and EDP applications. Transaction flows have been documented using narratives and flowcharts; the detailed flowcharts and narratives have been marked to indicate which controls are key and which are supervisory. As each audit begins, the documentation is reviewed and updated, starting with overview charts which show the broad flow of activities and documents between departments. During the current year only relatively minor systems changes took place at Stellar; the overview charts were not affected.

Conduct Interviews and Document the Understanding

Stellar's chief financial officer is familiar with the company's management information system, and especially with the accounting aspects of the system. Nonetheless, the auditors updated the flowcharts on the basis of individual interviews with frontline employees and supervisors responsible for particular financial or operational activities. Client employees were interviewed as to changes in systems, programs, and operating routines; they were also questioned as to the origin of the input to their operations, and about output to others. Most of the interviewing was done by the audit manager. Only minor changes were made to detailed flowcharts on the basis of the newly obtained information.

Stellar installed a new sales/accounts receivable system during the year. The auditors flowcharted this system by utilizing microcomputer software. They chose EasyFlow, a program which automates the charting process and makes the output more readable. As noted previously, flowcharts can be marked to identify key controls and supervisory controls.

The auditor has the option of confirming the accuracy of the charts by tracing one or more transactions of each type through the system from each transaction's inception to its burial in the accounts; the technique is referred to as a transaction review or walk-through. Instructions for performing transaction reviews appear in Figure 9-9. At Stellar, transaction reviews were waived by the partner. Systems other than sales/accounts receivable had been tested in the prior year and no significant changes had come to the auditors' attention; the accounts receivable system was still undergoing post-installation modification.

Internal Control Questionnaires: An Option

The author believes that while internal control questionnaires (ICQs) are effective memory joggers, they should be filled in on a selective basis only. The reason is that in many cases ICQs may not convey benefits commensurate with the effort involved in their completion. ICQs may actually have counterproductive effects. For example, staff members may complete ICQs in a mechanical manner, which can detract from the exercise of professional judgment; or, an ICQ may divert attention to a red herring (i.e., to a problem which may have no significance for a particular client). Worse still, ICQs may be given to a client for completion and may wind up in the hands of persons ill-prepared for the task; ICQs could even become part of the tool kit of an actual or potential perpetrator of fraud.

FIGURE 9–9
Transaction Review

Transaction reviews are desirable to establish that the auditor has understood and recorded the system correctly in narratives and flowcharts.

To the extent possible, transactions should be tracked from their origin to their recording in the accounts. Transactions are usually followed through the system on a basis of transaction types to which similar controls have been applied. Special attention is given to the reasons for branching in the flow of transactions—that is, to the birth of new transaction types; new types should be created only for valid reasons, and upon appropriate approvals.

Transaction reviews may have particular value in an audit of an automated system. However, transaction tracing in automated systems may become complicated and time-consuming through sorting and manipulation, commingling of transactions in common totals, and the subsequent need to track totals, and/or to test the totaling routine. Moreover, output may be represented by summary reports, depending upon the nature of the application. In other words, a high degree of data processing knowledge may be required to accomplish transaction reviews in a complex EDP system.

Since transaction reviews should mirror the flow of processing, transaction review workpapers should be images of flowcharts and narratives, with activities and documents referenced to the flowcharts or narratives. The controls, particularly key controls and supervisory controls, should be identified.

Transaction reviews usually involve:

1. Determination of transaction types.
2. If not evident from the documentation, description of the control procedures reperformed.
3. Identification of the transactions and documents reviewed.
4. Description of review results. In the absence of exceptions, such results may be marked by a checkmark, or by a simple OK.
5. Resolution of exceptions. If a transaction is not processed as understood and recorded, the flowcharts or narratives must be changed.

In any event, internal controls and ICQs need to be tailored to the needs of a particular client. The FitzGeralds' book contains a selection of controls helpful in dealing with virtually any type of threat to virtually any type of computer component.[8] A more tradi-

---

[8]Jerry FitzGerald and Ardra F. FitzGerald, *Designing Controls Into Computerized Systems*, 2nd ed. (Redwood City, Calif.: Jerry FitzGerald & Associates, 1990).

tional and less EDP-oriented approach is followed in the AICPA's Audit Program Generator (APG) disks which include an ICQ for medium to large companies.

Controls in the Focal Areas of Exposure

Regardless of uncertain benefits of ICQs in general, the auditor should jog his memory by reference to ICQs for the focal areas of exposure: physical security, computer access, and management representations. (Physical controls and computer access controls were discussed in Chapter 6, and management representations in Chapter 8.) Review of these reminders (see Figures 9–10, 9–11, and 9–12) should sensitize the auditor to possible exposures and assist in planning the nature, timing, and extent of substantive tests. Given the importance of these controls, further commentary seems appropriate.

Physical Controls
Controls in this area involve systematic management of the risks of thievery, sabotage, espionage, etc., an up-to-date security program, effective interaction between auditors and security officers, and security awareness on the part of employees at all levels.

Computer Access Controls
Company procedures should identify those allowed to enter each area of the computer facilities; access restriction requires a locked door and a key that unlocks the door only to authorized personnel. Access to terminals should be restricted wherever possible. Control over access to programs and data helps to prevent unauthorized access and to enforce segregation of duties. Terminal, program, and data use should be controlled by authorization schemes that designate authorized users and uses of the system. Identification controls should ensure that only authorized users can access the system for authorized purposes. Data communication lines and equipment should be controlled to restrict opportunities for unauthorized access to the system during transmission of messages between the terminals and the computer.[9]

---

[9]Donald A. Watne and Peter B. B. Turney, *Auditing EDP Systems*, 2nd ed. (Englewood Cliffs, N.J.: Prentice-Hall, 1990), p. 273.

FIGURE 9–10
Physical Security

Program Study

1. Has security, including physical security, been formally studied by the client?
2. In connection with such a study, was a comprehensive inventory taken of:
   a. Assets?
   b. Information resources?
   c. Consequential hazards that could arise through loss, such as business interruption?
3. Was a parallel inventory taken of threats, including:
   a. Earthquakes, floods, power failures, etc.?
   b. Fire prevention and detection?
   c. Air conditioning failures?
   d. Fraud and theft?
   e. Sabotage or other hostile acts?
   f. Computer viruses?
   g. Other possible emergencies?
4. Did the study result in the establishment of security objectives?
5. Did a formal security program result from the study?
6. Did this program include an orderly approach to managing security in terms of:
   a. Values of the items to be protected?
   b. Threats?
   c. Likelihood of their occurrence?
   d. Selection of risk management techniques?
   e. Cost/benefit determinations?
   f. Resource allocation?

Program Operation

7. Is the program reviewed periodically to see that it adequately addresses the then-current risk management requirements?
8. Are the following covered by the client's program:
   a. Property, plant, and equipment, including offices, plants, and warehouses?
   b. Contents of the facilities in the preceding item?
   c. Data processing:
      i. Hardware?
      ii. Software?
      iii. Systems?
      iv. Data?
   d. Other information resources and records?
   e. Pledges or assignments of corporate credit?
   f. Trade secrets and other confidential matters?
   g. Blueprints and designs?
   h. Patents and patents being developed?
   i. Employee fraud or theft?
9. In connection with the above, are recurring inventories taken of the items to be protected, and do these inventories take place at reasonable intervals?

FIGURE 9-10 *(continued)*

10. In connection with these inventories:
    a. Are losses determined?
    b. Are losses investigated?
    c. Are the records promptly adjusted to reflect the losses?
    d. Are writeoffs approved by corporate officers?
    e. Is an attempt made to eliminate the causes of losses?
11. Are the threats also updated at reasonable intervals?
12. Are other elements of the plan, such as insurance, updated in similar fashion to reflect changes in values, threats, locations, and approaches to risk management?
13. To the extent that program elements are testable (such as security of warehouses and backup routines) are tests/rehearsals conducted?
14. Based on the test results, has the program been modified?

Organization

15. Based on its utterances, does management seem committed to security?
16. Has that commitment been evidenced in a formal statement?
17. Have security responsibilities been assigned?
18. Is the head of security at an appropriate organizational level?
19. Has security in general been coordinated with data processing security?
20. Is the aforementioned coordination evidenced in writing?
21. Have responsibilities been assigned for data processing security?
22. Does the security budget appear reasonable?
23. Is security evaluated periodically from a quality perspective?
24. If so, has that evaluation been conducted by qualified persons with an appropriate measure of independence?
25. Assuming the consultants made significant recommendations, were such recommendations evaluated and implemented as appropriate?

Policies and Procedures

26. Are there published security policies/procedures?
27. Do these policies/procedures cover:
    a. Discovered fraud, thievery, or illegal acts?
    b. Notification of the aforementioned to regulators/insurors?
    c. Notification to the board/audit committee?
    d. Prosecution of perpetrators?
    e. Publicity to be given to crimes as a deterrent?
28. Does discovered fraud give rise to:
    a. Reevaluations of audit programs?
    b. Revisions in controls?
29. Have standards been set for internal control?
30. If so, do those standards directly or indirectly refer to assets in danger of being converted, such as cash, accounts receivable, and inventory?

Activities

31. Do security personnel advise on the handling of classified materials, and on sensitive employee contractual matters?

(continued)

FIGURE 9–10 *(concluded)*

32. Do security personnel advise on employee bonding practices?
33. Do security personnel advise on employee reference checks and on integrity checks for current employees?
34. Has consideration been given to electronic "sweeps" of offices?
35. Do security personnel maintain appropriate liaison with internal auditing?
36. Does internal auditing have forensic auditing capabilities?
37. To the extent fraud was discovered, were such discoveries attributable to the functioning of the system and its controls?
38. Does the client, and do its internal auditors, have a credible record of claims settlements, based on appropriate documentation?

Access Controls

39. Are there access controls to facilities:
    a. Physical controls:
        i. Electronic surveillance?
        ii. Safes and vaults?
        iii. Access codes and cards?
    b. Logical controls:
        i. Biometric controls?
        ii. Controls to evaluate accessor's authority to act?
    c. Computerized controls:
        i. Identification numbers?
        ii. Passwords?
        iii. Encryption?
        iv. Automatic shutdowns?
40. Do warehouse layouts reflect a grasp of security considerations, such as sensitive items not being stored near an exit?
41. Are such traditional techniques as guards, car searches, and visitors' logs in evidence?
42. Has physical security been established over critical documents:
    a. Payment requests?
    b. Unissued checks?
    c. Receipts on hand?
    d. Purchase orders?
    e. Sales order forms?
    f. Invoices?
    g. Credit memoranda?
43. Is there physical security over check signing equipment?

Inventory Aspects

44. If the client's inventories are of a technological nature or present substantiation/valuation difficulties for auditors, is requisite consulting support arranged?
45. Will such support be rendered by persons with appropriate independence, using techniques agreed upon by all concerned?

FIGURE 9–11
Computer Access

---

1. As to the computer mainframe, is the computer secure and is physical access restricted?
2. In general, and with respect to data processing in particular, are the custodians of assets persons other than those who keep records for assets?
3. Are systems analysts and programmers precluded from operating the computer, except for specifically authorized tests of new systems, and even then are they subject to supervision?
4. Are computer operators, systems analysts, programmers, and persons engaged in activities such as electronic fund transfers bonded?
5. Are computer operators, systems analysts, and programmers forced to take regular vacations?
6. Are computer operators, systems analysts, and programmers subject to job rotation?
7. Does the computer department observe documentation standards relating to:
    a. Program development?
    b. Program changes?
    c. Computer operations?
    d. Computer output and reports?
    e. Errors and resubmissions?
    f. Testing and debugging?
8. Are program change forms under numerical control, preferably by utilization of prenumbered forms?
9. Are such numbers accounted for periodically, with a report going to management?
10. Are controls in effect to restrict access to sensitive programs or libraries, and also to procedure libraries, access control software, system software, and logfiles?
11. Are controls in effect to restrict the actions that can be taken by particular individuals, or classes of individuals, with respect to sensitive programs or data?
12. Are errors and resubmissions controlled, especially in terms of timeliness of resubmission?
13. Is an aged analysis prepared of errors not resubmitted, and given to those in a position to take corrective action?
14. Are computer logs (1) secure and (2) subject to review by persons independent of computer operations?
15. Where terminals are in use, does an audit trail for transactions exist in terms of:
    a. Terminal identifier?
    b. Transaction record?
    c. Person entering the transaction?
    d. Transaction date, time, or sequence?
    e. Transaction type?
16. Is terminal access restricted to individuals who meet criteria based on:

(continued)

FIGURE 9–11 *(concluded)*

    a. Something the person desiring access is?
    b. Something the person desiring access knows?
    c. Something the person desiring access has?
17. Is care taken to ensure that all information entered is authorized:
    a. Based on the authority of the person doing the entering?
    b. Based on the document being entered?
    c. Based on document cancellation upon entry?
    d. Based on electronically transmitted authority?
18. Are controls in place to ensure completeness of entry:
    a. Computer sequence checks of serially numbered documents?
    b. Computer matching with previously processed data?
    c. Agreement of pre-established control totals for key fields?
    d. Agreement of manually established document counts?
    e. One-on-one individual checking of documents?
19. Are controls in place to ensure accuracy:
    a. Key verification?
    b. Format checks?
    c. Parity checks?
    d. Existence checks?
    e. Check digit verification?
    f. Reasonableness checks?
    g. Dependency checks?
    h. Mathematical accuracy checks?
    i. Range checks?
    j. Prior data matching?
20. Are internal and external labels used to assure use of correct programs and files?
21. Are procedures in effect relating to:
    a. Backup?
    b. Restoration and recovery?
    c. Caution in downloading untested or public domain software?
22. Has an effort been made to create company-wide security awareness?
23. Do the internal auditors have an EDP audit capability that enables them to audit the computer and to use the computer as an audit tool?

In addition, completeness and accuracy of input should be safe-guarded by a combination of manual and EDP controls, as should changes to systems and programs.

Controls found present should be noted on flowcharts and posted to the master tracking sheet. The point is that the controls should be marked or recorded on the basis of the auditor's *own* knowledge, based in many cases on observation of evidence. (At Stellar, physical and computer access controls were generally lacking.)

FIGURE 9–12
Management Representations Questions for Auditors

1. Did the auditor request a management representation letter in accordance with professional rules? (Note: *Statement on Auditing Standards (SAS) 19* suggests a variety of matters for inclusion in representation letters.)
2. If so, did the client's letter cover all matters requested?
3. For example, did the letter cover:
   a. Management's responsibility for the financial statements?
   b. Availability to the auditors of all pertinent documents?
   c. Absence of irregularities?
   d. Provision to the auditors of regulatory reports?
   e. Plans or intentions bearing on values or classifications?
   f. Recording or disclosure of related-party transactions?
   g. Violations of laws?
   h. Contingencies?
   i. Unasserted claims or assessments?
   j. Material transactions and their proper recording?
   k. Inventories at net realizable value?
   l. Satisfactory title to owned assets?
   m. Provision for material losses on purchase commitments?
   n. Compliance with contractual agreements?
   o. Accuracy of accounting estimates?
   p. No subsequent events requiring adjustment/disclosure?
4. Did the representations in the letter generally conform to actual values, conditions, and events?
5. Were amounts for the letter determined subsequent to completion of work on significant accounts?
6. Do all amounts in the letter reflect and incorporate all known significant adjustments?
7. Was the client forthcoming in terms of consenting to and arranging all interviews requested with employees within a reasonable time frame and did such interviews take place reasonably on schedule?
8. Did the client submit all requested documents without serious delay?
9. Were complete files of regulatory reports made available to the auditors?
10. Were the on-line data bases, or other independent sources, used to the fullest extent possible to verify:
    a. Values of publicly held securities marked to market?
    b. Income from publicly held securities?
    c. Values of investments carried on the equity method?
    d. Existence of nonpublic investments?
    e. Valuations of restricted or nonmarketable securities?
    f. Valuations of joint ventures to co-venturers' statements?
    g. Existence and apparent health of major accounts receivable?
    h. Liquidity of inventories relative to sales trends?
    i. Valuation of intangibles relative to disposals?
    j. Valuation of property, plant, and equipment *viz.* industry?

(continued)

FIGURE 9-12 *(concluded)*

    k. Legal data bases, as to client and his key executives?
    l. Regulatory data bases as to violations?

11. Is the auditor reasonably satisfied as to certain indicators of managerial integrity:
    a. Executives do not view corporate funds as piggy bank?
    b. Constructive attitude toward accounting and auditing adjustments?
    c. Constructive attitude toward internal control?
    d. Willingness to consider prosecuting wrongdoers?

12. Does the control environment appear satisfactory in terms of:
    a. Tone at the top?
    b. Corporate audit committee's activism?
    c. Organization, staffing, schedule, and reporting of internal auditors?
    d. Ethics code?

13. Have major threats (identified by use of the on-line data bases)—which were not controlled by the client—been considered in terms of audit risk management?

Management Representations—Verification

This book takes the position that management representations should be verified independently to the extent possible to avoid the threat of anchoring—that is, of having the auditor arrive at a conclusion that may be influenced by a desire to avoid trouble with the client.

Tests of Controls

The objective of testing controls is identical in manual and computer systems: to see that controls are properly designed, in effect, and functioning as planned. However, the underlying rationales for testing may differ: (1) to test controls upon which the auditor may rely in order to restrict the nature, timing, and extent of his substantive tests; (2) to test controls which would not be tested adequately as part of substantive tests; (3) to test controls in the focal areas of exposure in order to gain additional comfort; and (4) to test controls based on regulatory requirements or client requests.

Technology has had only minor effects on control testing; many tests continue to involve reviews of organization charts, job descriptions, and operating procedures, as well as observations, inquiries, and reviews of reconciliations and internal management reports. What *is* new is the increasing reliance by management on operational controls, particularly those of a supervisory nature. Many such controls have been designed into computer-based systems. Frequently, these controls involve the production and distribution of an exception-type report. In some cases, auditors can test controls simply by inspecting the reports or by documenting corrective actions which may have been taken.

Guidelines to the conduct of tests of controls are set out in Figure 9-13; in effect, tests of controls comprise control objectives and test procedures, descriptions of the manner of document selection and of the documents selected, test results, and resolution of exceptions.

Specific tests in the focal areas of exposure are discussed in Figures 9-14, 9-15, and 9-16. In general, these tests concentrate on key and/or supervisory controls. Examples of tests involve the design, organization, and operation of the security program, internal control standards and their application, controls over computer access and the handling of rejections, and independent verification of management representations by use of the on-line data bases. (It was not practical to test physical controls or computer access controls at Stellar; as noted, there was a dearth of controls to test.)

ASSESS CONTROL RISK

Control risk assessments are made by the manager and approved by the partner. Separate decisions may be made for each subsystem or systems cycle; among other factors, the auditors should weigh the cost of unrestricted substantive testing on the one hand, and restricted substantive testing plus control testing on the other. Although Stellar's new sales/accounts receivable system appeared to be relatively well controlled, the auditors decided not to rely on internal control because of high inherent risk (uncontrolled threats) and the fact that the system was still in its installation shakedown phase. With respect to other subsystems they also opted for unrestricted substantive testing. See Figure 9-17 for the conclusions required for Stellar by *SAS 55*.

FIGURE 9–13
Guidelines for Tests of Controls

SAS 55 has replaced the concept of compliance testing with tests of controls. Compliance tests referred to procedures performed to test the effectiveness of operation of control procedures. However, the broader term *tests of controls* is directed toward both the effective design and effective operation of relevant control policies and procedures.*

Tests of controls, or compliance tests, are conducted in the following circumstances: (1) where the auditor wishes to be satisfied that the control is in effect and functioning as planned, in order to restrict the timing, nature, or extent of substantive tests; (2) when the auditor feels that the control will not be tested adequately in connection with dual-purpose substantive tests; (3) when the auditor wishes to gain additional comfort, particularly in the focal areas of audit exposure; (4) when required either by the terms of the engagement (such as in a government audit) or by the client.

Controls that may not be tested adequately by use of dual-purpose substantive tests can relate to pending or suspended transactions, or to the effectiveness of supervisory reviews of potential out-of-line conditions. Examples include review of unfilled sales commitments, periodic review and updating of credit limits, review of monthly accounts receivable aging schedules, and review of written-off memorandum accounts receivable.

In many instances key controls, and especially supervisory controls, may be prime candidates for testing. The test procedure generally involves the following:

1. Statement of the control objective and description of control policies and procedures that achieve that objective.
2. Description of the test procedures to be applied. Tests may, but do not necessarily, involve reperformance by the auditor of the control function. Milton Zall has put this point clearly: "A test is an attempt to verify that a particular process works the way it should. To test a payroll system, one would insert some dummy transactions into the system and then examine output to determine whether the transactions were processed. . . . To formulate a solid test plan, you should ask the people within the organization what they consider to be the most important controls to be tested."†
3. Statement as to the number of documents to be chosen.
4. Description of the technique used to select documents or reports for the test, and the time period covered by the selection.
5. Identification of documents or reports selected.
6. Description of test results.
7. Resolution of all exceptions. (Given the relatively small number of documents usually examined in tests of controls, there should not be *any* unresolved exceptions. The logic, reasonableness, and veracity of client explanations should be carefully evaluated.)
8. When appropriate, the modifications to be made in substantive procedures as a result of the test.

---

*Jane E. Morton and William L. Felix, Jr., "A Critique of *Statement on Auditing Standards No. 55*," *Accounting Horizons* 5, no. 1 (March 1991), pp. 1–10.

†Milton Zall, "Tips on Evaluating an Organization's Internal Controls," *Government Computer News* 6, no. 9 (May 8, 1987), p. 90.

FIGURE 9-14
Tests of Controls in the Focal Areas: Physical Security

Security Program

Objective:
Evaluate the accuracy, completeness, timeliness, and professionalism of any study upon which the auditee's security program may have been based.

Tasks:
Review the security study and supporting reports, studies and evaluations to determine whether all critical issues have been identified and evaluated and whether the findings of the study have been approved by all parties who should have been consulted. The review should involve:

1. Inquiring of persons performing, reviewing, and approving research to ascertain whether the procedures performed (and the resulting reports, recommendations, and other documents) appear to be complete and appropriate.

2. Examining the study to determine whether:
   a. Conclusions in the study are sound and supported by facts.
   b. Top management, the board of directors, or both, as appropriate, have reviewed and approved the study.
   c. The following points have been covered:
      i. Inventory of resources, assets, and components.
      ii. Listing of threats.
      iii. Selection of cost effective control approaches.
      iv. Security objectives.
      v. Recommendations as to continuing program.

3. Examining the documents comprehended by point 2 for specific aspects as follows:
   a. Cost/benefit evaluations to determine whether the following were reasonable and proper in the circumstances:
      i. The formulas or algorithms used, especially the probability assigned to the likelihood that a particular event will actually take place.
      ii. The extent to which alternative security solutions were explored in terms of costs and benefits, and the logic of the recommended approach.
      iii. The soundness of organizational recommendations.
   b. Inventories taken to determine:
      i. The appropriateness of inventory taking methodology, in terms of accuracy and completeness of descriptions and counts, participation of checkers and reviewers, and coordination with other inventories that have been or may be taken from time to time.
   c. The extent to which indirect results of threats, such as business interruption, were identified and considered.

Organization

Objective:
See whether the security organization is at an appropriate level, and enjoys the requisite management support.

Tasks:
1. Evaluate the de jure and de facto organizational level of the security director by reference to the organization chart and minutes of management committee meetings.

(continued)

FIGURE 9–14 *(concluded)*

2. Examine correspondence to determine the role the security director plays with respect to potential, suspected, or actual employee fraud.
3. Review correspondence relating to data processing security to see that the security director is active with respect to matters such as identification numbers, passwords, access authority, and encryption.
4. Discuss the adequacy of budgetary funding of the security organization with its director.
5. Review any consulting studies that may have been made of the security organization and determine whether significant recommendations were made, management's responses to those recommendations, and the status of implementation.
6. Discuss the results of any audits of the security organization with the head of the internal auditing activity.

Security Program Operations

Objective:
Evaluate whether the recommended program has been put into effect and is functioning, and whether the program is subject to appropriate tests, changes, and updating.

Tasks:
Review policies and procedures designed to promote security, determine whether they have been approved by the appropriate parties, and that they are functioning. The review should involve:
1. Determining whether security policies and procedures cover property, plant, and equipment, building contents, data processing systems, hardware, and software, and information intangibles, including patents.
2. Determining whether security policies and procedures have been reviewed and approved by management.
3. If management or employee fraud occurred, establishing whether notification of such acts was made to the appropriate authorities both inside and outside the client organization.
4. Visiting the client's facilities to inspect the functioning of physical security including:
   a. Passive surveillance, such as lighting, fencing, and alarm systems.
   b. Active surveillance, such as the presence of guards and trained dogs and the maintenance of sign-in procedures at security gates.
   c. Check-in routines, including maintenance of visitors' logs and badge issuance and retrieval; check-out routines, including inspection of shipping authorizations, and truck and personal vehicle inspections.
   d. Parking restrictions, including prohibitions against parking near storerooms.
   e. Segregation in a secure area of items thought to be especially subject to pilferage, such as small hand tools, flashlight batteries, etc.
5. Reviewing the results of client physical inventories, and especially the actions taken to determine whether shortages existed, the conditions or the identities of persons causing the shortages, and the need for strengthening security policies and procedures.
6. Seeing whether security procedures were tested, with consideration of:
   a. The reasonableness of the test procedures.
   b. The results.
   c. The extent to which a need was recognized for changes to the program.
   d. The degree to which such changes were implemented.
7. Reviewing the steps taken from time to time to update the program in terms of changes to underlying information, risk management approaches, and insurance policies.

FIGURE 9–15
Tests of Controls in the Focal Areas: Computer Access

Internal Control Standards (if Introduced)

Objective:
Evaluate the completeness and reasonableness of internal control standards, with attention to separation of duties relating to systems from computer operations.

Tasks:
1. Review the internal control standards, giving particular attention to:
   a. Seeing that the standards were conveyed to all concerned.
   b. Determining that the standards are implemented through policies, procedures, and operating instructions.
   c. Seeing that compliance is monitored by accounting department managers and supervisors and by the internal audit staff. Monitoring should be reflected in memoranda (for example, memoranda pertaining to reassignment of undesirable or conflicting responsibilities), as well as in internal audit reports.
2. Inspect assignment sheets, attendance records, and sign-off initials on documents to see that standards and related procedures are observed.

Access Controls

Objective:
Transactions are to be rejected if they do not comply with procedures and programs as to authorization, sender's authority to engage in the transaction, nature of the transaction, and its origin. The rejection should last until the underlying defects are cured.

Tasks:
1. Visit the computer room to inspect the functioning of facility access controls including:
   a. Passive surveillance, such as locked doors, electronic surveillance, and alarm systems.
   b. Active surveillance, such as the presence of librarians and receptionists.
   c. Check-in routines, including visitors' logs.
2. When in the computer room, observe persons in attendance, especially individuals who may have systems or programming responsibilities; note the nature of activities during their visit, and inquire into the manner in which their access was authorized.
3. When in the computer room, observe that data entry validity, authorization, completeness, and accuracy controls said to be in operation are in operation. The review should include:
   a. The steps taken by operators when the computer rejects a transaction. Presumably, the operators will endeavor to clear errors on the spot. Therefore, the question arises where they obtain information for clearance, and whether the clearance information has been, or should be, authorized. (The nature of authorization for clearance assumes particular importance in the case of permanent or semipermanent information that may be affected by the correction.) Another question relates to the nature of the error, and to the steps that might be taken to minimize that particular type of error in the future.
   b. Controls in effect to account for errors that cannot be immediately corrected, and that have resulted in a rejection from the system. Such rejections require adjustment to batch or similar manual control counts or totals, as well as to computer created counts or totals.
   c. User satisfaction with the accuracy of data in the system, or with the volume of errors slipping through the system.

(continued)

FIGURE 9–15 *(concluded)*

4. Consider using test data to see whether computer rejections take place as anticipated by the systems designers. If the test data were developed by the audited organization's systems analysts, the auditor should satisfy himself as to the adequacy of separation of duties. When using test data, care must be taken to avoid contamination of client records.
5. Review any entry in the computer-created log to identify access denials or restrictions in terms of:
   a. Nature of rejected transactions, with consideration of their significance from an internal control perspective.
   b. Terminal or site of attempted entry (and identity of the person attempting entry, if known).
   c. Time and frequency of entry.
   d. Nature and timeliness of response to access denials reported by the computer log.
   e. Referral to appropriate authorities for investigation and corrective action.
6. Review library controls with respect to programs and data files signed out; check this information to run schedules and to computer logs; see that materials are returned in a timely fashion.

Rejections and Resubmissions

Objective:
   Evaluate controls over rejections and resubmissions to see that rejections are carefully monitored, that proper authority exists for corrections, that the reasons for rejections are carefully evaluated, and that controls exist to ensure timely resubmission.

Tasks:
1. Inspect inventory of unresolved rejections, noting:
   a. Age of rejections.
   b. Effect on the financial statements.
   c. Evidence of attention given timely error clearance by auditee executives; such attention often includes some type of reminder.
   d. Trends in the inventory level.
2. See that adjustments to the inventory of rejected items, especially removals, can be made only upon proper authority.

Program Change Controls

Objective:
   Make certain that programs can be changed only by someone with proper authority, and on the basis of a program change notice that is physically and numerically controlled and approved.

Tasks:
1. Review accountability over program changes with respect to:
   a. Inventory of open changes.
   b. Justifications for changes.
   c. Computer access by programmers for testing and debugging purposes.
   d. Approval for the change.
2. Consider using a utility program to compare an authorized and controlled program to a program that has been used for a production run; investigate any differences. (Jerry FitzGerald has assembled a library of 28 audit/security programs.*)

---

*Jerry FitzGerald, *Online Auditing Using Microcomputers* (Redwood City, Calif.: Jerry FitzGerald & Associates, 1987).

FIGURE 9–16
Tests of Controls in the Focal Areas: Management Representations

Comprehensiveness of Management Representations

Objective:
Evaluate the accuracy, completeness, and timeliness of information developed in connection with management's expressed or implied representations.

Tasks:
Review the management representation letter together with supporting reports, studies, and evaluations to determine whether all substantive issues have been identified and evaluated in accordance with *Statement on Auditing Standards 19,* and whether the letter was prepared with the approval of all parties who should have been consulted. The review should involve:

1. Inquiring of persons performing, reviewing, and approving research to ascertain whether the procedures performed (and the resulting reports, recommendations, and other documents) appear to be complete and appropriate.
2. Making certain that any values in the representation letter have been referenced to the working papers, and that all adjustments have been reflected in the letter.
3. Seeing whether:
   a. The CEO, the CFO, the board of directors, and the audit committee have reviewed and approved the management representation letter.
   b. The letter includes all information requested.
   c. The letter has been reviewed by counsel.
4. Review data base output to determine whether there was discovery of any hitherto unknown effects on management representations. The review should involve:
   a. Evaluating economic conditions in the client's industry and markets based on articles and other published information, such as sales forecasts, reports on inventory levels and supplies, and price trends.
   b. Weighing the effect of regulatory or professional directives and initiatives on the company's financial statements, and/or on its operations.
   c. Analyzing the effect on the client of developments that carry inherent risk, such as technological changes, actions brought by regulators, and legal decisions.
   d. Noting any significant information that bears on the company's plans—especially involving acquisitions, financing, and facilities.
   e. Monitoring any information that could reflect negatively on the control environment.

Related Control Environment Aspects

Objective:
Evaluate the control environment in relation to the conduct of the audit engagement and management representations.

(continued)

FIGURE 9-16 *(concluded)*

Tasks:
Debrief the audit staff to determine whether the client cooperated in setting up and carrying through interviews, whether requested documents were made available without significant delay, and whether a professional and security-conscious atmosphere was maintained. Points covered should include:
1. Assuring that the audit staff maintained appropriate security over its working papers, and that the client respected such security.
2. Seeing that working facilities and physical comforts provided to the auditors were adequate.
3. Ensuring that no efforts were made to impede access to client facilities or personnel.
4. Ensuring that client personnel involved in financial statement preparation, and especially internal audit personnel, exercised their assigned functions pursuant to established procedures and related controls.
5. Seeing that the audit staff did not become aware of any negative aspects bearing on the control environment.
6. Seeing that all reporting issues were surfaced by the audit team and brought to the attention of the appropriate authorities within the audit organization.
7. Making certain that, insofar as known, based on knowledge of the client's industry, pertinent regulatory authority reports were:
   a. Made available.
   b. Reviewed by the audit team from the point of view of impact on the financial statements.
   c. Reflected in the accounts and in the representation letter as appropriate.

FIGURE 9-17
Stellar Corporation
Control Risk Assessment

Control risk is assessed at the maximum for all account balances or assertions.

(dated and signed)   _____ , _____

(dated and approved by audit
partner)   _____ , _____

FIGURE 9-18
A Suggested Technique for Allocating Substantive Testing Effort

Audit risk has been described as "a measure of how willing the auditor is to accept that the financial statements may be materially misstated after the audit is completed and an unqualified opinion has been reached." In general, most practitioners in today's litigious climate will seek low audit risk. Audit risk is affected by detection risk which represents "a measure of how willing the auditor is to accept that the audit evidence to be obtained for a segment will fail to detect errors exceeding a tolerable amount should such errors exist."*

In Chapter 2, it was pointed out that the Treadway Commission's research showed that instances of fraudulent financial reporting had been concentrated in receivables, inventory, accounts payable, accrued liabilities, and fixed assets. In Chapter 4, revenue recognition errors alleged to have been made by auditors were mentioned as relating to land, equipment, real estate, and construction projects; alleged asset valuation errors afflicted inventory, goodwill, receivables, natural resources, and real estate.

The master tracking sheet represents a listing of threats, identified as to their nature, seriousness, and the accounts affected. Uncontrolled threats are assumed to contain elements of audit risk. Audit risk can be reduced by increasing the amount of evidence examined, that is the extent of auditing performed.

One way to determine that extent is to consider each major account in the financial statements. Each pertinent account can be weighted 3 for high inherent risk, 2 for medium, and 1 for low; an additional factor of 1 can be added for accounts with high risk (or .5 for medium risk) in the focal areas of risk. Dollar values in the accounts are multiplied by these factors. The evidence gathering effort can then be allocated to accounts on the percentage which individual accounts as extended bear to the total.

*Alvin A. Arens and James K. Loebbecke, *Auditing: An Integrated Approach,* 4th ed. (Englewood Cliffs, N.J.: Prentice Hall, 1988), p. 242.

ALLOCATE AUDIT EFFORT

The auditor should prepare a time budget, based on the audit program. The primary purpose of a budget is to guide resource allocation—that is, to schedule the work, to assign professional staff, and to see to liaison arrangements with internal auditors, specialists, other public accounting firms as necessary, and client management. Figure 9-18 presents a simple technique for allocating time. (At Stellar nearly half of the audit time was to be devoted to the substantive audit of accounts receivable, inventories, and costs.)

The time budget is an important planning tool since it tells auditors what their responsibilities are, what objectives they are to achieve, and how their work fits into the overall schedule. But, the time budget should not assume undue importance in terms of straightjacketing the current year's work; and the time budget should not serve as an automatic guide for next year's budget. Given a climate of constant change, it may be to the auditor's advantage to estimate the time for each year's efforts afresh; the audit plan executed during the prior year does represent an excellent basis for reviewing accomplishments and for developing a focus for improvement in future years.

CONDUCT SUBSTANTIVE TESTS

The AICPA Audit Program Generator

The AICPA Audit Program Generator (APG) is a computerized tool which assists accountants in preparing and/or custom-tailoring all types of programs. The selection of individual procedures involves the master tracking sheet and the inventory and ranking of the uncontrolled exposures it reflects. Other selection criteria include prior experience in the audit of a particular account, the absolute value of the account and the related materiality, availability of documents necessary to carry out the procedures, test efficiency—in terms of performance time or of testing more than one account in one pass through the records—ease of testing, and effectiveness of the test procedures in detecting errors and irregularities.

Computerized substantive tests have advantages of thoroughness, accuracy, and discipline. Many types of procedures can be carried out by computer:

- Computation.
- Reperformance/recomputation.
- Comparison.
- Scanning.
- Analytical procedures.
- Search for out-of-line conditions.
- Selection.

General-Purpose Computer Audit Programs

APG can be enriched with steps calling for use of a general-purpose computer audit program, such as Interactive Data Extraction and Analysis (IDEA) which was mentioned in Chapter 6 and is available through the AICPA. It can be used for:

1. Importing, extracting, and displaying records.
2. Arithmetic functions.
3. Applying file sequencing, manipulation, and summarization.
4. Statistical sampling.

Author's Comment

At Stellar, IDEA could perform a variety of test procedures; for example, with respect to accounts receivable:

1. To add money value fields.
2. To verify aging (see succeeding paragraphs).
3. To select accounts for confirmation (see succeeding paragraphs).
4. To identify duplicate accounts.
5. To screen zero account balances.
6. To apply post–confirmation period cash receipts.
7. To ensure that a proper cutoff was made of year-end shipments by listing shipping document numbers and shipment times and dates.
8. To ensure that inventories were relieved of such shipments.
9. To verify the timing of invoicing by comparing shipping dates to billing dates.
10. To verify accounts receivable cash collections to computerized reports received from lockbox depositories.
11. To compare accounts receivable charges to closeouts of job orders.
12. To compare post–balance sheet date returns, claims, and allowances to year-end balances.

The aforementioned types of procedures can be added to the APG audit program. Two examples follow:

1. *Objectives:* independently verify the accuracy of the aged trial balance; obtain an aged trial balance of trade receivables as of the date selected for confirmation; and use IDEA to prepare an independent aging of accounts receivable.

    a. Import the client's accounts receivable file, using the total as the control field.

    b. Extract and summarize all negative balances.

    c. Utilizing the date-of-billing field, establish four buckets of days into which open invoices are to be classified: 0 to 30, 31 to 60, 61 to 90, and above 91. Summarize the results. Obtain explanations for any discrepancies from the client's figures.

    d. Consider the result of the aging in light of Stellar's usual terms (net 30 for domestic sales) and in light of the credit line agreement with Stellar's bank.

    e. Trace totals to the general ledger control account, and, if as of the balance sheet date, to the lead schedule and the working trial balance.

2. *Objectives:* support the existence and accuracy of accounts receivable, being watchful against overstatements; and select individual customer accounts for positive confirmation by reference to the aged trial balance.

    a. If the client requests that any accounts be excluded from the confirmation process, obtain explanations; review correspondence files to substantiate the explanation. Perform alternative procedures with respect to such accounts; if post–confirmation date cash receipts are used as part of such alternative procedures, trace the date of receipt and the payor to a control list of incoming receipts that should have been prepared in the mail room.

    b. Use IDEA to reclassify credit balances. Obtain explanations.

    c. Use IDEA to select all accounts above $500; summarize the value of accounts selected.

    d. Use IDEA to draw a systematic sample, using a random start, for the remaining accounts.

    e. Use IDEA's capabilities to export to a word processing program. Prepare positive confirmations. Mail confirmations bearing the auditor's return address.

f. Trace confirmation replies to the trial balance. Investigate differences. Inspect evidence supporting explanations for differences.

g. Obtain new addresses for all confirmations returned by the post office and remail.

h. Send second requests for all unanswered confirmation requests. Consider sending third requests by registered or certified mail, and performing alternative procedures.

Operational Information

References to operational records and fields can also be added to APG. The intent is to draw on quasi-independent operational information to validate financial data; furthermore, it is expected that operational information may yield early warning signals of financial problems. Three examples follow:

1. *Objective:* confirm the existence of sales by examining commissions paid to salesmen. (The assumption is that sales are required to be approved by persons other than the salesman on the account.) It is axiomatic that salesmen are likely to complain about underpayments of commissions, but not about overpayments. Discrepancies may reflect questionable or unsupported sales, erroneous exclusions from sales and accounts receivable, or overpayments of commissions.

   a. Sort sales compensation by transaction date, product, and customer.

   b. Verify commission rates for particular products: compute sales.

   c. Compare recorded sales with the sales computed in the preceding step.

   d. Obtain explanations for significant differences between the two listings and examine evidence backing the explanations.

   e. Assess the incidence of returns (which typically are not reflected against commissions) and prepare management letter comments.

2. *Objectives:* confirm the existence of sales by reference to evidence of shipments acknowledged by public carriers and validate sales

by extending units shipped (and acknowledged by a public carrier on a bill of lading) by selling prices. Discrepancies may reveal failures to bill customers and/or unauthorized shipments.

 a. Obtain shipping register and supporting bills of lading.

 b. Inspect bills of lading to see that all appear to be originals, that they bear acknowledgements of receipt, that product codes are shown, and that the file of bills is complete.

 c. Trace the bills to the shipping register.

 d. Extend the units shipped by sales prices, and total the result.

 e. Compare the result to recorded sales and obtain meaningful and documented explanations for significant differences.

3. *Objective:* see that accounts receivable carrying values will not need to be written down when pending customer claims are adjudicated.

 a. Examine an analysis of customer service reports for the period. Assess the accuracy and completeness of the list.

 b. Identify the nature of claims, and the dollar volume of claims which have historically resulted in adjustments to accounts receivable.

 c. With respect to the claims identified in the preceding step, determine processing lead time.

 d. Review the inventory of open claims at the year end considering the age of claims, the nature of claims, and the potential adjustment to accounts receivable.

 e. Determine whether a need exists to write down or reserve existing balances in recognition of likely adjustments; bring to client's attention.

Other Software

Stellar's financial statements were prepared using a series of AICPA programs, ACCOUNTANT'S TRIAL BALANCE (ATB) Version 2.1. This easy-to-use program automates trial balances, consolidations, and preparation of financial statements, together with appropriate supporting materials.

SUMMARY

This chapter has illustrated the use of the on-line data bases to brief the auditor with respect to client inherent risk and to update him as to professional and regulatory developments. The use of operational information was considered in relation to analytical review, tests of controls, and substantive tests. The auditor's awareness of operational matters should enhance client service, as well as audit efficiency.

Internal control questionnaires were discussed primarily as ticklers for reminding auditors of available controls; stress was placed on controls needed in the focal areas of exposure. Moreover, the auditee organization's view of internal control can represent an indicator of the control environment. Suggestions were made as to when controls might be tested, and comments provided as to the organization of certain working papers. In addition, sample control testing programs were provided for the focal areas of exposure. (At Stellar, because of uncontrolled threats due to high inherent risk and accompanying problems, control risk was assessed at the maximum.) Substantive tests were discussed in relation to test automation and the use of operational information to accomplish financial audit objectives.

CHAPTER 10

WORKING PAPERS

A people without history is like the wind upon the buffalo grass.

A Lakota chief

USER PERSPECTIVE: **Items of Special Interest**

EXECUTIVE HIGHLIGHTS: All readers

INTRODUCTION: All readers

WORKING PAPERS: QUINTESSENTIAL COMMUNICATION MEDIUM: All readers, especially audit committee members

THE COMMANDMENTS OF THE "YELLOW BOOK": External auditors, internal auditors

TYPES OF WORKING PAPERS: External auditors, internal auditors

THE ACTIVE REVIEWER: External auditors, internal auditors

COMMON WORKING PAPER DEFICIENCIES: All readers

THE PAPERLESS AUDIT: IT ISN'T HERE JUST YET: External auditors, internal auditors

SUMMARY: All readers

EXECUTIVE HIGHLIGHTS

The computer has not yet prompted the creation of fundamentally different working papers. Similarly, the paperless audit has not yet arrived and is not likely to arrive soon, at least in a pure form.

Working papers represent the platform upon which an audit is built. Auditors integrate new and existing knowledge as they design and complete their working papers; the skills used in preparing working papers have an important bearing on both audit effectiveness and efficiency.

The GAO has noted that working papers provide evidence that audit work has been adequately planned and supervised, internal accounting controls have been studied and evaluated, and accounting transactions, balances and financial items and related evidential matter have been examined.

Much of the importance of working papers lies in their uses by reviewers, particularly those within an audit organization. It follows that reviewers' needs must be considered when working papers are prepared. It could be useful to provide reviewers with a basic set of instructions to be used in accessing different types of information. Such review software could incorporate a menu or it could feature an interactive, conversational format.

More important, working papers have become a new medium for communication between auditors and users of financial information. For example, the successful accomplishment of an audit committee's mission centers on the effectiveness of the oversight it exercises. That oversight can involve two interrelated approaches: (1) inspection of documentation of the system and its controls and (2) review of output reports, which in themselves may constitute supervisory controls.

Changing technology makes it necessary to address working paper creation, access, and retrieval on an ongoing basis. The current trend toward linking microcomputers into central file storage will facilitate automation of the audit process.

INTRODUCTION

The subject of working papers receives little space in most audit books, despite its pervasive importance. In this book, the working paper topic has been placed in the central position of the three chapters concerned with implementing up-to-date auditing techniques.

Auditors integrate new and existing knowledge as they design and complete their working papers; the skills used in preparing working papers bear importantly on both audit effectiveness and efficiency. The professional literature states that working papers provide support for the auditor's report, evidence that the examination was made in accordance with generally accepted auditing standards (GAAS), and a means for directing, executing, and evaluating the examination. Working papers also indicate that the auditor has met the standard of due care, that she has discharged her professional responsibilities with competence and diligence, and that she has performed to the best of her ability.

The Challenge

Much of the importance of working papers lies in the uses made of them by reviewers within an audit organization. It follows that the reviewers' needs must be considered when working papers are designed and prepared, especially when computers are involved. It will be helpful to establish general rules setting out authorized hardware, software, guidelines to indexing and storage, instructions for both the reviewers and the reviewed, and rules for backup and security. In addition, the circulation to all audit personnel of examples of desirable and/or particularly successful working papers may improve both preparation and review. Essentially, partners and managers *must* understand what has been done by their subordinates and, more important, what should have been done; therefore, subordinates should leave a clear audit trail showing how they arrived at judgments. The papers should stand on their own—they should not require written or spoken supplements. The completeness consideration is especially important where the work may be used by a court of record (forensic accounting) or where important decisions are likely to be based on the auditor's work.

So far, the effect of computers upon working papers has tended to be cosmetic, rather than conceptual. (There are few indications of how the worksheet of the future will look. The matrix of components and threats, reflected in the master tracking sheet discussed in Chapters 8 and 9, could be a portent.) Stated differently, the computer has not yet prompted the creation of fundamentally different papers. However, working papers can now be prepared in a more understandable (and legible) fashion. Some tasks of working paper preparation have been automated, and software like IDEA (considered in the preceding chapter) permits the manipulation of client information to accomplish a wide variety of audit tasks.

This chapter considers some of the concepts which underlie working paper preparation, and discusses safeguards against typical errors of omission or commission.

WORKING PAPERS: QUINTESSENTIAL COMMUNICATION MEDIUM

Working papers have become a new medium for communication between auditors and users of financial information. The user audience is becoming larger and is likely to include members of audit committees. The tendency to think of a wider audience is reflected in auditors' increased use of graphic and other visual presentation techniques. (On the debit side, the computer also permits the creation—intentional or not—of a veritable paper avalanche which could induce confusion, rather than enlightenment, in working paper readers.)

Successful accomplishment of an audit committee's mission centers on the effectiveness of oversight: the committee must see to the introduction of controls sufficient to provide a measure of assurance that internal control and financial reporting–related responsibilities are being carried out. Therefore, an audit committee member should be aware of the significance of the following questions: (1) which controls are really important to the prevention and detection of financial fraud? (2) which of these controls have been put in place by my company? (3) what steps can be taken to prevent having these controls overridden by management? (4) how have the subject controls been documented by my company's systems personnel and auditors? and (5) how can an audit committee member satisfy herself that the controls are functioning?

Some of the oversight techniques available to audit committee members have been documented in Figure 6–13. Essentially, audit committee members can pursue two interrelated approaches: (1) inspection of documentation of the system and its controls and (2) review of reports which in themselves may constitute supervisory controls. With respect to the first approach, directors may wish to refer to working papers—especially papers showing test results—and to audit reports and management letters. For example, controls represented as present should be traceable to systems documentation; contrariwise, controls found absent should have been reported and explained in the management letter. Assurance that controls are functioning may be found in tests of controls and in dual-purpose substantive tests.

At least initially, the directors may find it helpful to start their review in the focal areas of exposure. They could look at flowcharts and/or narratives to ascertain that key controls and supervisory controls (i.e., controls designed to ensure that other controls are working) had been identified by the flowchart preparers and/or the auditors. In this way they could see that the flow of transactions had been recorded and analyzed from a control perspective. If they are interested in the control environment, they could examine pertinent procedures, collections of confirmations and other periodic affirmations required by those procedures, and descriptions of audit tests applied, as well as the resolution of audit findings.

An executive information system (EIS) designed to meet the information needs of a corporate audit committee may be able to access selected working papers prepared by either external or internal auditors. However, such a system would seem to be especially useful to directors seeking to review reports generated by the functioning of controls. The committee could also be provided with analytical reports developed to meet its own special needs; the possibilities are endless and depend on the directors' particular interests and concerns. For example, data base distributors could be asked to provide automatic updates of new developments relating to matters of audit committee interest. The update services are available at reasonable cost and tend to be highly effective. Other examples include:

1. Status report of open internal audit matters.
2. Report on audit adjustments and their resolution.
3. Report on compliance with specific aspects of the corporate code of ethics (e.g., a report on waivers of compliance with the conflicts-of-interest policy).

4. Inventory of unresolved computer input rejections.

5. Listing of program change authorizations, together with the reasons.

THE COMMANDMENTS OF THE "YELLOW BOOK"

This chapter makes considerable use of publications issued by the U.S. General Accounting Office (GAO). GAO pronouncements are particularly useful in the working paper area for several reasons: (1) GAO has pioneered in promulgating definitive working paper standards; (2) GAO resembles a large and very high-quality public accounting firm; fortuitously, its standards, pronouncements, and publications are in the public domain; and (3) GAO rules have significant direct effects on one third of U.S. audits, and indirect effects on the balance.

In July 1988, GAO issued a comprehensive restatement of its Government Auditing Standards, known as the *Yellow Book*. This revision became effective (for audits subject to Yellow Book standards) as of the beginning of 1989.

Changes in the appearance of working papers were recognized by GAO which said that papers "may include tapes, films, and disks." The agency elaborated on the nature of evidence and on how that evidence should be documented:

> Evidence may be categorized as (1) physical, (2) documentary, (3) testimonial, and (4) analytical.
>
> *a.* Physical evidence: Physical evidence is obtained by direct inspection or observation of (1) activities of people, (2) property, or (3) events. Such evidence may be documented in the form of memoranda summarizing the matters inspected or observed, photographs, charts, maps, or actual samples.
>
> *b.* Documentary evidence: Documentary evidence consists of created information such as letters, contracts, accounting records, invoices, and management information on performance.
>
> *c.* Testimonial evidence: Testimonial evidence is obtained from others through statements received in response to inquiries or through interviews. When possible, statements important to the audit should be corroborated with additional evidence.

d. Analytical evidence: Analytical evidence includes computations, comparisons, reasoning, and separation of information into components.[1]

The retention of the auditor's work in the form of working papers represents a long-standing GAO requirement. GAO expounded on the requirement in its revised field work standards for financial audits:

> Working papers are the link between fieldwork and the auditors' report. They serve as a record of the results of the audit and [of] the basis of the auditors' opinions. Supplemental working paper requirements for financial audits are that working papers should:
>
> *a.* Contain a written audit program cross-referenced to the working papers.
>
> *b.* Contain the objective, scope, methodology, and results of the audit.
>
> *c.* Contain sufficient information so that supplementary oral explanations are not required.
>
> *d.* Be legible, with adequate indexing and cross referencing, and include summaries and lead schedules, as appropriate.
>
> *e.* Restrict information included to matters that are materially important and relevant for the objectives of the audit.
>
> *f.* Contain evidence of supervisory reviews of the work conducted.[2]

Similarly, the significance of working papers was emphasized by the GAO in its standards for performance audits. It was stated that papers should:

> *e.* Be complete and accurate to provide proper support for findings, judgments, and conclusions, and to enable demonstration of the nature and scope of work conducted.
>
> *f.* Be understandable without oral explanations. Conciseness is important, but clarity and completeness should not be sacrificed just to save time or paper.[3]

---

[1] U.S. General Accounting Office, *Government Auditing Standards* (Washington, D.C.: U.S. Government Printing Office, 1988), pp. 6-16, 6-17.

[2] Ibid., p. 4-6.

[3] Ibid., p. 6-22.

Working papers were virtually positioned as the platform upon which an audit is built, when GAO stated that

> there are no substitutes for a working understanding of the audit objectives, the reasons for conducting a specific task, and knowing how the task will satisfy the objectives. This understanding comes from well-planned and well-organized work programs and effective instructions by supervisors. The practice of having all working papers contain clear statements of purpose is very helpful in ensuring that information accumulated is properly related to audit objectives and reporting.[4]

TYPES OF WORKING PAPERS

Carmichael, Meals, Huff, and Anderson have commented that working papers normally fall into three general categories: The permanent file, the general file, and the account balance file. The working papers in the permanent file represent either miscellaneous information about the client's organization and operations or specific documents supporting transactions that take place over several accounting periods. The general file contains forms, schedules, correspondence, etc., not directly related to financial statement components and supporting schedules. The largest part of the working papers consists of schedules supporting trial balance accounts.[5]

Concerning the major part of the papers, Kell, Boynton, and Ziegler have classified working papers into the following groupings based on broad characteristics: (1) audit plans and audit programs, (2) working trial balance, (3) adjusting and reclassifying entries, (4) schedules and analyses, and (5) audit memoranda and documentation of corroborating information.[6]

---

[4]Ibid.

[5]Douglas R. Carmichael, Dennis R. Meals, Bruce N. Huff, and Jerry Anderson, *Guide to Audits of Small Businesses*, 7th ed. (Fort Worth: Practitioners Publishing Company, 1989), pp. 5-7 and 5-8.

[6]Walter G. Kell, William C. Boynton, and Richard E. Ziegler, *Modern Auditing*, 4th ed. (New York: John Wiley & Sons, 1989), p. 126.

Montgomery's Auditing describes the nature of test documentation:

1. Tests of controls may be documented in narrative form by describing what tests were performed and which control structure policies and procedures were tested.
2. Substantive tests are most often evidenced by some kind of analysis; the form depends on the nature of the auditing procedures performed. The working papers should present both the account information and an indication of what evidence was examined and what other auditing procedures were performed.
3. Analytical working paper evidence usually consists of a narrative description of the procedures, their results, further investigation of matters identified as having a significant effect on the audit, and any resulting changes in the scope of the audit of related accounts.[7]

THE ACTIVE REVIEWER

The reviewer brings her own perspective and a degree of objectivity to her review. The reviewer should have a thorough understanding of detection risk, the risk that the auditor will not detect a material misstatement in a management assertion. This makes it essential that auditors, and especially reviewers:

- Understand the client's business.
- Understand computerized processing.
- Are aware of assets and other components and of the threats thereto.
- Have identified pertinent key and supervisory controls.

---

[7]Philip L. Defliese, Henry R. Jaenicke, Vincent M. Reilly, and Murray B. Hirsch, *Montgomery's Auditing*, 11th ed., college version (New York: John Wiley & Sons, 1990), pp. 176–79.

- Know control and substantive test procedures, the qualifications of the audit personnel assigned to the engagement and the degree of effort required to accomplish those procedures successfully, the documentation available for test purposes, and the relative merits of different types of evidence.
- Are able to assess the adequacy and results of tests actually performed.

An effective reviewer fills many roles: quality controller, confidante, sleuth, and teacher. Review represents a first line of defense against ineffective audit procedures. (This is especially true of engagements which require an understanding of EDP systems and of the related control procedures, plus use of the computer to carry out audit procedures.) Planning for reviews should represent part of overall planning; the review work should be performed while the work is ongoing and the facts are fresh in everyone's mind. When the review is conducted contemporaneously with the fieldwork, immediate corrective action can be taken on deficiencies observed in the conduct of the examination.

Item

It may be desirable to set aside original client documentation for inspection by the reviewer. In one situation, the client asserted that an inactive inventory, being considered for writedown, had suddenly become active. The client produced a number of sales orders which were said to have just been received. The reviewer, a partner, quickly established that the alleged orders, prepared on a nonstandard form and involving foreign customers, were fraudulent. This type of deception is more likely to be spotted by a senior reviewer than by a junior working paper preparer. (Readers might be interested in noting that the audit firm resigned the engagement.)

Item

In the case of the railroad referred to in an earlier chapter, two reviews (by an audit partner and the general auditor) took place contemporaneously with track construction. The reviewers scanned progress via their terminals daily. In analyzing variances, the reviewers concerned themselves with (1) the need to institute a new control, or to strengthen an existing one, (2) the need for possible changes in operations to be discussed with the division manager, and (3) the need to revise audit programs, especially those followed in the field by internal audit teams.

When reviewers become involved on a timely basis, hopefully while the papers are still in the planning stage, it is more likely that deficiencies can be avoided. Insofar as possible, the preparer should ease the reviewer's task by extending total cooperation to her and by surfacing actual or potential problems for her consideration and guidance. For example, preparers may wish to mark both paper and electronic working papers with flags, such as the following: + represents a finding, > represents that something remains to be done by the auditor, and # flags a situation rife with audit detection risk. Word processing programs have the ability to search for and identify words or strings of characters, thereby helping to focus a reviewer's attention.

A most important aspect in creating and maintaining working papers is the organization of papers to meet the needs of reviewers and others likely to retrieve information in the future. Reviewers, mostly audit partners and managers, may be unfamiliar with computer-prepared papers. It may be desirable to provide a basic set of instructions to be used by reviewers in accessing different types of information.[8] The reviewers may also find it helpful to be instructed on such matters as (1) whether the reviewer must perform cross-referencing, and to which documents, (2) the review techniques to be applied, and (3) the recording and clearance of review notes. Such information can be incorporated in software as part of a "menu" or in an interactive conversational format. It is possible that automated reminder techniques will be found superior to conventional questionnaires, instructions, and checklists.

---

[8]U.S. General Accounting Office, Information Management and Technology Division, "Using Micro Computers in GAO Audits; Improving Quality and Productivity," *Technical Guideline 1*, 1986, p. 28.

COMMON WORKING PAPER DEFICIENCIES

GAO has been concerned with the adequacy of evidence as reflected in public accountants' working papers. GAO reviewers examined a statistical sample of 328 audit reports to determine the nature of deviations from professional standards as identified by regional inspectors general (RIGs) of federal departments. GAO noted that working papers *should* have included evidence showing that audit work had been adequately planned and supervised, testing of compliance with laws and regulations had been performed and exceptions identified and resolved, internal accounting controls had been studied and evaluated, and accounting transactions, balances and financial items, and related evidential matter had been examined. Insufficient evidence led to nonacceptance of one in every five reports![9]

Montgomery's Auditing lists some significant working paper deficiencies, including:

1. Purpose of working papers not apparent; no explanation given.
2. Working papers sloppy, cluttered, or concerned with immaterial or unimportant aspects.
3. Exceptions or unusual items not properly explained or evaluated.
4. Amounts not in agreement with trial balance.
5. Poor quality, illegible photocopy.
6. Too much reliance placed on the prior year's working papers, resulting in a lack of focus for the current year.
7. Nature of auditing procedures not explained clearly.
8. Working papers prepared in redundant fashion, or without regard to economy in their preparation, reflecting poor planning.[10]

---

[9]U.S. General Accounting Office, "CPA Audit Quality: Inspectors General Find Significant Problems," *GAO/AFMD-86-20*, December 1985, pp. 16–17.

[10]Defliese et al., *Montgomery's Auditing*, p. 180.

The most typical cause of inefficiency in working paper preparation involves useless replication (often with a slightly changed format) of information previously prepared by the client. Another common problem relates to choices of procedures that are not cost-effective. In this connection, value analysis might be considered in selecting auditing procedures to do the best job at least cost. Purchasing agents use value analysis extensively. For example, in the paper industry there is a disposable tool called a chipper blade that makes little chips out of big trees. For many years the industry used cheap domestic blades until value analysis established that more expensive, imported blades had a longer life and therefore yielded more cuts per blade, resulting in lower operating costs.

Item

In applying value analysis to auditing, there must be knowledge of the cost of performing a particular procedure in terms of hourly rate and anticipated time, the risk of failing to detect an error, the materiality of the accounts, the numbers of items involved, and the possible client service potential. Example: assume there is a lack of control over the assignment of vendor codes. This could make it easier for improper, padded, fictitious, or duplicate payments to be routed to vendors of dubious lineage. The auditor has several choices in her tests. She could (1) arrange for a visit to vendors by company investigators, (2) obtain vendor confirmations, (3) look up vendor information in the on-line data bases, or obtain credit reports, (4) test compensating controls, or (5) establish that the services or materials were actually received. In most cases, the auditor would select a blend of approaches, depending on her value analysis.

The author has also encountered examples of carelessness involving working paper preparation or utilization: (1) lack of support in the working papers for findings in the report or in the management letter; (2) failure to carry findings forward from the working papers to the report or the management letter; (3) failure to act on review notes; (4) failure to clear review notes even though they had been acted on; (5) failure to discover accounting and auditing problems, and/or to signal those problems for consultation with technical or industry experts or with other senior personnel; and (6) last, but not least, questionable reviewers' judgments which may be reflected in sweeping or unsupported condemnatory statements.

THE PAPERLESS AUDIT: IT ISN'T HERE JUST YET

The paperless audit has not yet arrived, and is not likely to arrive soon, at least in a pure form. Even when it becomes possible to create or make available most engagement working papers in an automated format, it will remain necessary to maintain hard copy documentation for certain papers. Examples of hard copy include: (1) a master summary or index; (2) printed directories of all diskettes, along with information on their numbering and labeling; (3) printed documents requiring official signatures; and (4) printouts of important documents, which may also be used for backup. In other words, working papers are likely to represent a blend of information on paper and on electronic media. This makes a rational approach to indexing doubly important.

Indexing

The GAO has entered the following caveat:

> For each job, there needs to be a single master index or directory that lists all individual working papers and materials associated with the job. This master index should show the storage device and location of each working paper. It should also provide information as to the subject of the worksheet, its title, and its file type; e.g., a LOTUS spreadsheet. . . . Indexing can be facilitated by devising and using standard file names which contain coded information on the type of file, and the number of the working paper, or other information relevant to locating particular documents from a whole set of related documentation.[11]

With respect to file coding, the following use is possible of an available three-position file suffix: identify the type of worksheet,

---

[11]U.S. General Accounting Office, "Using Micro Computers in GAO Audits," p. 27.

its number in a sequence, and its purging or destruction date. For large engagements it may be useful to have an abstract of the content of important working papers; as already noted it may also be helpful to develop key words or symbols to facilitate searches. Standard word processing, data base, and spreadsheet software have some capability for supporting indexing and searching. Consequently, it may be possible to use available software to some degree for sorting, searching, and extracting information from individual working papers.

Bradford Hildebrandt has focused on the importance of word processing and related activities in law firms. He notes that

> an automated index system for firm research documents and other important work product from the various practice areas . . . also requires management and maintenance. The technology aspect of a work product retrieval system is not necessarily the primary issue. For the system to work, you must identify individuals responsible for gathering this information and maintaining and updating the data base.[12]

Author's Comment

The index that is developed depends, of course, on the audit organization's needs.[13] It may be useful to recall some of the retrieval aids used by the public on-line data bases. Key word arrangements used in some data bases may generate useful ideas. For example, a well-regarded data base, ABI/INFORM, includes the searchable segments listed below this paragraph; a possible auditor's equivalent appears next to the name of the data base field:

- Title: the client's name.
- Author: the engagement partner.
- Classification code: the Standard Industrial Classification (SIC) code.

---

[12]Bradford W. Hildebrandt, "Organizing MIS in a Legal Environment," *New York Law Journal*, December 12, 1989, Law Office Management Sec., p. 4.

[13]The firm of Deloitte & Touche determined that working paper preparation represented a pocket of significant clerical effort. Accordingly, a system, A+, was created to help process client balances. The A+ "core system" computerizes preparing, organizing, and reviewing working papers.

- SIC Classification name.
- Journal name: the type of file.
- Publication year: the year of the audit.
- Descriptor (a key word assigned from a controlled vocabulary): descriptors could identify business problems, accounting issues, or audit questions.
- Abstract.

Reference to indexes available elsewhere, such as the Accountants' Index, or the Electronic Index to Technical Pronouncements, could help in starting an in-house data base combining internal and external literature. Mead Data Central has experience in developing full text private libraries linked to LEXIS/NEXIS.[14]

Evidencing Supervisory Review

An unresolved problem relates to the addition of supervisory signatures and (possibly) dates of the supervisor's performance to working papers stored on diskettes. The GAO has mentioned some possibilities, such as including a signature block on the diskette labels or using supplementary paper files. (It would seem that this situation should be addressed by software manufacturers; they should be able to devise a means whereby supervisors access programs and data under appropriate security—probably using encryption—and affix an electronic approval; subsequently, data would be processed only with that approval or upon the performance of alternative routines.)

Use of Tickmarks

Tickmarks are notations on working papers next to an amount indicating the application of a particular procedure to that

---

[14]At Mead Data Central, inquiries regarding private data bases may be directed to Dale Heider, Esq., Director, Accounting Market, 9393 Springboro Pike, P.O. Box 933, Dayton, OH 45401.

amount.[15] Traditionally some auditors have endeavored to impart creativity and beauty to their tickmarks. Unfortunately, color and artwork are not easily transferable to computerized working papers. Therefore, to prepare for automation, the tickmark could be replaced with a letter or numeric code; also, a selection could be made of standard symbols.

Spreadsheet Problems

Much of the information required for good spreadsheet documentation can be entered directly on the spreadsheet. Separate sections of the spreadsheet can be used to list data sources, describe the variables included, detail the assumptions of the analysis, and describe models embedded in the spreadsheet. Other separate sections can be devoted to information on the preparer, the date, the version of the spreadsheet, and other facets of file management.[16] Similarly, a history or record of modifications should be maintained for permanent or protected information, including formulas.

The supervisory review of spreadsheets calls for two caveats: (1) make certain that the reviewer performs correct and complete steps, particularly to satisfy herself as to the integrity of the model; and (2) see that the supervisory review is evidenced in appropriate fashion.

Faye Borthick has recommended that spreadsheet models be audited by means of validation procedures designed to detect logic errors, likely opportunities for data entry errors, and unnecessarily difficult user interfaces: (1) model results should be compared with expected results for test cases; (2) the potential for errors should be reduced by minimizing the number of keystrokes, including cursor movement, required for data entry; all cells that are not data entry should be protected against data entry; and (3) documentation for spreadsheets must be complete and current. (Faye Borthick has also noted the availability of software which

---

[15]D. R. Carmichael et al., *Guide to Audits of Small Businesses*, p. 5-9.

[16]U.S. General Accounting Office, "Using Micro Computers in GAO Audits," p. 29.

detects errors by validating spreadsheets.) Spreadsheet documentation should include:

- Change log.
- Description or purpose.
- Explanation of how the spreadsheet works.
- Data entry directions.
- Sample output.
- Formulas and cell contents listing.
- Developer guidelines for enhancements.
- Security considerations.
- Systems diagram.
- Reference to prior audit reports.[17]

Security

Backup of all files is critical throughout each phase of the audit process. Lawrence Sawyer advises:

> Copies of disks holding working papers [should] be backed up every evening. After the fieldwork is done, backups should be made weekly until working paper reviews and all review notes have been completed. It is advisable that two copies of the finished audit disks be stored for future reference. In sensitive audits . . . the auditor may wish to consider keeping an additional set in a . . . high-security location.[18]

Limiting access to engagement files can help prevent unauthorized use and inadvertent damage. The efforts of hackers have been widely reported; however, auditors have not yet been discovered as promising targets. Still, the danger is real; auditors are reminded of reported endeavors by unethical clients to break into (or even change) auditors' conventional working papers.

---

[17]A. Faye Borthick, "Validating Spreadsheets: Minimizing the Potential for Errors," *EDPACS The EDP Audit, Control, and Security Newsletter* XVII, no. 3 (September 1989), p. 1.

[18]Lawrence B. Sawyer, *Sawyer's Internal Auditing*, 3rd ed. (Altamonte Springs, Fla.: The Institute of Internal Auditors, 1988), p. 361.

Item

An auditing professor prepared his final examination on his microcomputer. No identification code or password was required to access his computer; the exam file was not disguised or coded. Indeed,
this word processing file was simply called FINALEX. The door
was locked. However, persons unknown broke into the office, copied FINALEX, and marketed printouts to students. One of the potential customers reported having been solicited. An alternative
exam had to be developed on a crash basis.

Records Retention

There are no rules stating how long papers should be retained; the
period should be sufficient to meet the needs of the practice and to
satisfy pertinent legal requirements; however, it is important to establish a policy that is followed consistently.[19] The GAO says that
electronic working papers, "like any others," must be retained for at
least three years. GAO has also noted that storage of floppy diskettes may require special care, favoring cool and dry environments.

Records management has expanded its function, both in terms
of technology and management responsibility. Even the lowly file
folder has been changed, with its labels bar coded and its code stored
in a computer, allowing management to automate the records inventory function.[20] The electronic publishing industry has experienced unforeseeable and unprecedented growth; CD-ROM, compact
disk—read only memory technology, was mentioned in Chapter 6. A
data base on CD-ROM can be searched by a user from an appropriately equipped personal computer. The WORM (write once—read
many) disks present exciting possibilities for working paper storage.

The Future

Changing technology makes it necessary to address working paper creation, access, and retrieval on an ongoing basis. The current trend toward linking microcomputers into central file stor-

---

[19]D. R. Carmichael, et al., *Guide to Audits of Small Businesses*, p. 5-9.

[20]"Records Management: Technology Advances on All Fronts," *Modern Office Technology* 35, no. 1 (January 1990), pp. 50, 62.

age will facilitate automation of the audit process.[21] Further impetus will be given to the development of in-house data bases, and to development of related search techniques; the latter are likely to be similar to those applied to search on-line data bases.

SUMMARY

The chapter has brought out the need for a systematic approach to the creation, filing, and retrieval of working papers. Audit entities will develop procedures sufficiently flexible to accommodate major trends in technology, such as a blending of audit automation with automation of the accountant's office. Two major facets of protection over working papers are: (1) physical protection, and (2) control via records. Physical protection involves protection from natural as well as man-made catastrophes, especially given diverse working paper media. (The magic word is backup.)

The most important record control is the master index. It should reflect an orderly approach to record-keeping; users, and especially reviewers and authorized personnel, should be able to identify, classify, retrieve, and purge individual papers. Larger audit entities might wish to incorporate their working papers in an in-house, on-line data base, accessible in a manner similar to public on-line data bases. Such an arrangement would incorporate a capability of searching a variety of segments and of utilizing key words or terms for easy retrieval.

The paperless audit is not quite here yet. Major constraints involve making certain that audit supervisors understand what they are to review with respect to computerized audit approaches, how they are to satisfy themselves as to the quality of the work performed, and how they should evidence their review. Audit organizations may wish to take positive steps by formal and on-the-job training to reinforce the partners' and managers' understanding of the information provided to them and the review procedures to be applied by them.

---

[21]U.S. General Accounting Office, "Using Micro Computers in GAO Audits," p. 33.

CHAPTER 11

A ROAD MAP TO IMPLEMENTING NEW TECHNOLOGY

Within its field of learning, a profession has a responsibility to give leadership to the community which it serves. This is provided by research, experiment and innovation, constantly improving methods and techniques and better organization. It must therefore plan to keep abreast of, and preferably just ahead of, public thought and opinion.

Lord Benson*

USER PERSPECTIVE: Items of Special Interest

EXECUTIVE HIGHLIGHTS: All readers

INTRODUCTION: All readers

THE FIRST STEP: THE CHIEF TECHNOLOGY OFFICER: External auditors, internal auditors

A STRATEGIC PLAN FOR TECHNOLOGICAL DEVELOP-MENT: External auditors, internal auditors, audit committee members

INVOLVEMENT OF ALL PERSONNEL: External auditors, internal auditors

THE AUDITOR: THE BUSINESSPERSON: All readers

THE IMPLEMENTATION SEQUENCE: External auditors, internal auditors

---

*Lord Benson, the doyen of the British profession, formerly headed Coopers & Lybrand's U.K. operations.

IMPLEMENTING TECHNOLOGY: THE ON–LINE DATA BASES: All readers

IMPLEMENTING TECHNOLOGY: SOFTWARE: External auditors, internal auditors

IMPLEMENTING TECHNOLOGY: NEW PRODUCT LINES: External auditors, internal auditors

EVALUATING THE APPLICATION OF TECHNOLOGY: External auditors, internal auditors

SUMMARY: All readers

EXECUTIVE HIGHLIGHTS

The American Institute of Certified Public Accountants (AICPA) has endeavored to provide technological guidance to practitioners. Valuable products have been made available; several of these are referenced or utilized in this book.

However, many individual accounting firms or internal audit departments have been slow to embrace either research into technology or the mantle of technology leadership. An audit organization should formulate its own strategic plan to assess technology, coordinate the efforts of participants in its technology-oriented programs, avoid duplication and overlap, and ensure that key tasks are completed.

The preparation of a successful strategic plan requires (1) knowledge of technological developments in areas relating to the organization's practice, (2) in-depth knowledge of clients, employees, and practice administration, and (3) an understanding of the actions and action responses that have been taken historically and are likely to be taken in the future by significant competitors.

The plan should incorporate measures of performance, such as the effect on engagement profitability, increases in time charged to clients relative to time available, fee increases attributable to mastery of automation, resulting client accessions or special work, and planned versus actual penetration of a particular market.

The individual selected for the post of chief technology officer should have imagination, creativity, and a desire to have his firm assume leadership. The organization's culture should encourage research and experimentation; the audit organization should provide positive incentives to learning, rather than disincentives.

Technology might be implemented in the following sequence based on ease of introduction and early realization of benefits: on-line data bases, software, and new product lines, such as fraud auditing.

INTRODUCTION

Michael Sekora, a former official of the Defense Intelligence Administration, recently noted:

> In the past 10 to 15 years technology has continued to evolve very, very rapidly. Developments are very shortlived. . . . [A problem is] how people are using technology strategies to gain advantages over other companies. . . . We have identified 24 different technology strategies. . . . There is a misconception in the United States that you can control technology. You cannot. You must take all the action you can to increase your forward momentum.[1]

In the words of Ross Johnson of RJR Nabisco fame, the challenge is one of "understanding change, managing change, and explaining change to others." For a CPA firm or an internal audit department, this could be interpreted as knowing what technology is available, selecting that which will work to the advantage of the firm, and monitoring developments as they break; great opportunities are available to public accounting firms of all sizes. Yet, many accounting firms have been slow to embrace either research into technology or the mantle of technology leadership.

The American Institute of Certified Public Accountants (AICPA) and other professional organizations have endeavored to provide guidance to practitioners. Some valuable products have been made available; several of these are referenced or uti-

---

[1]Robert Wrubel, "The Frontal Assault," *Financial World* 59, no. 140 (July 10, 1990), pp. 22–24.

lized in this book. However, an audit organization should also formulate its own strategic plan or framework to assess technology, coordinate the efforts of participants in its technology-oriented programs, avoid duplication and overlap, and ensure that key tasks are completed.[2]

While some accountants may have de-emphasized automation of professional activities, as well as automation in the office, progress has been reported by lawyers. For example, as early as 1985 one major law firm had automated internal systems (including personnel management, message switching/routing, and accounting) and was conducting legal research via minicomputers. Research included the creation of briefs and other legal documents. The same computers were used to track the progress of client engagements, the firm's timely submission of documents, and performance of other litigation-related actions. (Failures to take such actions, and to submit documents when required, play a part in more than a third of lawsuits brought against attorneys.)

The relatively advanced character of law firm automation is reflected in an article by Daniel J. DiLucchio, who notes that "an external focus on outside threats and opportunities, rather than an internal firm focus, may mean the difference between success and failure for a firm in this decade." He elaborates:

> The firms that fail will be those that dwell only on internal matters. . . . Externally focused firms spend a predominant amount of time and energy with these issues: competitors; expansion. . . ; legislative, regulatory, or political changes that may affect the firm or its clients; the economy; business development; maintaining current clients. . .; and firm image. . . . The internal focus was [formerly] on staff service, such as automation and word processing. . . . What demanded the firm's time yesterday is not the same today. . . . The fittest firms will survive, and they will be those

---

[2]Highly useful information on strategic planning for accountants and on the strategic planning process can be found in a document published by the AICPA: AICPA 1986–1988 Strategic Planning Committee, "Strategic Thrusts for the Future," October 1988.

that have already settled their internal problems—or are at least well on the way to doing so—and have the energy and resources to focus on the external threats and opportunities.[3]

Thus, implementation of technology by internal and external auditors would seem to be urgent. Technological change has significant implications for the professional development of individual auditors, for their deployment, and for their specialization in particular industries. Among other things, the present chapter discusses the assignment of responsibility for harnessing technology. The appointee should monitor technological developments, evaluate their significance to the practice, set up plans for introducing new technology, and assess the effectiveness of such plans and the manner of their implementation. The technology leader's tasks will be complicated by continuing shifts in the subject matter and timing of audits, in the users and uses of audit reports, and in the composition of audit teams.

The chapter begins with a brief consideration of the responsibilities of the technology officer, followed by an outline of key steps to be taken toward implementing emerging technology.

THE FIRST STEP: THE CHIEF TECHNOLOGY OFFICER

Chief technology officers have been described as "men and women who commute between the down-and-dirty atmosphere of the laboratory or computer room and the rarefied atmosphere of the executive suite—and who try to make sure that neither side gives the other short shrift."[4] The individual selected for the post of chief technology officer should have imagination, creativity, and a desire to have his firm assume leadership. The ap-

---

[3]Daniel J. DiLucchio, "Balancing Internal, External Demands; Focusing the Resources of the Firm," *The National Law Journal*, May 21, 1990, Law Office Management Sec., p. 16.

[4]Claudia H. Deutsch, "Treasuring the Technology Guru," *Sunday New York Times*, July 22, 1990, Business Sec., p. 23.

pointee should be a trained auditor with a commitment to the auditor's role in a free society; he should also have comprehensive and practical knowledge of audit objectives and procedures. He will usually hold partner, manager, or equivalent rank. The time requirements of the position depend on the size of the firm, its product and service mix, and upon its current state of technological sophistication. (If the firm has to play catch-up, time requirements will rise.) In any event, the position will be part time in all except the very largest firms.

The duties and responsibilities of this officer may include:

- Advising the audit entity's management on matters of technology strategy and tactics.
- Developing a strategic plan for technological change (or to incorporate technology in strategic plans).
- Monitoring technological developments as they occur and interacting with accounting departments or schools at universities.
- Considering the possibilities of joint ventures with other firms, universities, or professional associations.
- Analyzing developments in terms of their impact on the organization and to draft any necessary recommendations to management.
- Disseminating news of significant technological changes to others in the organization.
- Conducting research designed to adapt technological developments to the firm's existing practice, and to the markets it serves. Normally, new products should be linked to existing product lines and to existing marketing capabilities.
- Monitoring quality with respect to applications of technology.
- Training staff in understanding technology and in seeking opportunities for its application.
- Acting as a resource to staff in utilizing technology.

A STRATEGIC PLAN FOR TECHNOLOGICAL DEVELOPMENT

The preparation of a successful strategic plan requires (1) knowledge of technological developments in areas relating to the firm's practice,[5] (2) in-depth knowledge of the firm's practice, clients, employees, and administration, and (3) an understanding of the actions and action responses that have been taken in the past, and are likely to be taken in the future, by significant competitors. All proposed activities should be classified into projects. Within each project, tasks should be defined, ordered sequentially, and accompanied by time and cost estimates. Of course, estimates relating to activities planned for the distant future will tend to be relatively soft compared to estimates for the near term. The projects should be evaluated on both tangible (costs versus monetary benefits) and intangible bases (quality improvements, new client accessions, sale of new client services, etc.) and ranked accordingly. Since many projects are related or interdependent, the overall plan should serve as an umbrella to coordinate projects.

The plan should incorporate measures of performance, such as the effect on engagement profitability, increases in time charged to clients relative to time available for client service, fee increases attributable to mastery of automation, any resulting client accessions or special work, and planned versus actual penetration of a particular market. The plan should also include milestone dates. Such dates could be utilized as "go" or "no go" checkpoints, at which performance can be assessed and decisions made as to whether to proceed with or terminate projects. Similarly, there should be a post-audit at which actual accomplishments can be evaluated in the light of original expectations.

While there is need for the discipline of a formal plan, control applied over use of hardware, software, and information re-

---

[5]The IC2 Center at the University of Texas at Austin publishes a quarterly newsletter which lists and briefly discusses developments in key technological areas. The newsletter may be secured by writing to: Leading Edge Technologies, IC2 Institute, 2815 San Gabriel, Austin, TX 78705.

sources by individual staff persons or partners should be relatively loose. The atmosphere should encourage research and experimentation; the audit organization should provide positive incentives to learning on the job, rather than disincentives. (Excessive control, or the lack of any control philosophy at all, have contributed to the entry of public accounting firms into the computer age at very different levels of sophistication.)

Author's Comment

Members of audit committees and others with oversight responsibility should be aware of the fact that different audit organizations are at markedly different stages in their mastery of technology. For example, the organizational responsibility for EDP auditing, the commitment to audit research, the nature of EDP audit training, the degree of staff persons' computer literacy and their ability to understand EDP processing and to use computers to enhance audit efficiency and effectiveness, differ from one firm to the next. Since audit organizations should interact with audit committees in synergistic fashion, audit committee members may have to engage in judicious questioning of auditors, together with review of documentation, to ferret out their level of sophistication.

INVOLVEMENT OF ALL PERSONNEL

Recruiting Well-Educated Auditors

Recent years have seen revisions to academic curricula, often in reaction to practitioner criticism. (According to Lawrence McKibbin, a former president of the American Association of Collegiate Schools of Business, the fundamental change relates to the profession's need for a broadly educated accountant/auditor.)

The trend toward broad-gauged auditing is reflected in increased employment of auditors who may not have been trained academically as accountants. For example, more than a third of hires by the U.S. General Accounting Office (GAO) reportedly are not accountants. Another indication: the general auditor of Exxon was quoted as having been disappointed by the performance of trained accountants in connection with the Valdez cleanup; reportedly, Exxon's auditor recruiting is being redirected to attract persons with backgrounds in diverse professional disciplines. The author is concerned with such developments; it used to be a virtual axiom that a good financial auditor tended to be a good businessperson and a good operational auditor. (An apparent plateauing in operational audit activity by internal auditors could be due to self-imposed restrictions; lack of self-confidence could have contributed to such restrictions. If so, steps should be taken to address the problem.) In a more positive vein, it is hoped that hires of liberal arts graduates or of persons from other professional disciplines will cross-pollinate knowledge among members of audit organizations.

Early Application of What Has Been Learned

Those trained in technology should participate in hands-on applications as early as possible upon completion of their training. Early doing, preferably repeatedly, causes the new material to be integrated into staff and partner mindsets. Conversely, if training is not followed by actual applications, its benefits will gradually evaporate.

Audit Team Specialization

Given the continuing risk of irregularities perpetrated by clients or their employees, auditors are advised to specialize in particular industries early in their careers, possibly at the time of entry into the profession. (There are precedents in other businesses for this approach. For example, some vendors of hardware and software assign new salespeople to particular industries at the beginning of their careers.) Writers recommending early specialization have cited the E. F. Hutton check overdraft scheme; the scheme was discovered by one of the affected banks' employees on the basis of a transaction pattern that indicated possible kiting. The authors noted that such a pattern would be familiar to someone who knows that facet of the banking business. But, they asked, would it be recognized by a generalist auditor?[6] The same authors suggested that audit *teams* should be supported by resource persons (i.e., by industry specialists). They observed, perhaps prophetically, that a firm with only one client in an industry could not afford an industry support strategy. The authors also commented that training on abuses peculiar to a particular industry might improve the audit teams' chances of uncovering irregularities. To lengthen the integral state and continuity of an audit team they urged incentives in terms of pay, fringe benefits, and additional time in grade.[7]

A recent survey of audit committee chairpersons also focused attention on audit teams, rather than audit firms. The directors consistently judged team factors more important than firmwide factors for preliminary assessments of audit quality. The team factors included the level of partner/manager attention given to the audit, the planning and conduct of audit team work, communication between the audit team and client management, independence exhibited by audit team members, provisions to keep auditors up-to-date technically, mix of skills and depth of experience of the team, and communication between the audit team and the audit committee.[8]

Partner and Manager Training

Since senior personnel on an engagement (i.e., partners and managers) are decision makers, they must receive exposure to and training in applied audit technology. Their training should inculcate diagnostic capabilities (i.e., recognition of deficiencies), together with the ability to guide corrective action. Such training

---

[6]Jan P. Muczyk, Ephraim P. Smith, and George P. Davis, "Holding Accountants Accountable: Why Audits Fail, How They Can Succeed," *Business Horizons* 29, no. 6 (November–December 1986), pp. 22–28.

[7]Ibid., p. 27.

[8]Mary S. Schroeder, Ira Solomon, and Don Vickrey, "Audit Quality: The Perceptions of Audit Committee Chairpersons and Audit Partners," *Auditing: A Journal of Practice & Theory* 5, no. 2 (Spring 1986), pp. 86–87, 91.

should simulate real world situations, problems, and remedies. To the degree practical, training sessions for senior people should be contemporaneous with those for employees in their charge.

THE AUDITOR: THE BUSINESSPERSON

The auditor's understanding of operational information under-lies the audit techniques described in this book. Moreover, *SAS 55* implies that auditors should have an operational orienta-tion. The former administrative or operational controls have for-mally reentered audit purview—at least to the extent to which these controls bear on the prevention or detection of material er-rors or irregularities in the financial statements. In earlier chap-ters, internal risk was considered and materials provided to guide the identification, evaluation, and testing of selected operational controls, particularly in the focal areas of exposure. Also, opera-tional information was suggested for use in analytical review and examples were given of tests of various kinds of controls.

Knowledge of the client's business, and a focus on that busi-ness in relation to the audit, is basic. Conveyance of an opera-tional orientation may require retraining of junior personnel in audit organizations; the more senior people may merely have to revert to old (and good) habits. Of course, knowledge of the client's business, as well as of technology, also underlies the introduction of the new product lines that will be discussed later on in this chapter.

THE IMPLEMENTATION SEQUENCE

Technology might be implemented in the following sequence, based on relative ease of introduction: on-line data bases, soft-ware, new product lines. The idea is to permit some benefits to be realized as early as possible. However, readers are cautioned that sequencing depends on the technology and/or general managerial strategy adopted by a particular audit entity relative to its vari-ous publics, including competitors. (Strategic choices also impact the nature of services to be rendered and the clientele to be served, together with the location of the services.) A possible order of introduction follows:

1. On-line data bases.
   a. External analytical procedures.
   b. External risk management.
   c. Evaluation of people risks.
   d. Professional and regulatory changes.
2. Software.
   a. Consolidation and financial statement preparation.
   b. Flowcharting.
   c. Internal control evaluations.

   Item

   Some interactive programs have been developed to assess the adequacy of a client's separation of duties. An example of such a program is Deloitte & Touche's ControlPlan; the availability of this program is restricted.[9]

   d. Substantive tests.
3. New product lines.
   a. Fraud auditing.
   b. Proactive auditing.
   c. The systems development life cycle (SDLC).

IMPLEMENTING TECHNOLOGY: THE ON–LINE DATA BASES

Assuming that the auditor has decided that on-line data bases make sense for him (and that he possesses the necessary equipment and software) he should (1) sign up with the appropriate on-line services; (2) learn to communicate with the services; and (3)

---

[9]Further information may be obtained from Mr. Trevor Stewart, Partner, Deloitte & Touche, 685 College Road East, Princeton, NJ 08540-6691.

learn how to do on-line searching.[10] (Other startup details appear in Chapter 6.)

Given the complexity of data base selection and usage, this book does not pretend to represent either a census of what is available, or a comparative analysis of the advantages and disadvantages of such offerings. The focus has been on data bases which the author has found especially useful. These data bases are vended by Mead Data Central (MDC), DIALOG, ORBIT, and COMPUSERVE; the addresses of these and other data base suppliers were shown in Table 5–1. The steps involved in implementing data base usage are:

1. Request literature and sign-up information.
2. Consider the suitability of alternatives to the development of information on-line. The possibilities include engaging information providers, purchasing software to select the most productive data bases, and complementary use of data bases available in CD-ROM (compact disk—read only memory) format.
3. Make a record of customer support telephone numbers.
4. Until some experience has been gained with usage patterns, billings by data base vendors should probably be based on actual usage. (Such usage will provide information for eventually deciding on an optimum invoicing arrangement.) On the other hand, it could be less expensive to teach partners and staff to use the bases while enjoying a discounted rate. In any event, an audit organization should make certain that it is put on the vendors' mailing lists for in-house periodicals; in general, such periodicals are filled with hints for improving usage efficiency.
5. Order supporting literature, such as DIALOG's (white page) data base chapters, which can provide additional explanations for data bases expected to have heavy usage. With some vendors, operating manuals may be part of the basic subscription; others may make separate charges for manuals. In any event,

---

[10]Jean M. Scanlan, Ulla de Stricker, and Anne Conway Fernald, *Business Online: The Professional's Guide to Electronic Information Sources* (New York: John Wiley & Sons, 1990), pp. 45–50.

the manuals are important for effective (and cost-effective) use of the data bases and represent an important part of the auditor's library.

6. Select training courses. Training courses are offered in convenient locales, the quality of instruction is generally excellent, the cost is minimal (because it may be partly or even wholly offset by the granting of complimentary computer time), and professional and regulatory jurisdictions may offer continuing professional education (CPE) credits.

7. Set access rules for professional auditors. (In order to encourage wide usage, experimentation should be encouraged and adverse criticism of the experimenters avoided.)

8. Establish operating procedures. The following ought to be covered:

    a. The nature, adequacy, and location of information resources available, including the practice office library.

Author's Comment

The audit research guide of one Big Six firm covers not only on-line data bases, but also local and regional library facilities in terms of specialization, number of volumes, and availability of reference librarians' help. Comprehensive coverage of information resources enhances research productivity and reduces the risk of false starts.

    b. When and how to initiate research.

    c. The names and telephone numbers of resource persons that may be contacted when needed.

    d. The extent to which research requests require approval or monitoring from either a quality or an expenditure control perspective. (Approvals should *follow* rather than precede usage.) Requirements for prior approval—that is, for seeking permission for data base use from people removed from the problems being solved—represent a disincentive which could sound the death knell of the program.

    e. The objective of the search request; it should outline:

        i. The desired end product of the search. Examples include: "List audit failures involving accounts receivable valuation"; "give examples involving a loss of usefulness of property, plant, and equipment, together with footnotes describing the resulting write-off"; "determine whether John Smith was involved in any adjudicated criminal lawsuits in his home state."

   ii. The appropriate service, library, and file (MDC) or the name of the data base (other data base distributors). (MDC has created easy-to-search combined files. DIALOG has a data base called DIALINDEX which identifies the number of postings of search terms to a particular data base. DIALINDEX is easy to use—it requires the selection of files to be searched, followed by the search statement. The output can be used to restrict subsequent searches to data bases with the greatest numbers of hits.)

   iii. The key search words.

   iv. The search statement.

   v. The result, together with recommendations for changes in the search approach, statement, or techniques.

   vi. Any comments which will enhance future search effectiveness.

 f. Billing arrangements with the client. The author sees no reason why at the conclusion of the initial learning period normal client billing arrangements should not obtain. Lee Nemchek, writing for a legal audience, discussed the need to adopt a profit-center approach toward service areas such as data bases and libraries. The following questions were raised: (1) are clients billed a surcharge over and above the actual amount paid by the firm for data base use? (2) is someone, preferably a librarian, responsible for processing monthly data base invoices and client charge-backs? and (3) is the data base budgeted so that its profit contribution can be assessed? The writer commented that a firm's practice specialization influences the nature of the data bases it utilizes, and the profitability to the firm of the particular data bases used.[11]

---

[11]Lee R. Nemchek, "The Dynamics of Data Base Profitability in Private Law Firms," *Law Office Economics and Management* 29, no. 4 (1989), pp. 447–55.

g. Arrangements for announcing significant search results. It may be desirable to (1) disseminate particularly valuable search results or results obtained through imaginative approaches throughout the organization, or (2) arrange to have results retrievable over the organization's in-house data base or message distribution network.

9. Develop a plan for initial client applications, and for gradually permeating the practice.

10. Evaluate the tangible and intangible results of progress achieved by on-line searching. Compare cost, timeliness, and quality of results to previous periods when conventional information resources were employed.

Truly effective searching cannot be achieved without constant practice. The practicing must be done, not by librarians or paraprofessionals, but by the auditors themselves. A recent article by Reva Basch dramatized the pitfalls of full-text searching: "A full-text data base may be a garden of earthly delights, but the garden is often overgrown and full of snakes." Ms. Basch sees parallels to the seven deadly sins in full-text searching: "Pride might be exemplified by the on-line system that took full-page ads in major national publications to declare that 'our service is a world of information at your fingertips.' Gluttony is a memory-gobbling full-text download. Sloth equates to slow processing time. And, avarice, of course, has something to do with pricing."[12]

IMPLEMENTING TECHNOLOGY: SOFTWARE

A caveat must be entered in connection with an audit organization's purchase of software. Thomas Hoar has observed that the first step in choosing a package involves identifying packages which meet proximate needs. Other factors include vendor support, current users' opinions, documentation, and pricing. Hoar points out that "a software package should allow [processing of]

---

[12]Reva Basch, "The Seven Deadly Sins of Full-text Searching," *Database* 12, no. 4 (August 1989), p. 15.

many different computer applications. . . . To ensure that the audit software does not disrupt the company's current operations, the package should be able to operate in a multiprogramming environment and terminate file processing before the computer file has been fully read."[13]

The software, discussed elsewhere in this book, follows:

- The Electronic Index to Technical Pronouncements (EITP).
- The NAARS Literature file (LIT).
- EASYFLOW.
- Audit Program Generator (APG).
- Interactive Data Extraction and Analysis (IDEA).
- Accountant's Trial Balance (ATB).

Steps Necessary to Implement the Software

The steps to be taken to implement the aforementioned software are similar:

1. Order the software. EITP, APG, IDEA, and ATB can be obtained from the AICPA; generally, programs are available on both 5¼ inch and 3½ inch disks. Access to NAARS and LIT can be arranged as part of a subscription to Mead Data Central's (MDC's) LEXIS and/or NEXIS services. (See Table 5–1 for the addresses of the data base distributors.) As mentioned in Chapter 6, EASYFLOW is available from HavenTree Software Limited, P.O. Box 1093-G, Thousand Island Park, NY 13692. The programs mentioned are accompanied by well-written manuals and instructions.
2. Establish operating procedures. The following ought to be covered:
   a. The nature of the information available via a service, library, or file.
   b. Guidelines to recognizing an appropriate application.
   c. The customer support telephone number.

---

[13]Thomas Hoar, "How to Select an Audit Software Package," *Journal of Accounting & EDP* 4, no. 4 (Winter 1989), pp. 30–36.

d. Examples of search requests, and of successful searches.

e. Quality control and feedback arrangements.

IMPLEMENTING TECHNOLOGY: NEW PRODUCT LINES

The attest function is being applied to new areas; moreover new audit services and products have become possible through applications of technology to auditing. Three innovative product lines will be discussed; they should be implemented only on the basis of a comprehensive marketing study, and, hopefully, completion of a successful pilot study.

Fraud Auditing

Those who would perpetrate frauds are older, better-educated, and more intelligent than the typical criminal. The societal response includes the creation of the auditor for all seasons: a good fraud examiner is part auditor, part investigator, part sociologist, and part lawyer.[14] Moreover, the private sector's responsibility to resolve fraud issues can be expected to increase. Nonetheless, relatively few auditors have chosen to practice in the burgeoning (and lucrative) fraud audit arena; for example, only one Big Six firm has been reported as offering comprehensive training in fraud prevention and detection. Yet, given widely reported public expectations, and an apparently continuing expectation gap, auditors are likely to find it to their advantage to enter this market.

Author's Comment

Fraud auditors are likely to use modern information resources, such as on-line data bases. A hypothetical example follows: if acts of omission or commission attributed to S&L officials were perpetrated as reported, the government should take steps to prevent a recurrence of similar actions by the same individuals. In this connection, regulatory agencies may wish to explore whether directorships held by the same individuals in *non-S&L* financial service institutions, such

---

[14]Joseph T. Wells et al., *Fraud Examiners Manual* (Austin: National Association of Certified Fraud Examiners, 1989), foreword, p. 1.

as banks, credit unions, insurance companies, and brokerage houses, are leading to undesirable effects. Entities that appear to have been affected negatively could be targeted for early audit attention. The purpose would be to mitigate or avoid serious problems.

Federal regulators are currently involved in searching for capable (and untainted) auditors to work with the Resolution Trust Corporation (RTC) and other agencies in liquidating the government's S&L portfolio and in investigating the principals of some of the failed companies and their culpable actions. The on-line data bases could be useful in these planned audits and investigations. In this connection, the GAO's "Investigators' Guide to Sources of Information" (see Appendix B) is likely to prove helpful. However, it should be pointed out that the available data bases tend to be weak in terms of disclosing either the perpetrator's modus operandi, or the manner of detection of the crime.

Item

The following example illustrates the advantages to an auditor of being aware of the culprit's modus operandi. Barry Minkow, the wunderkind who headed ZZZZ Best, had acquired some knowledge of audit procedures. He expressed himself as shocked by their ineffectiveness. Minkow knew that tracing post–confirmation date cash receipts was a widely applied substantive test technique. To deal with this procedure, Minkow simply "created" receipts. In his words: "Accounts receivable are a wonderful thing. They immediately apply a different [current] ratio. . . . One way you cannot dispute a receivable [is] if it's been paid. . . . It was easy to invent the receivables and invent the income. I was a paperwork manufacturing machine. . . . It tied together so nicely—what do they know?"[15]

Proactive Auditing

A proactive audit involves evaluation of business actions or decisions before the actions are completed or the decisions implemented. Such an audit focuses on control practices helpful to management, and utilizes all information that can be expressed

---

[15]"ZZZZ Best's Barry Minkow—A White Paper Interview," *The White Paper* 4, no. 6 (November/December 1990), pp. 13–14.

in numbers and verified. The proactive audit can be applied to all private or public sector plans and programs that are relatively discrete, subject to planning, managed by designated individuals, subject to measurement, and prone to control and accounting. Functions suited to the proactive audit include evaluation of the security program, intendance over the procurement program, and oversight over construction in progress. Here is an example of a major proactive auditing opportunity: the state of Florida plans to spend more than $50 billion during the next decade on infrastructure repairs; much of the responsibility for monitoring these expenditures will be placed on auditors.

Item

A proactive audit of a major construction project focuses on the framework of control established *before* construction begins. The auditor looks for systematic and complete planning efforts, observes the construction management systems selection, searches for existence of preferred control practices, and tests the functioning of controls by use of test data. Two examples: (1) a large public utility planning a billion dollar project decided to use a fixed fee, rather than the familiar cost plus fixed fee, approach. Competitiveness was not diminished; however actual costs were a surprising 5 to 10 percent below those experienced on a virtually identical (but cost plus) project five years previously. (2) A university hospital asked potential contractors to submit bids with and without workers' compensation coverage. As a result, the university elected to manage construction workers' compensation coverage, with savings of several million dollars per annum, due in part to improved loss control.[16]

The proactive audit eliminates the "Monday morning quarterback" image of the auditor. Since the technique is non-threatening, proactive auditing is likely to gain support of auditees. Some auditors have objected to the proactive audit on the grounds that it comes close to decision-making and therefore could affect independence. (The same objection can be made to op-

---

[16]The author described Coopers & Lybrand's Preemptive Auditing™ program in his book *Managing Capital Budget Projects: A Preemptive Audit Approach* (New York: John Wiley & Sons, 1984).

erational auditing, internal audit services by public accountants, and certain consulting services.) With respect to all of these services, the risk of criticism can be reduced by (1) drawing a line between providing inputs to managerial decision-making on the one hand, and actual decision-making on the other, and/or (2) rendering the services involved to nonattest audit clients.

The skills needed to practice proactive auditing include knowledge of the concepts and practices of risk management, management information systems, and planning and budgeting. The basic knowledge can be acquired by an auditor or consultant serving clients in a particular industry. However, that knowledge can be updated and honed by using the on-line data bases.

The Systems Development Life Cycle

The systems development life cycle (SDLC) simply refers to the phases involved in significant systems redesign and development. The SDLC may be viewed as a special type of proactive audit. The SDLC starts with the perceived need for a new system and extends through systems design, implementation, and turnover to operations. Ron Weber has identified 12 major phases in this process:

1. Problem definition.
2. Management of the change process.
3. Establishing a commitment to change; assessing feasibility.
4. Analysis of the existing system.
5. Organizational and job (employee work or task) design.
6. Information processing system design.
7. Software acquisition and development.
8. Procedures development.
9. Acceptance testing.
10. Conversion.
11. Operation and maintenance.
12. Post-audit.[17]

---

[17]Ron Weber, *EDP Auditing Conceptual Foundations and Practice*, 2nd ed. (New York: McGraw-Hill, 1988), p. 108.

There are important reasons for involving auditors in the SDLC: (1) to see that controls have been or are being built into the system, and (2) to ensure observance of the audited organization's systems development standards, especially with respect to documentation. Auditors *should* be involved with virtually *every* phase of the SDLC; particular attention should be given to the aforementioned phases 6 through 8, and to phase 12, the post-audit.

SDLC reviews by auditors permit designers to incorporate timely recommendations as implementation proceeds. When auditors get involved earlier, they are in a better position to avoid longstanding deficiencies: (1) absence of a systematic approach to the design of controls; and (2) lack of understanding of the technologies involved, and a consequent reluctance to exploit them.[18] The on-line data bases will acquaint the auditor with published materials concerning the latest design approaches, hardware and software, and the latest in current management theory and practice.

EVALUATING THE APPLICATION OF TECHNOLOGY

Benefits from the application of technology primarily affect audit efficiency and effectiveness. These aspects should have been incorporated as performance measures into the strategic plan for technology development. A discussion of some selected anticipated benefits follows:

1. Quality enhancement. Compliance with professional rules will be promoted by the capability of looking up the professional rules on-line. The Miami office of one Big Six firm reports that its staff delights in searching the NAARS literature file; the office's management believes that the popularity of the file, in addition to its merit, can be attributed to both a desire for guidance and an aversion to carrying volumes of literature. Moreover, this firm's in-

---

[18]Joanne Stidwell, "Improving the Systems Development Life Cycle," *CA Magazine* (Canada), 117 (July 1984), p. 117.

ternal data base facilitates on-line access to its own in-house advisories and technical decisions, thereby compounding its advantage over its competitors.

2. Positive effects on client relationships. Many clients have been critical of the auditors' slow adoption of automated auditing techniques. Juniors may still be seen reconciling bank accounts laboriously (and often inaccurately) when the task should have been eased by any of the following means, assuming that the auditor has satisfied himself as to program integrity: (a) reconciliation by the bank—when its procedures are acceptable from an audit perspective, (b) free public domain reconciliation programs (these may be located through the on-line data bases), (c) a selection of utility programs (such as those bundled with operating systems), (d) general-purpose computer audit programs, or (e) the reconciliation capabilities often furnished with disbursement packages.

3. Enhanced revenues resulting from innovative new product lines. For example, an estimate was previously cited relating to infrastructure repairs in Florida—$50 billion over a 10-year period; if just 1 percent were spent on construction management oversight—an activity for which auditors have outstanding credentials—the possible fees would be $500 million, or $50 million per annum.

4. Improved personnel utilization, and better control over administrative costs. Personnel with interdisciplinary qualifications may recognize uncontrolled client exposures, and thereby help to reduce audit detection risk. (For example, one firm found a civil engineer in its tax department; he was then utilized on construction oversight engagements and to advise client construction companies. He generated numerous control improvements.) However, technology may also help to evaluate, and possibly reduce, selected administrative costs. For example, OAG, the Official Airline Guides Electronic Edition (OAG is available on DIALOG and COMPUSERVE) provides unbiased, up-to-date travel information including schedules, fares, and seat availability; OAG can be used either for booking purposes or to monitor the activities of

an organization's travel agents. (Other purchased goods and services are available in electronic malls; however, the malls tend to be geared to the needs of retail buyers. Nonetheless, prices paid by or quoted to audit entities can be compared to on-line prices. Such comparisons may be especially interesting when they involve computers and related products.)

SUMMARY

The chapter has outlined the role of a designated individual to guide technological development in his audit organization. The need for systematic strategic planning was emphasized to establish an advantageous sequence of implementation priorities. Stress was also placed on the desirability of implementing on the job what has been learned, on involvement of senior people in the program, and on using technology to grow sophisticated new product lines.

The auditor's business acumen and his knowledge of the client's industry, business, and system are preconditions to implementation of technology-based techniques. Use of the on-line data bases was suggested as an initial step. Automation of audit procedures via audit software represented the second theme.

Compliance with *SAS 55* was mentioned; such compliance will be strengthened and facilitated by accessing the information contained in the on-line data bases. The point is that in order to improve audit effectiveness and efficiency, technology must become an integral part of the auditor's tool kit.

PART 4

THE NEW AUDIT IN ITS ENVIRONMENT

CHAPTER 12

RESEARCH ACROSS DISCIPLINES

There are questions which illuminate, and there are those that destroy. I was always taught to ask the first kind.

*Isaac Isador Rabi**

USER PERSPECTIVE: Items of Special Interest

EXECUTIVE HIGHLIGHTS: All readers
INTRODUCTION: All readers
THE RESEARCH DICHOTOMY: External auditors, internal auditors
PRACTICE RESEARCH: External auditors, internal auditors
RESEARCH REQUESTS: External auditors, internal auditors
THE FUTURE OF AUDIT RESEARCH: External auditors, internal auditors
RESEARCH ACROSS DISCIPLINES AND SECTORS: External auditors, internal auditors
SUMMARY: All readers

EXECUTIVE HIGHLIGHTS

All practitioners, regardless of individual inclinations, have become part-time audit researchers. The need for research has risen due to the rate at which innovative financial instruments have

---

*Quoted by Arno Penzias in *Ideas and Information* (New York: Simon & Schuster, 1989), p. 162.

been created, new threats have emerged, systems have become more complex, and the volume of transactions has increased.

There is a disconcerting lack of cohesiveness between academic and practice research. Typically, academic auditing research is conducted with a long-term perspective. Recently, much academic auditing research has been designed to understand the *demand* for auditing services within the context of the business and economic environment and the players' responses to that environment.

In contrast, practitioner research is likely to involve the audit process and its products. Practice research is usually driven by the need to complete a particular engagement, to respond to a regulatory initiative, or to develop a certain product.

Practitioners may be reluctant to read, much less apply, mathematically expressed or influenced academic research products; in many cases, the prejudice may be based on little more than lack of understanding. The solution lies in the creation of a basis for understanding.

Research conducted by an audit organization is likely to involve (1) emerging issues and (2) practitioner technical support. The nature of consultations between auditors, the placement within the organization of formal channels for such consultations, and the responsibilities of practice consultants differ from firm to firm. Technical support is usually given on request. There should, however, be a degree of assurance that support will be sought in all appropriate instances and that the right research questions will be asked.

The anticipated amalgamation of clients' management information systems, office automation, and computer-assisted manufacturing techniques will spur demand for audit research.

INTRODUCTION

The first three sections of this book have considered the effects of technology on an individual audit engagement and its personnel. The last section takes a broader view and discusses how these developments affect audit firms, internal audit departments, academic institutions, the profession, and the public—matters which concern auditors as professionals and citizens.

The present chapter deals with audit research in a time of rapid change. Audit research, which will be defined subsequently, means different things to practitioners and academics. However, the need for research is undeniable, given the rate at which innovative financial instruments have been created, new threats have emerged, systems have become more complex, and the volume of transactions has increased. Given the pace of developments, it no longer seems reasonable to expect others, including the AICPA, to perform required research and to issue guidelines and instructions within a relatively short time frame. To turn current problems into opportunities, all of the profession's research resources—including the best minds in academe and in practice—will need to be identified, encouraged, and enlisted in the cause of meeting the increased need for timely research.

When the term *research* is used in the context of accounting or auditing, an image of a scholarly paper comes to mind.[1] However, a significant segment of accounting and auditing research has historically emanated from practice. Firms and practitioners have made important contributions. Yet, the segment of practice output that has been published represents only a small part of total practitioner research. In a sense, all practitioners, regardless of their individual inclinations, have become part-time researchers. The challenge is to make their efforts as efficient and effective as possible.

The chapter explores the interaction of academics and practitioners, as well as the difficulties encountered in that interaction. Lack of cohesiveness between academic and practice research imperils the usefulness of research results to the practitioner and heightens the need for meaningful research answers. This chapter outlines audit research activities in which audit organizations, large and small, are (or should be) participating. Suggestions also are made for achieving better control over research conducted within firms and internal audit departments, and for

---

[1]*Deloitte & Touche Professors Handbook*, an adaptation of the *Handbook of Accounting and Auditing*, 2nd ed. (Boston: Warren, Gorham & Lamont, 1989), p. 35-2.

enhancing research productivity. There is also a brief discussion as to the possible application of audit research to solve broader social problems.

Author's Comment

While external and internal auditors are besieged by vocal critics, persons in scientific disciplines speak almost longingly of the desirability of conducting "audits" of research claims, attributions, and other verities in the physical sciences. Well-known audit techniques, including testing and sampling, would be used to promote the completeness and accuracy of scientific papers.

THE RESEARCH DICHOTOMY

In general, research can be classified into three categories: pure, applied, and product development. Pure research is intended to advance human knowledge, applied research is designed to convert laboratory ideas into pragmatic forms, and product development should result in commercial applications. Much academic research is of the pure variety, while practitioner research is largely concerned with developing, implementing, and supporting audit applications for the field.

The Nature of Academic Research

Typically, academic auditing research is conducted with a long-term perspective. Recently, much auditing research has been designed to understand the *demand* for auditing services within the context of the business and economic environment and the players' responses to that environment.

Wanda Wallace has written that sources of demand for audit services are explained by agency theory, information theory, and insurance hypothesis.[2] She considers each approach important to

---

[2]Wanda A. Wallace, "The Economic Role of the Audit in Free and Regulated Markets: A Review," in *Research in Accounting Regulation*, vol. 1, ed. John Gary Previts (Greenwich, Conn.: JAI Press, 1987), pp. 7–34.

the audit process, because of the "product attributes [of audits] including control dimensions, complementary services, enhanced reliability of the information system, and regulatory compliance." A brief discussion of each approach follows. The purpose is to convey the flavor of academic research, rather than to critique particular theories or the way in which they have been summarized.

Agency Theory
In Wallace's words, "Agency theory holds that agents [i.e., corporate managers], charged with certain decision-making responsibilities on behalf of principals [i.e., corporate owners] provide an incentive for being monitored [i.e., audited], in order to [protect] the principal's best interests."

Information Theory
Information economics holds that certain benefits, including reduction of risk, enhancement of decisions, and increased profits, may result from audits. Stated differently, the audit itself and the audit opinion are said to provide additional information of value to owners beyond management's financial statements. (Moves by the Securities and Exchange Commission (SEC) to make financial reports available on-line could significantly affect the timing, quantity, and quality of information submitted, and the auditor's role in its processing.)

Insurance Hypothesis
Wallace observes that the insurance dimension of an audit creates additional demand for audit services from trustees, investors, and creditors who wish to demonstrate their exercise of prudent care, and to ensure against losses by tapping the auditors' presumably deep pockets. An additional user group includes regulators who may wish to acquire some protection from public criticism by requiring auditor involvement.

The Relationship between Academic and Practice Research

Wallace has written that the theories discussed in the preceding paragraphs help to explain the market for audit services, as well as the regulatory activities that affect such services. She notes that "many unanswered questions persist . . . and [that research] has highlighted those aspects of the market for audit services and of the audit process which have yet to be explored."[3] In general, it seems fair to say that academic research has focused on the *demand* for audit services, while practitioner research is likely to have involved the audit process and its products.

In a university setting, research work often will be done by persons with academic credentials who may be educated in methodology but have little or no practical experience, especially at decision-making levels. In practice, relatively simple tasks, such as looking up examples of particular treatments, may be accomplished by the engagement team; more complex work will be guided by a research specialist—in relatively few cases, one with advanced academic training.

Practice research is usually driven by the need to complete a particular engagement, to respond to a regulatory initiative, or to develop a certain product. These needs involve tight target dates. The desire to achieve an advantage over a firm's competitors may be at the very core of a practice research project; hence, secrecy, (or even carefully managed disinformation) may be reflected in imposition of access restrictions on outsiders. However, in an academic environment, the research report is (in McLuhan's terminology) "medium and message"; moreover, time constraints tend to be less binding. Great effort may be expended in striving for perceived perfection; for example, comments may be sought from other academics, and resolved with considerable thought. Similarly, there will be a strong desire to gain professional and social preferment by sharing research results with one's peers by publishing in a refereed journal.

Academic research typically involves the construction of models and/or use of quantitative techniques. Practitioners may be reluctant to apply mathematically expressed, or even influenced, audit techniques; in many cases their prejudice may be based on lack of understanding. Academic research may be lim-

---

[3]Ibid., p. 27.

ited in scope by shoestring funding (which may even preclude data base searches) or by inadequate library facilities. Ironically, similar parochial tendencies exist with academic *and* practice researchers: both may draw on the literature available in such disciplines as economics, finance, philosophy, statistics, and psychology; and both may avoid law, medicine, and engineering. Ironically, the latter disciplines require professionals to cope with practice environments similar to that of auditing. (In other chapters, reference is made to risk management in law firms, and to the setting of practice standards in hospitals.)

Practice research has a significant advantage over academic research with respect to access to actual client data. Practitioners are traditionally reluctant to grant academics access to either clients or client data. This stems from professional requirements for confidentiality, a general disinclination on the part of clients and auditors to serve as guinea pigs or to see any benefit to themselves in a research venture, and auditors' frequent lack of understanding of research methodology.

Academic Research Has Had Little or No Impact on Practice

Over a decade ago, a workshop on the separate worlds of accounting and auditing research was held at Duke University; many attendees noted the need for achieving improved bonding between academic and practice researchers. Unfortunately, most problems explored then still plague present day researchers: (1) academics' lack of awareness of real world problems; (2) practitioners' poor comprehension of methodology; (3) academics' exclusion from access to data; and (4) practitioners' scant ability to understand academics' papers.

Author's Comment

The problem is to create a basis for understanding. One option, lending academics as faculty interns to audit organizations, has achieved moderate success. Unfortunately, many of the faculty persons' assignments have involved playing subordinated roles on audit engagements, rather than serving as audit researchers. Moreover, the problem also is one of involving practitioners more *directly* with academic research. Universities might find it useful to create advisory panels; the members could be given a title such as "distinguished practitioner." The practitioners could then be assigned to participate in specific projects; as they provide input, progress will be made in overcoming the problems mentioned earlier. A related aspect: in recent years there has been substantial growth in the number of incubators organized by far-sighted universities; an incubator is intended to convert ideas into products, and academic visions into the reality of an emerging business. Universities with incubators offer opportunities for research of all types and for the use of joint academic-practitioner research teams.

Sten Jonsson has argued for bringing practice and academic research into a tandem relationship. He observes that the American Accounting Association has distinguished three types of approaches to accounting theory: classical, decision usefulness, and information economics.[4] Sten Jonsson writes that the *classical* or *true income* approach has focused on a search for measurement techniques. Some authors have concentrated on income determination, others on valuation of balance sheet items; measurement has become increasingly complex due to such problems as inflation and currency fluctuation. The *decision usefulness* approach is intended to provide relevant and reliable information to decision makers. And, *information* theory marks a return to economics in that it treats information like other goods which should be produced according to market demand.[5] Jonsson points out that while there are several choices of theory, there is only one practice; hence the way to choose between theoretical approaches is to study practice and then to choose.

Jonsson says that the role of scientific research in the development of good accounting practices should *not* be overestimated. "It is not that rational arguments are not used in standard setting, but that there is a competition between bases of rationality." He goes on to say that

---

[4]Committee on Concepts and Standards for External Financial Reports, *Statement on Accounting Theory and Acceptance*, (Sarasota: American Accounting Association, 1970).
[5]Sten Jonsson, *Accounting Regulation and Elite Structures: Driving Forces in the Development of Accounting Policy*, (Chichester, U.K.: John Wiley & Sons, 1988), pp. 4–44.

there is little hope of finding the scientific quality of accounting through reasoning in terms of a measurement theory. . . . Even if it is obviously possible to increase the rationality of accounting procedures, accounting per se can hardly become scientific. The very foundation for that is missing, since accounting implies that someone is accountable to someone else. [Consequently], none of the parties can reasonably assume the independence and neutrality of the scientist. . . . The quest for methods . . . has to be reconciled with the awareness that general acceptance will be gained only by those accounting principles that are accepted by several parties.[6]

PRACTICE RESEARCH

Consultation

Some practice research had its origins in firm colleagueship; within an audit organization, informal consultation with one's peers promotes audit quality and furthers individual professional development. Usually, staff members seek the counsel of qualified individuals; this ad hoc consultation process can be highly successful, especially when it is endorsed and supported by an audit organization's management; eventually, such a firm's atmosphere will become charged with intellectual and professional excitement. However, at times it may be necessary to consult with others on a more systematic basis in accordance with policies established by the audit organization. (The AICPA's membership services also provide practitioner research support; as noted, the number to call is 1-800-223-4158.)

The nature of consultations between auditors, the placement within the organization of formal channels for such consultations, and the responsibilities of the consultants differ from firm to firm. In the case of smaller firms, such consultations may be handled by one person on a part-time basis.

In a large firm the consultations group may be centralized or decentralized; it may do its own research, or it may use the ser-

---

[6]Ibid.

vices of researchers, either assigned to or organizationally independent of the consultations group. Each audit organization should choose arrangements that best meet its needs, conduce to a free flow of information, and conform to the corporate culture. (The author prefers a centralized consultations group, supported by integral research, because the consultant(s) would be on-line with the world outside, as well as within the organization.)

The Emergence of Practice Research

As noted, audit research personnel may support practice office consultations at larger firms. Smaller firms are likely to engage in audit research on a more informal and part-time basis. (Parenthetically, it should be said that the time may be especially opportune for activating research consortia for groups of smaller firms.) In any event, research by audit entities is likely to involve (1) emerging issues and (2) technical support.

Emerging Issues

Communicate with Standard-Setting Bodies
Records maintained by standard-setters show that correspondence is received customarily from the very large firms, and from a revolving constituency of people who perceive that their "ox is being gored" by emerging rules. Surprisingly, smaller firms are generally not heard on the issues, even when their practice is directly affected.

Author's Comment

Several years ago the GAO redrafted its Yellow Book. One change involved a new continuing professional education (CPE) requirement for government auditing practitioners. The draft rules seemingly put smaller accountants into a disadvantageous competitive position. Moreover, the draft language was not clear and presaged difficulties in implementation. Yet, it was reported that very few smaller firms were heard from.

Firms should establish specific criteria to help decide whether to respond to invitations to comment on a particular issue being considered by regulators. Possible criteria include: the extent to which the audit organization is qualified to comment on the matter; the extent of public interest in the issue; the likelihood of disagreement and the importance of being recorded as disagreeing; the likelihood of agreement and the importance of being recorded as concurring; and the need for recommending clarification of an issue, or coverage of additional aspects.

The preparation of responses will be simplified and the contents of communications improved if the audit organization has (1) a policy statement or mission statement defining its posture vis-à-vis its various publics or constituencies—including clients, employees, financial statement users, and regulators; and (2) if it abstracts, maintains, and retrieves its prior comments. If *both* conditions are not present, the stage will be set for successive iterations of Walt Whitman's dictum: "Do I contradict myself? Very well then, I contradict myself." Even if self-contradiction has merit for a poet, the same may not hold true for an auditor.

Author's Comment

The input of the preparer community (i.e., of clients) can be useful for setting enforceable and realistic accounting and auditing standards; therefore, an auditor may wish to seek preparer views on important emerging issues. Solicitation of client views has obvious perils, which have drawn comments from the profession's critics; yet, the author is not aware of a single instance in which preparers leaned on a firm to submit a desired response. To the contrary, some preparers even applied their own perspective and suggested more efficient and effective compliance mechanisms; the positioning of the accountant between regulator and preparer may act as a filter that enhances the quantity and quality of feedback.

Recognize Emerging Issues

Audit organizations may benefit from timely recognition of issues as they emerge; such recognition may help to even out the audit organization's research work load and should alert all personnel to impending changes. Most importantly, an assessment must be made of the effect of new regulatory initiatives on audit risk management, as well as on particular audit procedures. In addition, auditors may be put in a better position to advise their clients on how to benefit from new rules, or how to minimize any resulting pain.

Develop Explanations, Policy Statements, Publications, and Training Materials

Partners and staff represent the primary audience for such releases. The creation of materials involves tasks similar to the following:

- Research the topic to obtain an understanding of the subject matter, determine the issues involved, and ascertain if positions have been taken on the issues previously.

- See whether any material developed by others is available and determine to what extent and with what type of permission this material can be quoted or adapted.

- Develop a problem solution approach with consideration of time restrictions, costs, and benefits. In some cases, the approach will include reviewing existing literature and soliciting the views of personnel knowledgeable in the area.

- Complete the work.

- Draft a memo documenting the research methodology, the sources consulted, the relevant issues, and the tentative conclusions.

- Circulate the memo for review and comment.

- If necessary, arrange field tests, or quality reviews.

Technical Support

Audit organizations primarily give technical support to those who request it. However, there should be a degree of assurance that support *will* be sought in *all* appropriate instances. To an extent, that concern can be met by bulletins, instructions, constant monitoring, internal quality control reviews, and peer reviews. Nonetheless, partners and managers must also be alert to unusual accounting, reporting, and disclosure, and should determine whether consultation and support were sought; for example, standing instructions could be issued to a report department or to a librarian to bring all variations from the norm to the attention of designated individuals, or to circulate unusual reports to partners.

The following types of research are likely to be performed in connection with technical support:

Auditing Procedures Problems

The complexity of the tasks makes it necessary for researchers to be highly knowledgeable with respect to efficiency and effectiveness of audit procedures. Representative assignments are as follows:

1. Participating in understanding and utilizing technology as implemented in the client's system, or as necessary to accomplish an effective audit.
2. Assisting in tailoring audit programs and procedures to the needs of companies in specific industries.
3. Designing or implementing an innovative or difficult audit procedure that may have become necessary because of inherent risk, deficient or questionable client documentation, or special regulatory requirements.
4. Helping to develop appropriate reporting language for special or unusual engagements.

Accounting Principles Questions

These may be prompted by difficulties in interpreting the professional literature. Searches of background materials assembled or developed by standard-setters may be helpful in establishing the regulators' intent. Reports issued by various enterprises (as shown in such data bases as NAARS, DISCLO, and 10-K) and the views of industry specialist partners and managers represent important resources helpful to arriving at correct interpretations.

Law and Regulation Implementation

Performance audits (a term which refers to economy and efficiency *and* program audits) for government units or nonprofit institutions represent an example of the type of audit likely to require research assistance. These audits may be complicated by difficulties experienced in determining lawmakers' intentions; very few legislatures set clear program objectives and/or measurement criteria, to say nothing of objective and controlled techniques for gathering feedback on program progress. Therefore, the researchers may have to (1) consult minutes of legislative committee hearings, (2) seek the assistance of individual legislators, or (3) work with the auditee in arriving at mutually acceptable measurement criteria.

Author's Comment

The Foreign Corrupt Practices Act, passed in 1977, included an adaptation of auditing terminology to accomplish very different government objectives. Consequently, many auditors performed research to determine the degree of documentation (or redocumentation) of control systems to be undertaken by their clients. Similarly, in 1989 and 1990 many clients consulted their auditors regarding the impact of the AICPA's expectation gap statements and the Treadway Commission's recommendations on their organizations and control procedures.

Item

Some years ago a review was made of results achieved by the Saudi Arabian literacy program.[7] While the results *were* impressive, no objective measure of literacy had been established at the beginning of the program. Thus, it was unclear whether *literacy* referred to ability to pass a specified elementary school grade, whether it meant passing a uniform exam, whether it was reflected in capacity to read from the Holy Quran, or all three. Such criteria could have facilitated measurement of program progress, redirection as necessary, and last but not least, the conduct of the program audit.

Auditing Theory Research

Such research is usually prompted by ongoing evaluations/modifications of an internal or external auditor's engagement approach. Not surprisingly, the technical parameters or audit approaches of audit firms and internal audit departments show similarities; however, most firms have added bells and whistles in a quest for brand identification. Unfortunately, some may have curtailed, deleted, or labeled "optional" otherwise desirable procedures in the hope of improving engagement profitability. Because of these differences, as well as differences among firms in their approach to technology, it behooves members of audit committees and others participating in auditor selection to ask probing questions to identify the auditor with the "right stuff"; in other words, an external audit firm should be a good fit with its client.

---

[7]This review represented research conducted by Salih M. Jadallah, who was a doctoral student at the time. Dr. Jadallah obtained his doctorate from Texas Technical University.

New Product Development

Practice in newer product lines (fraud auditing, proactive auditing, operational auditing, compliance auditing, etc.) is likely to require research support. Activities include identifying research resources and performing literature reviews, together with the design of new policies, procedures, and instructions, and possibly, the development of training materials.

RESEARCH REQUESTS

Practice office partners and managers, including the previously discussed practice consultants, represent the major source of research requests. Many requesters will merely seek references to authoritative literature concerning a particular subject, or an example or precedent for a certain accounting treatment or disclosure. They should be encouraged to perform these simple tasks by themselves with the aid of the research tools available to them, such as the Electronic Index to Technical Pronouncements (EITP), the public on-line data bases, or the firm's in-house data base.

The research request form bears on research quality and productivity. It helps to see that the right question has been asked and that the right guidance will be provided within an appropriate time frame. It should call for a description of the request, background information relating to the client, and a statement of the problem. The person assigned to respond must first determine whether the question should have been asked at all, or whether the requester should have developed the answer by himself.

A second concern is more important: there must be assurance that the *right* question has been asked; that assessment will be made by the assigned researcher based on the fact pattern, knowledge of the requester, awareness of actual and emerging rules, sensitivity to matters involving audit risk or possible litigation, and judicious questioning of the requester. Since the researcher may not discover the right question, the individual in charge of the activity should make a further review of research requests.

The research request form should also ask the requester to describe the type of information she desires; if examples of reports are needed, it should ask how many. The request form should also include space for indicating the reference source, such as the data base publisher, and the file. If a request involves the on-line data bases, the requester may also be asked to suggest search terms or key words helpful to searching. A research request form has been included as Figure 12–1.

Processing the Research Request

When the request has been evaluated, an approach must be developed to solve the problem. Research sources include: (1) on-line data bases, (2) CD-ROM, (3) an in-house data base together with supporting hard copy files, (4) the audit organization's library, (5) public and other libraries (or even other firms' libraries where exchange arrangements have been negotiated), (6) other firms' publications, and (7) miscellaneous resources; the latter include the AICPA's Financial Report Surveys (drawn from the NAARS data base), the Accountants' Index (available on-line from ORBIT Search Service, and the minutes and releases of the Emerging Issues Task Force (EITF), available on NAARS. Another resource should not be overlooked: academics represent a pool of trained resource personnel that is available and prepared to resolve research issues.

A supplementary comment seems appropriate in regard to CD-ROM offerings, which resemble cassette recordings and represent data base contents at a point in time. CD-ROM overcomes some weaknesses of the on-line products that are not readily predictable, such as difficulty of learning, undependable transmission, and charges that can be high, as well as difficult to verify. CD-ROM has brought searching to a much larger audience, resulting in an increased awareness of on-line services and their offerings. It is quite possible that over the long term, mixed CD-ROM and on-line solutions will become prevalent.[8]

---

[8]George Vaveris, "Peaceful Coexistence Between On-line and CD-ROM," *Searchlight* 18, no. 7 (July 1990), pp. 2–3.

FIGURE 12–1
Research Request

Client _____
Engagement partner _____
Requester _____ Date needed _____
Output or information desired, including number of examples _____

Problem statement or research objective and search terms, if known _____

Background, and results of research already performed _____

Authoritative literature (if known) _____

Research sources, search terms, and approach, if known _____

On-line data bases, if known _____

Scope, time, or cost restrictions and reasons _____

Researcher's comments, especially as to research objective and
approach _____

Research Management

In the future, most research is likely to be an ongoing process, rather than a one-shot deal. The essence of research management has been conveyed eloquently by Arno Penzias: "Managing successful research depends far more on ensuring the flow of ideas between individuals than on rigid direction from the top. . . . Once a research idea proves ready for development, a much larger number of people becomes involved and careful coordination becomes essential, but rarely before."[9]

THE FUTURE OF AUDIT RESEARCH

Jonsson's view that academic research should be anchored in practice represents a cogent call for bringing practice and academic research into synchronization. Time would seem to be of the essence. The urgency is created by the anticipated near-term amalgamation of management information systems, office automation, and computer-assisted manufacturing techniques. (Some academics have pointed out in Cassandra-like fashion that failure by academic researchers to deal with live issues may invite the creation by large professional or industrial firms or by practitioner organizations of their own "captive" universities. In this connection it was even reported that the New Zealand profession had given thought to the creation of a new university-level institution!)

A persuasive case for practice-oriented research was implicit in a recent monograph commissioned by the Institute of Internal Auditors Research Foundation. In the early phases of the study, a substantial number of prominent auditors were asked to list factors that they believed would have the most significant impact on auditing by the year 2000.

The output of the study consisted of a large number of forecast happenings classified into the following categories:

---

[9]Penzias, *Ideas and Information,* p. 206.

1. Auditor's future tool kit—powerful computer workstations.
2. The control environment and systems applications.
3. Audit testing—control testing and substantive testing.
4. The role of auditing.
5. Organizational structure of the auditing function.
6. Skills required of the auditor.
7. Education and training of the future auditor.[10]

The study forecast abundant opportunities for accounting and auditing researchers who have a flair for developing solutions to practical problems. A different study, which reached similar conclusions, was edited by A. Rashad Abdel-khalik and Ira Solomon. In this monograph, auditing was viewed broadly as a human evaluation process that measures adherence to certain norms; the outcome of that process is used to formulate an opinion which is communicated to interested parties. Auditors were described as *employing certain approaches and techniques* and *adapting to and using complex technologies* in *forming judgments/decisions* about a *subject matter* within *constraints* of the audit environment.

The research issues identified with respect to complex technology were subdivided into two groups: technology research topics and auditing research topics. An excerpt, which describes auditing research topics resulting from new systems applications, conveys the flavor of the publication:

- "The extent to which the auditor will need to be involved in the development of decentralized systems.
- The development of guidelines to determine when the auditor should be involved because a particular application is financially significant or sensitive for security and control purposes.
- The effect of new system development on auditors; that is, ongoing modification of the *auditor's* system may be neces-

---

[10]Gary L. Holstrum, Theodore J. Mock, and Robert N. West, *The Impact of Technology on Auditing—Moving Into the 21st Century*, (Altamonte Springs, Fla.: The Institute of Internal Auditors Research Foundation, 1988), pp. 175–180.

sary, thus increasing the costs of auditing *client* system changes.

- If dynamic change processes are being used by the client, ways of obtaining assurance that security exposure has been minimized."

Moveover, the authors evaluated each recommended research issue in terms of audit questions raised in the literature; these audit questions included: evidence type, sources, and quality, expansion of scope, and legal liability. This enrichment resulted in the publication of a virtual catalog of practice-oriented research projects.[11]

The *Deloitte & Touche Professors Handbook* puts the matter succinctly:

> Professional research by academic and practicing accountants is essential to solving the many complex problems faced by corporations, to keeping users of financial information informed, and to dealing with and mitigating professional risk. . . . For both academic and practicing professionals, the information explosion will necessitate much more use of sophisticated research tools, data bases, and methodologies.[12]

RESEARCH ACROSS DISCIPLINES AND SECTORS

For convenience, research may be classified into horizontal and vertical groupings. Horizontal research would seek information which cuts across different professions. In some cases, relatively familiar search statements may be used to search data bases pertaining to other professions. (The task could be complicated by a lack of uniform search protocols, the need for experience in modifying search strategies, and, given a nonfinancial environment, the searcher's encounter with unfamiliar concepts.) There are

---

[11]American Accounting Association, Auditing Section, *Research Opportunities in Auditing: The Second Decade*, ed. A. Rashad Abdel-khalik and Ira Solomon (Sarasota: American Accounting Association, Auditing Section, 1988), p. 75.

[12]*Deloitte & Touche Professors Handbook*, p. 35-17.

some options relating to cross-disciplinary searching. These are to obtain additional training in nonfinancial on-line data bases and integrate that training with one's background, or to utilize the services of an outside information provider, possibly one skilled in retrieving information from a particular data base.

The vertical approach represents an adaptation of search techniques beyond a particular engagement to meet broader needs. In other words, if a concept is valid on a particular engagement, it may be transferable to an audit entity's own operations, including such support functions as marketing, personnel management, or research, or to the solution of professional or even global problems. An international example may be appropriate.

Item

A committee of the International Section of the American Accounting Association assembled a monograph to show how shortages of accountants, and failure to address control issues in a timely manner, had resulted in the buildup of eventually insoluble problems in the "less developed countries." The monograph included a chapter on bureaucratic corruption which cited examples from three nations. A summing up of the corruption cycle highlighted the crucial position of auditing:[13] The phases include: a corrupt system. Reform. Extensive audit efforts; progressively more severe penalties. The achievement of an equilibrium between corruption and countervailing efforts. An easing up on such efforts. Collusion among corrupt officials. Ultimately, reform becomes the system.[14]

Two considerations stood out relative to the aforementioned corruption cycle: first, the timing of phases appeared to be predictable; second, there was some evidence that the negative phases could have been postponed and their effects mitigated, if (preventive, detective, and corrective) controls had been recommended and installed.

---

[13]Francis T. Liu, "A Dynamic Model of Corruption Deterrence," *Journal of Public Economics* 31 (November 1986), pp. 215–36.

[14]*Role of Auditors in Solving the Problems of the Less Developed Nations* (American Accounting Association, International Section, 1989) available as working paper 1989-X through Florida International University, School of Accounting, University Park, Miami, FL 33199.

It is easy to think of a *potential* application closer to home. Competitiveness, or lack thereof, has been singled out as an important problem confronting U.S. business. Robert Reich has suggested six steps to smooth the path to competitiveness:

- Scanning the globe for new technologies.
- Linking government research and development funding to commercial products.
- Integrating corporate research with production.
- Managing the establishment of technological standards.
- Investing in the technological learning of workers.
- Providing a good basic education to all citizens.[15]

With respect to most of the six points, one would think that the factfinding and documentation techniques honed by external (and especially by internal) auditors would be tailor-made for exploring whether there is a lack of competitiveness, what caused it, and how to redress matters.

SUMMARY

The rate of technological change will accelerate. Moreover, public expectations of the auditor, together with new legislative strictures, are likely to create new obligations and opportunities. Consequently, geometrically increased demand for audit research services can be anticipated, especially with respect to the supply of audit services and the nature of the audit process. In order to meet these expectations, it will be necessary to pool the resources of all parties—internal and external auditors, and academic and practice researchers.

Challenges exist in both the practice and academic environments: in practice, the cry is for a better-educated auditor; in academe, competent researchers, with solid training in accounting

---

[15]Robert B. Reich, "The Quiet Path to Technological Preeminence," *Scientific American* 261, no. 4 (October 1989), pp. 41–47.

and auditing, are at a premium. Steps should be taken immediately to increase supply in this very long-term pipeline.

Academic and practice research are two sides of the same coin. As noted elsewhere in this book, a profession must do more than simply meet public demand; it should anticipate that demand. In other words, it should become more causative, and less reactive. Researchers lead that effort. Accounting and auditing research can also be expected to have significant and beneficial effects on the efficiency and effectiveness of audits, and hopefully, on the development of solutions to national and international problems.

CHAPTER 13

THE ACCOUNTANT'S ORGANIZATION

Our organizational structure differs little from the one the Israelites adopted on their march from Egypt to the Promised Land—"Leaders of thousands, leaders of hundreds, leaders of fifties, and leaders of tens." (Exodus 17:21)

Arno Penzias*

USER PERSPECTIVE: **Items of Special Interest**

EXECUTIVE HIGHLIGHTS: All readers

INTRODUCTION: All readers

THE MARKET FOR IDEAS: All readers

THE ORGANIZATIONAL PYRAMID: External auditors, internal auditors

THE CHANGING FACES OF THE SPECIALISTS: External auditors, internal auditors

THE REALIGNMENT OF TECHNICAL EFFORT: External auditors, internal auditors

HUMAN RESOURCE MANAGEMENT: All readers

QUALITY CONTROL AND ASSURANCE: External auditors, internal auditors

RISK MANAGEMENT—SCREENING CLIENTS: External auditors

ADMINISTRATIVE MATTERS: External auditors, internal auditors

SUMMARY: All readers

**From *Ideas and Information* (New York: Simon & Schuster, Inc., 1989), pp. 194–95.*

EXECUTIVE HIGHLIGHTS

Contrary to Cassandra-like predictions, computers have strengthened individual creativity and influence. Hence, organizations should emphasize the development of people rather than methodology. Emphasis must be given to long-term planning and interaction with employees, especially as to their professional and personal development.

A deliberate response is necessary to adapt the impacts of technology and of public and regulatory expectations to audit organizations, to the systems which serve them, and to the people who work in them.

The free flow of ideas among audit partners and managers, and up and down the line, does not require organizational restructuring. Technology can make the existing order work by linking the participants in an integrated flow of information. However, the increasing complexity of engagements can be expected to lead to an expansion in the numbers of experienced personnel, relative to those who are more junior. Most observers think that the trend will continue; in time, the organizational pyramid may come to resemble a rectangle.

The industry specialist, knowledgeable and known within a particular industry, is a familiar species. A newer functional specialist will devote himself to aspects of auditing that require technical knowledge or experience. Functional specialists are likely to engage in two types of services: the first represents audit support; it may involve diagnostic approaches to determine whether more extensive specialized work ought to be performed. The second service represents an engagement, often nonrecurring, which is under the specialist's control.

Senior personnel will participate more actively in the sensitive aspects of audit engagements: understanding the business and its inherent risk, touring plants, and behavioral interviewing. The time required will be reallocated from internal staff work and administrative activities.

INTRODUCTION

The preceding chapter noted that what had long applied to tax persons now held true for auditors as well—they need to spend much of their time in research, an activity that bears significantly on audit efficiency and effectiveness. This chapter deals with the broad effects technology will have on the auditor's organization, the kind of people he hires, and the nature of the workplace he creates for them.

No aspect of the auditor's work has been immune from change. Government pressure has propelled many significant revisions to long-standing auditing practices. As a consequence, auditing threatens to become more compliance oriented (read: mechanistic). The present chapter endeavors to reemphasize the intellectual challenge of auditing and the humanistic interaction among practitioners.

In addition to government initiatives, change also has been paced by (1) new or reaffirmed social expectations and (2) technological tools, especially the microcomputer. Change, which previously affected every aspect of an engagement, has started to influence the organization of public accounting firms and of internal audit departments. The author believes that a deliberate response is necessary to adapt the impacts of technology and of public and regulatory expectations to audit organizations, the systems which serve them, and the people who work in them. The chapter content is overlaid by concern for the individual and his personal and professional development. The reason is this: an audit organization offers nothing to its clients (or, in the case of internal auditors, to corporate management), other than the individual and collective professional judgments of its practitioners.

THE MARKET FOR IDEAS

A Sea of Opportunity

Seven years ago John Naisbitt and Patricia Aburdene published *Megatrends*, a book described by one reviewer as a field guide to the future. The work turned out to be substantially accurate;

some attributed that accuracy to the authors' alleged penchant for dwelling on trends which were already well under way. (Even if that were true, the authors would still deserve credit for trend recognition.) In any event, Naisbitt and Aburdene's update should be of interest.[1] Only three trends will be mentioned:

1. The global economic boom of the 1990's.
2. The privatization of the welfare state.
3. The triumph of the individual.

The flavor of Naisbitt and Aburdene's book comes across in the following excerpts: "We are [building] an international information . . . system. In telecommunications we are moving to a single worldwide information network. . . . We are moving toward the capability to communicate anything to anyone, anywhere, [in] any form. . . . Financial services, the most evolved sector of the global economy, have more to do with electronics than with finance or services."[2]

What does *Megatrends 2000* have to do with auditing? Surely this: simple monitoring of trends should permit auditors to discern windows of opportunity! The on-line data bases are particularly valuable in identifying and analyzing possible opportunities. Each of the following examples relates to activities for which U.S. practitioners have good credentials.

1. With respect to the accountant's role in developing nations, Dr. Miguel Angel Alarcon Rios, the president of the Interamerican Accounting Association, has observed: "Every public accountant is necessarily involved in the social and economic development process of each country. . . . [h]is or her participation is a clearly established responsibility."[3]

2. Despite some speculation, little is known of the disposition intended to be made after 1992 of the European Economic Com-

---

[1] John Naisbitt and Patricia Aburdene, *Megatrends 2000: Ten New Directions for the 1990's* (New York: William Morrow, 1990).

[2] Ibid., pp. 23, 94.

[3] Miguel Angel Alarcon Rios, "The President Says," *Interamerican Bulletin*, November 1990, p. 1.

munity's accounting directives. Some think that no additional directives are likely. Nonetheless, if existing directives just continue to move toward implementation, accountants might soon have to review separate European and/or regional financial statements, along with reconciliations of such statements to U.S. generally accepted accounting principles.

3. Elsewhere, mention has been made of Electronic Data Interchange (EDI). The problem is that weaknesses in internal control, accompanied by inadequate security, are likely to go international along with EDI.

4. Whether to privatize typically involves a study of financial factors, as well as of intangibles, in order to arrive at a determination in the public (as well as private) interest.

An important statement in *Megatrends 2000* concerns the true effect of computers: "The very nature of an information economy shifts the focus away from the state to the individual. Unlike a widespread Orwellian-instructed view that computers would tighten the control of the state over individuals, we have learned that computers strengthen the power of individuals and weaken the power of the state."[4]

Organization Planning and the Individual

Planning mechanisms have been described in the accounting and auditing literature. In an earlier work the author provided this description of planning:

1. Establishing general goals, dealing with corporate purpose, mission, and organizational values.
2. Analyzing current and future environmental conditions.
3. Assessing corporate strengths and weaknesses.
4. Establishing specific objectives.

---

[4]Naisbitt and Aburdene, *Megatrends 2000*, p. 95.

5. Developing the plans.
6. Securing agreement among the planners.
7. Disseminating plan provisions.[5]

However, public accountants or internal auditors gain few tangible or psychic rewards by creating structured plans. The emphasis should be on people, rather than methodology. In the words of Arno Penzias: "Sophisticated technology leads to organizational complexity. But, technology builds on knowledge, and knowledge begins with the ideas that human beings create. Thus the technology to meet the future needs of our complex society will very likely owe its foundation to people who do their best work in groups of ones and twos." Penzias adds:

> We must never stray from the perspective of the individual, "the reason each of us chooses to be here." For most of us, that turns out to be the opportunity to work with others, doing something we think is important. . . . Making a meaningful difference on a global scale will take the best use of the minds and machines that our society can muster. Machines need direction from human minds, and human minds need inspiration from human leaders.[6]

Given today's emphasis on the individual and his contributions, it is all the more surprising that some professional firms may not have given sufficient attention to such basic matters as interaction among partners. With reference to this subject as it relates to lawyers, Bradford W. Hildebrandt has written:

> Partners [may not be] headed in the right direction:
> 1. They have different personal goals.
> 2. They have different expectations from . . . practice . . . and from partnership in a firm.
> 3. They have different approaches to the practice.

---

[5]Felix Pomeranz, *Managing Capital Budget Projects: A Preemptive Audit Approach* (New York: John Wiley & Sons, 1984), p. 28.

[6]Arno Penzias, *Ideas and Information*, pp. 206, 219.

Hildebrandt recommends attacking the problem of faulty or nonexistent communication among partners. He notes that strategic planning "must begin with a discussion of firm values and philosophies and how those will be melded into the firm's future profile, as well as the direction the firm must take to achieve that profile.[7] A similar emphasis on reconciling personal and firm goals appears in a recent article in *The CPA Journal*. The authors reported that a CPA firm's strategic direction had been influenced by a major planning study which addressed such matters as personal goals vis-à-vis firm goals.[8] Of course, the preceding references drew on firms of some size. Nonetheless, the same fundamental considerations apply to a small firm: long-term planning and interaction with employees, especially as to their professional and personal development.

With reference to staff management in accounting firms, Joseph W. Larson has observed, "firms that understand their staff's concerns will have fewer turnover problems." He said that "CPA firms . . . will have to understand how new staff members perceive their firms and which simple changes in operations and attitude can greatly enhance morale." For example, he suggested that "supervisors must understand [that] taking a vacation or long weekend isn't a sign of lack of dedication, but of the employee's recognition that he needs a break before he can be at his best again."[9]

The free flow of ideas among the partners, and indeed, up and down the line, does not require organizational restructuring. Technology can make an existing order work by linking the participants in an integrated flow of information. For example, in a recent article Terry Campbell advised auditors to "check the electronic room for a new way to make meetings work." He described

---

[7]Bradford W. Hildebrandt, "Personal Relationships at the Firm," *Law Office Management*, May 8, 1990, p. 4.

[8]Greg M. Thibadoux, John Alvis, and Marilyn M. Helms, "Management of an Accounting Practice: Questionnaire Used as Part of Long-Range Planning Study May Be Helpful," *The CPA Journal* 59, no. 10 (October 1989), pp. 70–74.

[9]Joseph W. Larson, "Firms that Understand Their Staff's Concerns Will Have Fewer Turnover Problems," *Journal of Accountancy*, February 1991, pp. 31–34.

such a room as providing an open forum for raising issues, identifying underlying assumptions, and allowing participants to rank their preferences—the very activities likely to take place in engagement planning.[10]

THE ORGANIZATIONAL PYRAMID

Partner-to-staff ratios differ from firm to firm; the ratio depends on the nature of the services rendered, the type of clientele and the perceived risk, the responsibilities assigned to or assumed by partners and staff respectively, firm size, and even firm philosophy. It is difficult to obtain reliable information on prevailing partner-to-staff ratios, let alone recommend guidelines; moreover, the title "partner" can describe differing employment or compensation arrangements. For larger firms, the ratio has been reported to range between 1:8 and 1:15; the ratio tends to be lower for smaller firms.

The bare statistics would be of interest primarily to recent graduates about to enter the profession; this is true because historically there may have been some correlation between partner earnings and the leverage which those partners exert relative to staff. In other words, higher ratios were likely to carry higher eventual rewards. However, the ratio can be expected to decline; the increasing complexity of engagements will lead to an expansion in the numbers of experienced personnel relative to those who are more junior. The lower partner/staff ratio could have an important bearing on individual career plans, as well as on firms' plans for personnel procurement. Most observers think that the trend will continue; in time, the organizational pyramid may come to resemble a rectangle. The most desirable practitioner response to this problem would involve enhancement of the value of services to clients followed by fee increases.

---

[10]Terry L. Campbell, "Technology Update: Group Decision Support Systems," *Journal of Accountancy*, July 1990, pp. 47–50.

THE CHANGING FACES OF THE SPECIALISTS

Two different types of specialists can be found; they may be referred to as industry specialists and functional specialists. Of course, the industry specialist, knowledgeable and known within a particular industry, is a familiar species. The newer functional specialist devotes himself to aspects of auditing that require technical knowledge or experience. The distinction between the two types of specialists is still evolving. The nature of the specialties, the number of specialists, the time devoted by them to their specialty, and the essence of their interaction with the practice depend on each audit entity's needs.

The Industry Specialist

A generation ago, specialties were recognized because clients were engaged in an arcane business or used unique terminology. Lately, government regulation, particularly the existence of statutory (i.e., non-GAAP) accounting treatments, has tended to define specialties. In any event, there has been a reduction in the *number* of industries considered to be the province of specialists, while life in specialty industries has become immensely more complicated. Some specialties are set apart by entrance restrictions; government—with mandated experience, education, and continuing professional education requirements—is an example. Other industries may become specialties because of high inherent risk or particular auditing difficulties; this category includes S&Ls, credit unions, pension plans, small insurance companies, and some health care providers. The author believes strongly that high-risk situations should be avoided by a firm unless it has a lot of clients in an industry, or one very large client. Certainly, a decision as to whether to specialize in an industry should be made only after profound study.

The Functional Specialist

The author believes that a shift has occurred from the industry specialist to the newer functional specialist. Functional specialists are needed for three reasons: (1) to deal with emerging technology, or with techniques that require a high level of technical experience or education; (2) to provide guidance with respect to audit risk management; and (3) to research, evaluate, and bring to market new product lines that promise to enhance the audit organization's performance or profitability. Among other things, functional specialists serve as resource persons to the audit staff, as discussed later in this chapter. The likely specialists include: (1) a management information systems auditor (reviews both general and application controls in computer-based environments; evaluates data base design and operation; assesses network controls; develops custom software, etc.; (2) a security analyst knowledgeable in matters involving control over protection of assets (conducts inspections; evaluates security program; arranges special surveillance, etc.); and (3) a forensic accountant (advises with respect to engagement strategy; supports insurance claims; conducts interrogations, etc.).

Management should avoid the establishment of unnecessary specialties, and the investiture of unnecessary specialists; audit risk and market demand should drive placements. Some of the questions that should be answered before installing functional specialists are:

- Will the specialist support the current audit practice only? Or, will he market his specialty as a separate service? How will his time be allocated and controlled?

- What credentials should be held by a specialist recruited into the firm? How can the specialist's professional development be assured? What is his career path? Is it possible to transfer to the specialty from the audit staff or vice versa?

- How is he assigned to engagements? Who recognizes a need for his services? What assurance exists that the specialist is involved in *all* of the *right* engagements? (The master tracking sheet, Figure 9–4, which offers an indication of the seriousness of uncontrolled threats, could be referred to when making specialist assignments.)

- What does the specialist actually do on an engagement? How will his performance be measured?

- To whom does he report technically and administratively for different types of engagements?

Functional specialists are likely to render two types of services. The first represents audit support; it may involve diagnostic approaches to determine whether more extensive specialized work ought to be performed. The second service represents an engagement, often nonrecurring, which is under the specialist's control. There are many advantages to such engagements: they showcase the organization's services, they are welcomed by the client—because they often help to solve known problems—and they may be highly profitable.

The author believes that a management information systems auditor should sign off on *all* engagements, unless the systems are *totally* manual; the management information systems auditor is in a position to apply professional judgment to determine the nature, timing, and extent of his involvement. Of course, if the functional specialist is to make an informed determination, he has to be provided with focused and meaningful information by the engagement team.

The Core Group

Assuming that at least one, and possibly more than one, expert has been assigned to a particular functional specialty, he may be established as a core group. A core group should be a separate profit center; in addition to rendering client services, the member(s) would engage in research in their specialty, maintain quality control, and act as resource personnel in staff training. When assigned to audit support, they would report to the audit manager, and would be accountable to him for proper performance of their duties. When assigned to an engagement in their specialty, they would work under the direction of a functional superior. Regardless of the nature of their current assignment and physical location, they would exchange technical and administrative information among themselves and with others with a need to know.

The core group concept is applicable to external, internal, or government auditing. In a decentralized audit organization which espouses centralized control and guidance, a core group at headquarters could render services such as quality control, audit research, training, technical support of field auditors, and overall coordination. (Some credit Exxon with pioneering the core group approach in its internal audit operations.)

THE REALIGNMENT OF TECHNICAL EFFORT

The audit guide *Consideration of the Internal Control Structure in a Financial Statement Audit* states: "Methods of assigning authority and responsibility . . . [inter alia] include consideration of employee job descriptions delineating specific duties, reporting relationships, and constraints."[11] Auditors should apply the audit guide's client oriented advice to their own job descriptions. They are likely to be surprised by the brevity of job descriptions for audit partners; an excessively short job description argues for its own revision and lengthening. The tasks discussed in this book could provide salient detail.

Given the sketchiness of job descriptions at some public accounting firms, partners tend to interpret their responsibilities in line with their own conceptions. There is no standard model. Many partners perform what may be described as a vicarious audit: they see the client and his problems through the eyes of junior staff; the same partners may question staff, generally on the basis of information contained in working papers, and usually without adding new knowledge; in some cases these partners try to compensate for other defects by engaging in extensive clerical checks of the financial statements, and tracing amounts to the working trial balance. (Automated approaches, such as that of the AICPA's Accountant's Trial Balance, further decrease the value of such activities.) Some writers have actually recognized *several* layers of vicarious reviews, none of which is likely to add significant new information. Conversely, other partners, perhaps those

---

[11]Control Risk Audit Guide Task Force, *Consideration of the Internal Control Structure in a Financial Statement Audit* (New York: American Institute of Certified Public Accountants, 1990), p. 28.

less trusting of their subordinates, may often be found in the client's office, immersed in detailed audit tests. A third group of partners may adopt a middle-of-the-road approach. A fourth, and hopefully large, group may already be engaged in the activities (e.g., behavioral interviewing, plant tours) that this book has recommended for partners. Given apparent freedom of choice by the partner, audit organizations may wish to redirect partner effort based on perceptions of audit risk and on the seriousness of exposures. (Mention might also be made of the second (concurring) partner review on public company engagements; it would be appropriate for the second partner to provide an audit risk management perspective.) In general, the time required for the partners to perform their recast responsibilities would be allocated away from internal staff work and administrative activities.

A major shift is taking place in the timing of partners' activities. Historically, much of the work done by partners came too late to impact the course of events; indeed, at the time of a partner's review, fieldwork could even have been completed and the audit team dispersed. Nowadays, however, supervision by partners tends to be performed more or less contemporaneously with the activities supervised. The partner should know what facts are coming to the surface, what those facts mean from an audit risk perspective, what redirection in audit procedures is necessary and when it should be carried through, and to what extent the client should be kept informed.

To recapitulate, the modern buzzwords are *active partner involvement*, bearing especially on such matters as understanding the client's approaches to managing internal and external risks. Moreover, for the reasons set forth in the next two paragraphs, partners may wish to participate in interviews of employees in sensitive positions and in the tour of the client's facilities.

Very few frauds have been detected by audit procedures, including interviews. This can be partly explained by the fact that the interviews are typically conducted by junior accountants, likely to have little experience with, or training in, behavioral interviewing. A young accountant may be pitted against a senior executive, an authority figure who may have spent a lifetime in the pursuit of planning and executing irregularities, and who may also be a seasoned prevaricator. The deck would seem to be stacked against the junior. The odds would improve if the partner or manager were to conduct the interview.

Similar reasoning may be applied to the plant tour. Again, a partner or manager will have a better chance than a junior person of noticing symptoms of unfavorable conditions and divining the underlying causes. There is a further benefit to be obtained as a result of active partner involvement: to a significant degree, the concerns of the partner with respect to such matters as the preparation of complete and accurate financial statements, and the effective functioning of internal auditors, coincide with audit committee concerns. Therefore, the partner should be able to anticipate directors' interests, the questions they are likely to ask, and the materials they will want to examine. Ergo, the partner should focus on these materials in his review, see that deficiencies are remedied and adjustments properly considered, and the parties provided with information that assists them in carrying out their responsibilities.

It is impossible to develop bogeys to assess how much time a partner should spend on an engagement, or what percentage of total engagement time should be represented by his contribution; in the good old days, numbers such as 5 to 10 percent were bandied about. The figures have gone up; the author has heard estimates ranging to 20 percent.

HUMAN RESOURCE MANAGEMENT

Juniors: Lessening Demand and High Turnover

Loss of chargeable time resulting from automation seems to be occurring at the low end of the wage scale. Thus, the audit organization of the future may be replete with partners, managers, specialists, supervisors, and seniors, but may need fewer juniors or semi-seniors. The unassigned junior is beginning to be a problem. One solution features sales of junior time; in a sale, the buyer's work-in-process account is only charged for a portion of the junior's cost.

Stated differently, the profession finds itself on the horns of a dilemma. On the one hand, juniors must be recruited and trained to serve as tomorrow's partners. On the other hand, unassigned

junior time represents an unacceptable charge on public accounting firms' profitability, especially in times of shrinking margins.
However, public accounting firms have historically provided a species of basic training for entrants who eventually (usually within
three to five years) choose to pursue careers elsewhere—as internal
auditors, government accountants and auditors, academics, and
industrial accountants. The merits of this pro bono training arrangement can be argued from a variety of perspectives, but it still
represents a substantial drain on the public accounting firms' profitability. The author believes that the following suggestions merit
consideration in order to bring the problem under control:

1. Public accounting firms should primarily hire people with
a predisposition to and the talent for a career in public accounting; similar selectivity should be applied by the other arms of professional practice, such as internal audit departments. This approach will become more accepted as universities put students
through specialized tracks—including internal auditing, government accounting and auditing, and management accounting.

Author's Comment

Currently between 50 and 100 people are hired to (ultimately) produce one partner. Therefore, some have spoken of a failure (*depar-
ture* would be a better word) rate of 98 or 99 percent. One cannot be
sure that departures represent failures; within the alumni ranks of
every Big Six firm it is easy to find the familiar names of presidents
of Fortune 500 corporations. Very little research has been done to
identify the causes of turnover. The author is acquainted with a
psychologist whose tests tend to show that turnover may reflect
performance expectations on the part of the employee that differ
significantly from those held by the firm.[12]

2. Employer and employee should have a mutual understanding as to the performance expected of employees and the
measurement criteria to be applied.

---

[12]Discussions with Robert W. King, Behavioral Science Associates, 2135 East University Drive, Suite 9, Mesa, AZ 85213.

3. Public accounting firms should reevaluate policies which force the separation (the current term is *outplacement*) from service of those who fail to achieve promotion within guideline periods. Few statistics are available as to the cost of turnover per employee; the lost investment in recruitment and training might serve as a surrogate measure—some estimates have ranged as high as $25,000 per employee. More importantly, the complexities of current practice argue in favor of retaining auditors with street smarts. (In the United Kingdom, much of the excitement and challenge of training staff on the job is assumed by very senior nonpartners, known as principal managers.)

Assignments, Audit Risk, and Professional Development

Many audit staff assignments continue to be made under conditions of crisis management. In the worst of all possible worlds, a staff assignment can become an unequal contest between a partner with clout in the personnel department and another partner who may lack connections. The assignment manager acts as "body merchant" in selling an alternative placement to the reluctant engagement partner. Two important matters may be lost in the shuffle: (1) audit risk management on the engagement; and (2) the professional development needs of the assignee.

Part of the solution lies in the design of a long-range career development plan for an individual staff person. The plan begins with (1) an inventory of the individual's strengths and weaknesses at the time of hire; (2) target dates within which particular accomplishments will be expected; (3) a preliminary schedule of experience and training designed to help the individual achieve targets; and (4) employer-employee agreement on the plan.

The organization may use the plan to remedy gaps in the employee's academic preparation or experience. For example, an employee could be assigned to train in fields mentioned in this book: technological developments, behavioral skills, mathematical skills, and knowledge of administrative or operational controls pertaining to business functions such as production, marketing, research, and procurement. Periodic counseling can be used to monitor and reinforce the execution of the career plan.

When staff is requested from the personnel department, the sought-after qualifications should be related to management of audit risk on the engagement. For example, if valuation of real estate represents a significant problem, it may be desirable to request a person who knows how to select appraisers, assess their qualifications, and evaluate the procedures applied by them. Normally, after the staff person has begun work on the client's premises, efforts should be made to retain him on the engagement (subject, of course, to professional rotation requirements for certain senior personnel). Auditors with experience with a client will display greater acuity in detecting material errors and irregularities than newcomers. In addition, few things are more likely to arouse a client's ire than frequent appearances of new faces on the engagement, especially when breaking in (i.e., orientation) is required by the client's people.

As already pointed out, clients evaluate audit quality, not on the basis of a firm's reputation, but by judging the work of the engagement *team* as reflected in its contacts with management. This facet presents another incentive to maintain the continuity of the engagement team.

Participative Management

In general, junior members of the engagement team are likely to have more client knowledge than they are credited with. Accordingly, every effort should be made to secure input by informal, but skilled, questioning of the members of the audit team. The objectives are: to limit audit detection risk (i.e., risk of missing a material error or irregularity and arriving at an incorrect opinion), to solicit client profitability improvement ideas, to enhance audit efficiency, and to enhance staff skills. For example, staff persons' recommendations for amending, strengthening, or eliminating audit program procedures, together with the reasons for their opinions, should be listened to with care; any necessary action should be taken with speed and diligence.

Debriefing of the staff blends the old-fashioned suggestion box into an unstructured version of industrial quality circles. A word of clarification may be appropriate: quality circles represent a disciplined effort by workers to agree on suggestions, and to see to their implementation. In most cases, quality circles involve the services of a trained director. Although several audit organizations have experimented with quality circles, efforts to date have not been successful. It is possible that an informal approach is most suitable in an auditing environment.

QUALITY CONTROL AND ASSURANCE

A distinction should be made between quality control on the one hand and quality assurance on the other. *SAS 25* and the *Statements on Quality Control Standards* set out controls intended to provide reasonable assurance that GAAS will be followed. The term *quality assurance* as used in this chapter includes inspections (*SQCS 1*) to determine whether quality control standards, policies, and procedures are observed. Quality control must be integrated into the audit organization's way of life; it focuses on complying with, and hopefully exceeding, the letter and spirit of professional requirements. Quality assurance represents an activity apart; the key issues involve the selection of engagements for review and the nature of the review procedures.

The selection of engagements for working paper examination involves a balancing of risk attaching to the engagement and risk linked to the engagement team and its leadership. In any event, the choice should be heavily influenced by audit risk on engagements. Other criteria include the results of reviews for compliance with rules, the degree of confidence reposed in the engagement partner (or staff), the outcomes of prior reviews, and his (their) receptivity to constructive comments. A further consideration relates to the quality of the person in charge of quality assurance—the individual should be a superb auditor with an understanding of audit technology. He should devote sufficient time to either performing or directing the review work. Stated differently, quality control should not be a sinecure for numerous part-timers; firms err badly when they assign part-timers, either because there is nothing else for them to do, or because it is thought that they would benefit from finishing school.

RISK MANAGEMENT—SCREENING CLIENTS

Lawyers have joined accountants and doctors as targets for law-suits. The president of the Austin-based Texas Lawyers Insurance Exchange has been quoted as saying that the average damage claim has increased from less than $20,000 in the early 1980s to several million dollars in the late 1980s.[13] An article in the *ABA Journal* suggests that lawyers should give more thought to a potential client or case *before* agreeing to the representation. Qualifying clients before accepting retainers may help to avoid frivolous malpractice claims; lawyers are warned against clients who don't understand billing procedures or the legal system, can't be satisfied, are in a hurry, are seeking psychological reinforcement, or are excessively optimistic. Lawyers are cautioned to avoid dabbling in areas outside their expertise. Engagement letters are also recommended as a must.[14] The advice given to attorneys seems pertinent and appropriate for auditors as well.

Medical malpractice rates have moderated, but hospital executives report that access to care is being restricted, especially in rural areas and with respect to certain medical specialties.[15] (The same provider shyness could manifest itself in public accountancy.) Given uncertain prospects for near-term reform of the tort laws, medical staffs have been urged to become active in risk management programs. Some professional liability insurance vendors are offering hospitals up-front financial incentives to participate. To receive a rebate, a hospital must have an entire risk management program in place. On-site visits are made to hospitals by the insurer's representatives; hospitals are presented with plans to correct any deficiencies.[16] It would not be surprising if this targeted risk management approach were to spread to other professions. For example, National Union Fire Insurance Company, the country's leading underwriter

[13]Darrell Preston, "Legal Malpractice Woes Mounting for Lawyers Hit With Huge Claims," *The Dallas Business Journal, Inc.* 13, no. 33 (April 16, 1990), sec. 1, p. 1.

[14]Duke Nordlinger Stern, "Know When to Say No," *ABA Journal* 73, no. 54 (July 1, 1987) Feature Section p. 54.

[15]Terese Hudson, "Tort Reform Legislation: Can It Help Hospitals? *Hospitals* 64, no. 10 (May 20, 1990), p. 28.

[16]Terese Hudson, "Vendors Offer Discounts for Risk Management," *Hospitals* 64, no. 5 (March 5, 1990), pp. 58–60.

of directors' and officers' insurance, grants certain concessions to companies which maintain an audit committee that follows the Treadway recommendations.[17] In any event, audit entities and their clients may wish to document their risk management program(s) for future reference in discussions with insurers.

ADMINISTRATIVE MATTERS

Internal Auditing

Internal auditing within public accounting firms is rarely accorded its deserved importance. Internal auditing requires the services of individuals dedicated to the activity, and aware of the problems and opportunities inherent in professional firm internal auditing. Operational auditing, with a focus on cost reduction or revenue enhancement, should occupy much of their time. For reference, a cost reduction checklist has been appended as Figure 13–1.

Item

A major public accounting firm had been spending more than a million dollars annually on stationery used for client financial statements and management letters. This stationery had an impressive appearance, said to reflect its very high rag content. An operational audit established that neither the firm's partners, nor the client recipients, cared about, or were even capable of distinguishing between, high-rag-content paper and cheap chemical paper. As a result of the audit, rag content in the firm's stationery was reduced to 25 percent; there was no visible deterioration in the appearance of the stationery, but more than $100,000 was saved on a recurring annual basis.

Marketing

The strategic dimension of marketing involves the *anticipation* of public demand and the marshaling of resources to meet that de-

---

[17]Those interested in details should write to Lawrence W. Ray, vice president, National Union Fire Insurance Company of Pittsburgh, PA., 70 Pine Street, 5th Floor, New York, NY 10270.

FIGURE 13-1
Checklist for Reducing Costs within Audit Organizations

Personnel Matters

1. Work to reduce personnel turnover; make job offers to individuals who display interest in making auditing their life's work.
2. Apply a targeted approach to seeing that partners and staff keep current; make certain that personnel receive input on a need-to-know basis. Consider using the on-line data bases and the updating services offered by data base providers.
3. Make sure that engagement personnel receive meaningful information for monitoring engagement costs and unfavorable cost variances within a time frame that permits corrective action to be taken without delay.
4. Maximize value from continuing professional education programs; endeavor to gear programs to the professional development needs of individuals.

Engagement Matters

5. Have a clear image of working papers as a communications medium; get the papers to serve more than one purpose.
6. Realign audit effort to parallel risk.
7. Avoid overauditing by seeing that each procedure (1) supports the attainment of audit objectives and (2) yields the greatest comparative value in the circumstances.
8. Avoid duplicating or redundant audit procedures; make sure that tests accomplish more than one purpose whenever possible.
9. Exercise quality control and supervision on a basis contemporaneous with fieldwork in progress; minimize false starts or work that will require redoing.
10. Encourage participative management, especially with respect to feeding back possible concerns involving audit inefficiency or—more importantly—audit ineffectiveness.
11. Broaden the scope of quality assurance reviews to incorporate matters of apparent audit inefficiency.

Firm Operations

12. Establish a systematic plan for productivity improvement, on engagements and with respect to office operations.
13. Compare time paid for and time billed to clients. Focus on pockets of nonproductive time; establish programs to reduce such time, and to make sure it is kept under control.
14. Optimize cash utilization with respect to collections, payments, and utilization of balances; bear capital needs in mind.
15. Eliminate dysfunctional support activities.
16. Apply sound purchasing principles to purchased materials and services, in terms of shopping the market, seeking bids, and negotiations.
17. Prepare an orderly plan for the implementation of technology; decide on policies for acquiring hardware and software.
18. Assess stationery and printing costs, bearing the recipients of communications in mind.
19. Control travel expenses; display cost consciousness with respect to charges to be rebilled to clients.
20. See to the automation of records management with a view toward reducing its cost, while improving retrievability.

mand. The tactical dimension of selling is concerned with mundane aspects such as identifying leads, qualifying leads, cold calling, etc. The author believes that accountants should *direct* the marketing efforts, and also engage in direct selling.

Popular wisdom denigrates the worth of accountants and auditors as salespersons. Yet, when in a selling mode, auditors are armed with a thorough knowledge of their product—a prerequisite to an intelligent selling effort. A lack of sales incentives can weaken sales performance by auditors. Some firms offer no bonus, commission, or other reward to partners who bring in engagements; those that offer incentive payments may differentiate between recurring work and nonrecurring work. Ironically, low-margined recurring work may carry a higher bonus than high-margined nonrecurring work. Accordingly, audit organizations are advised to examine their incentive/disincentive structure.

The emergence of the multifaceted executive is another beneficial result of the new technology. In the words of Bill Conlin, president of CalComp, a division of Lockheed: "With multitasking software there is no reason a single person couldn't act as a designer, engineer, purchasing agent, or even salesperson. . . . The way companies will measure progress in the future is to determine whether an individual's span of responsibility has increased."[18]

The Accountant's System

In general, accountants' own systems have suffered from benign neglect, offering proof of the accuracy of the adage that the shoemaker often goes barefoot. The situation may no longer be excusable, given the large number of software offerings related to professional firms' accounting, timekeeping, and project control systems.[19]

The system should accommodate both administrative and technical needs. The technical part of the system encompasses au-

---

[18]Quoted in Ralph Carlyle, "The Tomorrow Organization," *Datamation* 8, no. 3 (February 1, 1990), p. 24.

[19]The AICPA publishes an annual software catalogue. The 1991 listing includes "Engagement Manager," described as "the on-the-job project management system with the ability to analyze, document, and correct specific problems in the timeliness of . . . engagements." The AICPA is located at 1211 Avenue of the Americas, New York, NY 10036-8775.

dit programs and procedures described in other chapters, communication, word processing, research, and the in-house data base. The administrative system includes human resource management, marketing, engagement budgeting and timekeeping, and client billing and general accounting.

Of course, the accountant's system should demonstrate awareness of the need for security, as well as informed applications of technology. With respect to security, much guidance is available, some of it geared to particular systems or environments.[20] As to technology, the following represents an example: an audit organization could arrange for an electronic bulletin board whose members would be practicing accountants and auditors. The bulletin board would promote a congress of views among users. Over time, arrangements could be worked out with practitioners and others for exchanging information bearing on selected technical and research issues.

In addition, data entry should be automated insofar as possible. For instance, time charged could be entered by means of hand-held units. Each day the system could generate a series of variances for review, analysis, and immediate action.

SUMMARY

This chapter has been concerned with the impact of technological change on practitioners and their firms. The blessings may be mixed: on the one hand, the age of the perceptive, sensitive, and thinking auditor is (or will soon be) at hand. On the other, there may be a need for increased numbers of technical specialists, risking diminished audit profitability. Partners will actively participate in and control all phases of the audit with the aid of modern communications. Their employee associates will be carefully groomed and nurtured and will engage in participative management.

---

[20]See, for example, the *Technical Reference Series*, published by the Association of the Institute of Certified Computer Professionals, 2200 E. Devon Avenue, Des Plaines, Ill. 60018. This series, which deals with control, audit, and security matters, was prepared by the firm of Ernst & Young.

Hiring patterns may shift, benefiting those who would make auditing their life's work. Careers are likely to require broad-gauged creativity, leavened by mastery of a technical specialty. While the new environment will be more stimulating (and more fun) than the old, the rewards will go to the thinking auditor who is also a good businessperson.

The author thought it appropriate to end this chapter by quoting five of the venerable W. Edwards Deming's "Fourteen Points":

- Create constancy of purpose for improvement of product and service.
- Adopt the new philosophy.
- Improve constantly and forever every process for planning, production, and service.
- Break down barriers between staff areas.
- Put everyone in the company to work to accomplish the transformation.[21]

---

[21] As quoted in Martin K. Starr, "Winning the Business Olympics," *Hermes* 16, no. 3 (Summer 1990), p. 21.

CHAPTER 14

PUBLIC POLICY AND AUDITING

Society either accepts or rejects the role that a professional group assumes for itself; in time the group either finds a role acceptable to society or the group disappears . . . . Professional groups must continually be alert to the desirability of role modification and revision.

*Robert Mautz**

USER PERSPECTIVE: Items of Special Interest

EXECUTIVE HIGHLIGHTS: All readers
INTRODUCTION: All readers
THE MAKING OF PUBLIC POLICY FOR AUDITING: All readers
RELATED PUBLIC POLICY ISSUES: External auditors, internal auditors
THE FREE MARKET AND AUDITORS: All readers
FOREIGN POLICY AND AUDITORS: External auditors, internal auditors
EDUCATIONAL POLICY AND AUDITORS: All readers
SUMMARY: All readers

EXECUTIVE HIGHLIGHTS

Most auditors have uneasily watched public policy-making; they have tended to wait for the proverbial other shoe to drop. Rarely are auditors heard on issues which directly concern them, on is-

---

*Noted accounting educator.

sues which are tangential to their work but in regard to which they possess special expertise, or, indeed, on most issues which relate to the economy or to the interests of the business community.

The very first (1933) regulatory act was already influenced by ideology. Therefore, the profession should participate in shaping any legislative agenda that seeks to expand its obligations. This makes it important to close the real expectation gap which involves law makers on the one hand and the reality of what an audit can accomplish on the other.

In general, the SEC-AICPA partnership, backed by state regulation, has fostered high standards and emphasized independence in fact and appearance. Current trends at the SEC appear contradictory; on the one hand, there are proposals for a management report on controls; at the same time, some foreign corporations may be exempted from complying with U.S. disclosure requirements.

The composition of the FASB's membership invites questions. Legislators are likely to discern a credibility gap in that preparers being regulated can be seen as participating in their own regulation. The eventual legislative response cannot be predicted, but it is likely to include intensified oversight.

Individual state courts balance policies in the public interest to determine the party to whom auditors owe duty of care. However, there is no uniform interpretation of the public interest and no uniform rule governing auditors' duty of care to foreseeable third parties.

External and internal auditors should be heard on public policy issues that relate to auditing, such as ambiguous laws relating to computer crime, lying to auditors, EDI standards, privacy, and deregulation of markets for international auditing services.

INTRODUCTION

The preceding chapter noted the effects of technological and social changes on the audit entity and on the auditor's career path. This chapter explores the pervasive effects of public policy-making *on* auditing; policy-making is eventually reflected in laws, administrative rules, and professional regulations.

It is apparent that some kind of rapport should exist between the expectations of the policymakers on the one hand, and the reality of what an audit can accomplish on the other.

David Flint put it this way:

> The social machinery for interaction between auditors and audit policymakers . . . is informal and unstructured, but it is important that it should be effective. A failure on the part of auditors or audit policymakers to recognize the dynamic nature of auditing or to respond to legitimate societal pressure will result in frustration of the social purpose and emergence of [an] expectation gap . . . . The onus is on auditors and audit policymakers constantly to seek to find out what is the societal need and expectation for independent audit and to endeavor to fulfill that need within the limits of practical and economic constraints, remembering at all times that the function is a dynamic, not a static one.[1]

Some have written that virtually every significant development in the profession during the last 100 years can be attributed to governmental pressure and that the profession has been too reactive and insufficiently causative. Others have described the politicized aspects of policy-making, at times in vivid terms. Most auditors have uneasily watched public policy-making even when it could directly affect them; in many cases they simply waited for the proverbial other shoe to drop. Rarely are auditors heard on issues which directly concern them, on issues which are tangential to their work but in regard to which they possess special expertise, or, indeed, on most issues which relate to the economy or to the interests of the business community.

This chapter discusses current trends in policy-making. The purpose is to stimulate auditor interest in the process, and to motivate auditors to become more active in aligning the expectations of their various publics and the realities of efficient and effective audit engagements. As Flint pointed out, "auditors who see a corporation and its shareholders as their only 'client' and

---

[1]David Flint, *Philosophy and Principles of Auditing: An Introduction* (London: Macmillan Education Ltd., 1988), pp. 15–17.

resist moves to recognize other representative bodies, such as regulatory or supervisory agencies . . . or employee groups, as legitimately entitled to be directly addressed by auditors, understand neither the nature of the concept of accountability nor the social function of the audit."[2]

THE MAKING OF PUBLIC POLICY FOR AUDITING

Congressional Initiatives

Historic Perspective
Auditing was in demand long before government discovered the accounting profession. That demand was driven by the desirability of independent verification of accounts and reports rendered by a manager to an owner. By 1932 the New York Stock Exchange had required all listed companies to provide financial statements audited by qualified accountants. (The original 1933 and 1934 Acts mandated CPA audits of *all* listed companies, regardless of stock exchange.)

The 1933/34 Acts
Haim Falk searched after reasons for congressional actions. He found that while audits added value, politics were also a factor. Three kinds of added value accrued to the public from mandatory audits by CPAs:

> First, although the traditional role of the voluntarily hired auditor was to detect and report breaches of implicit or explicit contracts, . . . the auditor's role intended by legislation was to monitor management disclosure of information assumed to be used in investor decisions. . . . Second, auditors' independence was enhanced by the imposition of the legal liability provisions in the Act. Third, granting audit rights to members of an organized profession created an

---

[2]Ibid.

improved mechanism to convey information concerning independence and competence of professional auditors.[3]

Added value notwithstanding, Falk concluded that the motivation for a positive congressional vote was ideological, that it resulted from the conviction that "that is the right thing to do." According to Falk, statistics cited by Chairman Rayburn on the day the 1933 act (unanimously) passed the House may have influenced the vote; Chairman Rayburn had observed that between the end of World War I and 1933, $50 billion in new securities had been floated, of which half subsequently proved worthless.[4]

Current Events

Chairman Rayburn's concerns are being echoed today. Legislation introduced by Rep. Ron Wyden (D–Ore.) would have required, among other things, auditor whistle-blowing on fraud and illegal activities.

Although the Wyden legislation was not passed by the Senate, consideration of "similar or more onerous legislation" is foreseen.[5] In the words of Gilbert Simonetti,

> important congressmen do not want to be told about the objectives and limitations of financial statement audits. They believe that auditors are supposed to detect and blow the whistle on illegal activities. They want greater assurance about the ongoing financial condition of an entity . . . . If the proposals are ultimately successful, the independent auditor will face a collection of compliance and internal reviews and direct reporting requirements to a number of different government agencies, and even to the public.

Simonetti concluded with an admonition: "The profession must be aggressive in shaping any legislative agenda that seeks

---

[3]Haim Falk, "A Comparison of Regulation Theories: The Case for Mandated Auditing in the United States," *Research in Accounting Regulation*, vol. 3, ed. Gary John Previts (Greenwich, Conn.: JAI Press, 1989), p. 115.

[4]Ibid.

[5]Ernst & Young, "Financial Reporting and Accounting 1990 Update," (1991).

to expand its public obligations. Anything less would be an abdication of its professional responsibilities."[6]

Author's Comment

John Burton, a former chief accountant of the SEC, has cautioned that, if the accounting profession defines its role narrowly and creates a standardized compliance-oriented audit product, it is going to find that neither corporations nor governments will be prepared to pay the kinds of fees that have traditionally been paid for audits.[7] The aforementioned Simonetti comments are pertinent with respect to future legislation; auditors should carefully analyze detailed provisions to identify those which merit support. Of course, the obverse aspect involves the auditors' own practices; they must heighten their staffs' sensitivities to fraud and increase the rigor of their examinations, especially in high-risk industries. If their efforts are successful, the cry for legislation may be muted.

The Securities and Exchange Commission

Historic Perspective

Shortly after passage of the 1933/34 Acts, there began what has been described as a unique partnership between government and the public accounting profession. Carman G. Blough, the first chief accountant of the SEC, "influenced the establishment and affirmation of private control over the accounting/auditing function and over . . . accounting rule making."[8] Interestingly, it seems that neither the government nor the profession had any particular interest in establishing accounting rules; however, the profession hoped that government would *not* make the rules.

In general, the SEC-AICPA partnership, backed by state reg-

---

[6]Gilbert Simonetti, Jr. "The 1990s: More Public Scrutiny," *Accounting Today*, January 8, 1990, p. 6.

[7]John C. Burton, "Information Development in the Future," *Moret & Limperg (Arthur Young & Company) Symposium 1983* (Rotterdam, Netherlands: Moret & Limperg, 1983).

[8]Robert Chatov, "The Regulatory Philosophy of Carman Blough," in *Research in Accounting Regulation* vol. 2, ed. Gary John Previts (Greenwich, Conn.: JAI Press, 1988), p. 96.

ulation, has fostered high standards and emphasized independence in fact and appearance. Much of the credit should go to the SEC's chief accountants who have continued to be a positive influence on the development of accounting and auditing standards through technical publications and by making themselves available to practitioners as catalysts and resource persons.

Although the SEC's powers extend to both accounting and auditing, the focus of SEC oversight has been on accounting and disclosure (presumed to be helpful to investor decision making) rather than on auditing. Through the years the usefulness of the disclosures has been studied; at times the SEC took vigorous action to improve the meaningfulness of the disclosures. For example, the Commission currently plans a close look at what disclosure has accomplished in the financial services industry. A task force of 25 attorneys will scrutinize past disclosures for possible enforcement recommendations. The principal enforcement weapon is to bring fraud charges based on misrepresentation or omission of material facts. According to Thomas M. Leahey and Jonathan N. Eisenberg, microscopes will be focused on the following:

- Adequacy of allowances for loan losses; attention is to be given to less developed country (LDC) loans, real estate lending, and junk bonds.
- Excess mortgage servicing. Questions will be asked such as: was the initial valuation of excess mortgage servicing appropriate and subject to periodic reassessment?
- Investment versus trading accounting. Was the portfolio correctly categorized?
- Real estate investments. Were investments correctly classified and accounted for?
- Management discussion and analysis. Were disclosures adequate?
- Leveraged buyout (LBO) financing. Did reporting reflect the condition of these portfolios?
- Real estate markets. Was the potentially adverse impact of local markets disclosed?

- Participation. Was management's analysis of value consistent with the analyses by other participating lenders?
- Proper disclosure of new financial institution rules. Was the impact discussed, particularly in the area of required capital?[9]

Author's Comment

The questions posed by Leahey and Eisenberg should be taken as something of a clarion call to financial institutions. However, auditors should also think through the implications of the questions from an audit perspective. The regulatory concerns as enunciated could be used to set priorities in current and future audits of financial institutions.

As noted, the SEC has concentrated on accounting, rather than on auditing matters. The author has been told that, in the absence of special circumstances, SEC examiners are likely to request audit working papers for fewer than 100 registrants yearly. This could also change. The Commission has set up a special unit with five lawyers to sue advisers to public companies, mostly lawyers and accountants, whom it views as guilty of unethical or improper professional conduct. The Commission hopes to curb what it contends is a growing temptation by accountants to bend professional standards in a highly competitive time.[10]

Current Events
A pending SEC proposal would require public companies to assess the effectiveness of their internal control structures and report the results to the public. More specifically, the SEC would require representations relative to management's assessment of the effectiveness of its internal control structure, management's response to significant recommendations of internal and indepen-

---

[9]Thomas M. Leahey and Jonathan N. Eisenberg, "SEC Is Ready to Examine Financial Firm Disclosures," *American Banker*, March 21, 1990, Comment Sec., p. 4.

[10]Alison Leigh Cowan, "Audit Firm: Victim or Accomplice?" *New York Times*, July 17, 1990, Business Digest sec., p. D-6.

dent auditors about the internal control structure, and an acknowledgment of management's responsibilities for preparing financial statements and establishing a system of internal control.
This proposal does not call for attestation; however, the SEC also
indicated that independent auditors should determine whether
there are any material misstatements of fact in management's report. (Along parallel lines, the Auditing Standards Board (ASB) is
developing an attestation standard.[11] Further, the Committee of
Sponsoring Organizations of the Treadway Commission has
sponsored a project intended to produce a framework in which a
common definition of internal control is established and control
components are identified.)

An insightful analysis of the SEC's internal control reporting
proposal was developed by Leonard P. Novello, general counsel of
a Big Six firm. According to Novello,

> most commentators supported requirements for management to
> acknowledge its responsibilities for preparing GAAP financial
> statements and establishing and maintaining an internal control
> system . . . . Less than half agreed that management should assess
> the effectiveness of its internal control structure. And there was
> overwhelming opposition to the proposal that management re-
> spond to significant recommendations of internal and independent
> auditors.

Novello also observed that "many believe that the incremen-
tal costs of this documentation will outweigh the benefits, especially for smaller companies.[12]

Author's Comment

Guidance is still being developed; therefore, final judgment must be
deferred. However, there is a distinct danger that the proposed documentation will add little or no useful information; on the other hand,
the cost to registrants, especially smaller entities, is certain to be

---

[11]Morton B. Solomon and Joe R. Cooper, "Reporting on Internal Control: The SEC's Proposed Rules," *Journal of Accountancy* 169, no. 6 (June 1990), pp. 56–63.

[12]Leonard P. Novello, "Internal Control: Reliability in Financial Reporting," *New York
Law Journal*, June 28, 1990, Corporate Update Sec., p. 5.

substantial. In terms of the SEC's direction, one might question whether the proposed reporting on internal control presages future coverage of other controls, and/or of risk management techniques generally. If that is the direction, another expectation gap could be created, given the lead time and preparatory work that would be necessary to establish standards for evaluating operational controls!

The Financial Accounting Standards Board (FASB)

Historic Perspective

The decisions of the FASB are implemented through auditing. Therefore, the nature of problems addressed by the FASB and the sequence and timing of its pronouncements have an effect on how the public perceives auditors. Many agree that the FASB has dealt with the right issues; it is less certain that the order in which issues were worked on and pronouncements released met the needs of the auditors' varied constituencies. This may have contributed to some regulators' harsh views of accounting principles. Timothy Ryan, Jr., the director of the Office of Thrift Supervision, has called for an overhaul of generally accepted accounting principles to reflect institutions' market values. He stated that accounting principles will become irrelevant as a regulatory tool if they do not reflect economic reality.[13]

Lee Seidler has commented upon the FASB's record in acidulous terms, mentioning "low production, avoiding the big issues, lack of consistency, barely acceptable accounting principles, and lack of leadership." Seidler avers that the "self-defeating cookbook approach stems mainly from the view that the CFOs of American corporations will, given the slightest opportunity, manipulate their financial statements to serve their own purposes. Their auditors will permit anything that is not expressly forbidden." He is not worried about the possibility of a government takeover of rule-making, since "it is difficult to envision

---

[13]Debra Cope, "Ryan Reads the Riot Act to Auditors," *American Banker*, September 6, 1990, p. 1.

any accounting rules more bureaucratic than those of the FASB."[14]

Others have faulted the FASB for catering to too narrow a group of financial statement users, and for favoring the short term over the long term in its rule-making horizon. One writer described small businesses as having been bound to standards derived from assumptions based on a user perspective that appears irrelevant, if not nonexistent, to these entities. Moreover, the FASB's bias toward investors and creditors was said to be such that it resulted in dictation of *non*public entity reporting and auditing needs by users of financial information for publicly held entitles.[15]

Current Events

As of late, critics have questioned the regulatory *structure*, the membership of the FASB and its parent, the Financial Accounting Foundation (FAF), and the voting rules of the FASB. Some have been disturbed by a trend toward increased representation of the preparer community on the FASB and the FAF. Arthur Wyatt said it this way:

> [originally] there was an agreement that representation from the practicing profession would be in the majority. Four of the seven FASB seats were allocated to those from public accounting; that is down to three. And, a majority of the trustees of the FAF were from public accounting; that is now down to one third. I come back to the notion of acting in the public interest and developing standards that are fair and unbiased in the sense of being neutral, not trying to promote any particular interest.[16]

Others have been equally concerned about the *appearance* of the voting arrangement. Legislators are likely to discern a credi-

---

[14]Lee J. Seidler, "What Ails the FASB," *The CPA Journal* 60, no. 7 (July 1990), pp. 46–48.

[15]Frederick M. Richardson and C. T. Wright, "Standards Overload: A Case for Accountant Judgement," *The CPA Journal* 56, no. 10 (October 1986), pp. 45–52.

[16]Quoted in Floyd Norris, "Users and Abusers: Here's the Bottom Line on the Accounting Profession," *Barron's*, September 14, 1987, p. 48.

bility gap in that the preparers can be seen as participating in their own regulation. The eventual legislative response cannot be predicted, but is likely to include intensified regulatory oversight.

Timely issuance of professional guidance is another concern which transcends the identities of issuers of pronouncements. The Emerging Issues Task Force (EITF) of the FASB, which focuses on accounting issues, has been a substantial success. (Both the FASB and Clarence Sampson, then chief accountant of the SEC, deserve to be complimented on the EITF's creation.) Therefore, it is not surprising that some have called for the creation of a similar body to address emerging auditing issues. According to a letter from the AICPA's Dan M. Guy, such a body already exists, known as the Audit Issues Task Force (AITF); he reports that this group is "responsible for reviewing and providing timely guidance in response to emerging technical auditing issues." AITF may request the AICPA's Auditing Standards Division to issue timely guidance in the form of notices to practitioners. (Although there is some resemblance between EITF and AITF, there are also differences; for example, AITF's output and minutes are not widely disseminated, and it is not clear whether output does or should represent a level of generally accepted auditing standards.) In any case, the AICPA's Special Committee on Governance and Structure has recommended a reassessment (by the Auditing Standards Board and the Accounting Standards Executive Committee) of the manner in which emerging issues are identified and the manner and timing of the guidance developed.[17]

The Courts

Historic Perspective
Individual state courts balance policies in the public interest to determine the party to whom auditors owe a duty. However, there

---

[17] "Addressing Emerging Technical Auditing Matters," *The CPA Journal* 60, no. 7 (July 1990) News & Views, p. 6.

is no uniform interpretation of the public interest and no uniform rule governing auditors' duty of care to foreseeable third parties.[18] In much of the United States, including New York, the privity rule, discussed later in this paragraph and first set out by Justice Cardozo in *Ultramares Corp. v. Touche*,[19] has endured. In the words of one of the AICPA's lawyers:

> The rule does not provide an arbitrary advantage to the accounting profession; rather, it exists to prevent what would be an untenable situation in its absence, and it has repeatedly been found consistent with established principles of tort law. Broad liability should exist where an accountant is accused of fraud. But where the accountant's alleged wrongdoing amounts to negligence only, and where the accountant stood to gain nothing from the wide dissemination of his work product . . . equally broad liability is neither fair nor expedient.[20]

Current Events

The U.K. high court, the Law Lords, applied privity more narrowly in a recent decision. The Lords held in *Caparo Industries PLC* v. *Dickman* (1989) 2 W.L.R. 316 that auditors are *not* liable to third parties who rely on the accounts to make investment decisions. The interpretation was based on the "original, central and primary purpose" of the legislative provision involved—protection of the company, and informed control by the shareholders as a body. The decision could turn into a Pyrrhic victory for auditors, in that it could prompt a debate as to the need for an annual audit.[21] While some subsequent Canadian decisions have cited *Caparo*, there has been no apparent effect in the United States; in any case, developments bear watching.

---

[18]H. David Brecht, "Auditors' Duty of Care to Third Parties: A Comment on Judicial Reasoning Underlying U.S. Cases," *Accounting & Business Research* 19, no. 75 (Spring 1989), pp. 175–78.

[19]255 N.Y. 170 (1931).

[20]Deborah C. Cooper, "Accountants' Liability; Privity Rule Is Necessary in Today's Market Place," *New York Law Journal*, April 9, 1990, Outside Counsel sec., p. 1.

[21]Raymond Ashton, "Law Lords Take Narrow View in Caparo Ruling," *The Independent*, February 13, 1990, Accountancy and Management Page, p. 22.

RELATED PUBLIC POLICY ISSUES

External and internal auditors should be heard on public policy issues, particularly when those issues relate to auditing. The four issues discussed in the paragraphs which follow involve internal control and security matters which, if properly addressed by new laws, would strengthen the hands of external and internal auditors.

Ambiguous Laws Relating to Computer Crime
Hackers who gain access to computer information without authorization may avoid criminal charges because of legal technicalities. The difficulty in prosecuting these cases stems from the many conflicting theft and computer trespassing laws that exist throughout the individual states.[22] There is no federal act proscribing unauthorized entry, or insertion of computer viruses, into civilian computer systems. When laws are drafted, initial difficulty will be encountered in defining a computer virus. Since a virus does the same type of thing that a normal program does, the virus has to be defined to exclude normally functioning programs. Further, the definition would have to include the circumstance that entry into the system was unauthorized for the purpose of inserting that particular program. (Many individuals who input viruses have authorization to enter the system for other purposes, since they are employees of the organization.)

Lying to Auditors
It has been made a crime for government contractors to try to obstruct, influence, or impede a federal auditor in the performance of her official duties. The term *federal auditor* means any person employed full time, part time, or on a contractual basis to perform an audit or quality assurance inspection for or on behalf of the United States. The new crime carries a maximum punishment of five years in jail and a fine of up to $250,000 for individuals, and

---

[22] James Connolly, "Patent Disputes, Hacking Major DP Law Issues in '85," *Computer World*, January 21, 1985, pp. 14–15.

$500,000 for corporations.[23] Auditors should think through and express their views on this question: will auditing become more effective if the proscription against lying to auditors is extended to other industries?

EDI Standards

As pointed out in an earlier chapter, standards for electronic data interchange are set by groups largely representing industrial corporations and software houses. Generally speaking, the groups seem to be falling behind in terms of meeting the demand for standards; the problem is likely to get worse when EDI goes international. It would seem that progress could benefit from increased representation of or participation by internal or external auditors on key committees.

Privacy

Given the geometric increase in types of electronic dossiers, together with the sparseness of protective legislation on the books, the climate does not appear favorable to protection of privacy. Moreover, many uncertainties exist. First, there is no clear definition of what constitutes personal information. Second, many types of information are not covered by statutory protection. Third, no constitutional procedures exist for guaranteeing the accuracy and integrity of stored information.[24] Auditors, especially internal auditors, could help to protect companies from possible legal exposure; corporations need to be particularly careful when operating across national borders, given the very strict privacy protection laws in some European nations.

THE FREE MARKET AND AUDITORS

The author believes that auditors should be active competitors, as well as participants in the national debate on competition. Michael Porter recently made some insightful, if controversial, comments

---

[23]"Obstructing Government Auditor Made Subject to Criminal Fine, Jail Term," *BNA, Inc., Federal Contracts Report*, November 14, 1988. (The reference to the law is 50 FCR 744.)

[24]Gerald Salton, "A Progress Report on Information Privacy and Data Security," *Journal of the ASIS* 31, no. 2 (March 1980), pp. 75–83.

about what he called a "national retreat from competition." He explained that competitive advantage results from "rapid improvement, innovation, and upgrading"; he added that "high levels of productivity are achieved when companies continuously upgrade by improving quality, adding new features, penetrating new and more sophisticated market segments and applying new technology and skills to produce their products more efficiently."

According to Porter, innovation and upgrading do not result from a comfortable environment in which risks have been minimized, but from pressure and challenge. He downgraded the relative importance of the vaunted Japanese cooperative research projects. These projects take place through independent entities to which government and companies contribute personnel and modest amounts of money. However, Porter noted that the individual companies invest much more internally on proprietary research on the same technologies, stimulated by the fact that all their competitors are working on them too.

Porter believes that the lesson is that competition works, not that we should limit it. He argues that instead of relaxing antitrust enforcement, we should be tightening it. "Mergers and alliances between leading competitors should be prohibited . . . . Cooperative research and development involving leaders should be sanctioned only when it is through independent entities involving the majority of industry participants and represents a modest proportion of companies' overall research efforts."[25]

Author's Comment

Some of Porter's perceptions have implications for audit organizations, even if the megamergers in public accounting may have passed into history. The author believes that firms of all sizes should be able to compete effectively for audit engagements; the prerequisites would be that the auditor has carefully selected her practice niche, has the human and material resources to service the engagements, has made her practice as effective and efficient as possible, and takes advantage of what should be her encyclopedic knowledge of her client's business.

---

[25]Michael E. Porter, "Japan Isn't Playing by Different Rules," *New York Times*, July 22, 1990, Business sec., p. 13.

Competition may be encouraged by the AICPA's agreement with the Federal Trade Commission, which (primarily) removes certain restrictions on advertising. Coming back to Porter's thinking, it may also be possible for the AICPA to borrow a leaf from the Japanese book by engaging in cooperative research. An American example will make the point:

Item

In the early 1980s the American Bar Association (ABA) created its National Legal Malpractice Data Center. The Center's statistics can be of help in understanding the causes of claims and creating a risk management program. For example, the Center has found that a large number of claims can be attributed to a faulty time/docket control system or to a system which is not being used properly.[26] The ABA sponsorship of the Center makes it worthy of study, and possibly, of emulation.

FOREIGN POLICY AND AUDITORS

The European Economic Community

As a result of recent actions, particularly during the Uruguay Round of the General Agreement on Tariffs and Trade (GATT) and the Group of Negotiations on Services (GNS), liberalization of markets has become an imperative. John Hegarty, the executive director of FEE (Federation des Experts Comtables Europeens) has noted that introspection and protectionism are not appropriate responses to the European Economic Community's (EEC's) single market program.

Hegarty has described himself as surprised that more attention has not been devoted to the service sector in the past. The European Economic Community, with a market share estimated at $168 billion per annum, is the world's largest service exporter. Liberalization implies that the Community would not have to wait for rules and regulations to be the same everywhere before

---

[26]Duke Nordlinger Stern, "Reducing Your Malpractice Risk," *ABA Journal* 72, (June 1986) Feature Sec., p. 52.

frontiers disappear. Instead, the barriers would fall, allowing free movement of goods, services, capital, and labor, even while differences remained.

A new directive on mutual recognition of professional qualifications is expected to come into force in the EEC in 1991. Subject to several types of conditions which may be imposed by member nations, the directive will permit an accountant carrying on certain activities in one state, and using a professional title to do so, to move to another member state and have the right to the equivalent title necessary to carry on the same activities in that country. The impact of the mutual recognition directive is not so much to create a single accountancy market, as to recognize the continuing existence of 12 separate national markets, each with its own characteristics, and to facilitate movement between these markets.[27]

Douglas MacDonald has observed that barriers within countries (i.e., barriers erected by states or provinces) are incompatible with multilateral trade agreements. He noted that procedures should be reassessed, and, if necessary, brought into line with those of other developed countries.[28]

Author's Comment

To smooth interstate reciprocity, the AICPA and the National Association of State Boards of Accountancy (NASBA) are developing a Uniform Accountancy Act to be offered to state CPA societies and state boards. This Act will be used to convince state legislatures to change current laws. Nonetheless, according to a U.S. representative to the GATT talks, prevailing trends appear to be reinforcing states' rights.[29]

FEE has taken a close interest in the slow-moving Uruguay Round negotiations to liberalize world trade in services, especially accountancy services. An evaluation made of accountancy services as a subsector indicated that the accountants were likely to benefit from any agreement. In other words, the accounting

---

[27]John Hegarty, "Leading The Way," *CGA Magazine*, March 1990, pp. 23–28.

[28]Douglas J. MacDonald, "Breaking down Barriers," *CGA Magazine*, March 1990, pp. 19–22.

[29]Thomas S. Watson, Jr., "Impacts of EC 1992," *New Accountant*, February 1991, p. 33.

profession has a potentially rewarding opportunity to lead in liberalization of worldwide trade in services.[30]

Douglas MacDonald reported on an FEE-organized two-day symposium in early 1990 at which the attendees developed a list of points and conditions which they believed should be contained within a GATT agreement on services.[31] The principal points included:

1. The accounting profession's support of liberalization.
2. The recognition that the accounting profession should be self-regulating.
3. The requirement for developed countries to assist developing nations in establishing their accounting profession.
4. The necessity for an operational commitment to market access, with choice of mode of delivery (that is, partnership, corporation, etc.).
5. The profession's support of national rules that emphasize that professional accreditation should be based solely on competence and ability.
6. A commitment to progressive liberalization, achieved through immediate freezing of existing regulation, followed by a rollback of regulation.
7. A stipulation that the agreement (should) contain provisions to ensure that obligations accepted by national governments are enforceable at state, provincial, and local levels.

Author's Comment

In the final analysis the internationalization of auditing does not depend upon treaties, state agencies, or even on accounting and auditing guidelines issued by supranational groups. The answer involves individuals. Practitioner(s), working with or advising other practitioner(s) abroad—directly or through the local professional society—are essential to making international auditing work.

---

[30]Hegarty, "Leading the Way."
[31]MacDonald, "Breaking down Barriers," pp. 19–22.

EDUCATIONAL POLICY AND AUDITORS

Accounting is on its way toward truly becoming one of the learned professions. Parallels exist with medicine. Herbert Pardes, Dean of Columbia University's Faculty of Medicine, has been quoted as saying:

> It is conceivable that by the year 2000 you will go to a doctor who will be able to run a genetic screen on you and give you a list [showing] every disease to which you are genetically predisposed. The technology will be overwhelming. Medicine, which began with the notion of a person taking care of another, will have increasing amounts of technology interjected. Medical education hasn't yet come to grips with the potency of technology and the need for medical personnel to manage it with humanity and compassion.[32]

The genetic screen has a counterpart in external and internal auditing. For example, the screen could represent controls, accompanied by a listing of the consequences (potential findings) that may result from their absence or weakness, and by a menu of special audit procedures to be applied in recognition of the deficiencies and in a search for potential cures.

Other similarities can be cited between accountancy and medicine. For example, there are medical studies to see how the physical shape of substances affects their function; in auditing, the nature of resources affects vulnerability to threats, and the selection and design of controls. Medicines are being developed which zero in on disease causing organisms; in auditing there are programs which search for evidence of contamination of records by means of viruses.

Exchanges of ideas are not limited to accounting and medicine. Similar exchanges are desirable between arts and sciences, law and economics, philosophy and medicine, chemistry and engineering, and criminology and auditing.

It is no longer acceptable or practical to separate a generally educated person, the product of a liberal education, from a professionally competent person who has mastered the extraordinary

---

[32]Michael I. Sovern, Jonathan R. Cole, Martin Meisel, and Herbert Pardes, "The Now & Future University," *Columbia*, Summer 1990, pp. 16–23.

demands of a technologically advanced society in a narrow field. William D. Hall, a well known retired practitioner, has stated the problem bluntly: "Persons who major in accounting normally concentrate on specialized accounting and related courses and . . . slight the humanities. Because of this, many accountants may be incapable of understanding or influencing the broad forces that shape business and society."[33]

The managing partners of the former Big Eight firms have called for a broadly educated accountant in their paper *Perspectives on Education: Capabilities for Success in the Accounting Profession*. They have asked educational institutions to produce graduates who possess a broad array of skills and knowledge. The managing partners have pointed out that "the professional environment is . . . characterized by rapidly increasing dependence on technological support, [and that] no understanding of organizations could be complete without attention to the current and future roles of information technology in client organizations and accounting practice."[34]

Robert Elliott, a prominent audit researcher, has written that information technology results in a closer relationship with customers, improved quality, and increased global competition through telecommunications. He has concluded that the accounting curriculum must become more relevant by integrating accounting, business, and general knowledge. Technology in the curriculum should give students the ability to function in the information era.[35]

SUMMARY

The unique partnership between government and the accounting profession has served the nation well. It would be desirable to enroll a broader group of auditors in this partnership; auditors

---

[33]William D. Hall, "The Education of an Accountant," *Massachusetts CPA Review* 62, no. 3 (Summer 1988), pp. 34–38, 43.

[34]The Managing Partners of the Big Eight Firms, *Perspectives on Education: Capabilities for Success in the Accounting Profession* (April 1989), pp. 5, 8.

[35]"Peat's Elliott Calls for New Education," *Accounting Today*, May 14, 1990, p. 20.

should express their opinions on issues which directly and indirectly affect their welfare and that of the nation. While Congress is moved by populist traditions, the SEC doggedly pursues disclosure, and the FASB's structure comes increasingly under scrutiny, regulators will continue to be responsive to those who exercise their right to be heard.

It is no longer possible to separate a generally educated person from a professionally competent person, a realization echoed by the managing partners of the Big Six firms. The increasingly international aspects of the profession and Europe's projected economic unity will bring new demands to remove trade barriers, abroad and at home. Moreover, steps need to be taken to maintain a strong U.S. position in international accounting and auditing services. One way this can be done is by enlisting auditors in the quest to encourage competition within the United States.

CHAPTER 15

A DISTILLATION OF EXPERIENCE (AND A FORECAST)

I see a continuing acceleration of technological knowledge and capabilities—especially in the utilization of electronics and electronic data processing. Here, it seems inevitable that we will have a gap that continuously widens between what we know and what we do to use that knowledge in a practical sense.

Victor Z. Brink*

USER PERSPECTIVE: Items of Special Interest

EXECUTIVE HIGHLIGHTS: All readers
INTRODUCTION: All readers
EYEWITNESS TO AUDITING HISTORY: All readers
POSITIVE FUNDAMENTALS: All readers
THE CONTINUING BOON OF TECHNOLOGY: External auditors, internal auditors
THE EXPECTATION GAP REVISITED: External auditors, internal auditors
SUMMARY: All readers

EXECUTIVE HIGHLIGHTS

The size of the S&L fiasco, between 10 and 30 times as great as the 1929 stock market crash, together with strains which have be-

---

*Widely regarded as a founder of the modern internal auditing profession.

come apparent in other financial services businesses, could turn into a catalyst for government action.

The role of auditors in the S&L crisis was peripheral; auditors represented only one link in the regulatory chain, albeit an important one. Nonetheless, the profession and its practitioners should take steps to minimize the risk of further embarrassment. In essence, greater emphasis should be placed on the management of audit risk. Attention should be focused on uncontrolled threats, especially in the focal areas of exposure. Unrestricted substantive testing would become routine, and partners and managers would be heavily involved in performing audit steps that involve sensitive matters.

The fundamental conditions underlying the practice of auditing continue to be positive. First, there is the internationalization of business, fostered by freer markets abroad as well as by computerized technology transfers across national borders. Second, auditors will resume their traditional role as business advisers to clients, drawing to some extent on computer based ability to review operational data. The AICPA's expectation gap statements have reintroduced operational controls into audit concerns; and the proactive audit—an operational audit conducted prior to operations—invites cooperation from operating managers.

Most important, technology will make it possible to conduct audits that are both efficient and effective. (See Appendix D for a summary of improvement opportunities.) Technology will continue to spawn positive audit developments. Neural computing, chaos theory, and, more immediately, artificial intelligence and knowledge-based systems warrant attention from audit organizations' technology officers. Success is most likely for those firms whose technology research represents an integral part of a soundly conceived audit research program.

INTRODUCTION

The different sections of this book have described the twin challenges of audit effectiveness and efficiency, the opportunities for improvement made possible by technology, the implementation of a modernized audit approach, and its effects on the engagement, the firm, and the profession.

This chapter describes important trends likely to influence the professional lives of accountants and auditors during the next decade. These developments are discussed within the context of the accounting and auditing environment that existed during the author's years in practice.

The chapter's objective is to reassess and update what has been covered. The experience of writing the book has confirmed the author's sense of optimism. The underlying conditions are positive, particularly in regard to technology which will enable auditors to conduct the more efficient and effective audits needed to meet public expectations.

Technology has contributed to the emergence of a new humanistic working environment which pertains to audit entities of all kinds and sizes, but which speaks especially to the smaller practitioner. Vaclav Havel, the playwright-president of Czechoslovakia, suggested that "the most important thing today is for economic units to maintain—or, rather, renew—their relationship with individuals, so that the work those people perform has human substance and meaning." He adds: "I would tend to favor an economic system based on the maximum possible plurality of many decentralized, structurally varied, and preferably small enterprises that respect the specific nature of different localities and different traditions, and that resist the pressures of uniformity." He concludes that regulation of a variegated economic scene "should be based on nothing more than a highly evolved sensitivity to what contributes to the general good of the human being, and what, on the contrary, limits and destroys it."[1]

Recently, a book was published with the intriguing title *Eyewitness to History*.[2] Unfortunately, not a single accountant appears in this anthology as either subject or reporter. This could be due to the fact that accounting and auditing events have not received their deserved share of attention throughout recorded history. Moreover, trends in auditing may not become clearly de-

---

[1]Vaclav Havel, "Work, by Any Other Name," *Columbia*, Fall 1990, pp. 40–41.

[2]John Carey, *Eyewitness to History* (Cambridge, Mass.: Harvard University Press, 1987).

fined until some cataclysmic event brings them into focus. The author will make a modest attempt to remedy the deficiency.

EYEWITNESS TO AUDITING HISTORY

The Past as Prelude

The author assessed the accounting environment in an article published in 1979, and noted these trends:

1. Increased consumer demand for accountability.
2. Increased construction by the courts of the public as the auditor's client.
3. New initiatives pertaining to responsibility to detect fraud.
4. An increasing role for the accountant in corporate governance.
5. Growing prevalence of audit committees.
6. Computerization, including continuous auditing.
7. Increased emphasis on the international aspects of accounting and auditing.
8. Performance auditing, spurred by governmental demand.
9. Attestations for social purposes.[3]

In general, the forecast was reasonably accurate. As to point 2, judicial opinions, recent experience has been mixed; however, U.S. courts have generally tended to hew to the *Ultramares* decision, which was discussed in Chapter 14. Social reporting, point 9, appears to have gone into eclipse; it is possible that interest in this topic is cyclical in nature. The remaining trends can be expected to go forward. Before certain aspects are discussed, some comments seem appropriate in regard to recent events in the securities markets.

---

[3]Felix Pomeranz, "The Attest Function Trends and Prospects," *The CPA Journal* 49, no. 4 (April 1979), pp. 41–47.

The Decade of Greed

Roberta S. Karmel, a former commissioner of the Securities and Exchange Commission (SEC), has characterized the past 10 years as the "decade of greed." She admits that there may be a distinction between greed and market-based solutions to economic and social problems, but asserts that the two had become synonymous by the end of the 1980s. Karmel observes that greed was not always illegal. She says that "program trading and the resulting stock market crash of 1987 sprang from the same impulse for an edge, the same substitution of speculation for investment."

She notes the development of theories to justify free-market, libertarian policies, rather than government regulation of corporations and security markets; she quotes one commentator as noting that "there is something sick about a financial culture that seriously listens to claims that dishonesty is tolerable because it's efficient." Karmel says that the SEC shifted its regulatory policies to accommodate the infatuation with markets: "Although the SEC maintained a tough enforcement stance . . . in insider trading cases, it favored the market for corporate control that fueled the leveraged buyout, and did not campaign for regulatory reform after the 1987 stock market crash."

Perhaps prophetically, she expects that after a decade of economic overindulgence, the president and Congress will deflect blame from themselves. She predicts a "hue and cry . . . for tougher securities regulation and the prosecution of all available scapegoats: . . . Prosecuting those who went too far will be easier than dealing with international competition, serious economic dislocations, and a financial services industry regulated for the benefit of its special interest groups."[4]

If Karmel is correct, readers of this book have reason to be concerned. The size of the S&L fiasco—between 10 and 30 times as great as the 1929 stock market crash—and strains which have become apparent in other financial services businesses, such as

---

[4]Roberta S. Karmel, "A Decade of Greed," *The New York Law Journal*, Securities Regulation Sec., March 1, 1990, p. 3.

credit unions and insurance companies, could turn into a catalyst for government action.

At the time of this writing, the role of accountants and auditors in the savings and loan collapses had not become clear. For example, it remains uncertain whether, to what extent, and how effectively, internal and external auditors had reviewed loan portfolios, assessed related controls, and conveyed pertinent findings to management. Still less information is available as to management's responses to audit findings, any proposed corrective measures, and the auditor's reactions to management's actions or inaction.

The author believes that the role of auditors in the S&L crisis was peripheral; auditors represented only one link in the regulatory chain, albeit an important one. Nonetheless, it would be desirable for the profession and its practitioners to minimize the risk of further embarrassments. Practitioners could apply the lessons of the S&L crisis to improve audits of other financial service organizations. In essence, greater emphasis should be placed on the management of audit risk. Attention should be focused on uncontrolled threats, especially in the focal areas of exposure; unrestricted substantive testing would become routine, and partners and managers would be heavily involved in performing audit steps that involve sensitive matters or that are of an information-rich nature.

While auditors wait for the S&L cloud to dissipate, they may take comfort from the fact that the fundamental conditions which underlie auditing are quite positive. The specific aspects which will be mentioned include the internationalization of business, the auditor's posture as a businessperson, and ongoing advances in technology.

POSITIVE FUNDAMENTALS

The Internationalization of Business

Before World War II the international aspects of external auditing were mirrored only in the large firms' maintenance of offices in a few European cities. (These offices performed U.S.-style services for the foreign branches of U.S. transnational corporations.)

Item

Lybrand, Ross Bros. & Montgomery (the predecessor to Coopers & Lybrand) operated offices in London, Paris, and (before World War II) Berlin; the Berlin office was closed by the National Socialist regime. Colonel Robert H. Montgomery, one of the firm's founders, recorded his sense of outrage at this action in his memoirs. In 1949 the author mentioned the office closure to an aged Colonel Montgomery. The Colonel leaned back in his chair and said: "I want you to understand why this made me so angry: it was done without due process." That single sentence was a reflection of Robert Montgomery's world view, and probably of that of many of his accountant contemporaries.

The moves toward economic collaboration in Europe in the 1950s were reflected in the emergence of so-called international public accounting firms. However, (with one important exception) these organizations represented more or less informal associations of local firms, rather than monolithic one-world structures.

Some firms endeavored to improve audit quality and consistency on a worldwide basis, especially for international audit clients which filed reports with the SEC. The new international audit approaches incorporated the best procedures that could be found within the family of member firms. In addition, the materials developed for the international audit approach explained differences existing from country to country in accounting principles, disclosures, and auditing standards.

The strongest feature of these approaches has been mentioned. It involved worldwide searches for the best available national audit techniques so that these could be incorporated in the international package. The worst feature was that in many countries the new audit approach was used only on international engagements; audits of local clients proceeded as heretofore. This parochial reaction was caused by the expense of conversion to the international approach, and by local laws which mandated procedures and reports inconsistent with an international perspective.

Since the first international audit approaches were developed, accounting and auditing standards and procedures have become more transparent and more comparable through the efforts of many groups and individuals. The 1992 single market program of the European Economic Community may lead to a further rise in developments such as: (1) the emergence of additional truly international accounting firms; some large firms and their associates abroad are experimenting with innovative organizational arrangements; (2) exchanges of research information facilitated by electronic networks; in effect, researchers of different nations will be able to work together on projects without being in physical proximity to each other; and (3) collaborative working arrangements of firms and individual practitioners will assume a more personal character; also, local professional committees and societies may display greater interest in transnational projects.

Give Us a Businessman

It has been said that when the Athenian city-state was threatened by the Persians, the cry was not for a military leader, but: "Give us a businessman!" In the 1950s a similar shout went out for business-oriented auditors to perform "operational auditing." The extent to which operational auditing succeeded in *internal* audit organizations is difficult to determine. The phrase *operational auditing* can mean very different things to different people with respect to depth of application and the degree of discipline applied to this type of practice, such as the establishment of preferred control practices. In any event, use of operational auditing is believed to have peaked among U.S. internal auditors. These days approximately half the U.S. internal audit effort still appears to be devoted to operational tasks. Reportedly, operational auditing has been implemented somewhat more widely by internal audit departments in Europe, especially in the United Kingdom.

Operational auditing did not fare as well with U.S. *external* auditors. Two of the Big Six made serious attempts at operational auditing; one firm actually integrated "operational control reviews" into its audit practice. In the author's opinion an integrated audit approach covering all controls and requiring testing of both financial and operational information contemporaneously was and is the right way to go—both then and now.

The operational reviews met with a mixed reception from clients; ironically, but perhaps understandably, well-managed clients welcomed the practice; clients with deficiencies were either unenthusiastic or angry. Engagement profitability varied markedly; factors bearing on profitability included the experience and skills of the engagement team and the quality and extent of direction provided by the audit partner. A combination of threatening or negative factors made survival of the operational audit practice tenuous at best. When auditors were swamped by seemingly more important service demands, such as the conduct of special reviews to ascertain compliance with the Foreign Corrupt Practices Act, operational auditing was made optional; in other words, its eventual eclipse at public accounting firms was assured.

Item

The following story is not atypical of negative attitudes toward operational auditing existing among executives of the 70s and 80s. Mayor Frank Rizzo of Philadelphia wished to restrict the city's internal auditors to financial matters; he indicated that he would "not stand for being second-guessed on operational issues." City Comptroller Klenk sued the mayor; facing the likelihood of losing in the courts, the mayor reached an accommodation with the comptroller who was (formally) granted rights of unrestricted audit access.

Those who attempted to assess the reasons for slow acceptance of operational auditing by executives in industry and government usually blamed lack of understanding by the auditees, shortage of audit resources, and lack of auditor training opportunities—not without justification.

However, a rebirth of the operational audit ideal may not be far away. Past mistakes are likely to be avoided or their effects controlled. More important, today's circumstances favor implementation: (1) the expectation gap statements of the AICPA's Auditing Standards Board (ASB), especially *SAS 55*, have reintroduced operational controls into the mainstream of audit concern; (2) client data bases make it easier to draw on operational data to accomplish financial audit objectives; and (3) the proactive audit—an operational audit conducted in advance of operations—

invites cooperation, rather than dissent, from operating managers.

Proactive auditing represents an example of change in both timing and subject matter of audits. The idea is to install and test controls *before* money has been spent and to extend the subject matter of the audit to include operational information. Such an audit may consist of a planning or prestart-up phase, followed by a substantive or compliance phase. The proactive audit permits operating managers to gain comfort that suitable control practices will be put in place and tested while programs and/or systems are still under development. The compliance phase of the audit involves testing to see that the controls which have been installed are in effect and functioning as planned. Deficiencies are subject to immediate correction; consequently, the proactive audit helps to turn potential adversaries among operating managers into allies.

A highly disciplined approach can be applied to a proactive audit, since its scope can be well-defined in advance and controlled as the engagement progresses. The effectiveness and efficiency of such an audit can be boosted by the involvement of functional specialists. Accordingly, partners and staff are likely to be supportive of such audits, given the intellectual challenge, the opportunity to improve the client's system and controls, and the possibility of enhancing client profitability.

A different thrust in the direction of the evaluation of nonfinancial information involves the expansion of the audit function to newer forms of attestation. An *attest engagement* is one in which a practitioner undertakes to issue a written communication that expresses a conclusion about the reliability of a written assertion made by another party. As the definition implies, verification procedures may be applied to types of information or processes extending beyond financial data.[5]

The renewed emphasis on knowledge of the client's business, operations-oriented audit services, and use of operational infor-

---

[5]American Accounting Association, Auditing Section, *Research Opportunities in Auditing: The Second Decade*, ed. A. Rashad Abdel-khalik and Ira Solomon (Sarasota: American Accounting Association, Auditing Section, 1988), p. 157.

mation in the financial audit, re-creates and reinforces the auditor's traditional role of business adviser to his client.

The Systems Analyst/User/Auditor Axis

A renaissance is likely to occur in the importance of the management information systems analyst, and in the auditor's value to both systems analyst and information user. Early systems analysts frequently engaged in clumsy attempts to find out what end users needed by asking: "What do you need?" Occasionally, the question drew the rejoinder: "You are the expert, you tell me." The facetiousness of the questions began to change in the 1960s when systems steering committees came to be chaired by operating executives who had risen through nonfinancial disciplines and professions; emphasis began to be placed on providing operating personnel, not necessarily financial personnel, with timely, accurate, and complete information.

> **Item**
>
> In 1965 Westvaco Corp.'s executive vice president, a chemist by training, chaired the corporate systems steering committee. After critical subsystems had been identified, task forces were assigned to document, study, and, when necessary, redesign each subsystem. Every task force was *guided* by a professional systems analyst; but, the task forces were *staffed* primarily by user personnel, including salesmen, production schedulers, and stores supervisors. The committee made certain that users were heard, top management's support did not waver throughout the life of each project, and task force members had acquired cross-disciplinary skills, together with an empathy for controls.

User involvement became universal in the late 1980s with the availability of microcomputers. Indeed, the pendulum may have swung too far in the users' direction; the times were marked by hasty acquisitions of ill-matched hardware and software; seesawing battles occurred between traditional management information systems officers, and newer "PC managers." The users' lack of appreciation of internal control was sometimes matched by the vendors' lack of a "security ethic."

Control deficiencies could and did lead to bad data, erroneous software logic, reliance on inaccurate data, inadequate error handling, and incomplete information trails. In many instances, personal computers were not cost-justified; when attempts were made in that direction, the emphasis was put on clerical cost reduction, rather than on productivity increases. Nonetheless, the overall effects may have been salutary in terms of making more people computer literate, stretching their minds, and making them more receptive to new ideas.

One of the results of the aforementioned difficulties was the restoration to influence of the systems analyst. Fertile conditions now exist for judicious and reasoned interaction among users, systems analysts, and auditors. Such interaction is a prerequisite to a successful proactive audit, and especially to an audit of a system under development. With respect to such systems, the prospects are excellent for averting losses due to control deficiencies and for avoiding costly alterations of systems after they have gone into operation.

Kinder, Gentler Decisions by the Courts

There has been no perceptible change in the inclination of unsuccessful investors (or career litigants) to hold those with presumably deep pockets responsible for imagined, inferred, or, possibly, even actual failures. (The author finds it difficult to believe that many of the persons bringing such suits, together with their attorneys, are incapable of grasping the limitations of financial audits.) Doctors, and of late, lawyers, have been targets of similar lawsuits, including frivolous actions. The prevalence of these suits, and the fact that they have virtually come to represent an indiscriminate attack on *all* professions, enhance the prospects for eventual relief.

A cure for the litigious society would require uniformly equitable treatment of accountants by the courts, reform of the laws applying to torts, statutory limitations of liability, and safe harbor provisions in appropriate instances. Prospects for action are uncertain; therefore, accountants are advised to continue to mount their own defense. For example, accountants had long hoped that client communications with auditors would come to be protected by privilege (i.e., would not need to be disclosed to regulators or litigators). However, state laws have remained diverse and/or ambiguous in this regard; therefore, corporations and taxpayers should conduct themselves without any expectation of testimonial privilege for information conveyed to public accountants.[6]

THE CONTINUING BOON OF TECHNOLOGY

Computing Capacity Continues to Increase

The continuing explosion in computing capacity has been the bedrock of the technologically driven audit. Kenneth Kellar believes that the availability of computing power has become such that any problem that can be conceived of as amenable to calculation will soon be doable at an acceptable cost and in a reasonable period. By the end of this century, computer designers expect to see a supercomputer that can calculate more than a trillion mathematical operations each second. Thus, there is interest in advancing the limits of what can be reduced to calculations.[7] Neural computing, chaos theory, artificial intelligence, and knowledge-based systems are moving toward implementation by auditors, and should be carefully monitored by audit organizations' technology officers.

Neural Computing
The brain operates as a parallel distributed processor, combining both memory and processing elements. While conventional computers are programmed with expertise that lets them perform specific tasks, neural networks are programmed to learn from experience and to figure out a correct course of action.

For the past 20 years, the development of expert systems has

---

[6]Denzil Causey and Frances McNair, "An Analysis of State Accountant-Client Privilege Statutes and Public Policy Implications for the Accountant-Client Relationship," *American Business Law Journal* 27, no. 4 (Winter 1990), pp. 535–51.

[7]Kenneth H. Kellar, "Science and Technology," *Foreign Affairs* 69, no. 4 (Fall 1990), p. 128.

been dominated by an attempt to create artificial intelligence which takes rules developed by human experts and applies them to new data. However, a neural computer can also become an expert at doing its job. The first tentative applications for neural networks involve monitoring products on an assembly line, assessing credit risks, picking out forged checks, and rating bonds. While it seems that a good start is being made, problems are foreseen; neural applications typically do not produce either an audit trail or step-by-step disclosure showing how decisions are being reached.

Based on similarities to early artificial intelligence applications, it appears that neural computing could warrant significant audit usage. Consequently, audit researchers should begin to participate in neural computing applications; they should provide inputs to ensure that computer decisions will be traceable, assessable, and subject to validation. In this way, the auditability of neural computer applications will be protected, and the successful use of neural computers as audit tools assured.

Chaos Science

Chaos science looks for patterns and meanings in seemingly random events. Robert Scheier has pointed out that computing environments are not neat, orderly, and predictable; new products, new demands from users, and new problems crop up unpredictably and with little apparent relation to one another. The chaos science concern with boundary conditions may help to explain some of these events; each boundary raises unique issues, such as the need to establish common file formats or to educate users about proper data backup. If the effect is large, and the immediate cause is not apparent, it may be desirable to focus on what it is in the environment that multiples the effect.[8] From an audit perspective, these environmental factors could be identified as a basis to their management and control; again, the potential audit usefulness seems significant, and may become

---

[8]Robert L. Scheier, "Applying the Laws of Chaos to Computing; Chaos Science in Microcomputer Systems," *PC Week* 7, no. 17 (April 1990), p. 125.

more so when more frequent interaction is achieved between different systems.

The Action in Telecommunications

Kellar has noted that inexpensive, multiple, and worldwide networks for communicating information have shifted power from governments to individuals and have given major impetus, at a practical level, to the heretofore rather abstract notion of a linked world.[9]

Telecommunications, including electronic data interchange, are likely to receive priority attention from auditors in the future, given tremendous growth in applications and difficulties in ensuring accuracy and completeness of transmissions. Further impetus will come from the construction of a gigabit network of fiberoptic cables. (A *gigabit* represents an information unit of a billion bits.) Such a network is viewed by many scientists and executives as both a vital research tool and an essential part of the country's information infrastructure for the next century. Federal financing to develop a high-speed nationwide computer network failed in Congress in 1990. However, the setback is likely to be only temporary, given the huge array of information, entertainment, and business services that would be created.

Ron Weber has described five major audit concerns that arise in data communications: (1) technological complexity increases; (2) exposures are higher—and the technology needed for their control is in an unstable state; (3) systems users, wherever located, depend upon each other, to some extent at least, with respect to compliance with controls; (4) privacy issues are becoming important; and (5) possible illegal use of the system may become a concern. He notes that satisfactory solutions to these problems should be based on a combination of research and practical experience.[10]

---

[9]Kellar, "Science and Technology," p. 127.

[10]Ron Weber, *EDP Auditing: Conceptual Foundations and Practice*, 2nd ed. (New York: McGraw-Hill, 1988) p. 931.

Expert Systems and Knowledge-Based Systems

According to Miklos Vasarhelyi,

> many CPA firms are committed to programs of audit automation. Some of these efforts involve expert systems technology . . . . The complexity of modern . . . means of production leads to a web of entangled and often conflicting professional standards, jurisprudence, and good professional judgment . . . . The areas of most immediate application potential are constrained problems where a clear domain of judgment exists.[11]

In light of these conditions, success is most likely for those firms whose expert systems research represents an integral part of a soundly conceived audit research program.

Those who wish to introduce expert systems into their practice may purchase an already developed system or seek to develop their own. In the latter case, they may either write the software, or utilize commercially available developmental software. In this way, relatively modest beginnings may be made by audit organizations of virtually any size. (Nonetheless, *true* expert systems may often not be commercially available, but will be utilized by the companies which developed them.)[12]

Research has been reported on the development of intelligent, knowledge-based systems, the successors to today's expert systems. The true intelligence of a system is evaluated by its ability to acquire and apply knowledge in different situations. If an organization is to make critical decisions on the basis of these systems, the auditor will need to consider the integrity of the facts and knowledge embodied in them and the ways in which they make inferences; presumably he will be able to gain some satisfaction by considering the methodology used to *develop* the system. However, a greater problem, with an unknown solution, will be posed

---

[11]Miklos A. Vasarhelyi, *Artificial Intelligence in Accounting and Auditing* (New York: Markus Wiener Publishing, 1989), p. xx.

[12]Thomas R. McKee, "Does Your Practice Have a Place for an Expert System?" *The CPA Journal*, January 1988, The Practitioner and the Computer Dept., pp. 114–18.

when he assesses the quality of the knowledge *embodied* in the system.[13]

Reprise: The Impact of Technology on Auditing

Ron Weber has offered some comfort to those concerned with the impact of continuing technological change on auditing. Weber writes that technology will *not* have a major impact on such audit activities as evaluation of general controls, application controls, and data quality in an organization's data base. He describes these aspects of auditing as invariant. However, he identifies five marginal areas of impact:

1. The auditor will need to understand the new technology.
2. Levels of EDP auditing work may emerge, classified on the basis of the need for the auditor to become involved with system details and of his technical skills.
3. More systems may (or at least, should) contain features that facilitate auditing.
4. In the short run, systems design audits may become increasingly important. (Over the longer term systems are likely to become easier to modify in the light of experience gained with them.)
5. In some areas there may be a temporary scarcity of audit tools.[14]

An Emerging Issue: Capital Requirements

The need for acquiring hardware and software, installing integrated systems in the auditor's own office, and engaging in stepped-up research could impose unwonted capital requirements on auditors. As a corollary to such requirements, questions arise as to how the expenditures should be financed. The author believes that any needed financing should be generated through operations, or that equipment should be purchased via loans se-

---

[13]Weber, *EDP Auditing*, p. 929.
[14]Ibid., pp. 926–27.

cured by that equipment. Public ownership of equity securities issued by firms engaged in attestation audits does not appear to be a viable alternative. While the author is aware that minority stock ownership has been explored in the United Kingdom, such a solution is not likely to be acceptable to U.S. practitioners as well as to state boards of accountancy. In any event, the new capital-intensive nature of auditing and financing alternatives should be considered in practitioners' strategic planning.

THE EXPECTATION GAP REVISITED

As has been seen, the profession has attempted to narrow the expectation gap in two ways: first, it expanded communication with users, clients, and CPAs; second, the Treadway Commission endeavored to define the responsibilities of the parties—audit committee members, chief financial officers, and external and internal auditors—relative to financial fraud.

Don Giacomino has succinctly explained a special expectation gap said to exist between legislators on the one hand, and auditors on the other: "Congress believes [that] there is a need to expand the auditor's role to include greater responsibility for detection of fraud and disclosure of financial problems. Auditors propose that the profession attempt to better educate financial statement users about the auditor's role and responsibilities."[15]

The expectation gap *SAS*s were intended in part to clarify the role of the audit in the market for information. The author is not optimistic that the statements will achieve this objective, although they may represent a step in the right direction. It is questionable that financial statement users will be influenced by seemingly innocuous wording changes in reports, or by the *SAS*s themselves. These doctrinaire communications largely represent the profession's point of view; they tell the reader what an audit is not. However, they do not explain the benefits of an audit to the user—and no such explanation appears to be in the cards.

---

[15]Don E. Giacomino, "Narrowing the Expectation Gap: A Comprehensive Approach," *Journal of Accounting and EDP* 4 (Spring 1988), p. 4.

The Treadway Commission's recommendations were designed to clarify the roles of all parties relative to the prevention and detection of financial fraud. However, the recommendations are likely to have only tangential effects. What is possibly Treadway's most significant recommendation called on public companies to establish *independent* audit committees. Of course, the creation of the committee is only the first step; if an independent audit committee is to have value, conditions favorable to its success must be created. In order to play a meaningful role in preventing and detecting fraudulent financial reporting, independent directors must be provided with complete, accurate, and pertinent information within an appropriate time period; they need time to digest the information they have been given; and they may need access to clerical or professional support staff.

The National Association of Security Dealers (NASD) and the American Stock Exchange (ASE) have endorsed the establishment of audit committees primarily composed of independent directors. In most other respects, the status of Treadway implementation is uncertain, especially as to the activation of internal auditing activities by public companies regardless of their size. It seems that companies that were following a recommended practice *before* Treadway have continued to do so. Those firms upon which new costs would be imposed do not seem to have rushed to compliance.

The United Kingdom profession has taken a focused approach to closure of the expectation gap. An auditing guideline published by the six main accountancy bodies directs auditors, after considering the need for legal advice, to "disclose [fraud discovery] to a proper authority in the public interest or for other specific reasons." The aim, said Ian Brindle, vice-chairman of the Audit Practices Committee, is to close the expectation gap in what the public wants auditors to do, while still maintaining confidentiality with the client.[16] In the United States, the same objective is accomplished by the more circuitous approach of the auditor's resigning from the engagement, having the client report the resig-

---

[16]Michael Beckett, "Auditors Must Disclose on Fraud Discovery," *The Daily Telegraph*, March 2, 1990, p. 22.

nation to the SEC, and disagreeing with the client's report on Form 8-K if necessary, all within an increasingly constricted time frame.

The introduction of ethics committees by public accounting firms could help to narrow the expectation gap. Hospital ethics committees have been found useful in various functions, including education, advice on policies, assistance in developing positions on ethical issues, and assistance to individual physicians facing ethical dilemmas.[17]

One English writer has taken the expectation gap beyond the technical. David Waller has commented on the reluctance of some public accounting firms to issue meaningful financial information:

> It is high time that the UK's top 20 accountancy firms started publishing their profit figures . . . . [a] move toward glasnost would be in the public interest . . . . Any [corporate] chairman . . . bragging . . . that sales had gone up a lot . . . would be denounced . . . . Yet senior partners get up regularly and say how marvelous it was . . . . Partners and staff become inculcated with the idea of growth for growth's sake . . . . The expectation gap has widened to become first a gorge and now a canyon. It can be narrowed to gap-shaped proportions by the simple expedient of publishing profit figures . . . . Openness will help."[18]

SUMMARY

Environmental conditions likely to have a favorable impact on the profession include: the internationalization of business; the need for auditors with a broad business perspective; and rapid technological change. Internationalization will be fostered by freer markets abroad as well as by knowledge transfer across national borders. Auditors will resume their traditional role as busi-

---

[17]Stephen E. Loeb, "Ethics Committees and Consultants in Public Accounting Firms?" *Accounting Horizons* 3, no. 4 (December 1989), pp. 1–10.

[18]David Waller, "Profits Disclosure Is in the Public Interest," *Financial Times*, March 29, 1990, p. 13.

ness advisers to clients, drawing to some extent on computer-based ability to review operational data. Technology will make it possible to conduct audits that are both efficient and effective.

The rate of technological change has not abated; computing capacity continues to expand. The influence of professional systems analysts is in the ascendancy, a consideration beneficial to the audit of systems while they are being developed. New nonfinancial audit services will continue to evolve, based on the auditor's knowledge of his client's business.

Any possible extension of the auditor's responsibility for the detection of management fraud will be influenced by congressional assessment of the profession's performance on S&L and other financial services engagements. However, there has been some improvement in the accountants' legal posture as a result of reluctance by some state courts to extend auditors' due care obligations to third parties, especially unforeseen third parties.

The last paragraph in this book includes the conventional exhortation to begin. The beginning could be represented by a review of individual engagements selected on a basis of audit risk and perceived inadequacies. A typical engagement could then be chosen as a prototype for improvement; audit objectives and procedures would be reassessed and streamlined in line with the revised audit model. Uncontrolled threats would be identified, especially in areas considered particularly exposed. Technology would be employed to accomplish unrestricted substantive tests; the on-line data bases would be introduced to help in assessing inherent risk. Selected audit software would follow. In addition, the professional and business judgments of senior personnel would be brought to bear to improve client service along with audit efficiency and effectiveness.

APPENDIX A

DISCOVERY SAMPLING TUTORIAL*

Discovery sampling is a technique that is widely used in fraud examination when a very small number of material irregularities are presumed to exist in a given population. The procedure allows the examiner to determine the minimum number of items to select in a random sample so that there is a specified probability of having at least one example of the irregularity appear in the sample.

In spite of its great value and widespread use, discovery sampling does not appear to be well understood. This is not due to any deficiency on the part of those who use the procedure, but rather a lack of exposure to the process.

Discovery sampling is usually taught with the use of a formula, a table or both.[1] Such information allows the fraud examiner to effectively use discovery sampling, but it is often at the expense of understanding the procedure.

An examiner may be questioned about sampling methods by senior level management during the course of an investigation or later by an attorney in court. To properly address these questions, the examiner must understand the procedures.

---

*Source: Dallas R. Blevins, "Discovery Sampling: The Basics." Reprinted with permission of the National Association of Certified Fraud Examiners, Austin, Texas. This article originally appeared in *The White Paper* 4, no. 6 (Nov.–Dec. 1990), published by the National Association of Certified Fraud Examiners.

[1]Ernst & Whinney, Audit Sampling, 1980, pp. 41–43; Dan M. Guy, *An Introduction to Statistical Sampling in Auditing* (New York: John Wiley & Sons, 1981), pp. 4, 16, 38, and 66–70; The Institute of Internal Auditors, *Sampling for Modern Auditors* (Altamonte Springs, Florida: The Institute of Internal Auditors), pp. 5–1 through 5–17; and B. J. Mandel, "How Statistical Methods Can Detect Possible Fraud or Abuse," *The White Paper,* May-June 1990, pp. 6–9.

The discovery sampling formulae provide answers that are: (1) easier to determine, (2) faster to obtain, and (3) more precise and less costly than the answers obtained from a set of tables.

This article takes the fraud examiner through the development and use of the formulae which comprise discovery sampling. The two primary formulae and a hand held calculator will relieve the fraud examiner of the necessity of carrying, referencing and interpolating a book of tables.

MODEL DEVELOPMENT

The logic of discovery sampling is based upon chain reasoning. Although the logic is not extremely difficult to understand, it does require some concentration and patience.

Combinations: The Total Number of Samples

Assume that a population is comprised of the smallest possible number of items: $N=2$. Suppose one of these is an error or an irregularity: $X=1$. With a population (N) of 2, the only possible sample size (n) is 1.

This means that there are two possible samples in the population under investigation. This is because there are only two possible combinations of "N" things taken "n" at a time (written $_NC_n$). Equation 1 is the standard used for the computation of the number of combinations of "N" things taken "n" at a time.[2]

Note that in a combination, the *order* of items in the sample does not matter. The mathematical symbol !, used throughout this article, means: take any number, X, preceeding the ! and multiply X by $X-1$, $X-2$, $X-3$, ... until X minus the number equals one. Example: $5!=5(4)(3)(2)(1)=120$. Also, 0! always equals one.

Equation 1:

$$\begin{aligned}
_NC_n &= N!/[n!(N-n)!] \\
&= 2!/[1!(2-1)!] \\
&= [(2)(1)]/[1(1)!] \\
&= 2/[1(1)] \\
&= 2
\end{aligned}$$

---

[2]David F. Grobner and Patrick W. Shannon, *Business Statistics: A Decision-Making Approach,* 2nd ed. (Columbus, Ohio: Charles E. Merrill Publishing Company, 1985), pp. 136–40.

Permutations: The Distribution of Irregularities within the Population
If "A" represents an acceptable observation and "I" an irregularity, the population can be conceived as being in one of two arrays. Equation 2 below is the standard used in the computation of the number of permutations of "N" things taken "n" at a time, with each new order constituting a separate permutation.[3]

Notice that order is of significance in a permutation, but not in a combination as discussed above. There are two possible samples (permutations) of a population consisting of two elements when the sample size is taken two at a time.

Equation 2:

$$\begin{aligned}
{}_N P_n &= N!/(N-n)! \\
&= 2!/(2-2)! \\
&= 2!/0! \\
&= 2!/1 \\
&= 2! \\
&= (2)(1) \\
&= 2
\end{aligned}$$

These two orderings can be identified as "AI" or "IA".

If the population is in the "AI" array, then the sample of one (n=1) will select the "A", and no irregularity will be found in the sample. If the population is in the "IA" array, then the sample of size one (n=1) will select the "I", and the irregularity will be found in the sample.

Probability: The Chance that a Sample Contains an Irregularity
In our example, since the fraud examiner has no way to tell which of the two possible arrays happens to exist, the overall probability (P) of selecting the "I" is .5. This is because there are two possible samples ($_N C_n$), one of which (X=1) contains the irregularity (I). Equation 3 below quantifies this reasoning process.

Equation 3:
$$\begin{aligned}
P &= X/{}_N C_n \\
&= 1/2 \\
&= .5
\end{aligned}$$

---

[3]Groebner and Shannon, pp. 132–36.

The probability of selecting a sample which does *not* contain an irregularity is one minus the probability that it does: $(1-P)$. Equation 4 specifies this relationship. Statisticians call this the "alpha error" (α).[4]

Equation 4:
$$\begin{aligned} \alpha &= 1.0-P \\ &= 1.0-.5 \\ &= .5 \end{aligned}$$

Equation 4 provides a second way to compute the probability of selecting a sample of size "n" that contains at least one of the "X" total number of errors or irregularities existing in a population of size "N". Solving Equation 4 for "P" gives rise to Equation 5 as follows:

Equation 4: $\alpha = 1.0-P$
Equation 5:
$$\begin{aligned} P &= 1.0-\alpha \\ &= 1.0-.5 \\ &= .5 \end{aligned}$$

This brief illustration has introduced and explained five variables:

X = the number of irregularities in the population (=1)
N = the population size (=2)
n = the sample size (=1)
P = the probability of selecting a sample of size "n" from a population of size "N" which contains at least one of the "X" total number of irregularities; the level of confidence (=.5)
α = the probability of selecting a sample of size "n" from a population of size "N" which does *not* contain at least one of the "X" total number of errors or irregularities (=1.0−P=.5)

Statisticians have noted a relationship among these variables as stated in Equation 6.[5] Equation 6 is a key relationship used in discovery sampling.

Equation 6:
$$\begin{aligned} P &= 1-[1-(n/N)]^x \\ &= 1-[1-(1/2)]^1 \\ &= 1-[1-.5] \\ &= 1-[.5] \\ &= .5 \end{aligned}$$

---

[4]Groebner and Shannon, p. 358.
[5]The Institute of Internal Auditors, p. 5–5.

Equation 6 provides a third way to calculate the probability of selecting a sample which contains an irregularity "P". If Equations 5 and 6 are analyzed simultaneously, the following relationship emerges:

	Equation 5	**Equation 6**
	$1.0-\alpha$	$= 1-[1-(n/N)]^x$
	$-\alpha$	$= 1-[1-(n/N)]^x-1.0$
Equation 7:	α	$= [1-(n/N)]^x$
		$= [1-(1/2)]^1$
		$= [1-.5]$
		$= .5$

Equation 7 reveals a second way to compute the probability that a sample will *not* contain an irregularity "a". Since (n/N) is the percentage of items existing in the population that are taken in the sample, $[1-(n/N)]$ is the percentage of items in the population that are left out of the sample. This means that "a" is a function of the sample size.

Equation 6 can be manipulated to disclose the required sample size. Equation 8 is the result.

Equation 6:

$$P = 1-[1-(n/N)]^x$$
$$= 1-[(N-n)/N]^x$$
$$[(N-n)/N]^x = 1-P$$
$$[(N-n)/N] = (1-P)^{(1/X)}$$
$$(N-n) = N[(1-P)^{(1/X)}]$$
$$-n = -N+\{N[(1-P)^{(1/X)}]\}$$
$$n = N-\{N[(1-P)^{(1/X)}]\}$$

Equation 8:
$$n = N[1-(1-P)^{(1/X)}]$$

Equation 8 is the formula that is listed in those few publications that do not provide a table for sample size determination in discovery sampling situations.[6] Remember that Equations 6 and 8 are basically identical. The two forms are simply designed to solve for a different variable.

In the case we have discussed, N=2, P=.5 and X=1, thus:

Equation 8:
$$n = N[1-(1-P)^{(1/X)}]$$
$$= 2[1-(1-.5)^{(1/1)}]$$
$$= 2[1-.5]$$
$$= 2(.5)$$
$$= 1$$

---

[6]The Institute of Internal Auditors, p. 5–17.

This means that the fraud examiner needs a sample of one (n=1) from a population of two (n=2) in order to be 50 percent sure (P=.5) that the sample will contain one example of the irregularity (X=1). This computation confirms the value of the formula for sample size determination.

PRACTICAL APPLICATION

In our prior example, the results are obvious. Now let's apply these same formulae to the following example.

Scenario
A fraud examiner discovers that over the past year the firm has made 1000 payments to suppliers (N=1000), but only 970 invoices are on file. The examiner wishes to select at least one of the 30 payments which does not have a supporting invoice (X=30). Any such accounts selected are to be analyzed to determine if a possible fraud has been committed. Recognizing that all sampling techniques involve the chance of being wrong, the examiner wishes to select a sample that has a 95 percent chance of containing one of the unsupported payments (P=.95).

Suppose that the researcher already has access to a random sample of 75 of these accounts (n=75). If any additional accounts are necessary, they can be obtained at additional search cost.

Using the Probability Equation
Since 75 of the total 1000 payments are already available, the fraud examiner will review these first to see if any are unsupported by an invoice. The first question to answer is: "What is the probability that at least one potential irregularity will be found in the 75 accounts?" Equation 6 provides the answer.

$$
\begin{aligned}
P &= 1-[1-(n/N)]^x \\
&= 1-[1-(75/1000)]^{30} \\
&= 1-[1-.075]^{30} \\
&= 1-[.925]^{30} \\
&= 1-.0964 \\
&= .9036
\end{aligned}
$$

There is about a 90 percent probability that at least one irregularity will be found. This same information can be obtained by referencing discovery tables, but the process is much more time-consuming.

Use of the Sample Size Equation
Presuming that none of the 30 unsupported payments are found in the original sample of 75, the researcher desires to know how many more should be extracted in order to be 95 percent sure that at least one will be found in the total sample. Equation 8 provides the answer.

$$n = N[1-(1-P)^{(1/X)}]$$
$$= 1000[1-(1-.95)^{(1/30)}]$$
$$= 1000[1-(.05)^{(1/30)}]$$
$$= 1000\ [1-.904966147]$$
$$= 1000\ [.0950339]$$
$$= 95.0339$$

This solution suggests that a sample of 96 (95.0339 rounded upward) will include at least one example of the irregularity 95 percent of the time. Since the fraud examiner already has 75, only 21 additional units need to be selected.

Again, although tables can be used to reach the same result, the time involved is much reduced by using the formula.

APPENDIX B

INVESTIGATOR'S GUIDE TO SOURCES OF INFORMATION*

Electronic data bases are a relatively new and rapidly growing source of information. Generally, data bases do not provide any more information than can be accessed from other sources. However, data bases have two distinct advantages—search speed and constant access.

INVESTIGATIVE AND LAW ENFORCEMENT DATA BASES

El Paso Intelligence Center (EPIC)

EPIC, located in El Paso, Texas, is a multi-agency operation that provides information about narcotics traffickers, gun smugglers, and alien smugglers. The center is designed to collect, process, and disseminate such information, and it is capable of providing a continuous exchange of intelligence between member agencies.

EPIC, the center of a network of telefax, teletype, telephone, and computer systems serving law enforcement, is managed by the Drug Enforcement Administration. Other participating agencies are the Immigration and Naturalization Service; the U.S. Customs Service; the Federal Aviation Administration; the U.S. Coast Guard; and the Bureau of Alcohol, Tobacco and Firearms.

---

*Source: U.S. General Accounting Office, Office of Special Investigations, *GAO/OSI-88-1* (1988), pp. 65–73.

Note: All statistics presented herein were pertinent as of the time the guide was written.

One of the primary functions of EPIC is to provide timely responses to queries from agents and officers in the field to support ongoing investigations and enforcement operations. Any state, county, city, or federal law enforcement agency may make an inquiry in person or by telephone, teletype, mail, or law enforcement computer.

The EPIC Watch operates on a 24-hour-a-day, seven-day-a-week basis to provide needed support for law enforcement. When queries are received, the Watch Section performs a check of hard copy and automated systems, and it responds by radio, telephone, or teletype to the inquirer. The following can be obtained from EPIC:

- Input and follow-up on vehicle, aircraft, and vessel lookouts.
- Information to aid in the establishment of probable cause.
- Coordination with participating federal agencies.
- Full-time contact with other agencies, such as state and local law enforcement, for call-back purposes.
- Intelligence support for ongoing field investigations.
- Professional support for any emergency in the field, such as relay of communications or requests for assistance.

The Watch is primarily concerned with inquiries and lookouts. It first attempts to fully identify the person or vehicle under investigation, and then tie it in with available information, such as methods of operation or criminal organization.

All inquiries received by EPIC are thoroughly researched and coordinated to furnish up-to-date, timely feedback. This could relate to a weapons or narcotics activity, alien, trafficker, pilot, aircraft, vehicle, or vessel.

Immigration and Naturalization Service Integrated Network Communications System (INSINC)

INSINC contains INS Aircraft Arrival Inspection Reports (form 192A), INS index of known alien smugglers, and INS index of various schemes involving fraudulent documents and false claims to U.S. citizenship. Inquiries should be limited to narcotics-related cases or files and/or smugglers of funds, other contraband, and aliens. INSINC is accessible through EPIC.

Narcotics and Dangerous Drugs Information System (NADDIS)

Inquiries should be limited to narcotics-related cases or files and/or smugglers of funds, other contraband, and aliens. NADDIS is accessible through EPIC.

National Crime Information Center (NCIC)

NCIC, located at the FBI Headquarters in Washington, D.C., is the best known law enforcement computer system. Most major law enforcement agencies have NCIC connections.

NCIC is often compared to a large "file cabinet," with each file having its own label or classification. Such a cabinet of data contains information concerning the following:

- Stolen, missing, or recovered guns.
- Stolen articles (must have a serial number).
- Wanted persons (for questioning or arrest).
- Stolen/wanted vehicles (autos, aircraft, motorcycles).
- Stolen license plates.
- Stolen, embezzled, or missing securities, stocks, bonds, and currency.
- Stolen/wanted boats.

NCIC can also provide an investigator with computerized criminal history (CCH) files as an additional source of information. These files give specifics on a subject's prior offenses, arrests, and dispositions, in addition to background information. For example, if a subject's name, date of birth, race, and sex were entered, the investigator would receive the following:

- FBI number.
- Full name.
- Sex.
- Race.
- Date of birth.
- Height.
- Weight.
- Eye color.
- Hair color.
- Fingerprint classification.
- Alias.
- Total arrests.
- Charges.
- Convictions.
- Dispositions.

National Law Enforcement Telecommunications System (NLETS)

NLETS is a sophisticated computer-switched communications network linking all the law enforcement agencies in the continental United States, Alaska, Hawaii, and Puerto Rico. NLETS communications facilities are also used by other state agencies, such as the various departments of correction, courts, and wild life management. It is available to such federal agencies as the U.S. Secret Service, the U.S. Customs Service, the U.S. Marshals Office, the U.S. Postal Inspection Service, the Internal Revenue Service, the Military Provost Marshals, and the Naval Investigative Service.

Inquiries into NLETS should include the subject's name, date of birth, sex, and race. Driver's license, motor vehicle registration, and criminal information records are available through NLETS. For example, if the required query information were provided to NLETS, the following information would be provided:

- Subject's full name.
- Last known address.
- Race.
- Sex.
- Date of birth.
- Height.
- Weight.
- Hair color.
- Eye color.
- Social security number.
- Driver's license number.
- License expiration date.
- Restrictions.
- Status.

If the investigators inquired about any vehicles registered to a subject, they could receive:

- Subject's full name.
- Last known address.
- Race.
- Sex.
- Date of birth.
- Auto tag number.
- Description of vehicle and year.
- Vehicle identification number.

If the investigators provided descriptive information and queried a state law enforcement agency, they could receive a complete criminal history of the subject.

Treasury Enforcement Communications System (TECS)

TECS is a system of telecommunications terminals located in law enforcement facilities of the Department of the Treasury. These terminals are connected to a computer in San Diego, California.

TECS contains information on wanted persons, identifiable stolen or missing property, and computerized criminal history (CCH) files. TECS also has access to the National Law Enforcement Telecommunications System (NLETS).

Participants include the U.S. Customs Service; the Bureau of Alcohol, Tobacco and Firearms; the Drug Enforcement Administration; the Immigration and Naturalization Service; the Department of State; the U.S. Coast Guard; the Federal Bureau of Investigation (NCIC Section); the U.S. Marshals Service; the Internal Revenue Service, Intelligence Division and Inspection Service; EPIC; NNBIS; and INTERPOL (National Central Bureau).

TECS works on a soundex-type system. If an inquiry is made regarding a certain name, then all similar sounding names on record are provided to the inquirer. Inquiries on TECS may be made by name alone, even if no identifying number, such as date of birth, FBI, or social security number, is available.

When a similar sounding list of names is provided by TECS, the various subjects' names are printed out along with sex, race, and date of birth. These factors can be reviewed by the inquirer who can determine which subject, if any, is the subject of interest. If a name is selected, then the name and date of birth are again queried and additional information is provided by TECS. This additional information may include, but is not limited to, the following:

- Special instructions (such as armed and dangerous).
- Full name.
- Race.
- Sex.
- Height.
- Weight.
- Hair.
- Eyes.
- Date of birth.
- Place of birth.
- Fugitive (which agency).
- Remarks (background information).
- Address.
- Citizenship.
- Miscellaneous numbers (such as FBI).
- Warrant held where and by whom.
- Warrant number and date.
- Date of offense.
- Alias.
- Treasury I.D. number.
- Case number.
- NCIC number.

Treasury Financial Law Enforcement Center (TFLEC)

TFLEC's Financial Information Data Base can provide the following information:

- Currency Transaction Reports (CTR), IRS Form 4789.

- Reports of International Transportation of Currency or Monetary Instruments (CMIR), Customs Form 4790.
- Reports of Foreign Bank and Financial Accounts (BA), Treasury Form 90-22.1.

Also available from TFLEC's Financial Information Data Base are special computer runs summarizing CTR & CMIR data.

Washington Area Law Enforcement System (WALES)

WALES is one of the state level law enforcement computer systems and is listed here to illustrate systems available in nearly all of the states.

WALES is sponsored by the Washington, D.C., Metropolitan Police Department and the state of Maryland, and it is available to state and federal investigators, when coordinated with the Washington, D.C., Police Department. WALES operates on a soundex system, and all that is needed for a query is the subject's name, without any identifying numbers. The system also interfaces with NCIC and NLETS. This system can provide investigators with information such as the following:

- Stolen property.
- Wanted persons.
- Filed complaints (lists violations by address).
- Gun registration information (in D.C. or Maryland).
- Court case disposition and status.
- Driver's license and motor vehicle registration.
- Business licenses.
- Traffic accidents.
- Lorton Reformatory inmates (prison-type information regarding prisoner location, status, disciplinary action, and type of custody).

COMMERCIAL DATA BASES, RESEARCH AND REFERENCE SERVICES

Dialog Information Retrieval Service (DIALOG)

DIALOG now offers more than 290 data bases (soon to be 320). DIALOG contains in excess of 80 million records, including references and abstracts of published literature, statistical tables, full text of selected articles, and directory, business, and financial data.

Dun & Bradstreet (D&B)

D&B has several data bases regarding corporations that are available through DIALOG, including a listing of 4.8 million businesses. Also available from D&B are 280 microfiche, sorted either geographically or alphabetically, containing listings that show assumed names (doing business as) or true names (corporate/partnership style).

Federal Procurement Data Center

The Federal Procurement Data Center maintains a computerized compendium of the Federal Acquisition Regulations (FAR), many agencies' supplements to the FAR, and information relative to all active (and some completed) government contracts. It is accessible through DIALOG.

General Accounting Office Documents Retrieval System (GAODOCS)

GAODOCS contains excerpts from GAO reports and is searchable by subject, GAO division, and report name or number.

General Services Administration Consolidated List

The GSA Consolidated List is a computerized list of suspended and debarred bidders.

House Member Information Network (MIN)

MIN is a group of on-line information-retrieval systems, which include the following: government statistics; the substance and present status of bills and resolutions; floor amendments; floor proceedings; pre-award grants (pertaining to all federal assistance programs contained in the Catalog of Federal Domestic Assistance (CFDA); post-award grants; and available contracts and awarded contracts, listing every civilian contract of $10,000 or more and every defense contract of $25,000 entered into by the federal government over the last four quarters. MIN also provides full text of the Congressional Record since the 99th Congress.

Justice Retrieval and Inquiry System (JURIS)

JURIS is a full-text, computerized information system (similar to LEXIS) developed and operated by the Department of Justice to provide attorneys with rapid access to relevant legal documents. JURIS is widely used in legal offices throughout the country and is available through the Library of Congress, American Law Division. JURIS contains headnotes and full text for 145,000 federal decisions and headnotes for 350,000 state decisions from *West's General Digests*. It also contains the following:

- Federal statutes and regulatory material.
- Attorney work products.
- Special files of evidentiary materials in support of ongoing litigation.

LEXIS

LEXIS is the largest and most widely used full-text legal data base. Available from Mead Data Central, Inc., LEXIS contains legal cases from federal and state courts, federal statutes and regulations, and law reviews and other publications that analyze current legal trends.

National Texts and Periodicals Database (NTP)

NTP consists of selected articles from over 200 law reviews and bar journals.

NEXIS

NEXIS is a full-text data base consisting of general news, business and financial information from more than 150 newspapers, magazines, wire services, etc. Magazine data dates from January 1975; newspaper data dates from January 1977.

Online Retrieval of Bibliographic Information, Timeshared (ORBIT)

ORBIT is an on-line, interactive retrieval system designed and implemented by the SDC Search Service Division Development Corporation,

Santa Monica, California. The ORBIT user interacts directly with the retrieval program via a terminal and telecommunication line, i.e. the user is "on-line" with the ORBIT program at a remote terminal.

Scorpio

This research service contains several different data bases, to include *abstracts* of the following:

- The Library of Congress Computerized Catalog (LCCC) contains all English books published in the U.S. since 1978.
- The Bibliographic Citation File (BIBL) is a file of selected citations to journal articles of interest to Congress from 1976 to the present.
- Congressional Status Files (CG Files) are bill status files, which can be searched by subject (e.g., acid rain) or by bill number to determine bill resolution, ratification, amendment, etc. This file can also be searched by committee, subcommittee, or member's name.
- The National Referral Center Master File (NCRM) is a data base consisting of approximately 14,500 trade organizations and professional societies (also lobbies). A popular use for this data base is searching for experts in particular subject areas. Searches are by subject.

Securities Information Center (SIC)

The SIC, located in Wellesley Hills, Massachusetts, is operated by Itel Corporation under contract with the Securities and Exchange Commission. All banks and brokerage houses, etc., that receive bad securities are required to report this information to the SIC. They are also required to run a check with SIC if they receive $10,000 or more in securities. Information is recorded as of October 1977.

Standard & Poor's (S&P)

S&P has several data bases regarding corporations. These data bases are available through DIALOG, including information on 36,000 corporations and 340,000 "key executives," with 74,000 profile biographies. S&P can also provide substantial information on financial institutions, including a list of the corporate officers and directors, mailing address, total deposits, primary bank, and primary law firm.

WESTLAW

WESTLAW is similar to LEXIS and JURIS, and contains many of the same files.

APPENDIX C

STANDARDS FOR INTERNAL CONTROL IN NEW YORK STATE GOVERNMENT*

EXPLANATION OF GENERAL STANDARDS

General internal control standards apply to all aspects of internal controls.

Reasonable Assurance

Internal control systems are to provide reasonable assurance that the objectives of the systems will be accomplished.

The standard of reasonable assurance recognizes that the cost of internal control should not exceed the benefit derived. Reasonable assurance equates to a satisfactory level of confidence under given considerations of costs, benefits, and risks. The required determinations call for judgment to be exercised.

In exercising that judgment, agencies should:

- Identify (1) risks inherent in agency operations, (2) criteria for determining low, medium, and high risks, and (3) acceptable levels of risk under varying circumstances.
- Assess risks both quantitatively and qualitatively.

*Source: Office of the State Comptroller, State of New York, *Standards for Internal Controls in New York State Government*, 1987, pp. 4–12. Portions reprinted with permission.

Risk assessment should be done following the information prepared by the Governor's Office of Management and Productivity: *A Guide to Conducting Vulnerability Assessments,* August 1985.

Cost refers to the financial measure of resources consumed in accomplishing a specified purpose. Cost can also represent a lost opportunity, such as a delay in operations, a decline in service levels or productivity, or low employee morale. A benefit is measured by the degree to which the risk of failing to achieve a stated objective is reduced. Examples include preventing an improper activity; enhancing regulatory compliance; or increasing the probability of detecting fraud, waste, abuse, or error.

Supportive Attitude

Managers and employees are to maintain and demonstrate a positive and supportive attitude toward internal controls at all times.

This standard requires agency managers and employees to be attentive to internal control matters and to take steps to promote the effectiveness of the controls. Attitude affects the quality of performance and, as a result, the quality of internal controls. A positive and supportive attitude is initiated and fostered by management and is ensured when internal controls are a consistently high management priority.

Attitude is not reflected in any one particular aspect of managers' actions but rather is fostered by managers' commitment to achieving strong controls through actions concerning agency organization, personnel practices, communication, protection and use of resources through systematic accountability, monitoring and systems of reporting, and general leadership. However, one important way for management to demonstrate its support for good internal controls is its emphasis on the value of internal auditing and its responsiveness to information developed through internal audits. Similarly, management should be supportive of and responsive to information developed through external audits made by organizations such as the Office of State Comptroller and independent CPA firms.

The organization of an agency provides its management with the overall framework for planning, directing, and controlling its operations. Good internal control requires clear lines of authority and responsibility; appropriate reporting relationships; and appropriate separations of authority.

In the final analysis, general leadership is critical to maintaining a positive and supportive attitude toward internal controls. Adequate supervision, training, and motivation of employees in the area of internal controls is important.

Competent Personnel

Managers and employees are to have personal and professional integrity and are to maintain a level of competence that allows them to accomplish their assigned duties, as well as understand the importance of developing and implementing good internal controls.

This standard requires managers and their staffs to maintain and demonstrate (1) personal and professional integrity, (2) a level of skill necessary to help ensure effective performance; and (3) an understanding of internal controls sufficient to effectively discharge their responsibilities.

Many elements influence the integrity of managers and their staffs. For example, personnel should periodically be reminded of their obligations under an operative code of conduct and the Public Officers Law. In addition, hiring and staffing decisions should include pertinent verification of education and experience and, once on the job, the individual should be given the necessary formal and on-the-job training. Managers who possess a good understanding of internal controls are vital to effective control systems.

Counseling and performing appraisals are also important. Overall performance appraisals should be based on an assessment of many critical factors, one of which should be the implementation and maintenance of effective internal controls.

Control Objectives

Internal control objectives are to be identified or developed for each agency activity and are to be logical, applicable, and reasonably complete.

This standard requires that objectives be tailored to an agency's operations. All operations of an agency can generally be grouped into one or more categories called cycles. Cycles comprise all specific activities (such as identifying, classifying, recording, and reporting information) required to process a particular transaction or event. Cycles should be compatible with an agency's organization and division of responsibilities.

Cycles can be categorized in various ways. For example:

- Agency Management.
- Financial.
- Program (operational).
- Administrative.

Agency management cycles cover the overall policy and planning, organization, data processing, and audit functions. Financial cycles cover the traditional control areas concerned with the flow of funds (revenues and expenditures), related assets, and financial information. Program (operational) cycles are those agency activities that relate to the mission(s) of the agency and which are peculiar to a specific agency. Administrative cycles are those agency activities providing support to the agency's primary mission, such as library services, mail processing and delivery, and printing.

The four types of cycles obviously interact, and controls over this interaction must be established. For example, a typical contract award cycle would be concerned with proper contracting procedures and, if awarded, administration of the contract. At the time of the award, the contract (program) and disbursement (financial) cycles would join together to control and record the payment authorization.

Complying with this standard calls for identifying the cycles of agency operations and analyzing each in detail to develop the cycle control objectives. These are the internal control goals or targets to be achieved in each cycle. The objectives should be tailored to fit the specific operations in each agency and be consistent with the overall objectives of internal controls as set forth in the New York State Governmental Accountability, Audit and Internal Control Act of 1987.

In the New York State Accounting System User Procedure Manual, Volume XI *Controls and Special Procedures* has, in Section 3.000, suggested guidelines for internal controls applicable to the major financial areas of payroll, cash, account coding, equipment, materials and supplies, and travel. Agencies should consider this material when designing, operating, and evaluating their internal control systems.

Control Techniques

Internal control techniques are to be effective and efficient in accomplishing their internal control objectives.

Internal control techniques are the mechanisms, whether manual or automated, by which control objectives are achieved. Techniques include, but are not limited to, such things as specific policies, procedures, plans of organization (including separation of duties), and physical arrangements (such as locks and fire alarms). This standard requires that internal control techniques continually provide a high degree of assurance that the internal control objectives are being achieved. To do so they must be effective and efficient.

To be effective, techniques should fulfill their intended purpose in actual application. They should provide the coverage they are supposed to and operate when intended. To be efficient, techniques should be designed to derive maximum benefit with minimum effort. Techniques tested for effectiveness and efficiency should be those in actual operation and should be evaluated over a period of time.

In developing control techniques, management must recognize that there are both prevention controls and detection controls. Prevention controls are designed to influence behavior to ensure that transactions are processed properly. Detection controls are designed to identify deviations from expected norms which should be investigated to verify that transactions are executed properly.

Continuous Monitoring

The systems in place should be evaluated on a continuous basis to identify weaknesses and allow management to take corrective action.

Internal control systems that have been put into place by management should be reviewed periodically to verify that they are working as intended, are still needed, and are cost effective. Controls that are not working should be identified and, if still needed, changed so they are working. In addition, agency heads should closely monitor agency action initiated to correct internal control weaknesses identified by internal or external auditors.

Management must recognize that internal control evaluations are accurate only at the time they are made and that procedures and the effectiveness of related internal controls are subject to change. For example, controls can change when employees change or when work flows are changed. Continuous evaluations help to ensure that established procedures and controls are being followed and continue to be appropriate.

EXPLANATION OF SPECIFIC STANDARDS

A number of techniques are essential to providing the greatest assurance that the internal control objectives will be achieved. These critical techniques are the specific standards discussed below.

Documentation

Internal control systems and all transactions and other significant events are to be clearly documented, and the documentation is to be readily available for examination.

This standard requires written evidence of (1) an agency's internal control objectives and techniques and accountability systems and (2) all pertinent aspects of transactions and other significant events of an agency. Also, the documentation must be available as well as easily accessible for examination.

Documentation of internal control systems should include identification of the cycles and related objectives and techniques, and should appear in management directives, administrative policy, and accounting manuals.

Documentation of transactions or other significant events should be complete and accurate and should facilitate tracing the transaction or event and related information from before it occurs, while it is in process, to after it is completed.

Complying with this standard requires that the documentation of internal control systems and transactions and other significant events be purposeful and useful to managers in controlling their operations, and to auditors or others involved in analyzing operations. This standard applies to both manual and automated systems.

Recording of Transactions and Events

Transactions and other significant events are to be promptly recorded and properly classified.

Transactions must be promptly recorded if pertinent information is to maintain its relevance and value to management in controlling operations and making decisions. This standard applies to (1) the entire process or life cycle of a transaction or event and includes the initiation and authorization, (2) all aspects of the transaction while in process, and (3) its final classification in summary records. Proper classification of transactions and events is the organization and format of information on summary records from which reports and statements are prepared.

Execution of Transactions and Events

Transactions and other significant events are to be authorized and executed only by persons acting within the scope of their authority.

This standard deals with management's decisions to exchange, transfer, use, or commit resources for specified purposes under specific conditions. It is the principal means of assuring that only valid transactions and other events are entered into.

Authorization should be clearly communicated to managers and employees and should include the specific conditions and terms under which authorizations are to be made. Conforming to the terms of an authorization means that employees are carrying out their assigned duties in accordance with directives and within the limitations established by management.

Separation of Duties

Key duties and responsibilities in authorizing, processing, recording, and reviewing transactions should be separated among individuals.

To reduce the risk of error, waste, or wrongful acts or to reduce the risk of their going undetected, no one individual should control all key aspects of a transaction or event. Rather, duties and responsibilities should be assigned systematically to a number of individuals to ensure that effective checks and balances exist. Key duties include authorizing, approving, and recording transactions; issuing and receiving assets; making payments; and reviewing or auditing transactions. Collusion, however, can reduce or destroy the effectiveness of this internal control standard.

Supervision

Qualified and continuous supervision is to be provided to ensure that internal control objectives are achieved.

This standard requires supervisors to continuously review and approve the assigned work of their staffs. It also requires that they provide their staffs with the necessary guidance and training to help ensure that errors, waste, and wrongful acts are minimized and that specific management directives are achieved.

Assignment, review, and approval of a staff's work requires:

- Clearly communicating the duties, responsibilities, and accountabilities assigned each staff member.
- Systematically reviewing each member's work to the extent necessary.
- Approving work at critical points to ensure that work flows as intended.

Assignment, review, and approval of a staff's work should result in the proper processing of transactions and events including (1) following approved procedures and requirements, (2) detecting and eliminating errors, misunderstandings, and improper practices, and (3) discouraging wrongful acts from occurring or from recurring.

Access to and Accountability for Resources

Access to resources and records is to be limited to authorized individuals, and accountability for the custody and use of resources is to be assigned and maintained. Periodic comparison shall be made of the resources with the recorded accountability to determine whether the two agree. The frequency of the comparison shall be a function of the vulnerability of the asset.

The basic concept behind restricting access to resources is to help reduce the risk of unauthorized use or loss to the State, and to help achieve the directives of management. However, restricting access to resources depends upon the vulnerability of the resource and the perceived risk of loss, both of which should be periodically assessed. For example, access to and accountability for highly vulnerable documents, such as check stocks, can be achieved by:

- Keeping them locked in a safe.
- Assigning or having each document assigned a sequential number.
- Assigning custodial accountability to responsible individuals.

Other factors affecting access include the cost, portability, exchangeability, and the perceived risk of loss or improper use of the resource. In addition, assigning and maintaining accountability for resources involves directing and communicating responsibility to specific individuals within an agency for the custody and use of resources in achieving the specifically identified management directives.

EXPLANATION OF THE AUDIT RESOLUTION STANDARD

Prompt Resolution of Audit Findings

Managers are to (1) promptly evaluate findings and recommendations reported by auditors, (2) determine proper actions in response to audit findings and recommendations, and (3) complete, within reasonable time frames, all actions that correct or otherwise resolve the matters brought to management's attention.

The audit resolution standard requires managers to take prompt, responsive action on all findings and recommendations made by auditors. Responsive action is that which corrects identified deficiencies. Where audit findings identify opportunities for improvement rather than cite deficiencies, responsive action is that which produces improvements.

The audit resolution process begins when the results of an audit are reported to management, and is completed only after action has been taken that (1) corrects identified deficiencies, (2) produces improvements, or (3) demonstrates the audit findings and recommendations are either invalid or do not warrant management action.

Auditors are responsible for following up on audit findings and recommendations to ascertain that resolution has been achieved. Auditor's findings and recommendations should be monitored through the resolution and follow-up processes. Top management should be kept informed through periodic reports so it can assure the quality and timeliness of individual resolution decisions.

APPENDIX D

AUDIT EFFICIENCY, EFFECTIVENESS, AND PROFITABILITY IMPROVEMENT OPPORTUNITIES

	Efficiency	Effectiveness	Profitability
With Respect to the Engagement			
Use the on-line data bases to assess current developments in the economy, industry, and company		X	
Use the on-line data bases for background on key executives		X	
Use the on-line data bases for external analytical procedures		X	
Use the Electronic Index to Technical Pronouncements to identify regulatory or professional pronouncements		X	
Use the on-line data bases to obtain details of professional rules		X	
Assess the client's approach to risk management; uncontrolled business risk may become audit risk		X	
Identify components and threats, and record them on the master tracking sheet (MTS)		X	
Arrange for the support of functional and/or industry specialists; also arrange for other experts that might be needed		X	

	Efficiency	Effectiveness	Profitability
Identify significant internal risks and carry them to the MTS		X	
Perform internal analytical review, drawing on operational data to the extent such data is controlled		X	
Review other audit reports, evaluate such reports, and consider them in the substantive test program as appropriate		X	
Review internal audit program; focus on: Charter Compliance with schedule Qualifications of individuals Conformance to standards		X	
Assess the control environment: In terms of "pulses" In terms of guidance such as that in *SAS 55,* and in the related audit guide		X	
Take plant/office tours: carry apparent deficiencies to the MTS		X	
Conduct behavioral interviews with the support of senior personnel		X	
Update overview flowcharts		X	
Arrange for updating of detailed flow charts; this should usually not be done by the external auditor		X	
Carry controls believed to be present to the MTS; on flowcharts identify: Key controls Supervisory controls		X	
Perform transaction reviews to the extent practical		X	
Review internal controls, especially: Physical security Access to the computer Management representation-related controls		X	

	Efficiency	Effectiveness	Profitability
Consider testing controls for: Physical security Access to the computer Management representations		X	
Make audit risk assessment; allocate audit effort on the basis of uncontrolled threats		X	
Compile substantive test audit program by reference to the Audit Program Generator	X	X	
Assess each step in terms of its effectiveness in accomplishing general or specific audit objectives; eliminate any work that does not support audit objectives	X		
Apply value analysis to each step	X		
Enrich the program by operational steps, again assuming that the information is appropriately controlled	X	X	
Identify those steps which can be accomplished by computer-based approaches, especially by a general-purpose computer audit program	X	X	
Program any tests of controls which may be necessary because the controls are not tested adequately as part of dual purpose testing		X	
Seek to have working papers serve more than one need	X		
Carry out the program; evaluate any discovered errors or irregularities in terms of their effect on controls and audit tests		X	
Search for control breakdowns using discovery sampling		X	

	Efficiency	Effectiveness	Profitability
With Respect to the Firm			
Marketing			
Provide general business advice bundled with auditing services			X
Given any expectations of serving clients abroad, build contacts to individuals or through local societies			X
Consider entry into high margin lines: Fraud auditing Proactive auditing Auditing systems under development Other attest engagements			X
Apply risk management concepts to new client acceptance, or to continuance of existing clients			X
Administration			
Initiate a productivity improvement program			X
Introduce an office security program			X
Establish an internal auditing program			X
Observe sound procurement concepts with respect to purchased materials and services			X
Practice tight cash management			X
Update the office systems; consider combining technical and administrative systems			X
Technology			
Appoint a chief technology monitor	X		X
Develop a strategic plan for taking advantage of technology as it develops		X	X

	Efficiency	Effectiveness	Profitability
Plan to computerize working paper storage; begin by developing a master index	X		
Consider the activation of a private data base which combines firm materials with information in the on-line data bases		X	
See to internal control over spreadsheet applications		X	
Engagement Support			
Create network for consultation		X	
Establish functional specialists		X	
Activate research capability, based on analysis of need		X	
Encourage free flow of ideas up and down the line	X	X	
Involve partners in sensitive aspects of audits		X	
Conduct quality control reviews while work is in progress		X	
Direct the firm's quality assurance review program on a basis of perceived audit risk		X	
Personnel			
Develop personnel career plans	X	X	X
Encourage participative management; especially, seek ideas bearing on audit effectiveness and efficiency	X	X	

INDEX

Also Available from
Business One Irwin...

THE BUSINESS ONE IRWIN GUIDE TO
USING THE WALL STREET JOURNAL
Third Edition
Michael B. Lehmann

More than 165,000 copies in print! Discover how you can use the comprehensive information in the *Journal* to make more profitable business and investment decisions.

ISBN: 1-55623-242-X

THE BUSINESS ONE IRWIN
BUSINESS AND INVESTMENT ALMANAC, 1992
Edited by Sumner N. Levine

This classic reference tool is the most comprehensive fact book available today! Gives you major and group stock market averages, price/earnings ratios, reviews of the major futures markets, and much more so you have one resource to turn to when you need the facts from 1991.

ISBN: 1-55623-532-1

THE COMPLETE
WORDS OF WALL STREET
The Professional's Guide to Investment Literacy

Allan H. Pessin and Joseph A. Ross

Now you can have at your fingertips the most comprehensive guide to the latest jargon used in the financial industry. Helps protect against financial loss due to miscommunication with clients and industry professionals.

ISBN: 1-55623-330-2

RAGING BULL
How to Invest in the Growth Stocks of the 90s

David Alger

Your guide to making the move from stable, slow-growing blue chips to smaller stocks with potentially higher growth. Alger shows you how to discover the next Apple Computer, Nike, or Amigen (Cellular One).

ISBN: 1-55623-462-7

INVESTING FOR A LIFETIME
Paul Merriman's Guide to Mutual Fund Strategies

Paul Merriman

Shows you how to make successful investment decisions in healthy or weak financial markets. Includes strategies and tactics for beating the market using Merriman's own successful timing techniques.

ISBN: 1-55623-485-6